ÉDOUARD GLISSANT, PHILOSOPHER

SUNY series in Contemporary French Thought
____
David Pettigrew and François Raffoul, editors

ÉDOUARD GLISSANT, PHILOSOPHER

Heraclitus and Hegel in the Whole-World

ALEXANDRE LEUPIN

Translated by Andrew Brown

French Voices Logo designed by Serge Bloch.

This work received the French Voices Award for excellence in publication and translation. French Voices is a program created and funded by the French Embassy in the United States and FACE Foundation (French American Cultural Exchange)

Cover painting entitled "The Quest for a Tree" is by Sylvie Sema; used by permission.

Published by State University of New York Press, Albany

© 2021 State University of New York

All rights reserved

Printed in the United States of America

For information, contact State University of New York Press, Albany, NY
www.sunypress.edu

Library of Congress Cataloging-in-Publication Data

Names: Leupin, Alexandre | Brown, Andrew, translator.
Title: Édouard Glissant, philosopher : Heraclitus and Hegel in the whole-world / Alexandre Leupin, translated by Andrew Brown.
Description: Albany : State University of New York Press, [2021] | Series: SUNY series in Contemporary French Thought | Includes bibliographical references and index.
Identifiers: ISBN 9781438483252 (hardcover : alk. paper) | ISBN 9781438483269 (pbk. : alk. paper) | ISBN 9781438483276 (ebook)
Further information is available at the Library of Congress.

10 9 8 7 6 5 4 3 2 1

for Sylvie

When a poet dies, his most beautiful images,
his most influential works,
as well as his most everyday words,
are immediately safeguarded
in imperceptible fissures of the improbable,
and in the mysterious cracks of time,
where those bold enough can consult them.

—Glissant, Philosophie de la Relation

All philosophy is an art.

—Glissant, Une nouvelle région du monde

It is not the system that needs to be challenged.
    What needs to be challenged
is any system that seeks to be systematic.

—Glissant, L'Imaginaire des langues

A living poetry must be part of life itself.

—Hegel, Esthétique IV

The death of poets also has a certain allure
which much more overwhelming
or terrifying sorrows do not possess. It is because we
feel that a great poet,
here among us, enters into a solitude
that we cannot conquer.
And once he has gone, we know
that if we were to follow him that minute into the endless shadows,
never could we see him or touch him.

—Glissant, Philosophie de la Relation

Embraces
Wholes and not-Wholes
An accordance, a discordance
Consonant and dissonant
And of all things one
And of the One all things

—Heraclitus, Fragment X

Contents

Abbreviations

CC   *La Case du commandeur* [*The Commander's Hut*] (Paris: Le Seuil, 1981)

CL   *La Cohée du Lamentin, Poetics V* [*La Cohée du Lamentin, Poetics V*] (Paris: Gallimard, 2005).

DA   *Le Discours antillais* [*Antillean Discourse*] (Paris: Le Seuil, 1981)

DG   *Discours de Glendon* [*Glendon Speech*] (Toronto: Éditions du GREF, 1990)

EBR   *Les Entretiens de Baton Rouge* (*The Baton Rouge Interviews*), with Alexandre Leupin (Paris: Gallimard, 2008). English translation: *The Baton Rouge Interviews with Édouard Glissant and Alexandre Leupin*, trans. Kate M. Cooper (Liverpool, 2020)

FM   *Faulkner, Mississippi* (Paris: Stock, 1996)

IBM   *L'Intraitable Beauté du monde. Adresse à Barack Obama* [*The Intractable Beauty of the World. Address to Barack Obama*] (Paris: Éditions Galaade, 2009)

IL   *L'Imaginaire des langues* [*The Imaginary of Languages*], with Lise Gauvin (Paris: Gallimard, 2010)

IP   *L'Intention poétique* [*The Poetic Intention*] (Paris: Le Seuil, "Pierres vives," 1969), republished as *Poétique II* [*Poetics II*] (Paris: Gallimard, 1997)

IPD   *Introduction à une Poétique du divers* [*Introduction to a Poetics of Diversity*] (Paris: Gallimard, 1996). English translation: *Introduction to a Poetics of Diversity*, trans. Celia Britton (Liverpool, 2020)

L   *La Lézarde* [*The Lizard*] (Paris: Le Seuil, 1958). English translation: *The Ripening*, trans. Michael Dash (London: Heinemann, 1985)

ME   *Mémoires de l'esclavage* [*Memories of Slavery*] (Paris: Gallimard, 2007)

MI   *Le Monde incréé* [*The Uncreated World*] (Paris: Gallimard, 2000)

MPHN   *Manifeste pour les produits de haute nécessité* [*Manifesto for Products of Prime Necessity*] (Paris: Éditions Galaade, 2009)

NRM   *Une nouvelle région du monde, Esthétique I* [*A New Region of the World, Aesthetics I*] (Paris: Gallimard, 2006)

O   *Ormerod* (Paris: Gallimard, 2003)

PC   *Poèmes complets* [*Complete Poems*] (Paris: Gallimard, 1994)

PhR   *Philosophie de la Relation, Poésie en étendue* [*Philosophy of Relation, Poetry in Extent*] (Paris: Gallimard, 2008)

PR   *Poétique de la Relation, Poétique III* [*Poetics of Relation: Poetics III*] (Paris: Gallimard, 1990)

QLMT   *Quand les murs tombent: l'identité nationale hors-la-loi?* [*When the Walls Fall: National Identity as Outlaw?*] (Paros: Éditions Galaade, 2007)

QS   *Le Quatrième Siècle* [*The Fourth Century*] (Paris: Le Seuil, 1964)

S   *Sartorius, le roman des Batoutos* [*Sartorius, the Novel of the Batoutos*] (Paris: Gallimard, 1999).

SC   *Soleil de la conscience* [*Sun of Consciousness*] (Paris: Éditions Falaize, 1956), republished as *Poétique I* [Poetics I] (Paris: Gallimard, 1997)

SR   *Le Sang rivé* [*The Blood Bound*] (Paris: Présence africaine, 1961)

TeM   *La Terre magnétique, Les Errances de Rapa Nui, L'Île de Pâques* [*The Magnetic Earth, The Wanderings of Rapa Nui, Easter Island*], in collaboration with Sylvie Séma (Paris: Le Seuil, 2007)

TFEV   *La Terre le Feu l'Eau et les Vents, une anthologie de la poésie du Tout-Monde* [*Earth Fire Water and Winds, an Anthology of the Whole-World*] (Paris: Galaade, 2010)

TM   *Tout-Monde* [*Whole-World*] (Paris: Gallimard, 1993)

TTM   *Traité du Tout-Monde, Poétique IV* [*Treatise on the Whole-World, Poetics IV*] (Paris: Gallimard, 1997). English translation: *Treatise on the Whole-World*, trans. Celia Britton (Liverpool, 2020)

Acknowledgments

First and foremost I wish to express my deep appreciation to Sylvie Glissant, whose vision of Édouard Glissant's work and the generous information she has provided have been an invaluable contribution to the writing of this book. Without her encouragement and support, this project would have been abandoned many times.

Thanks also to Jean-Claude Milner for his many clarifications on the question of universality, and to François Raffoul for his evaluation of the Hegelian dialectic.

Thanks are also due to Deans Guillermo Ferreyra and Gaines Foster of the College of Humanities and Social Sciences at the University of Louisiana, who have so often supported me, as well as the Manship family, thanks to whom I have been able to benefit from many scholarships. The Regents of the University of Louisiana deserve a special mention: in conjunction with the College of Humanities and Social Sciences, they granted me a sabbatical year without which this book would not have seen the light of day.

Thanks also to Chelsea Rye and Jeanne Jégousso for preparing the manuscript.

Translator's Note

With Alexandre Leupin's agreement, I have used the French versions of several canonical authors (from the Pre-Socratics to Heidegger) as the basis for my own translations, rather than quoting from "standard" English versions. The French and English versions of a philosopher such as Heidegger can be startlingly different in tone and even sense, and Glissant's intellectual world is imbued with a very francophone take on the philosophers he quotes. Despite the existence of several excellent English translations of Glissant's other works, I have also translated all of the texts quoted by Leupin afresh.

—Andrew Brown

à Alexandre Leupin.

Sur l'Imaginaire

Ce par quoi le concept échappe à son
enfermement, c'est dire à son propre système.

Ce par quoi toute communauté échappe
à son propre enfermement, pour entrer dans le
système non systématique du Tout Monde.

L'Imaginaire dépasse le dit, le vécu, le
concept, dans une dynamique qui est une
poétique.

Édouard Glissant

Baton Rouge le 20 avril 2002.

To Alexandre Leupin

On the Imaginary
*It is what enables the concept to escape its enclosure, in other words its
own system.*
*It is what enables every community to escape its own enclosure to enter the
non-systematic system of the Whole-World.*
*The Imaginary goes beyond what is said, what is lived, the concept, in the
dynamic movement of a poetics.*

—Édouard Glissant
Baton Rouge, April 20, 2002

Chapter 1

"The immense foliage of a Louisiana oak, like a flattened palaver tree"

On April 20, 2002, Édouard Glissant wrote a short text for me during a stay in Baton Rouge:[1]

On the Imaginary

It is what enables the concept to escape its enclosure,
in other words its own system.
It is what enables every community to escape its own
    enclosure to enter the non-systematic system of the
    Whole-World.
The Imaginary goes beyond what is said, what is lived, the
    concept,
in the dynamic movement of a poetics.

Today, I belatedly decipher, in this text addressed to me personally, an affable, firm, and delicate admonition not to allow myself to be confined within the concept and the system, but rather to question my training and my thinking. This is a formidable demand, one to which I have tried to respond in the present work.

But above all, the text goes far beyond its restricted address: these few lines sum up in an aphorism the totality of Édouard Glissant's thought. There is something astounding about this ability to compose everything as a whole, so that the slightest fragment points to the entire path of his thought and brings it together in a synthesis. Each word in this terse text names all (or almost all) of the places opened up by the work in its entirety. Meditating retrospectively, in a painful absence, this poem in prose (is it a manifesto? a Heraclitean fragment? the preamble to a novel? a hymn? a minimal epic? a line of verse?—the form itself overrides the distinction between traditional literary genres), I see a massive, graceful coherence arise, with repercussions for all Glissant's texts.

I thought that after the publication of the *Entretiens de Baton Rouge*, and after several articles and conference papers (which now strike me as quite inadequate), I had said everything I had to say about Édouard Glissant. But this was not the case: when he died, I was asked to give papers and interviews and to write articles, and I re-read the texts. His work then appeared to me much more systematic, rigorous, and nourished by certain traditions than I would have thought: it could be assessed anew—one just needed to come at it from a different angle.

In this regard, Sylvie Glissant often assured me, so as to help me overcome the many moments of asthenia that marked the writing of this book, that "Édouard knew that you would join him one day." I have the somewhat uncanny realization that Glissant had made this explicit on the back cover of the *Entretiens*. He mentioned various reasons for this belated publication, seventeen years after the recording of our conversations: "Why so long after? Probably to give time to what we would both need to write or think, then and since, and to return to what we had so tranquilly discussed between ourselves, outside of any limit." By some miracle, this time has been granted me; I must now give the results of this long lapse of time their opportunity—for it was, without my knowledge, a period of waiting and, beyond the grave, a response to Glissant's wish or divination.

In many ways, this tribute is fragmentary. First, the whole of Glissant's work, written with the greatest precision and detail, should be commented on word by word: but this would take an entire lifetime, which I no longer have. Second, I discuss only Glissant's essays and his theory. A topography of the gigantic monument comprised by his œuvre in its entirety would have needed to include his poetry, dramas, and novels. Similarly, his specific relation to the Caribbean, especially to Frantz Fanon and Aimé Césaire, would have required examination: the absence of these two key reference points is enough to indicate the partial nature of my project. An exhaustive account of the work would require a reading of its literary and poetic side (in fact, these themes have already been explored by the critics).[2] But if we are to speak intelligibly of a rhizome where "everything is in everything," where the smallest piece is connected to the whole, we need to distinguish, to fragment, to break, to truncate, so as not to fall into an amorphous mess.

I have therefore limited the field of my study to Glissant's intimate relationship with the "Western" philosophical tradition that pervades and informs his work. This relationship is both conflicted and welcoming— and, so far, this area of research has, with few exceptions, been neglected by critics.

My title might seem misleading. *Édouard Glissant as Thinker* might have been more apt, if we follow Jean-Claude Milner's definition of thought as "something whose existence is imposed on those who have not thought of it,"[3] which is an apt description of the effect produced by Glissant's work. Or else, *Glissant as "Rethinker,"* since he reassesses the themes of the philosophical tradition. Alexandre Kojève's definition of philosophical discourse also suits him perfectly: "It is a discourse, not just any discourse, but one that is different from all others insofar as it speaks not only of that whereof it speaks but also of the fact that it speaks about it in a way that other discourses do not."[4] Indeed, no word, no phrase in Glissant is ventured at random; very few discourses have such an awareness of their own nature.

In the antithesis that opens *Poétique de la Relation*, two categories of thought are contrasted: abstraction and concreteness. The latter is always given priority, breaking with the "Western" philosophical tradition, which usually tends toward abstraction. For Glissant, thinking is a matter of becoming entangled in a realm far from abstraction, individualization, and solitude, located amid the realities of the world, in the sharing of a community, even if this community is still to come. Thought as an act transforming the past and opening up the future differs from the philosophy faithful to the tradition inaugurated by Socrates. Thinking is a shared gesture in the real world, not in the solitude of ideas:

> Thinking about thought often comes down to withdrawing into a dimensionless place where the idea of thought alone persists. But thought is really spaced out in the world. It informs the imaginary of peoples, their diversified poetics, which in turn it transforms—and in which its risk is realized.
>
> Culture is the pretension of those who claim to think thought but stand aside from its chaotic journey. Evolving cultures infer Relation, the transcendence that underpins their unity-diversity.

> Thought draws the imaginary of the past: a knowledge
> in the making. We cannot halt it to assess it, nor isolate it to
> utter it. It is a sharing, and no one can stray from it or, by
> halting, take advantage of it. (PR 13)

Thought remakes the past and sketches out a knowledge in the making; it is not an affirmation of scholarly mastery, for no one can anticipate becoming; the philosophical tradition usually thinks what is and what has been, not what will be.

That Glissant was a poet, novelist, and playwright is common knowledge; that he thought according to these modes of writing is obvious. More unnoticed is his debate with the Western philosophical tradition as such: here his practice is allusive, metaphorical, and implicit. This is partly to avoid all pedantry, but above all to produce an interbreeding and interweaving that incorporates this tradition into the very material of his own work. This amounts to transforming philosophy into a poetics with its own distinctive tone of voice.

There is in Glissant, when he debates with philosophy or with the world, a patient hastening toward content, toward what he calls the "full-meaning" ("*le plein-sens*," PR 168, 217): "The meaning (linear), the full-meaning (in circularity)" (PR 236). His discourse does not obey any formal, required, or obligatory norm, except that which his poetic inspiration gives him. The formal requisites, languages, and rhetorics of philosophy, criticism, and literary history, the constraints to which those whom he calls the "literati" or the "scholars" are subjected, do not impress him because, in his vision of things, they are too often a way of muffling the truth and skewing meaning and reality. Rationalism and structure stifle truth/poetry. If, on a profound level, we think that the poetic is capable of truth, it need not conform to established rules. To restore the poetic to its inaugural place: that is the task.

Following Glissant, then, we need to draw an essential distinction, not only between "common thought" and "scholarly thinking" (EBR 151), but above all between "objective knowledge (*savoir*)," of whatever kind, historical, philosophical, linguistic, or critical, and "subjective knowledge (*connaissance*)," a word that echoes Claudel's *Art poétique*.[5] Subjective knowledge—the meaning of objective knowledge, the meaning of truth: such is the stake of Glissant's discourse: "Thus the theory of Relation cannot constitute a science, that is to say generalize by drawing up statutes and definitions for distinct roles. Relation is not objectively known, only subjectively knowable" (DA 251). This presupposes that we replace the *concept* and the abstract system on which it depends with *notions* founded in intuition, in the imaginary and materiality. So we will see that the operation does not in any way lead to an artistic blur.

Glissant's imposition of new meanings on the discourses that preceded him often causes misunderstandings, the first being to regard him as a "paraphilosopher" indulging in the gossip of a "poetic" subjectivity. Furthermore, for certain interpreters, the precipitate movement toward meaning is the sign that Glissant's thought is born out of nowhere, that it is inaugural and has emerged fully armed from a blank canvas. Nothing could be further from the truth: this thought draws on a concrete philosophical anthropology whose sources are often found in the West; it was therefore necessary for me to exhume them, partly according to the rules of academic knowledge, in order to determine Glissant's originality in relation to any tradition, always keeping in mind that the purpose of interpretation is subjective, not objective knowledge: even a very high level of culture does not guarantee understanding.

To take Glissant's propositions as so many certainties born out of nothing is both to reduce the questioning they deserve and to diminish their importance. A critical tabula rasa will flatten the historical depth of this thought into an achronic expanse. But we must remember that Glissant was first and foremost a thinker of and in history.

Le Sang rivé, a collection of his first poems written between 1947 and 1961 and published in 1961, includes, by way of exordium, an opening passage in which the writer is already reflecting on his act of poetry by placing himself "outside" the latter:

Poems—throughout the work of poetry, aimed at marking out the surroundings—not the strained, dull, monotonous or flat work in the image of the sea, endlessly sculpted—but splinters, tuned to the effervescence of the earth—and opening within the heart, beyond care and torment, something like a stridency of beaches—always cast away, always taken back, outside any completion—not works of art but the matter itself through which the work makes its way—are, all of them, related to some project that soon rejected them—first cries, naïve rumors, weary forms—witnesses, however inconvenient, of this project—which meet in their imperfection and thus find a perfect sense of solidarity—and here can convince us to tarry with uncertainty—with that which trembles, wavers and ceaselessly becomes all over again—like a land that is ravaged—scattered. (SC 9)

This exordium makes the anthology a composite object, somewhere between a collection of poems and a reflection on their production. It relegates the poems to obsolescence in the name of a new project that led to *Soleil de la conscience* (published in 1956). In addition, the exordium of *Le Sang rivé* is the announcement of a gap between the poet's aims and intentions and their inadequate materialization, something that in 1969 was to form the major theme of *L'Intention poétique*. But, immediately, this lack becomes the very sign of a future full of optimism: the failure is pregnant with a poetic future in the making, of a "matter," a "path," a "trembling" opening out on an uncertain tomorrow. *Soleil de la conscience* and *L'Intention poétique* amplify this interbreeding and interweaving of discursive types, mingling together poetry and reflection. Right from the start, *Le Sang rivé* establishes Glissant's specific mode of poetic production, which consists in going back over his past writings—what could be called a "becoming again," a self-critical mulling over his past that relaunches his project each time by modulating it.

With regard to the critical or conceptual title we file his work under, Glissant is, strictly speaking, unclassifiable; he has produced a work that lies beyond Belles-Lettres, the Republic of Letters, literature, and philosophy. At the very least, his project goes beyond the traditional notion of what is conceived as "literature." In 1958, *La Lézarde* still obeyed the conventions allowing it to be classified in the genre of the novel, but Glissant increasingly practiced a form of radically mixed writing, mingling genres so that the books he produced became uncategorizable. In fact, his œuvre, with a cross-generic aspect almost unprecedented in the tradition, appeals to new readers:

> Relation is unpredictable, and does not conceive of any rheto-
> ric. [. . .] The Chaos-World is unpredictable, and creates many
> rhetorics. Also, a system can be conceived in such a context only
> if it includes all possible rhetorics and also all the possibilities
> of a non-universalizing trans-rhetoric. (TTM 114)

There is thus no need to parrot Glissant in an adulatory and repetitive way, but to understand him and to consider him critically. If Glissant's reservations about systems and reason (as opposed to the imaginary) are to be valid, they must be completely rethought; they must not be simply restated in a mimetic reading. It is not enough for the interpretation to "quote" a critique (of the West, of identity, of Being, of universality, etc.) to become critical in its turn; the interpretation must reassess this critique's significance, trace its archeology, and ensure that assessment becomes an organic part of the knowledge being conveyed.

Academic knowledge may not give us an adequate grasp of Glissant's work, despite the very rich insights that this discourse has already produced: forever turned to a past that it inventories, this knowledge can admittedly produce indispensable insights. But how can it proceed to embrace a dynamic thought, endlessly becoming and intent on emerging from the library so as to embrace the world? How can it proceed with an object that is not literary knowledge (or objective know-how), but subjective knowledge, notions that Glissant always distinguishes between?

Glissant has no intention of constructing a literary work. In this sense, literary theory and criticism are of little use to those who wish to read and express the world, its cultures and its objects. Glissant's thought is in no way a reflection on the singular status of literary fiction,[6] on the role of the simulacra that literature shapes into an infinite parade (see his remarks in EBR 83–84); literary techniques, of which he makes so great and so subtle a use, are not objects of thought for him (see what he says of artistic techniques in *Une nouvelle région du monde*). In this sense, a purely "literary" analysis of the work will always fail to capture it, regardless of the richness of its insights.

Except for *Le Discours antillais*, the entire work could be read as a critique of academic discourse, with its many rigid distinctions and specializations, with its separation between subject and object, self and others, author and work, form and substance, with its ghettoization of national literatures and languages and literary genres, its contrast between philosophy and poetry, its cacophonies of methods and theories, its prioritizing of concept over experience, and its ideological contrast between the West and its Others. Glissant's thought rejects these segregations. Everything must be integrated into the uniqueness of the poetic dimension; the work must create the subject as much as the subject writes it, and thus follow Montaigne who, in his *Essais*, writes: "I have not made my book any more than my book has made me, a book consubstantial with its author, with a proper occupation, a limb of my life; not with an occupation and end that is a third party, foreign like all other books."[7]

Le Discours antillais has a special status in the problematics of Glissant's various discourses. In its first form, it was presented in 1980 to an academic jury at the University of Paris-VIII in order to obtain the symbolic recognition of a specific degree, namely a doctorate granted on the basis of published works. *Le Discours antillais* marks Glissant's entry into academic discourse; it is therefore not surprising that it is quite different from the rest of his writing: evidence, documentation, and argument (the logical sequence of propositions) occupy a more important place than in the essays that precede and follow it. In *L'Intention poétique*, for example, the argument does not rely on quotations; in *Poétique de la Relation* and later works, the concrete examples and particular cases that could illustrate or refute the theory are reduced, most of the time, to summaries that assemble them without presenting them in detail.

Glissant declares brutally: "Relation has no reality principle, it has only principles of relation" (EBR 102). This is not to be understood as a dismissal of reality or of the real, but as the mark of a discourse that does not have to provide evidence or documents, since it is projected toward an unpredictable future that has yet to happen. Therefore this discourse, in its openness to the future, does not stem from the discourse of the master or the discourse of the university (nor from paranoid psychosis and obsessional neurosis), but from an unpredictable act of healing wrought by Relation. Everywhere, in poetry, philosophy, and theory, in novels and plays, the discourse of theoretical mastery is fully integrated by and into a poetic form. The work is unified by an unmastered discourse in which the partitions between genres are made deliberately porous, so as to encourage us to envisage a future in which new genres will arise:

> From the integration or erasure or resurrection of all literary genres, theater, essay, novel, poetry, perhaps these other genres will be born. Perhaps we will experience some unprecedented interbreeding between the arts? But what they will be, we do not as yet know. (EBR 122)

Since Plato and Aristotle, poetry has been concerned with symbolic knowledge, the philosophy of the Being of rational knowledge, the myth of the "existence of the community in the world" (EBR 79), the epic of its constitution by defeat, the novel of "recounting history, the world" (IL 115) or, among the Romantics, the novel that expresses the self. It is this fragmentation and specialization of the poetic to which the Whole-World and Relation comprise an objection: the unity and totality of subjective knowledge have been lost in the compartmentalization of disciplines and forms of knowledge; the point is to recompose them and project them into a new becoming.

Le Discours antillais deals with one contemporary situation, the symbolic and economic status of the Antilles, while the other essays describe a future. As is appropriate for such an exercise, the theory is separated from its object: there is an observing subject and an observed object. The status of *Le Discours antillais* in Glissant's work is therefore an exception; this book comes closest to the discourse of the university, though it does send a tremor of anxiety through the latter. To create a book out of articles and conference papers, the latter were rewritten: this allowed Glissant to transfer them from out of the discourse of the university, and to set them back within the general movement of the work. For example, the Hegelian bedrock of the analysis of Martinican jouissance remains allusive, and the source is not explicitly mentioned—a major crime in academic circles. Moreover, affects and passions are not supposed to be part of the arsenal of a doctoral student, except under the category of the animal kingdom of Hegel's "spirit" (specialists in their ivory tower think that their discipline represents objective knowledge as such), or in the shape of a merely simulated passion. There is nothing more foreign to creolization than this kingdom; for Glissant, the "ivory tower" is a good thing (he spent much of his life there from 1989 onward), but only if its portal is open—to such a point that it agrees to its own abolition by excess of openness to the world and the Whole-World.

Glissant appropriates the affect explicitly, and thus decenters the animal kingdom of the spirit: "From a methodological point of view, this presentation will perhaps be marked by passion and affectivity, which in my view are among the components of the subject." Once again, the (academic) distance between subject and object is erased.

We must then question the question of control and jouissance in Glissant himself. Glissant rejects the *plus-de-jouir* of the master, the identification with the slave, the *plus-de-jouir* of both consumer and producer (of novels, of consumable prose). He also questions the mastery of the discourse of the university, not in the sense that *Le Discours antillais* does not deserve a doctorate (any doctoral program would be proud to have such a "candidate" among its applicants), but by rejecting the obsessional neurosis manifested in the mania for quoting (inherited from the medieval scholasticism that gave birth to the first universities). In addition, as far as the Republic of Letters goes, he rejects the jouissance of the popinjay sought by the leaders of sects or schools, such as André Breton in literature and Sartre in philosophy. The figure of the leader of a school is outdated, in his view. Like the partitioning of genres, it belongs to a world of rigidities now rendered obsolete by the Whole-World: literary and philosophical sects are the whited sepulchers of ideology.

It is a narrow path that Glissant traces to his jouissance (and not to his *plus-de-jouir*, which would bring it back into the discourse of *Das Kapital*).[8] The only possible way it can be made concrete is through poetic writing in relation. The potentiality of relation is the key to pleasures and jouissances: it is in relation that the fruits of a deferred accumulation and expenditure of knowledge await, and Glissant's work presents a materialized image of this process.

Finally, academic discourse is entirely directed toward the obtaining of a dominant mastery ("Dr. X masters his/her subject"); it is therefore not appropriate for a work that claims to be one of nondomination and nonmastery, and is moving toward a radical freedom.

Nevertheless, academic discourse remains indispensable when approaching Glissant's work: in particular, we cannot do without philosophy, which since Kant has been an integral part of the humanities. We cannot do without the history of philosophy, either, as it clarifies the implicit or allusive philosophical references in Glissant. But the sheer amount of the (quite immense) knowledge that the work deploys must in the final analysis bend to the requirement of poetic, intuitive, and material knowledge (*connaissance*), which is the supreme goal. Objective knowledge must be permuted by subjective knowledge, in the alchemical operation of the imaginary.

Since I am above all an academic, I have had to write against myself (against my way of being and thinking): to dampen down my systematizing trends, and rid myself of a gaze turned solely to the past, one which took the rationality of the concept to be the sole and supreme measure of all interpretation. Édouard Glissant gave me the freedom to write beyond myself: literature and poetry are the "first necessity," beyond objective knowledge, systems, and universals, and prior to all subjective knowledge. To write this book, I had to unmake and remake myself.

At the same time, as will be seen below, a "political" analysis will never grasp Glissant as an object; for example, while many of his interpreters are apparently unaware of the fact, he absolutely rejects interpretations that stem from postcolonialism. For him, this is a discourse that is abstracted from the poetic, turning the latter into a sort of pamphlet in the service of a noble cause. To reject postcolonialism does not in the least mean automatically repeating the misdeeds of the colonialists. No, thinking about the world and the future of the world, in poetry, the "novel," the essay, is a properly philosophical attempt to overcome these obsolete contradictions; this is the ultimate ambition of Glissant's program. It presupposes a multidisciplinary "method" or "theory," borrowing its tools from the most diverse fields. I recognize the contradiction presented by my choice of the philosophical field above all else: but we can speak of the unlimited only by limiting it.

Among the critical taxonomies that Glissant rejects, Francophonie figures prominently:

> We have arrived at a moment in history when we see that the imaginary of human beings needs all the languages of the world and, as a consequence, in the unavoidable place from where the literary work is broadcast, in the Antilles, the imaginary of the Antillean people needs the Creole language and the French language. That, indeed, is why I have never been able to accept the kind of vague alliance constituted by Francophonie. (IPD 41)

Francophonie, in his view, is merely an ideological symbol of France's effort to maintain its position in the interplay of international relations: "Francity is first and foremost an element of strategy. Francophonie is its sign" (DA 179). In addition, Francophonie is an extension of a past that must be remembered not so that we will get trapped in nagging resentment, but so as to extract new creative possibilities from it:

> It is clear that any attempt at a community of this kind ["francophone"] can only be a continuation of the colonial enterprise. [. . .] What we need is not to forget this old relationship; rather, the various memories of this old relationship should come together and combine. For forgetting is not a form of reunion. It is not a form of solidarity. But neither is a memory driven by the desire for revenge. (IL 100)

The rejection of labels and reductive descriptions (including both continuity and vengeful retaliation) is essential: to become trapped in them would be to prolong the old contradictions, whereas we must embark on the task of imagining many forms of sharing:

> If Francophonie rids itself of its ghosts, which still stammer the precepts of an all-ruling unity, it may well, in all beauty, finally join in the world's adventure and cease to be a bureaucratic imposition or a lofty prejudice, and become instead an inspiration and a breath of fresh air. (NRM 172)[9]

Postmodernism is just as sternly challenged. Glissant describes Antillean modernity in its relationship to the cultural heritage:

> We [Antilleans] do not have a literary continuum. This is what makes me say that we can enter fully into the modern world, that we are not atavists [. . .]. It is not from constructed works that we draw our continuity, but paradoxically from the historical impossibility of continuity. (IL 21–22)

Now, postmodernism reaffirms an underground continuity, one anchored in the recycling of the aesthetic results of its own past:

> What is known in Western cultures as the postmodern is an attempt to find an order in (and bring order to) this reality lived as chaos, without however giving up the vitality of this chaos. To manage modernity, by making it serial. That is to say, anchoring itself as much as possible in the continuum of its own production. [. . .] But, we have repeatedly suggested, aesthetic and philosophical thoughts, from whatever culture they were engendered, will have to break with the birth of their history, to compromise with every contamination. They will have to implement their Other of thought. (PR 235)

This critique of the continuity that postmodernism restores extends to postcolonial theory, when it is merely a repetition that relies on continuity and thus bars the emergence of anything radically new. Thus Glissant underlines the disappointing and often absurd results of anticolonialist struggles, criticizing the revival of old policies, and, implicitly, of traditional poetics: "Decolonizations were absolutely necessary, but [. . .]

they were not accompanied by a sufficient work of critical reflection on the very ideas that the West had proposed to the world" (EBR 59). If postcolonial theory is content to simply reverse the cultural themes of the colonizer, then it traps itself within a continuum of poetics that should have been broken. In short, it is never sufficiently Other, never sufficiently irreducible to what preceded it.

A poetics transparent to ideological positions, to social and political problems, ignoring what makes it literature rather than a pamphlet, a manifesto or a sociological study,[10] is also the exact opposite of what Glissant has in mind: "It is not the function of writing to precipitate politics" (EBR 60). This rejection of the ideological transitivity of writing is fundamentally anti-Sartrean, and aims to avoid any reduction of literature to politics:

> It seemed to me that if we dedicated writing solely to bringing a people's struggle, the struggle of a community or a nation, to completion—if, in the process of writing, we forgot what lay behind all struggles, that is to say the most discreet bases of a culture, the opacities of Being and the tremors of knowledge—we were not performing a writer's task but the equally necessary task of a pamphleteer or committed journalist or activist in a hurry to obtain such results. (EBR 60)

After post-Francophonie and postmodernism, postcolonialism also, quite consistently, is sent packing:

> I do not feel like a postcolonialist, because I am part of a never-ending history. The history of the Caribbean is not a fixed history. There is not a postcolonialist period in the history of the Caribbean, and even the Americas. There is a discontinuum that still weighs on us. If we call postcolonialism the fact that we can reflect on a past phenomenon called colonialism, I say that this is not true. We are still in the colonial period, but it is a colonialism that has taken another form. It is a colonialism of the big multinationals. A colonizing country no longer needs to occupy another in order to colonize it. There is something recapitulative, synthetic and conclusive in the term "postcolonialism" that I reject. (IL 64–65)

Let us generalize this example: the reproach addressed to the current critical categories is the way they are closed and fixed, which by definition excludes the history that is being made, a "never-ending history." This refusal of a direct politicization of the poetic follows quite consistently from the rejection of what I would call victimology, identification with the victim, often prevalent in francophone and postcolonial criticism (but not only there: feminist studies and gay studies suffer from it too). These schools of thought seek to save themselves from domination and to purchase a good political conscience for themselves on the cheap. Admittedly, no one is entitled to stifle the victim's cry; but those who have not experienced this cry and appropriate it for the benefit of an (academic) discourse are providing themselves with a good conscience at little cost to themselves. The "victimologist" is a subspecies of the Hegelian beautiful soul, who appropriates the supposed sufferings of the martyrs (of capitalism, the West, phallocentrism, etc.), while he or she often benefits in a privileged way from the surplus material wealth that bourgeois society offers him or her as a university professor. Victimologists may indeed walk a road paved with all the "good intentions" in the world, but they shift from academic work to an essentially ideological discourse in which, by acting as the voice of the martyrs, they secretly aspire, through them, to the place of the master. Why not, after all? But one must not claim, by virtue of this identification, to be adopting a revolutionary posture that will change the world. The profound structure of the discourse of the master is in no way reversed—it is reinforced by such an aspiration:[11] any victimological interpretation is then a piece of Hegelian chatter, since it never provides itself with the means to carry out any real action in the world; it is the direct heir of the beautiful soul and the intellectual. Glissant's position, in my view, is much more correct: by rejecting resentment, he delivers the oppressed from aspiration to the place of the master.

One example will be enough: "Enough laments! Let us dare more! Let us bring down the narrative into our present, let us push it into tomorrow! Let us dig into the sufferings that are here and now, to prevent those that will appear" (TTM 61). Lamentation imprisons us in the linear continuum of history without giving us any way of transforming it.

Victimology enslaves poetics to a monolithic, unique, and centered political vision of the world. Glissant's ban on "laments" also expresses a mistrust of the quasi-universals constituted by political alliances that reach a consensus. The commonplaces of victimology enclose its supporters in a negative attitude of resentment and perpetual protest. Victimology is anachronistic, since it requires those *who are no longer* victims and those *who are no longer* masters to identify themselves immediately with the masters or slaves of the past. Victims thereby fit into a predetermined dialectic that reproduces the old order ad infinitum. The same applies to anticolonialist struggles: "I had the presentiment that these struggles had followed the same model imposed by those who opposed them" (EBR 58).

Thus, in the whole of Glissant's work, in his stories and essays, one will not find any trace of elegy, as this would rehearse the same old resentments and complaints, both real and imaginary: in Glissant, as in Hegel, negativity is not a pretext for a jeremiad, but a propitious opportunity for affirming a positivity. To give just one example from a thousand others: "But what was a consequence of European expansion (the extermination of the Pre-Columbians, the importation of new populations) was precisely what founded a new relationship to the land: not the absolute sanctity of an ontological possession, but relational complicity" (PR 161). The negativities of history are required if we are to open up to a future of affirmation that will take advantage of constraints to overthrow them and lead to the joy of overcoming:

> As for us, we were taught to tell . . . a story. To consent to history. To gild ourselves with the brilliance of its style, which we believe to be ours. We were put on the leash. But the tale does not tell a story, the tale takes no account of wretchedness, the tale hurtles down to the hidden source of suffering and oppression, and it rejoices in unknown and perhaps obscure forms of happiness. (TTM 61)

Of course, the rejection of identification is not limited to victims. Glissant obviously opposes anyone becoming akin to a master, and any discourse of tutelage, whether political, rhetorical, poetic, national, or conceptual. His work aims to prevent the naturalization of the filiations comprised by aesthetic traditions, whether national or ethnic, from whatever source. The slightest assertion of dominance and exclusiveness must be questioned. By pointing out the flaws and the blind spots in systems and universals, Glissant hampers and disturbs any recourse to an established doctrine, whether "Western" or otherwise.

Glissant's thought suffers no exclusiveness: art can be produced as much by the master as by the slave. This is true of Faulkner, among others: "What a prejudice it is, inherited from the norm of the oppressors, to claim that a work cannot emerge from the house of the master as much as from the shack of the oppressed" (FM 29). Any precedence granted in literature and criticism to the victim merely inverses the old prejudice that only the master could produce, or cause to be produced, masterpieces for his sole use. No, masterpieces can emerge from everywhere, unpredictably: literature does not have to submit to the ideological splits of history.

In writing these lines I am put in mind of the times when, talking to Glissant, I praised Racine, who created a world with a vocabulary of five thousand words, or when I made him listen to Johann Sebastian Bach's "Canzone in D Minor" performed by Marie-Claire Alain on a restored organ in the Netherlands. In spite of his preference for Baroque literature, and in spite of his judgments on the "Western tradition," he enthusiastically approved of Racine and Bach. This benevolence, this welcome, of course, must be extended to the master philosopher, Hegel: the latter may have forgotten Africa, but that does not mean that he should not be read.

The new will emerge only if the oppressed emerges from the dialectic in which the slave simply aspires to mastery.[12] It will be noticed that there is never, in all his work, any personal complaint. From the beginning, Glissant leaves to his words the task of demonstrating and propagating his sovereignty, without laying any claim to recognition. In his work, there is no identification with any inferiority, racial, intellectual, or social (though this does not exclude listening to the weak and the oppressed). From the beginning, he engages in uninhibited dialogue with the greatest thinkers and poets, in life as in work, as an equal who does not have to establish his authority or gain recognition for it. This is a refreshing break from the never-ending complaints of privileged academics or successful writers, giving voice to real and imagined victims, past or present, with whom they have very little in common.

The rejection of victimology rules out any reading of the work that would reduce it to an ideology: "This is also because the poetics of Relation is forever conjectural and does not presuppose any fixed ideology" (PR 44). Glissant's mistrust of ideology is displayed everywhere, and should be respected as a fundamental principle of interpretation: "Against generalizing pontificators. Against self-sufficient ideology. Against local poppinjays [. . .]" (PR 217). Glissant never wraps himself him in the flag of the revolutionary, except when it comes to promoting Relation and the Whole-World: the upheavals he produces are all the more effective and fundamental:

> The domination inherited from conquest and possession per-
> sists and embellishes, but it is in those circularities in volumes
> where the lines have been lost: the light shed by ideological
> analysis is no longer enough to flush this domination out.
> [Under the word "ideology" I also include the critical and
> political philosophies that have helped to "reveal" ideologies].
> (PR 74)

His note on Trotsky and Marxism in *Poétique de la Relation* is revealing. The permanent revolution remains ethnocentric, linear, universalizing, and confined to the ideological domain—outside Relation: "The generalizing universal was latent in this thought: it authorized the monstrosities of Stalin. His imaginary, on the contrary, if he had been freed from the obsession with taking power, would have provided material for Relation" (PR 235).[13]

Édouard Glissant never lost interest in politics, just as he was not indifferent to the lot of the humble, the poor, or the oppressed. On the contrary, he engaged in many political activities.[14] He signed the *Manifesto of the 121* against the Algerian War in 1960 (which got him into trouble with the immigration services in the United States); together with Paul Niger, he founded the Antillean-Guyanese Front, which pursued independence and then autonomy in 1961 (which led to his being placed under house arrest in France between 1959 and 1965); and he wrote several works, such as the *Mémoires des esclavages*,[15] the 2007 manifesto *Quand les murs tombent: l'identité nationale hors-la-loi?* (co-authored with Patrick Chamoiseau), attacking the immigration policy of the Sarkozy government, and (also with Chamoiseau), *L'Intraitable Beauté du monde. Adresse à Barack Obama* (2009), as well as collaborating on the 2009 *Manifeste pour les produits de haute nécessité*.[16]

This latter manifesto clarifies Glissant's position (and that of Chamoiseau, one of the co-signatories) on the occasions when he is supporting a movement whose claims are purely economic and political. The Liyannaj Kont Pwofitasyon, or LKP ("Collective against outrageous exploitation"), created in 2008 in Guadeloupe, does indeed demand a better distribution of the *plus-de-jouir* of merchandise; in this sense, it merely strengthens the system, which it calls on to release the sums necessary for greater consumption. Glissant and the co-signatories of the *Manifeste* (Ernest Breleur, Patrick Chamoiseau, Serge Domi, Gérard Delver, Guillaume Pigeard de Gurbert, Olivier Portecop, Olivier Pulvar, and Jean-Claude William) add to the products of "primary necessity" demanded by the LKP the articles of "high necessity":

> Hence, behind the prosaic level of "purchasing power" and the "shopping basket," what we can see is the essential dimension that we lack and that gives meaning to existence, namely: the poetic. Every moderately well-balanced human life is shaped between, on the one hand, the immediate necessities of drinking-surviving-eating (in plain language: the prosaic) and, on the other, the aspiration to self-fulfillment, where our food consists of dignity, honor, music, songs, sports, dances, reading, philosophy, spirituality, love, free time assigned to the fulfillment of the great intimate desire (in short: the poetic). (MPHN 2)

The demand for the poetic superimposes itself on the prose of profit, production, and economic consumption, a move that goes beyond the first dialectic of material demand; this is a necessary step, and perhaps the only possible way out of the trading system (we will see why below). If the last manifestos share with the first interventions a political intention (the denunciation of the wrongs of nationalism or globalization), they affirm the poetic as a realm outside the political, which is thus deprived of its globalizing claim to gather everything together: "To head off to the Whole-World just like a young poet! This, perhaps, is the most realistic of policies" (IBM 33). Glissant's relation to politics takes the form of a chiasm: we need to disengage from a committed political poetry and put forward a politics of poetry. In the *Entretiens*, Glissant notes the radical inversion that he is imposing on the dialectic of the individual and of the social (political) bond. Political necessity applies not to a collectivity, but to the maintenance of individuality. The poetic, for its part, has the task of shaping the collective:

> There are these two approaches: in the first place, not to be lost as an individual in the rigorous attempt to establish a continuum of the biography of the collective; that is what I express by saying that the poet must be both solitary and solidary, as Albert Camus puts it in a phrase that I had lost and then found. Solitary: there is a preservation of the individual as a resource, and solidary: there is a quest for the collective continuum in time, in the form of the poetic [. . .]. As you will notice, *I*

reverse the function of these terms, "political" and "poetic"; they are no longer as commonly envisaged, but sketched out in a new dialectic. (EBR 38, my emphasis)

If we apply this chiasm to Glissant's very first essays, we see that they stubbornly reject the whole essence of the project proposed by Jean-Paul Sartre, the project of the committed writer whose works have the primary mission of being transparent to a political issue. And this happened at the very moment when Sartre's influence was at its apogee. The commitment here is an individual resistance to reducing the subject to the social agglomeration. As for writing, it must commit itself to the pursuit of a poetics of the community:

> The political is reinforced by the direct vision and the imaginary of the world, and bolsters its actions by agreeing at one and the same time to these two poetics [that of Relation, and that of place and detail], linked to a non-totalitarian totality (there is no internationalism of ideologies) and to a sense of belonging to particular places (countries and peoples) which are preserved from both entanglement and mimetic weakness. (PhR 86)

Glissant returns to the question in 2010, in an interview with Christian Tortel; he confers on politics what seems an impossible task, but one with an impressive ambition and nobility, as it goes beyond the mere agglutination of those shopkeeper's interests that comprise the daily bread of politics. What politics, after all, accords with the trembling of the world? What politics can conceive of Relation as anything but the mutual adjustment of particular demands? What politics can envision a vision other than the political vision of the world?

A politics must understand and accept that there is a trembling of the world, and that there is no weakness, no lack or omission, in consenting to this trembling: it involves giving up the single thought, the ready-made thought, and seeking connections, relations of thought. I believe that our poetics today must no longer be a poetics of *definition*, it must be a poetics of *relation*. And if we have a poetics of relation, we have a politics of relation. And that's all to the good.[17]

So the work cannot be grasped by preconceived categories that stick inappropriate labels on it, be they political, ideological, or critical. Neither

Francophonie, nor postmodernism, nor anticolonialism, nor postcolonialism can shed light on the texts. I do not intend to engage in sterile polemics here, but it is a fact that Glissant explicitly and consistently rejects these categories. First, they take us back to a past without transforming it, and confine themselves to endlessly mulling over a negativity without extracting a positive poetic affirmation from it; second, under their subversive appearance, they often fall back on a "bad" filiation; last, and above all, in their sometimes backward-looking fixity, they ignore the future and any dynamic becoming, thus blocking the path of the unpredictable, which is the fundamental desire of all that Édouard Glissant has written. We must read Glissant without labeling him.

Glissant's cultural relativism, of which Relation is the foundation, differs profoundly from multiculturalism. The latter is founded, legitimized, and imprisoned in a logic of identity, thereby prolonging a confinement: its essence is segregation. This is a ruinous error, which is the very antinomy of creolization. Glissant did not hesitate to criticize multiculturalism, taking the United States as an example, whether rightly or wrongly (largely wrongly, it seems to me); he contrasted multiculturalism with creolization:

> One of the peculiarities of the sociocultural structure of the United States is precisely that there is a multiculturalism, but without creolization, without any profound interpenetration. These cultures do not become contaminated, they are absolutely impervious to each other. The United States will become a great land of creolization the day these cultures can resonate with each other, with unexpected results.[18]

Creolization is not hybridity, the melting pot, crossbreeding, a juxtaposition of cultures that tolerate each other in the indifference of partitionings and the lack of all contact that a culture of selfishness produces; these representations are only passing phenomena, an expectation of something that does not express itself because it lies in the future:

> *The thought of creolizations*: the inexpressible aspect of the relationship between cultures, with very many unexpected extensions that so clearly distinguish creolization from mere hybrids. But we (ethnic, societal, cultural, continental or archipelagic) cannot at first conceive of these unexpected factors which introduce us to the uncertainties of Relation. Yet we have long understood that creolization is neither the obvious fact of this

hybridization alone, nor the melting pot, nor the mechanics of different forms of multiculturalism. It is process, not fixity. There is an alchemy of creolization which crosses crossbreeds even further, and yet is transmitted through them. (PhR 64)

Glissant's thought allows for a vast reassessment of the "Western" past; the originality of his vision of tradition enables us, as he writes, to "prophesy the past," to identify in this dense, diverse, multiple history the moments where the first outbursts of creolization occur, where the originary attempts of the Whole-World are born (we will come back to this), and also the periods in which these experiments are dismissed:

In all my novels, there is a quest for memory and a conception of time. Now, in his work, Proust builds a temporal cathedral. His memory goes back up, in a harmonious and continuous way, to the first principles of society. With us Antilleans, colonization has split us off from our temporal memory. It would be absurd to try to find a fluid, continuous and harmonious temporality. We do not go in search of lost time (a *temps perdu*) because this time is something we have never possessed and so cannot lose. It is a distraught time (*un temps éperdu*). We cannot build a temporal cathedral. We can only leap from rock to rock. We can recover a time of our own, but in a fragmented way only. We are inevitably in a state of temporal complexity. I will add that we must have a prophetic vision of the past. We must not put the past in a cage in order to decide on our future, but take into account the uncertainty of the past to think about the future. We need to go beyond historical analysis—this latter is necessary but not sufficient. We must not have a vision of the past that determines the present, but a vision that opens up to all possible presents.[19]

There are very few thinkers who have managed to subsume a Western (or, to avoid confusion, "European") tradition dating back three millennia so that we are enabled to see it in a completely new way and are freed from the sometimes oppressive drone of cultural constraints accumulated over the centuries. Glissant actively rejuvenates the "Western" tradition, drawing both on its inner resources and on elements from outside, rejecting the passivity of a faithful but inert transmission.

Chapter 2

"Repetition is not an unnecessary duplication"

From Glissant's first forays into the genre of the essay, *Soleil de la conscience* (1956) onward, mulling over (*le ressassement*) is posited as the dynamics of writing, on the basis of a twofold experience: the partial republication of his first poems and the assessment of these in the light of a project that gradually becomes clearer. The writing of *Soleil* is from the very start a crossbreed between poetry and essay, the Antilles and Paris, subject and object. In this process, one becomes the "ethnologist of oneself," both poem and commentary: "Thus, when the time of the New Reason came, presenting the reader with old texts—the first ones for example that one really wrote—means having the courage (while still being unsure of anything) to return to these pages of the beginning in an attempt to lay bare the motives, the dream of origins" (SC 34). This is a mulling over of oneself and one's work, a deliberate choice from the beginning, and constantly reaffirmed. In 2000: "So repetition is, here and there, an acknowledged world of subjective knowledge. Resuming without respite what you have always said. Consenting to the infinitesimal impulse and to the (perhaps unnoticed) addition which persist in your more objective knowledge" (PR 59). In 2009:

> We often used to privilege the practices of repetition, in an attempt to know or try to catch hold of the implicit or already obliterated meetings between the peoples in the world and in the histories of the world, but it is one of the principles of the Aesthetics of the Whole-World that no one ever utters the

> same words twice to form the same ideas, in this river of the
> world. So we utter infinitely imperceptible variants that act as
> a ferment and revealer of all repetition. (TTM 161)

In its turn, *Poétique de la Relation* is "the recomposed echo or the spiraling restatement of *L'Intention poétique* and *Le Discours antillais*" (PR 28). At the end of this itinerary, the *Philosophie de la Relation* will also be the modifying restatement of *Une nouvelle région du monde*: "The unordered sequence of images that I will here propose finds its common places in *Une nouvelle région du monde*, a work whose statements it summarizes or repeats" (PhR 25).

Mulling over is not a static return to the identical; it produces "infinitesimal" variants, from which arise new senses: the detail is never one of these senses. The flow of the Heraclitean river of becoming makes repetition different from itself and produces variants, a dynamic change through which thought continues to advance. This also applies to the mulling over of the many cultural and artistic traditions that the work embraces. Finally, repetition is driven by the failure of "poetic intention." "To say is something other than to do," wrote Montaigne (*Essais*, II, 31). Between what we mean, what we want (to say/write) on the one hand, and what we do on the other, there is always distance and difference. The intention is never fulfilled in the way we had hoped. From this general maxim made manifest in human destiny, Glissant draws the poetic consequences: what he has written never corresponds to what he wanted to formulate; so, right from the start, we must always restate, always repeat, in the pursuit of an end that is constantly disappearing into a new distance.

Re-reading his own texts is a fundamental driver of Glissant's writing: it is like an inaugural moment of Relation. The first moment, "the dream of origins," is one of poetry, and the essay comes later; then they become entangled. This interweaving will be accentuated even more at a later stage, when poetry and reflection engender each other and eventually merge. Re-reading is an act that combines theoretical or philosophical reflection and poetic creation, from beginning to end of the work. In the final analysis, mulling over is indistinguishable from the creative act and the path of thought:

> Wandering is the place of repetition, when the latter arranges
> the tiny (infinite) variations that each time distinguish this
> same repetition as a moment of subjective knowledge. Poets

and storytellers instinctively give themselves to this delicate
art of listing (by accumulated variations) which shows us that
repetition is not an unnecessary duplication. (PhR 61–62)

We are closer to the circle that Nietzsche created with the eternal
return of the same: "I would finally try to join the beginning to the
end" (SC 52).

One day in 1993, putting the last touches to *Tout-Monde*, Glissant
exclaimed point-blank: "It's a good thing that I re-read *Mahagony*, I was
going to write some really stupid things in *Tout-Monde!*" From which
we can infer, on the level of novelistic writing, a radical demand for
consistency from one book to another, extending, of course, beyond the
genre of the "novel."

Thus, repetition is what, in an apparent paradox, produces the completely new: "You repeat yourself, you venture into the risk of the commonplace, you dare to wander along the path, you dare the unexpected"
(PhR 94). Or again: "The result is something unexpected" (CL 253). This
process must be applied not only to the work itself, to the literary and
philosophical traditions that it incorporates, but also to the places and
landscapes of the world that it revisits in an incessant two-way journey.

Glissant is a radically original thinker. However, he arrives at the
completely new by a stubborn reiteration: of himself, and of others (Hegel,
Heraclitus, Faulkner, etc.). This is why it is essential to identify in his
work those others whom he has incorporated and who are often hidden
in allusion, ellipsis, and euphemism. Note that this rhetoric of the implied
is deliberate: its aim is to avoid the enumeration and exhibition of forms
of objective knowledge (inevitable for the commentator), absorbing them
into a poetics of subjective knowledge.

In the dialectical clash between Antillean culture and French culture,
Glissant begins with himself, in a composite inaugural movement, like
the psychoanalyst, the saint and the poet, just as the first troubadour,
Guillaume IX of Aquitaine, Count of Poitiers, had wished: "I will take
my poem as an authority. *Auctor*, he writes for 'authority'; this could be
translated: *my poem will be author of itself.*" But we must go further; from
the start, poetic creation, the solitary side of Camus' solidarity is constitutive of identity: "It is literally my language (*langage*) that *institutes me*"
(SC 50).[1] The writer makes himself, engenders himself, in "the work
of the self-arousing being, born from its own will (a clay that is allied,
without any demiurge, to its own breath)" (SC 15). This institution of the

writing subject, however, does not produce an incantatory tautology by which the work would be trapped in its own mirror, but clears a space for its exteriority: to be self-born is not to close the poem on oneself, to enclose the individual in his artistic realization, to make him or read him so that he stands in a desolate solitude; it is to be born to the world and to put the poem and oneself in relation, a poetic birth that does not lead to any completeness, and that recalls once again Claudel's *co-naissance* (subjective knowledge as co-birth): "To be born into the world is finally to conceive (to live) the world as relation: as a composite necessity, a consented, poetic (and not moral) reaction of otherness. As an unfulfilled drama of this necessity" (SC 20).

Glissant's birth was twofold, taking place both in the Antilles and in Paris, in the Sorbonne. It is compared to an immunization, an almost organic viral transplant that indelibly marks body and mind: "Leaving behind the tragic joy of the House, and resuming the course of the snow. This experience of Europe has 'taken', as one can say of a vaccine; and I can no longer go back on it" (CS 51). The Western tradition is thus a "vaccine": an element at first foreign to the body, but which the body appropriates and transforms into an organic part of itself. This re-appropriation, which transforms cultural constraints into a deliberate and conscious choice, depends on its evocation, and thus its writing: "But to evoke [this experience of Europe] is to know it. And this subjective knowledge (which comes after the unfolding, after the period of testing) is alone a matter of free choice. It introduces the subject–object to the realm of its future discoveries" (SC 51).

The journey to the West and to its culture is not experienced as a trauma, diaspora, or uprooting from a foundational soil; rather, it is a double graft in which the Antilles and Paris change places without our being able to distinguish, in this mix, between the original trunk and the graft: a true digenesis, which merges, while still distinguishing between them, two parallel and equally important origins that do not impose themselves as binding roots but as openness to new possibilities. The beginning (in the twofold Antillean and Western tradition) is not absolute, and the new beginning points to a fresh dawn based on recomposed legacies.

From this birth, in which the writer and the work, in a way, man-ufacture their own childbirth and baptize themselves, Glissant's work develops in a spiral, always ruminating over the same material, extending to and embracing an immense expanse of living multiplicities, which are the ferment of new discoveries: "The imaginary first. It works in a spiral:

from one circularity to another it encounters new spaces which it does not transform into depths or conquests" (PR 216). Of course, *Soleil de la conscience* works as a prelude here, as it develops, amplifies, and modifies itself; but Glissant's work is a rhapsodic symphony, consisting only of an immense "overture" to the future; whether it is deciphered retrospectively or prospectively, we will always hear a kind of basso continuo that modulates the "little phrases of Vinteuil." The work is similar to these huge prehistoric ammonites: starting out from a tiny shape, a few poems, a short essay, it grows out to embrace an infinite multiplicity, in a circle always broken and reshaped in the organic spiral of a vast growth.

Beyond the metaphors of ammonite and spiral, there emerges another figure, more secret and more real, of the construction of thought: this is the Moebius strip that twists on itself, registering contrasts and divisions on a unilateral and unifying strip while leaving them distinct: Paris/Antilles, narratives/essays, literature/philosophy, work/life, world/ expression of the world, etcetera—multiple facets of the same creative act that overcomes all division, all binarism. The Moebius strip allows us to endlessly amplify themes and to mull over the objects of thought, not just to nuance them, but to provoke them into some new shape, continuously relaunching them afresh. And, in the center of the Moebius strip, there will be not a void, but the world, or even the Whole-World, inextricably surrounded by the work.[2] When Glissant meditates on the rhizome, it corresponds exactly to a Moebius strip. The rhizome is not "a pure avatar or a prototype of flatness, or of some motionless or static thing; its infinite diversity *unfolds in an expanse twisted in on itself, underlying all directions, by a non-linear multiforce,* so that its heights as much as these depths swap places in a permanent movement across our spaces" (NRM 108–109; I have italicized the features that apply as such to the Moebius strip).

Almost all the major themes of the work as a whole, whatever the genre, poetry, novel, theater, essay, interview, or piece of circumstantial writing, are already latent in *Soleil de la conscience* and *L'Intention poétique.* This is evidence of the massive consistency that governs Glissant's thinking; the singular voice of the poet thinker can already be found in the first essays, and all the works that follow are merely a powerful amplification of this. In addition to what it retrospectively reveals about the profound unity of his thought, *Soleil de la conscience* manifests the interbreeding, the inextricable interweaving of reflection and poetry, displayed everywhere in the style.

At this point, a brief selection can stand as an inventory. Of course, *Soleil de la conscience*, like other texts, can stand alone and deserves its own detailed "internal" reading. But the very continuity of Glissant's work means that an analytical close reading would fracture the text and break up its integrity. It would also take several lives to produce an exhaustive commentary on each text: the real of the work always exceeds the possibilities of interpretation, which is the sign of the writer's greatness. It is true of Glissant as it is of Dante: nobody will ever say the "last word" about them—their texts produce an inexhaustible meaning.

Following the practice of listing that Glissant is fond of, here is a nonexhaustive inventory of the themes in *Soleil de la conscience*:

- The dialectic, a union of antinomies, refers implicitly to Hegel and Heraclitus and anticipates the process of the thought to come: "Outside, it is French truth that opposes mine—by this revealed covenant between a contrary and its other, of which we know that all truth is the dialectical consummation" (SC 16).

- The imaginary re-inscribes singularity in a community and establishes the dialogue between the silence of the individual and the shared, spoken word: "Imagination is shared, and can only bolster a common impetus; it is, however, dependent on silence, that of the individual" (SC 26).

- Against this desire for sharing stands the individualism of Western art, at the end of a long historical evolution: "Literary meticulousness, however lucid, announces a disintegrated Body. Today, the general character of Western art, what it shares among artists, is the absence of community" (S 62).

- From this Glissant derives the only form of "political" action to which, in the final analysis, he will consent: "the collective dimension of the literary phenomenon (a dimension that enables sensibility to be enriched by basing it in subjective knowledge)" (SC 62).

- The "Western" solitude of writing is challenged by the community founded by the "oraliture" (oral literature) of the fable and the tale; it leads to the need for a *common* poetic place: "We are here [in Paris] at the opposite pole from collective literatures, legends known a thousand times but always listened to, fervent attention to texts, vigils around the storyteller, the meaning of the word as everyone's common place: what made literatures the living weapon, living because tried and tested, of civilizations" (SC 13).

- Measure and chaos announce excess: "From the elucidation of chaos to the illustration of measure lies the long distance initially created first by the slow approach of objective knowledge and then by the muted task of suffering" (SC 20).

- The measured quality of a tradition or literary and rhetorical filiation is a betrayal of poetic intention: "When we use the material of the alexandrine (twelve syllables, a rhyme) as the measure of this verse, then we betray it" (SC 40).

- The poetic intention, in turn, means that the poem never corresponds entirely to the author's will: "The poem after the poem paves with momentary acquisitions those routes that everyone leads along into himself in order to learn forever" (SC 20).

- The project of the *Discours antillais* is anticipated: "We need to talk about racism [. . .]. I mean, we need to stop turning it into an absolute—to elucidate the motives that drive racism, whether we decide that they are social, economic or political—motives that authorize it, still, to wreak havoc" (SC 53).

- The suspicion of the abstract and universals that Glissant propagates, and his preference for the concrete, are announced: "[Man] abstracts concrete forms and makes them general: he wrings them dry and makes of them wan things" (SC 35).

- The Whole-World, decentering, the Relation, the importance of history in the intermingling of the poetic, all arise: "I sense that maybe there will be no more culture without all cultures, no more single civilization that can be the metropolis of all others, no more poets unaware of the movement of history" (S 11).

- The importance of the landscapes and places, already inextricable, of the Antilles and Europe, comes to light in a dialectical opposition.

- The first charting out of the question of Being is established: "Thus man runs to meet the world; and rids himself as he runs of the weight of his being, as a useless burden" (SC 41).

- Chaos (the chaos-world) is an origin that comes before all else, and forces us to think:

    > Chaos first. What we live is derisory until thought has corrected it. Man shouts out his volcano, he piles lava on lava. He is gauche; he proposes and struggles among what is obvious and yet remote. (SC 35)

- Finally, and above all, the preeminence of poetry as a practice of writing is affirmed—the poetic as the primordial means of the subjective knowledge of the world: "(Yes, I here engage it—poetry: may it grant me the meaning of my language, to testify to the meaning of my story. May it accomplish its work through me, to illustrate through itself the work of my consciousness holding me in its grasp)" (SC 40). Poetic knowledge is posited as the foundation of an understanding that goes beyond rationality by including it: "No art as much as poetry is linked to the apocalyptic momentum of human knowledge. [. . .] No art more than poetry has the task of opening up on man this reason for all things, a reason that will sublimate reason" (SC 41).

Soleil de la conscience is also a chronicle of Glissant's comings and goings between Martinique and Paris. The hybridity and digenesis of the origin are in evidence in the earliest essay, and the geography of the place is almost immediately a topography of subjective knowledge: "In truth, the answer is twofold: for wherever I go, I will feel solidarity with this 'piece of land' [. . .]; and on the other hand, it is undeniable to me that a whole part of me, the most arid and the most movably furnished at the same time, is here in Paris, where I have known so many other faces of subjective knowledge" (SC 64–65). But these two places are not the points of arrival and departure of any trivial trip: Martinique is "already," in 1956, the symbol of a new sense of subjective knowledge, of an enlargement and critical revival of a whole philosophical and poetic tradition; Paris is "already," not the mimetic acceptance of a French-style acculturation, but the possibility of "another face of subjective knowledge," which I think is none other than the face of philosophy, grasped "already" from a particular angle, "other" in a difference that mulls over it and at the same time goes beyond it.

Soleil de la conscience is also the discovery of others, which explains how we are also different, divided between "the gaze of the son and the vision of the Stranger" (SC 11), how "we are both subject and object" (SC 16), observer and observed, and how everyone must therefore be the "ethnologist of [himself]." The digenesis is not only that of cultures, but also that of the subject Édouard Glissant, shared between an inside and an outside brought into a dialectical relation. And "the discovery of the disparate, of the fundamental Other, which nourishes the nostalgia for unity" (SC 60) is the ferment of a long quest, not centered on a single origin, but as a union of opposites crossbred by a poetics.

There is thus a double distance and a double vision, something whose singularity has been emphasized by Alain Ménil:[3] the distance from the land of origin, modified by the perception of the *other* gaze acquired by learning about the Western tradition, and the distance from this West created by an Antillean origin. The place of utterance that Glissant chooses for himself is unlike any other. But Glissant, always unclassifiable, cannot be reduced to a double origin (a digenesis) that would constrain his thinking: he was a meteor, coming from Elsewhere, not just from the Antilles and Paris, but from a radically Other place that his work has constructed and which he will later call the *Other of thought* (PR 169).

As a result, his returns to Martinique will never be pastorals marked by nostalgia for a lost paradise. At the same time, the reinterpretation of the West will not be a matter of an uncritical parroting, nor of obedience to cultural filiation, nor of any resentment or thirst for revenge: the reassessment of Europe will be based on a gaze from elsewhere. Glissant has no patience for the songs of the homeland, nor for submission to universals inherited from a tradition, nor for the semblances of subversion. He writes between these places, between-lands or between-times, in a round trip where navigation is a relation between antinomies. This is a crossing both literal and symbolic, where the sea plays a fundamental role, and where (re)crossing from Fort-de-France to Le Havre reverses, positively, the route of the slave trade: "Now, I am again crossing the Atlantic. Either this ship, with the name of an apparently virgin land (it is called *Colombie*), is bearing me away; or, not stirring from the gray stone, I again find my voice and begin the dialogue across Paris. Now, I am not going up the Mountain—wait, wait: the Sea is growing through me" (SC 43).

L'Intention poétique is a mulling over of *Soleil de la conscience*, where continuity and coherence are reaffirmed. But repetition is dynamic progression: "(You write the same word.) So many restatements, 'obvious points,' for such a long time [. . .]. *Soleil de la conscience*: Wandering introduces us to diversity, and then diversity forces Being toward its 'meaning'" (IP 15). In this way a furrow of unifying writing is traced out, whose aim is non-linear: "Lands gradually accumulated, with the ceaseless glint of an unfurling furrow anticipated ever since those distant times" (IP 15).

In 1969, the idea of "relation," not yet dignified with a capital letter, became clearer: it is not "prophetic" or a "substitute for the absolute" (IP 24). The definition of it there given anticipates in germ all the themes (the detail, beings, the Whole-World, the concreteness of everyday life) that will be incorporated into it later: "[relation] implies that in lived experience, multiplied for oneself and for the other, the mass of daily life can be comprehended in its detail: relation is not prophetic, it is played out every day of the world" (IP 24). Last, relation is closely linked to a negativity that we will call, in anticipation, Hegelian: "To express relation is to calculate its negative fullness: the procrastinations, the errors, the denials. [. . .] To live relation thus means that everyone can cry the song of his land, and sing at length the dawn where that land *appears to itself* and, already, starts to melt away" (IP 207, 209). *L'Intention poétique*, moreover, defines relation not as a conceptual absolute, but as a real concreteness: "relation is not lived as an absolute (in which it would be denied), it is tried and tested in reality" (IP 21–22). Therefore, quite logically, the difference between the Same and the Other is no longer grasped as an antinomy between one being and another, but as the intertwining of a relational modality: "It is not the Being of the Other that impresses itself on me, but the modality of my relation to that Other: and vice versa" (IP 23). And already, the totalization of these different modes of relation form as it were the shadow of the Whole-World, anticipating what I call below the "logion" of relation:[4] "And again—what, in return, is totality, if not the relation of each matter to *all* the others?" (IP 16).

In *L'Intention poétique* there is also the problem of the universal. Right from the start, there are two sides to it: first, that of a never final concreteness that announces the ambition of the Whole-World, with no privileged orientation or fixed destiny, presaging the chaos-world and the inextricable nature of place. This universal is a universal of inclusion and must always be particularized, concretized, and respected in its opacity (its "secret"): "It is a universal as wish, in which Being without orient is caught. [. . .] No end is possible here: from all infertile chaos unraveled, there proceeds a *deep* chaos which must all be cleared. The aspiration (the claim) to universality must bury itself in the dense secret breeding-ground where everyone lives the relationship to the other." Second, there is another universal, let us say a philosophical one, that puts an end to all discussion—a universal of exclusion and closure: "The universal that [Western man] promoted was as a result so abstract, ideal, in the conception people had of it and in the way they expressed it, that it became possible to confuse it with just any particular value, provided that this value was audacious enough to forbid its being questioned" (IP 27). From Glissant's second sally into the genre of the essay there emerge traces of the quest for a universal totality that differs from the philosophical tradition.

The distrust of the abstract universal goes hand in hand with the suspicion of rational and critical analysis, which detaches the observing subject from its object. Here, relation (without a capital) must always be present, always lived; it must not be extracted from the living—it must be sung and its perceptible figures drawn; no subject can be exempt from the chaos within him, which is also the chaos of the world. Before being comprehended, the world must be lived: "The world as relation is indeed today a fertilizable drama, a mortal melee, a Promethean chaos. Neither the *constitutive gaze* nor analysis are enough to disentangle them: if you are not drama, and mingled into this chaos, you will dry up in your remote light" (IP 24–25). The project of the "ethnology of the self," which presupposes the separation of subject and object, is now merged with the drama of the living and the lived.

The "man of the West" is, in *L'Intention poétique*, essentially divided and solitary: isolated by abstraction, reduced by a universal that is not really universal, divided because he knows he is provided with an unconscious—from which one can deduce that psychoanalysis is a discourse specific to the West:

> After having learned with psychoanalysis that he has a "fallow" side, the man of the West feels the pressure of those "parts" of humanity that he had not realized or had not imagined

(despite Montaigne's warnings) that he needed to "consider": those aspects that inhabited the chasms. [. . .] He has been the world's irresistible vehicle. But he has been torn between the function that was his, that he had fulfilled (the function of being the world's mediator) and the ambition he actually experienced (of being the world's absolute). (IP 27)

The schizoid split in the subject of the West, the excluding universal of abstraction, is what prevents him from entering into relation and the Whole-World. This schizoid split means that the notion of the unity and the Whole of knowledge is lost. Glissant contrasts the ideal and dreamt-of One, and the realized or to-be-realized unity of the world: "For what is eternally lacking in the One is this realized dream—the work of art—that we would like to offer, from our awakenings; but what is needed for the unity of the world is that part of the world that, quivering in its being, is burdened with non-existence" (IP 13).

The writing that is inaugurated is not the writing of a subject assured of its unity, but of a poet who knows himself to be divided, between the here and the there, between philosophical knowledge and poetry, between poetry and politics. In *Les Entretiens*, Glissant spoke of the constitutive division of his being between poetic activity and political commitment in terms of "schizophrenia." But, unlike Hegel's unhappy consciousness, which brands the man of Western history with its seal, this schizophrenia is happy: "This kind of schizophrenia in my work was not really schizophrenia" (EBR 54). Why? Because division is redeemed as a quest for unity, not for the "harmonious One" (IP 13), going beyond the divided subject and the unhappy consciousness in order to seize the world with both hands:

We, the Antilleans and French of this generation, were looking for a new poetics, that is to say, a new sense of presence to the world. I remember a text by Henri Pichette: "Literature is beautiful only when read in the bed of the world." There was no break with my belonging to the Antilles. The vain duplication did not irritate, it was a mere appearance. Indeed, it seems to me that in these meetings and at this time a form of poetic logic was consolidated which continued in one di-rection and another: here-there." (EBR 54)

Henri Pichette appears in the anthology of the Whole-World, with a fragment of the *Épiphanies* that insists on "the book of the world," as opposed to the book about the book: "It is the book of the world, the wind turns the page, here is the fragment of the singular heart, here are the plurals in their unison, it is the species in all tenses of the verb, everything brought up to date under the immemorial eye" (TEFV 192).

Who can fail to see here the desire that runs through Glissant's multifaceted work, the desire for a unity beyond all division, fracture, and dissimilarity? This is not an additional but a fundamental reason for seeking the unity of Glissant's work.

The back cover states that *L'Intention poétique* is "a search for poetry through poetry." But this interpretive dynamic is not a folding of the literary object back on oneself (as with reflexivity or mise en abyme as practiced in the literature of the West since Homer). The reflexive *topos*, in fact, is absent from Glissant's work; it is not a book about the book or a writing about writing. The writers illuminated by *L'Intention poétique* (Mallarmé, Reverdy, Segalen, Claudel, Faulkner, Saint-John Perse, Char, Leiris, etc.) are not read according to a formal or rhetorical system limited to the interiority of the work; they are evaluated by the yardstick of the gap between their intention, or what they want to say, and the work as a realization of this intention that fails to live up to the project. The work is always imperfect—an activity whose conclusion is postponed, such as poetry. Thus does it open in its heart to the infinity of a becoming:

> Thus, for the writer, what he writes is little by little merely the rough draft of what he is henceforth (there, endlessly) going to write. Better still, what he will write will be only the shadow of what he should write (of what in eternity he would have been destined to write, if eternity were his). For writing, like the one, is a lack to which we consent. [. . .] The writer is always the ghost of the writer he wants to be. (IP 35–36)

The originality of the readings in *L'Intention poétique* consists in the "unfolding" ("to explain," *ex-plicare*, literally means "to unfold") of works onto the world, onto their relation to the world. In the critical landscape of the 1960s, preoccupied with textual, intertextual, and even "textic" analysis, *L'Intention poétique* is striking in its originality and its isolation; it is centered on the question of the poetic knowledge of the world, the question of a writer (of any writer), a question that in general so-called "literary" criticism, concerned with the interiority of works and authors, is reluctant to tackle. Reading Glissant by way of Glissant will thus involve, not turning the work into a mirror of itself, but considering it as an opening onto the cosmos or *chaosmos.*

In the dynamics of unfolding, outside becomes inside and, conversely, the intimacy of writing is turned inside-out in the extimacy of cultures. The One and diversity, the system and the non-system, universality and creolization, literary traditions and the Whole-World, the root and the rhizome, the Antilles and Paris are not only the symbols of a division and fracture that run throughout Glissant and his work: they are also the contradictions of the real world. Glissant's poetics sets itself the task of unifying, reconciling, and systematizing antinomies, and his work is the theater of this dialectic. The œuvre is thus always unfinished, and this incompleteness is a desiring positivity that impels him to write and rewrite (to mull over in order to produce something new): such is its immense vitality.

From the first two essays, in 1956 and 1969, Glissant's thought is virtually present, and it reserves its becoming (its "poetic intention"): an unpredictable future here finds its foundation. Everything is in relation: Relation is also, first of all, the unifying, organizing and gathering principle of what Glissant has written.

The whole of Glissant's work is consistent through and through. This means that Glissant is one of the most systematic writers in the world, no matter how strong the suspicion with which he constantly views the spirit of system. The oxymoron of the "unsystematic system" mentioned above clearly indicates a desire for homogeneity: there is always a system, an organization, a coherence, an ordering, a unity in his work, even if what they systematize is a chaos. If we treat the nonsystematic system as a simple rhetorical paradox, that is, according to the Greek etymology of the word, a statement "next to" (*para*) "common opinion or knowledge" (*doxa*), we trivialize Glissant's thought by obliterating its essential dimension.

We need to understand the work's systematic nature; it is not closed in on itself, like the Aristotelian or Thomist *summae,* but open, unpredictable, and unfinalizable: thus it is both part of the Western philosophical tradition and goes beyond it:

> It is not the system that is to be rejected. What is to be rejected is the idea that the system is systematic. We can have

non-systematic systems. We can have chaotic systems. [. . .]
A systematic thought or a system of thought is what obeys
systematic laws. So it is not the notion of system that is open
to criticism, it is the notion that the system obliges you to
accept unique forms of pathway, unique forms of progression,
linearities which no longer correspond to the current situation
of the world and its chaotic organization. (IL 77–78)

There is indeed a unified system or *summa* in Glissant without
which his thought, and the present book which aims to shed light
on him, would have no meaning. Contrary to a philosophical system,
which expels from itself the contradictions that the world may bring to
it, Glissant's system is open to the challenges with which the world, or
even the Whole-World, faces it—challenges that it does not claim either
to anticipate or to govern. The system, once it is denied its power as a
superego, ceases to be systematic; it therefore has no value as an absolute, fixed law but remains open to its own transgression, shaped by the
unpredictable wandering of world and word.

As soon as we try to decipher the systemic cohesion of the work,
it appears as perfectly "clear," contrary to the reproach of obscurity that
has often been addressed to it. Indeed, there is a methodical will and a
design that are relentlessly pursued—nothing is left to chance; everything
is meticulously calculated. This unity and this coherence in the project
yield to multiplicity and diversity to bring these together in Relation.

The philosophical, in Glissant, and as befits the requirements of philosophy, is totalizing, unified, and consistent: a monolith worthy of the best
conceptual constructions from antiquity to the present day. But as soon
as this monolith finds expression, it draws fresh air from the poetic and
its becoming, just as it did at the beginning of philosophy in Greece, in
the poetic settings scattered through the essays themselves, and in the very
material of Glissant's writing. This writing is a fusion and total integration
of the poetic and the philosophical, beyond genres and their limitations
(which are also prescriptions and ordinances for thought), a fusion that
Plato had banished from the City. A poetic philosophy, a philosophical
poetics, subject to the phrasing and the demands of the poetic: such is
Glissant's resumption as well as his radical innovation.

Proving that Glissant's work is a coherent whole—that is to say, a
philosophical one—is not meant to produce the lukewarm reassurance that
would result from the retrieval or re-inscription of his thought into any

tradition, even the "Western" tradition. Glissant brings out the unthought of the great themes of the philosophical tradition to open them up to their other and their elsewhere. Glissant does not construct himself as "other," as a place for his readers' projections and identifications, but as radically "Other": irreducible to critical analysis, to labels, to ideologemes of whatever kind. Defining his relationship with the Western philosophical tradition is, in the final analysis, only a way of highlighting his irretrievable difference. But the only way to perceive the originality of Glissant's contribution to thought and its history—that is, to really read it—is to measure it in the light of the "Western" tradition. Separating the work from its base in that tradition means reducing it to slogans and catchphrases, enslaving this thought to issues that are foreign or indifferent to it: no one has been more attentive than Glissant to the ravages that thought produced when it converted itself into an ideology.

Glissant's work is unclassifiable, the "Other of thought" (PR 236). It rejects categorization on principle: it challenges conformism of every tendency since the latter submits the work to the reification of a fixed object:

> The work of collection, accumulation and interpretation performed by historians, sociologists and psychologists, which is half a matter of compiling, and half a matter of synthesizing (the two things do not necessarily go together), should perhaps not hesitate to extend itself into an unexpected hypothesis, and will thus have accomplished its meaning only if it does not serve as a pretext for rejecting the multiplication of the thing known as "story" in the thing known as "world": these are things that cannot be treated as things. (PhR 76)

The poetic and the philosophical, in Glissant, are "intransitive": they do not express a sense external to them but create a new world of meaning of which they are the origin and the beginning—the work is irreducible to what comes before it. But, at the same time, the new meaning remakes the old meaning, which implies that we gain access to it via a detour—via what comprised Glissant's culture. The detour allows us to measure his radical originality. Speaking of the world, and of poetry in the world and in history, Glissant is a polymath who demands from his reader an unlimited knowledge that goes beyond so-called "literary" criticism. The relationship of the work to its outside must be taken into account, whether it goes through the real world or through many poetic and cultural traditions.

The "Western" tradition produces immense zones of silence and repression; and this negativity produces a new space, which will in turn need to be brought into Relation with this very tradition. The beginning is at once absolute and radically new, but also relative to a negativity: it will be necessary to give voice to the absences created by the weight of tradition. In Glissant's work, these absences often take the shape of a cry that breaks the silence, and renders necessary a new language that will give this cry its breath of life, of poetic writing, outside the negativity of the cultural traditions that created this blank page in an act of repression: "What does natural language (*langue*) matter, when we need to measure the implantation of the cry and the spoken word in it? In any authorized language (*langue*), you will build your language as idiom (*langage*)" (IP 45).

L'Intention poétique poses the profound relationship between unheard and tradition, both intimately linked to poetics:

> And if I listen to the voice of the West, the greatest politicians, the profoundest dogmaticians, the most subtle creators, I hear the silence whenever it is a question of this future in which the different abysses of man are to be shared. In these we are equally new, all of us, in the new injunction. And I do not forget the enormous denials throughout this history of the West, which are opposed, as if by preventive action (to prevent, to suspect, to deny), to relation. Only the poets here listened out for the world, and fertilized the ground in advance. We know how much time it takes to hear their voices. (IP 42)

Thus, Glissant meditated on and incorporated the Western philosophical tradition, from Heraclitus and Parmenides to Deleuze. However, when he was asked who was the most important philosopher, the answer flashed back, instantaneous and unhesitating: "Hegel!"

As soon as we decipher Glissant's work with an eye to Hegel's philosophy, the shadow of the Berlin philosopher appears everywhere—his shadow, that is, because it is unusual for Glissant's theoretical discourse to operate according to the quotational model of the university, with its apparatus of explicit references. In his essays, everything is allusive, implied, implicit, subjected to vision and metaphors. Philosophy is not a "source," but a homology consubstantial with the thought of Glissant who, like any great philosopher, reads his peers by metamorphosing them. Here is played out, on two levels, what we might call "the principle of extension" of Glissant's argument and his writing: in the first place, this principle works in his work, which grows not by deepening primary intuitions but by extending and varying them for use in ever-wider and at the same time more precise applications. On a second level, his reinterpretation of the monuments of the cultural past is always built as an extension: when he encounters the founding notions of his philosophy in the tradition, he always magnifies them to erase their limits and give them a generality that is concrete, and broader than what these notions originally represented.

The Ariadne's thread of the present book will be philosophy, even if it ultimately shows that Glissant, by re-reading the whole of the philosophical tradition, in the final analysis proposes a transcendence of philosophy. One might legitimately wonder why one should dismiss various tendencies and labels that discussions of Glissant so readily apply to his work: but, if the work is unclassifiable, it rejects in advance any reading that reduces its opacity to the transparency of the already known. Glissant never fails to point out the inadequacy of these categories when it comes to interpreting his work.

Chapter 3

"I do not reject, I establish correlation"

Two great figures were the mediators of philosophy for Édouard Glissant during the studies at the Sorbonne on which he embarked in 1946: Jean Wahl (1888–1974) and Gaston Bachelard (1884–1962). Thanks to Jean Wahl, Glissant became acquainted with Hegel, Kierkegaard, Kant, and Heidegger. Now Jean Wahl was the author of one of the earliest readings of Hegel in France to emphasize the *Phenomenology of Spirit* instead of reducing Hegel to the *Science of Logic*, as was the custom in French academia.[1] With *Le Malheur de la conscience dans la philosophie de Hegel* (*The Unhappy Consciousness in Hegel's Philosophy*),[2] published in 1929, Jean Wahl introduced into the French university tradition a Hegel read from the perspective of history and anthropology, somewhat earlier than Alexandre Kojève's lectures at the École normale between 1933 and 1939. In addition, Jean Wahl's Hegel is closely related to the figure of the poet Hölderlin, whose texts are considered as philosophical fragments that provide an access to the *Phenomenology of Spirit* and illuminate it. Wahl also highlights Hegel's intimate relation with art and literature, not only in his *Aesthetics* (where all artistic traditions, in the West as well as in the East, are called on, in a vertiginous accumulation of knowledge, to illustrate philosophical reflection), but also in the *Phenomenology of Spirit*.[3] Despite its purely philosophical and abstract sides, the *Phenomenology* is anchored in the concrete detail of history and anthropology; in addition, its itinerary is based on art as an originary moment of ideas, which reveal a conceptual dialectic only after poetry and aesthetic creation:

It would be wrong to imagine that these representations of, and reactions to [the gods of ancient Greece], already existed in an abstract form in consciousness before poetry, as propositions and religious determinations of a general character, and that only afterward were they clothed with images by poets, receiving the outer adornment of poetry. On the contrary, engaged in artistic activity, poets could express what was fermenting in them only in this determined form of art and poetry.[4]

A cursory reading of the *Aesthetics* shows how indebted Glissant's thought is to Hegel: for both of them, poetry is constitutive of and homologous to thought; the first moment of philosophy is a poem.

In Glissant's work, the Greek word *poiein*, "to make, to create," from which comes the semantic field of "poetry," is found in many guises. There is "poetry," one of the categories—the supreme category, as far as Glissant is concerned—of literary genres. There is "poetics" as such, not literary criticism as it was defined in France in the 1970s by the famous theoretical journal of the same name (*Poétique*), but poetics as a writing and an act of thought: hence *Poétique de la Relation*. There is the "poetic," a more general class, since it can arise in the poem (even if not all poems necessarily fall into the class of the poetic), but also in prose, painting, landscape, or beings. Glissant also distinguishes between "making poetry" (writing one or more poems) and "pursuing a poetic work and not a work of poetry"[5] (to think out a work, in its entirety, and whatever its genre, through poetry): the poetic is not in any way limited to being an anthology of poems. In poetics or poetry, the emphasis is placed on the necessity of artistic creation, without which there is for Glissant only non-meaning. To take the example of wandering: "The thought of wandering is a poetics, one which implies that at a certain moment it utters itself" (PR 31). Let us note in passing that meaningfulness is not limited to texts or words aligned on the page: poetry also springs from matter and from the elements.

Wahl thought of himself as a poet as well as an academically accredited philosopher. This alliance between philosophy and literature was very infrequent in France in Wahl's day, when they were opposite domains and philosophy was a territory reserved for academic specialists; this is very probably one inspiration for Glissant's philosophical poetics. Wahl was also the intermediary between Glissant and Heidegger, present in the former's work under the auspices of the problematic of Being and beings. Finally, in 1953, Glissant's graduation thesis, "Découverte et Conception du monde dans la poésie contemporaine" (The Discovery and Conception of the World in Contemporary Poetry), was supervised by Wahl. Thanks to the latter, Glissant confirmed his fundamental intuition: art thinks and philosophy is also an art.[6]

With Gaston Bachelard, a historian of science and the creator of the notion of the epistemological break, Glissant came into contact with Heraclitus and the Pre-Socratics. He also came across the notion of the "imaginary," which Bachelard developed in several of his works. The Bachelardian imaginary is constructed by a return to the four primordial elements familiar to ancient "science": earth, air, fire, and water. These four elements provide, almost word for word, *La Terre le Feu l'Eau et les Vents* (*Earth Fire Water and Winds*), an anthology of the Whole-World that Glissant published in 2010 and in which Bachelard plays a large role. One of the three fragments of Bachelard included in the anthology is titled "Fire and Water," the other "Earth": only "the winds" are lacking to form the complete title of the anthology of the poetry of the Whole-World and to complete the series of elements by adding the fourth, the air, this time in motion. The zephyrs find their place in Glissant's work, as a breath that animates and connects all the texts in the collection. In passing, let us emphasize that the Heraclitean thought that inspires Bachelard is also an epistemology, built up as a series of equivalences: "fire" is also soul and meaning, "water" is seed and word, "earth" is the body and the work of art.[7] Bachelard confirmed Glissant's interest in everything that stems from a poetics of nature and the elemental, as against Hegel this time, for whom "trees do not speak."

Contrary to a French Cartesian tradition, Bachelard was one of the first philosophers to postulate that rationality even extended to the imaginary; this showed the influence of psychoanalysis and, perhaps, of Hegel, who says in the *Aesthetics* that art must give its full share to *Phantasie*, the German word for the imaginary.[8] For Bachelard, poetic knowledge is of the same value as scientific knowledge, whether it opposes it or corroborates it. This importance of the poetic imagination in the anthropology of knowledge is evident in Glissant's work. He pays tribute to Bachelard in *Une nouvelle région du monde*: "In amazement, we finally receive the lesson taught us by the investigations of Gaston Bachelard" (NRM 73).

Finally, thanks to Bachelard, who created the notion, Glissant came across the concept of the epistemological break, to which I will return later.

There is no doubt that Glissant's encounter with the words of these great masters who paid due attention to both philosophical rigor and the poetic imaginary was a confirmation of the young poet's first intuitions.

Soleil de la conscience attests to this, affirming first of all his solidarity with Martinique, that "piece of land," while adding another place: "and on the other hand, it is undeniable to me that a whole part of me, the most arid and the most movably furnished at the same time, is here in Paris, where I have known so many other faces of subjective knowledge" (SC 65). No doubt he found in this discovery of the "Western" tradition (an inversion for him of the sixteenth-century explorations from east to west) the specific, crossbred origin of his thought, the thought of a poet who thinks and of a philosopher who poeticizes, the thought of a writer who incorporates the Western philosophical and literary tradition from a place that is split between the Antilles and Paris, a place that is no longer the space of an author owing strictly national and monolingual allegiances.

In his first essays, *Soleil de la conscience* and *L'Intention poétique*, the references to philosophy remain implicit. But with *Le Discours antillais* (1981) and *Poétique de la Relation* (1990), philosophical discourse appears in its full light, treated with the greatest freedom and the greatest rigor, without the poetic dimension being rejected, since it is part and parcel of the philosophical game (and vice versa).

From 1997, Glissant classified his essays in a systematic list in the "By the same author" sections that conclude the first or subsequent publication of these works in Gallimard: *Poétique I* (*Soleil de la conscience*), *II* (*L'Intention poétique*), *III* (*Poétique de la Relation*), *IV* (*Traité du Tout-Monde*), *V* (*La Cohée du Lamentin*); and *Esthétique I* (*Une nouvelle région du monde*). The list mainly displays a coherence and unity of thought discovered *after* the essays had first been written, and thus organic. We can compare Glissant to Balzac, who used the recurring characters in *The Human Comedy* as a way of bringing order to his *summa*.

Glissant's systematizing concerns only his reflections on art and literature; it could have also included a new category (Philosophy I, II, etc.), with *Le Discours antillais* and especially *Philosophie de la Relation* (2009), subtitled "poetry in extent." By being excluded from the list, the philosophical sphere is, as it were, cast into shadow, taken up by and into the aesthetic and the poetic, dedicated to an existence all the more active and powerful as it is only explicitly declared at the end of the work. Poetry and aesthetics come first; they too think, and are openly displayed; the philosophical, on the other hand, is something that Glissant partly seeks to conceal: it must therefore be the object of an exhumation that will bring it out into the light of day, into the "sun of consciousness" (*soleil de la conscience*). As a shadow cast by and inseparable from poetic luminosity, philosophy is the reverse side that comes to light in the *Philosophie de la Relation.*

Socrates gave philosophy a radically different aim from that of his predecessors and contemporaries. Philosophy was no longer responsible for thinking about the relation between human beings and the world (the *physis*); its task rather was to examine reasons and give a coherent account of their sequence: it became a logical technique (*technè*), and folded in on itself. Its coherence was now internal to its own discourse and it submitted itself to a requirement of conceptual and logical rationality; this was respected for twenty-five centuries, from Socrates up to (but not including) Kierkegaard. In the history of Greek philosophy, the moment of Socrates, in Hegel's view as well as Glissant's, was a catastrophe, a Fall from the paradise of the "primordial poem": it was the moment when everything collapsed under the repeated blows of a narrow version of reason, in which the Beautiful and the True became abstract notions empty of sense, and irony corroded all certainty. It was the same with Nietzsche: Socrates was "the instrument of Greek decomposition, [. . .] the decadent-type" (*Ecce homo*), he was the moment when, "in a single night, the evolution of philosophical science, hitherto so marvelously regular, but too hasty, was broken" (*Human, All Too Human*, I, § 261).

To label Glissant a philosopher would be to make him part of this rational tradition, and to ask him to explain his reasons. But even a superficial reading shows instantly that he has no intention of emulating Socrates, Plato, or Aristotle. On the contrary, throughout his work, reason as an absolute is rejected. Might Glissant's discourse be a prisoner of irrationalism, or a para- or non-philosophy?

This, however, would be to ignore the fact that Socrates challenged, or indeed silenced, a tradition, that of the Sophists and Pre-Socratics, whose philosophical vision was based on a different rationality from the logical sequence of reasons, and whose content also differed: for the Pre-Socratics this content was the world, for the Sophists, politics. The old rationality of the founders of philosophy in Greece (Heraclitus, Gorgias, Protagoras) did not separate subject from object, thought from world, poetry from philosophy or politics, and it did not enclose any system of thought in an eternal fixity: the pre-Socratic "system" was open to becoming and the appropriate moment of philosophical intervention (the *kairos* of the Sophists), which itself was open to the future. It was from this pre-Socratic tradition, as well as from Hegel, that Édouard Glissant would draw his tools of thought. It is in the light of this tradition, which gives equal weight to the philosophical and the poetic, that he must be measured if we are to decide whether the title of philosopher suits him. Glissantian rationality does exist; but, in the last analysis, it takes its source not in any logic but in a poetic imaginary whose pre-eminence it constantly affirms. Thought does not refute philosophical rationality, but weaves and interweaves it, breeding and crossbreeding it into an imaginary and cosmic form. Glissant could not be any clearer about this radically new digenesis, which intertwines rationality and irrationality, and which is not a simple regressive return, a restoration of originary ideas lost and then found:

> The question now is to know whether one can *integrate* within one form of subjective knowledge both the indissociated values that were those of the Pre-Socratics (which we can sum up in a crude way by saying that they were the values of the cosmic and the raw imaginary) and the principles of rational knowledge that developed from Plato and are still in us. These principles *do not incorporate* the dimension of the cosmic, the irrational or the autonomous imaginary. Not to mention the fusional attachment to language. (EBR 146, my emphasis)

The basis of thought is none other than the poetic coherence of the imaginary: poem and thought intertwine and enable one another, in a rhapsodic melting that creates their deep unity: "The poetics of Relation is thus always a philosophy, and vice versa: they preserve each other from false objectives. Then we discover in amazement that the language of the philosophers is first and foremost the language of the poem" (PhR 87).[9]

Glissant's nonsystematic system gives an account of its reasons by going back to a pre-Socrates and a pre-Aristotle, and by paving the way to a post-Hegel, opening philosophical coherence to the world and the poetic by renewing our reading of the Sophists and the Pre-Socratics.

The totalizing aim is asserted everywhere by Glissant; the philosophical coherence is perhaps more secret, but, at the end of the journey, the *Philosophie de la Relation*, by its very title, openly proclaims how Relation is positioned within the history of philosophical discourse. This may seem to contradict his attacks on the systematic spirit, on an over-rationalizing rationality deprived of poetry, and his resistance to seeing himself as part of any "Western tradition," one of whose unique and singular characteristics is precisely to have founded, de facto and de jure, the philosophical tradition itself: despite this, he thought of himself as a philosopher—and he was.

The truth of a theory will come from its outside, from what it has not taken into account, and from what is not integrated into its system. Every theory must be measured by an external criterion if it is to be called true; the only truth is a truth in context, whatever that may be (historical, symbolic, cultural). However, this assessment from outside is precisely what Glissant practices, pointing out the nonuniversality of philosophical systems, whether or not they stem from the Western tradition. Glissant does not fear the world and the unexpected forms that it constantly creates, in or outside of a system. The process of accumulation of the truth is both circular and open to a reality testing that is often postponed.

Moreover, nothing proves that a homogeneous and ordered system is true: for example, a psychotic delusion is coherent in all its parts, but it is so only by rejecting any reality testing (this is its hidden truth). In *Totem and Taboo*, Freud had not hesitated to compare psychosis with the caricature of a philosophical system because of the denial of reality that the two shared. Philosophical systems, and literary theories in their wake, often create a sense of unreality, as they elude any specific context and take refuge in abstraction to achieve maximum generality. In fact, a theory is consistent only when it amputates its relation to some real that it excludes and cannot envisage. It is *against* this truncation, indispensable to the constitution of a system or theory, that Glissant has always written and thought.

When *Poétique de la Relation* came out, Glissant said to me that Gilles Deleuze had told him that nobody had ever attempted such a venture: an assessment that at the time roused my skepticism, but one that assumes its full significance when you are aware of Deleuze's profound philosophical and literary culture, and is confirmed when you interpret Glissant's work from a philosophical standpoint. This was not a matter of Édouard boasting to reassure himself in his uncertainty, but an injunction to read him as he was—something that unfortunately came too late for me.

But what *is* a philosopher? First, it is someone who engages in a dialogue or a dialectic with the philosophers of the history of philosophy, as it began in Greece and as it continues today. The philosopher is the one who argues or palavers with his or her predecessors: it is Socrates/ Plato committing parricide with regard to Parmenides, it is Plato being contradicted by Aristotle, and so on until Nietzsche and Deleuze. Philosophy is a matter of signing into and out of a filiation that goes back two and a half millennia. To be a philosopher is partly to repeat, to mull over, as Glissant did. One does not become a philosopher by having one or more ideas, however brilliant and original, but by taking part in a dialogue with philosophy, from its origin in Greece, whether so as to insert oneself into a tradition or to challenge it. Second, then, a philosopher, ever since Heraclitus, is someone who constructs a coherent system of thought. Third, after Heraclitus and since Plato, a philosopher is someone who subjects this edifice to an evaluation that confirms or invalidates these premises. Fourth, a true philosopher, like a poet or a writer, but in a different way, weighs his or her words, and does not engage in the chatter of the Intellectual (what Hegel called "conversation"). And, finally, a philosopher (and not a historian of philosophy, though the distinction is somewhat artificial since all philosophers re-read their predecessors) builds an original edifice of thought: that is to say, to a greater or lesser degree, he or she distances him- or herself from the filiation of his or her predecessors by arguing with and against them.

Édouard Glissant meets all these criteria. We must understand that philosophy is not linear in the sense that it has an ancestor, and then heirs who develop it in a harmonious and unproblematic filiation from its genesis to its final goal: the first word of philosophy is not taken up and then erased by the second, the second by the third, and so on. Take Heraclitus, for example: Aristotle says, in order to silence him and replace him, that Heraclitus did not himself understand what he was saying (*Metaphysics*, K 5, 1062 a, 31). But the first word (that of Heraclitus) can return and become the last word. To paraphrase Gérard de Nerval: "The thirteenth thought returns, and it is still the first."

Hegel, the first modern philosopher to renew an authentic dialogue with the philosopher of Ephesus, declares: "There is not a single formula in Heraclitus that I have not taken up in my logic."[10] The first word thus becomes the last word, the newest. Similarly, the young Nietzsche writes: "The world, having eternal need of truth, will eternally need Heraclitus" (*Philosophy in the Tragic Time of the Greeks*). Closer to us, Heidegger writes: "With Heraclitus and Parmenides, the very foundation of Western thought is realized. It is to them that goes back, as to the secret of the source, what is still alive and always lively in the depths of our thoughts." And so philosophy does not advance in a straight line, but in a circle that returns to the first thought, and that develops it "in a spiral," renewing it by rendering it contemporary with us (it is different from what it was originally).

We need first to lay bare the archeology of Glissant's thought and the influences that presided over his development—not an inventory of "sources," which never explains a way of thinking, but an active journey, taking the form either of a return, or of a projection into the future, or of a reading of the present world. Without this re-reading, any critical engagement with Glissant's thought would not live up to its name: it would be tilting at windmills erected for the mere purpose of demonstration, it would be blind to what it is calling into question, it would remain at the level of intellectual chatter, an essentially "literary" digression, unable to grasp its object in any lasting way. Revealing the background on which our re-reading of Glissant is built will ensure its validity.

Archeology is indispensable; we cannot content ourselves with making Glissant begin with Glissant even if, in many respects, his words have an inaugural force thanks to their originality. To measure his contribution is to make him dialogue with those who came before him. If Glissant begins with Glissant—and this is one of the frequent errors made in the secondary literature devoted to him—there is a great risk of transforming philosophical meditation into slogans, progress into an absolute and a universal, the Whole-World into a totalitarianism that nothing can escape.

To read Glissant is not to anamorphose his propositions into impositions: Relation rejects such a move, absolutely and always.

Starting with Glissant alone, seasoning him with a pinch of history, a bit of sociology, a smidgeon of ideology, amounts to erasing a historical and philosophical depth, making a clean sweep of a context that gives its density to the new truths in his work:

> You see, the text that is utterly new and never looks back, the phrase that does not duplicate something, and the innovation devoid of any echo, even if they flash forth, would still often end up as a bunch of dried grass, in traces and furrows, between two harvests that, miraculously, repeat each other. Like different literatures, the *Philosophie de la Relation* is simultaneously a mulling over and a displacement (PhR 94).

Nothing new is of any value unless it repeats what preceded it, and there is no tradition of any value unless it is re-read from the standpoint of what it has engendered. And mulling over, finally, is the figure of the obstinacy of someone who wants to be understood and who knows that he still has not been understood: "These propositions must be repeated, until they are at least heard" (TTM 39).[11]

In this sense, this work aims at the legitimization of Glissant as one of the great thinkers of philosophy as a whole. To call him "subversive" or "revolutionary" is too facile, unless we have taken the measure of what it is that Glissant is transgressing. A "subversion" conceived of in this way empties the work of its full-meaning (*plein-sens*), and a fortiori of all meaning; it falls into the pure verbalism of the beautiful soul. People will object that I am trying to return to the hackneyed old ideas of legitimacy, territories, and filiations (including those of an intellectual kind)—in short, all that Glissant criticizes. This is not the case: it must be shown that Glissant's work is constructed in a living dialogue with very old utterances that return in their renewed presence to haunt our contemporaneity. It is about seeing how Glissant transforms the cultural past to project it into the future, not to reduce it to some tradition. In a certain way, we do not "surpass" Heraclitus and Hegel—we re-read them; we reactivate them; we modify them; we do not inherit the legitimacy of philosophy in a linear fashion; we return to it in a circle, and suddenly it is changed by this retrospective gaze. If there is any potential legitimization, it is of the order of what, by an apparent paradox, gives bastardy its patent of nobility, and canonizes heresy. It is a question of assessing how Glissant's philosophy is not a chapter added to a "history of philosophy" or an established tradition, but how it is a contribution of unprecedented boldness and originality *to philosophy itself*, which means that, in its rigor, it exceeds the Western tradition of thought.

The thought of Glissant is not a flight into irrationalism and confusion—it is a rationalism open to the imaginary with which it engages in dialogue; at the same time, it is an imaginary that does not give way to solipsism or fantasy, to error or to failure, but that breaks free from the constraints of a pure and solitary reason. Rather than being a matter of mechanical subversion or challenge, Glissant's work is one of recognition, in all the many meanings of this term: it revisits very old thoughts but does not fail to disturb them with a renewed knowledge, reaffirming the validity of these thoughts, recognizing (even implicitly) a spiritual debt, and finally, paving the way to a new kind of knowing.

Certainly, there is in Glissant a rejection of filiation in all its forms, including those of the family; there is a clear rejection of rooted identity, of the weight of conceptual inheritance: it is a thinking that knows that it no longer has any fathers, not because it has killed them but because it has incorporated them and gone beyond them. The belief in filiation is the neurosis of the son, who restores the Father by challenging or reaffirming him: patrilineal values return in his revolt. Thus, Glissant's rejection of filiation is never expressed by declamation, proclamation, or arbitrary decision, as this would empty the move beyond the past of all meaning and renew its weight. The overcoming of different inheritances is first brought about by a careful, attentive, alert re-reading of the philosophical and literary traditions, then by their quasi-organic incorporation into the work. This is not the subversion of traditions, then, but a way of relating them to one another: "But I do not reject, I establish correlation" (IP 42). Every thought, every art, is brought into relation with its Other.

The rejection of filiation also demonstrates Glissant's circumspection with regard to the various forms of the theoretical and thus systematic superego, and especially their dark internalization by the thinker, which renders them inaccessible to the "sun of consciousness" (*Soleil de la conscience*) or to any lucid revision.[12] It is a question of gauging the measure (*mesure*) and the excess (*démesure*) of this organic relationship to a cultural heritage. Glissant does not offer a traditional reading of cultural traditions: he does not solely consider what they once were, but above all what they open up as possibilities, as forms of becoming, and the potential which these traditions obscured, forgot, or repressed.

If the philosophy of Glissant is now original, it is also because it combines, right from the start, quite unapologetically, reason and the imaginary, the traditions of the West and elsewhere. His reflections are expressed as much in poems, novels, and plays as in essays; poetry and literature are "thought," though they are not poems or novels dictated by any thesis—this would make literature a romanticized avatar of philosophy (as, for example, often happens in Sartre, apart from his *Words*). And philosophy is a poetics, though Glissant does not fall into an incoherent, pseudo-literary mystique. This double characteristic was also a tradition: the Pre-Socratics, Plato himself, Montaigne, and Nietzsche are the most important moments in it. But Glissant today has very few peers among his contemporaries—people who can who handle with so much virtuosity the genres in which he has deployed his inspiration. He is one of the few moderns to have combined the poetic and the philosophical dimensions without necessarily holding them to be contradictory, and to have done so with a poet's talent demonstrated both in treatises and in the very numerous interviews that he gave. The whole work is thus a creolization blending philosophy and poetry, a poetic connection of two imaginaries and two ways of knowing that, ever since Plato, have been conceived of as distinct, even opposed.

We must warn ourselves against the illusion that Glissant indulges in vagueness, in an "artistic blur," that his thought is devoid of the philosophical foundations that ensure its consistency, its coherence, and its truth: when he speaks of the philosophical tradition, he has a clear and precise idea of it; when he advances propositions that renew or subvert this tradition, he does so with equal exactness, gauging repetitions and radical new angles word by word, with singular precision. Édouard Glissant is a philosopher.

Chapter 4

"This need to go beyond one's own subjectivity"

In Hegel's *Aesthetics*,[1] the German Romantic movement is represented by
the brothers August Wilhelm and Karl Wilhelm Schlegel, the editors of
the journal *Athenaeum*, published in Jena around 1800, when Hegel was
Privatdozent at the University of Thuringia. Hegel rejects the poetics of
the *Athenaeum* because it reduces everything to the Self, the only object
that interests the Romantic mind. From then on, concrete actuality and
the world are emptied, and what emerges is an unhappy and dissatisfied
conscience (that of Protestant Christianity); it knows that it does not
have the power to modify the world concretely, and consequently retreats into itself, declining into the "langors of the beautiful soul dying
of boredom."[2] For Hegel, Romanticism is the end point of a Western
process of individualization that has exhausted its resources and can no
longer intervene in human history.

The risk that the Romantic runs is "chatter," or according to the
beginning of the *Phenomenology*, "conversation," where only the Self and
its self-centered emotions count.[3] In the last analysis, Hegel reproaches
Romanticism for its extreme narcissism, which results in the melancholy
constitutive of the unhappy consciousness. The Hegelian condemnation
of Romanticism, his rejection of any refuge in the Self, the rejection of
melancholy and the unhappy consciousness, are all unhesitatingly endorsed
by Glissant: the poetic must be of the world, and in the world, in order to
modify it. In parallel, melancholy, the elegy, and the palinode are banished
from his poetics, as is clear in all of his work: "I am resolutely optimistic
but that does not mean that I am founding a new system of humanism.

Optimism is the trust in the effectiveness of interrelationships between many systems of cultures, languages, landscapes and countries. It is not a humanism, it is a poetics" (IL 85). The rejection of humanism indicates that the Romantic Self, atomized by extreme individualism, can no longer be taken as the "measure of all things": the instrument of measurement must be a poetics of Relation, placed in common and shared out between individuals. The expression of the Self, in fact, counts for nothing in Glissant's project; at the time of the *Entretiens*, for example, he refused point blank to talk about his life, except to sketch a brief history of his relations with French poets and his Martinican friends, and to immediately draw from it a more general poetic apologia, which made his singular biography part of the continuum of a community: "the collective biography, the story that the poem seeks to restore (and which is not a story to be narrated) can only correspond, not with rigor, but with *poémie*, or *poétrie* [translator's note: these terms are explained below], to the individual biography" (EBR 36). If there is lyricism in his work—and it is indeed very much in evidence—it has nothing to do with the emotions of individual lyricism, and everything to do with the song of communities in gestation.

In the Hegelian interpretation, Romanticism and the French Revolution together give rise to new actors in history, and to a completely new profession: that of the Intellectual. The French Revolution exhausted the possibilities of the transformative political action of society: we cannot go back before it unless we are to regress into the repetition of acts that have already taken place. In this context, the Intellectual is "the man with the good heart" who realizes himself by constantly criticizing the society in which he lives; in other words, his action is purely verbal. Never managing to get as far as revolutionary Action, the Intellectual's unconscious interest is to maintain the existing society of bourgeois citizens, so that he can continue to criticize it. He is a beautiful soul who is satisfied with a merely "literary" existence and projects his inner disorder into the world, finally becoming convinced that the world is the cause of this very same inner disorder.[4] The Romantic complacently reveals the only thing that interests him: himself. Only his self seems to him worthy of interest—he flees the world, and finds refuge in his "ivory tower"; his critique of the world is a meaningless semblance, as it is not meant to produce any change: for Hegel, Romanticism is essentially verbiage with no real effect on the world. The contemporary proliferation of confessions, autofictions, and exhibitionism in today's media demonstrates how much we are still in thrall to Romanticism: the harmful virus of the beautiful soul has infected nearly the entire field of criticism and creation in the West.

The means of action of the Intellectual is his talent, which he demonstrates in a circular way by speaking and writing. This is how he obtains the recognition of his mastery by others: through words. For Hegel, the world of intellectual life ("the animal kingdom of the spirit," *das geistige Tierreich*) is the world in which everyone criticizes everyone else, and where everyone criticizes everything: it is the Republic of Letters that was born in the fifteenth century and reached its peak in the eighteenth century.[5] Glissant develops and extends the Hegelian criticism of the Intellectual, contrasting the work of the cane cutter with the political illusions of the class of scholars: "The drama of the intellectual: the full range of illusions (of oneself) will never be worth the assent of a single cane cutter. Intellectuals *believe in themselves*. That is why, servile or pusillanimous, supposedly free or falsely barking, they always serve those who exploit the cane (and their literary class was created for this purpose)" (IP 189).

Glissant's refusal of any incorporation into the Republic of Letters is explicit:

> What does it mean, to create a "school"? It means that there are people who "follow" you down a track, who listen to what you say. It does not go beyond that. In the Whole-World, authors try out their feathers and wings individually, there is no systematic thinking, no ideology of ideology. If there were systematic thoughts and ideologies, we would fall back on the old mistakes, and in that case we would not have to attribute so much importance to the phenomenon of the "school." (IL 55)

From *Soleil de la conscience* onward Glissant paints a rather black picture of the Republic of Letters: "This city [Paris] rejects itself as much as it is denied, I mean in the early days. In these parts there is an unusual Freemasonry, a ritual necessity for initiation, at every moment disconcerting; these, even in the air, solicit attention and arouse irritation" (CS 12). On a lower level, the Republic of Letters appears as a collection of atomized individuals, united by belief in a fantasy: "Everyone is in his room; and how much this situation (the very expression) suggests the insular or the tropical. Here it is: a reverse exoticism" (CS 12). The Freemasonry of Belles-Lettres, whose rites provide a social bond and found a community, is organized to resist meaning and poetic knowledge: "But who would have the imprudence to claim, unless he has already made a 'name' for himself, that art or the search for an art mean for him the ambitions of some subjective knowledge? [. . .] Paris merely plays at the literary, at art" (CS 13). Thus, the Republic of Letters is reduced to a scene of fictional theater, a string of pretenses aimed at making people believe in the reality of its activity.

By rejecting the status of Intellectual, and thus any absorption into the Republic of Letters, Glissant escapes their curse: confinement in the chatter that does not change the world as it is. The state of the Intellectual is, for Hegel, a disease: the beautiful soul dies of boredom, of being interested only in itself.[6] This withdrawal is expressed by the mise en abyme, where the writer concentrates mainly not on the world, but on his art. Kojève points out: "The pinnacle of romantic expression will be the novel of a Novel, the book of a book."[7] One immediately thinks of Proust and, to a lesser extent, Michel Leiris and the French New Roman, the latter being merely (with a few exceptions) the laborious, schoolboy caricature of the text that folds in on itself. Hegel sees Romantic art, the last state of literature as he knew it, as a dead end, an exhaustion of expressive possibilities. In this respect, Proust's *In Search of Lost Time* is the breviary of the last writer of the Romantic kind. On the other hand, it is striking to note the absence of a "book about the book" in Glissant's work, something that goes hand in hand with the almost total silence on literary techniques, style, rhetoric, and so on in his essays and interviews. The only indication he gave me (verbally) about his writing technique was to tell me that he began with a general idea, and the details came flowing along afterward. What matters to Glissant is to transmit a vision, not to be distinguished by the imposition of a style, a rhetorical or literary technique that would grab the attention of his readers. Nothing is more foreign to him in this respect than the "book about the book."[8]

This explains, from *L'Intention poétique* onward, the mistrust of rhetoric, and also of any reading of literature that would be content merely to point out its mise en abyme, that is to say the process by which fiction allegorizes its own production of writing: "Of course, the concern for an organized language should not lead to the sterile bloatedness of a rhetoric with which we would be satisfied first and last. And such a rhetoric, by seeing itself as both object and subject of the poem, would be abolished in a perpetual and vain effervescence" (IP 62).

The individual solitude of the Intellectual of the Bestiary and the Republic of Letters results in the "unhappy consciousness," the end point of Romanticism, the products of whose intellectual activity are marked by Romantic irony (emblematized for Hegel by the brothers Schlegel and Jean-Paul), which derides everything:

> But the ironic, which is characteristic of brilliant individuality, consists in the self-destruction of all that is noble, great and perfect, so that, even in its objective productions, ironic art is reduced to the representation of absolute subjectivity, since everything that has value and dignity for man is non-existent as a result of his self-destruction. This is the reason why not only justice, morality and truth fail to be taken seriously, but also the sublime and the best, since in manifesting themselves in individuals, in their characters and actions, they deny and destroy themselves, in other words they are merely an irony of themselves.[9]

Let us re-read *L'Intention poétique*; its Hegelian bedrock is obvious:

> At another level, that of the highest nobility and responsibility (where the human being suffers what he says), the systematic intellectual attitude of derision is outlined in the unconscious refusal to share oneself, to live the world and the thought of the world with the other person. The unhappy consciousness then represents all generosity—all seemingly unmotivated im-pulse—as naivety. (IP 28–29)

For Glissant, the generosity of thought is not candor, but necessity; derision and irony (but not humor) are in fact banished from his work.

Based on his personal experience—the misunderstanding that his ideas came up against again and again in the course of his life—Glissant goes beyond derision to call on us to share ourselves out so as to smash the prison of the Romantic. For Glissant, the West is dying of its individualism, which is why it is necessary to bring subjects, including the subject-writer, back into the plural of a community in Relation. It is also in the name of this trenchant Hegelian judgment that Glissant dares to declare Proust "sickly" (IL 115), not because he was ill, or talked about illness, but probably because of his idolatrous love of the work of art as salvific.

Glissant sounds the death knell of Western literature because in his view it has exhausted its possibilities of expression. The realism that follows Romanticism does not mean that it escapes from its dead end:

> In the exercise of prose, as far as our literatures are concerned, writers believe all too easily that the description of the real accounts for reality. It is rather like those artists who produce pictures of everyday customs or genre paintings: a tropical market or Caribbean fishermen. They think they are giving an account of reality. This is just not true. They are absolutely *not* giving an account of reality; reality is something other than this appearance. (IL 29)

Let us not be mistaken. On the one hand, Glissant never says that the West cannot renew itself, but that any renewal from its sources can take place only if it opens itself, without denying itself, to Relation, to other cultures. On the other hand, this noting of the "end of history," the exhaustion of the expressive resources of the (Romantic) Self, does not imply that we must reject the "Western" tradition; on the contrary, it must be reinterpreted, but with a new eye and a new sensitivity. The Whole-World presupposes the inclusion of all cultural traditions.

Glissant does not conceive of poetic practice as a representation of the world, but as *an enactment of and in the world.* The poetic work functions as the evidence of a practical action, and this explains the intertwining of the poetic with reflective thinking in the texts: the poetic is testimony *against* the chatter of the Hegelian Intellectual—the philosophical proves itself in acts intertwined with History and other narratives. The poetic again becomes the Action that it had ceased to be in Romanticism: "It will be seen that poetics is not an art of dreams and illusions, but that it is a way of conceiving of oneself, of conceiving of one's relationship to oneself and to the other and expressing it. All poetics is a network" (IP 135).[10] The paradox, or the cunning ploy, lies in the fact that the poetic relation must remain virtual. This theme appears very early on, in the second essay: "The intention, even if deliberate, will die from being realized" (IP 12). It is repeated in a later text: "And I call *Poétique de la Relation* this possibility of the imaginary [. . .]" (TTM 22). The poetic act, however definite its realization, must always preserve in itself something unfinished; when it thinks it is manifesting itself completely, it must face its dissolution. The realization, the act (the book), always reveals how big a gap there is between the intention and its materialization: "The work which realizes its intention reveals another (hidden) intention of the author, one which remains open: to be fulfilled. The writer is always the ghost of the writer he wants to be" (IP 36). The power of the poetic, saved from novelistic and Romantic decomposition, is expressed in the future tense. Mallarmé's ambition to write a book that would express the totality of the world—a Book that itself remained an uncompleted project—is absent from Glissant's intention: the totality, never attained, can be glimpsed through the many different works and remains forever in a state of becoming.

According to the Romantic doctrine, the poet is a genius who expresses his self or expresses "the essence of his nation" in his poetic work. But every self is held to be different from every other self. From this postulate derives the necessity of originality, which is, in the last analysis, a very recent criterion in the critical evaluation of literature. Pre-Romantic writers were not in search of originality: they had at their disposal a large body of generic models, canonical works of antiquity, collections of *topoi* (those commonplaces shared by every educated writer), and even manuals for writing—those ancient treatises of rhetoric constantly updated by the medievals and the classics until recently: in the French education system, the "rhetoric class" that covered these subjects was suppressed only in 1885 by Jules Ferry, under the pressure of Romanticism, which had itself by now become a commonplace. Fundamentally, if literature before Romanticism was innovative, this novelty appeared in spite of and against its rigorously prescribed rhetorical nature. With Romanticism, the common heritage of the literate was replaced by the self of the genius. The Republic of Letters then changed fundamentally in nature and content; the once-living cultural heritage became a mere empty reference point whose sole purpose was to enable atomized individuals to recognize themselves as members of a community.

Glissant can be defined as an anti-Romantic. He does not "express himself in his works," and Relation is not self-expression. He has no Romantic claim to an originality based on the genius of his own self: "We abandon the claim to find the truth only in the narrow circle of our own subjectivity, and that, I think, is also an invariant, this need to go beyond one's own subjectivity, not to move toward a totalitarian system but to move toward an intersubjectivity of the Whole-World" (IL 44). At the same time, when he incorporates the literary and philosophical past, it is not to fit into a tradition, contrary to what the medieval thinkers and their successors, always bent on restating and transmitting cultural traditions, would have done. His work in its entirety is projected toward a future. The past, in Glissant, is remade, whether it is the story of his ancestors, a history erased by the slave trade, or the history of culture.

If he exalts the commonplace, it is to give it a concrete meaning in addition to its rhetorical meaning; it is also to make it a constituent element of the Whole-World, a mulling-over that becomes generalized. Moreover, the commonplace is displayed as such; it is not camouflaged by the Romantic demand for originality: "As people have guessed, one of the traces of this Poetics involves the commonplace. [. . .] You suppose an idea, they take it greedily, it is theirs. They proclaim it. They lay claim to it. This is the commonplace. It mobilizes, better than any system of ideas, our imaginaries, but only if you are alert enough to recognize it" (TTM 23).[11]

Rejecting Romanticism, Glissant rejects the pastoral, the self that projects itself into the delights of the spectacle of nature, a symptom of the impotence of the beautiful soul (think of Jean-Jacques Rousseau); the landscape serves only as something onto which we can project a state of mind and is not considered as such, in its specificity and otherness as an object in the world: "We know the romantic error, according to which the landscape was mainly a *consenting decor.* There is also a realism-of-purity of fields and greenery. The pastoral lurks" (IP 86). And it is not only the Western tradition that is targeted here, but all literature that justifies itself by its native territory, which succumbs to exoticism and folklore: the pastoral is outdated; when it returns, we need to rid ourselves of it, to oppose it with irreducible places.

We can now sketch out a Glissantian program, one that goes beyond the Romantic program and is inspired by Hegel's radical critique:

- The "Western" self has exhausted its possibilities of expression and representation. As a corollary, there is no longer any place for the "psychology of literary characters," even character itself as the representation of an autonomous individuality. Any criticism of Glissant's work that relies on Glissant's psychological motives or, even worse, on those of one or other of his fictional characters, as if these had the spiritual depth of the living, is wanting. Based on the fantasy of an identification with or projection onto the characters, this type of reading is one of the most frequent pet sins of so-called francophone criticism.

- The writer thus does not have to "describe" (*décrire*) himself, or to describe the world (passively); what is needed is to "write" (*écrire*) the world in its totality—in other words to produce it in act, through a poetics that does not reflect it but constructs and interprets it all at once. To write is not to hold up a mirror to objects, whatever they may be, but to remake the world from the imaginary.

- The book about the book can no longer be justified; the unique Book cannot and must not be realized.

- The Republic of Letters and the Ivory Tower, collections of isolated individuals, factitious communities, must be rejected, first by refusing to be absorbed into them, then by creating new communities (the first of which would be Glissant's readers). Glissant has paid dearly for this refusal to be absorbed: he does not really occupy a "position" in the Republic of Letters. Besides, this was indifferent to him, apart from the feeling that he was not really being read.

- The "unhappy consciousness," derision, irony, self-destruction are negativities that must be overcome by a poetic affirmation.

- There is no longer any place for the pastoral. The landscape, rid of the Romantic projections that idealized it, must be reaffirmed in all the detail of its reality.

- The original genius of the isolated Self must be replaced by new languages, which place real or future communities in relation: "And just as I think that the poetic fulguration is the acme of the exaltation of the self, I can likewise surmise that the mulling over of discourse is the measure of a We. But this We is not given as transcendence. We are even entitled to assert that it naturally presupposes the first datum of Relation, namely crossbreeding" (DA 250). The Romantic self has the obligation to shine in an original way every time, in every poem, but this demand, however brilliant it may be, only confirms the isolation of its narcissism, even when it turns itself into the voice of the "genius of the people." The modern (anti-Romantic) poet, on the other hand, *mulls over*, and this repetition produces selves that differ from each other, but also opens the possibility that this multiplicity of selves will lead to a community. Glissant's mulling over here

> takes on an additional dimension: restatement is constitutive
> not of the I, but of the We. It places subjectivities in relation.

If we can flee from gossip and verbiage only by giving ourselves over to the twofold consubstantiality of the philosophical and the poetic, "to enter philosophy" entails a new risk, that of believing that philosophy says (or can say) everything, that it exhausts reality. This was the avowed ambition of Hegel, and he thought he saw it realized when, according to legend, he saw Napoleon galloping down the streets of Jena in 1806. Thought, brought to its completion by Hegel, was realized by Napoleon's Action, and absolute knowledge was achieved.

But Hegel is not the last word of philosophy. In particular, his historical totalization omits the case of Africa: "What we understand, in short, under the name of Africa is an undeveloped ahistorical world, entirely prisoner of the natural spirit and whose place is still on the threshold of universal history."[12] The Africa left fallow by Hegel denies *in actual fact* the totality of absolute knowledge, and undoes it as a totality: "In truth all history (and therefore any Reason of History projected into it) has definitely been an exclusion of others: this is what consoles me for having been excluded by Hegel from historical movement" (IP 37). Beyond the Romantic exhaustion of "Western" individuality, other histories and other aesthetics are being built.

Glissant's deep connection to Hegel is neither one of contradiction nor of revenge. There is no trace of resentment "against" Hegel; for the philosopher, in his very incompleteness, opens the door to the poetic affirmation that goes beyond him by including him, and makes it possible to define a *Dasein* ("my condition in the world") that he did not foresee: "And if I want to understand my condition in the world, I see that if I tend to delve into my history, this is not for the malicious pleasure of contradicting Hegel a posteriori, nor taking a naive revenge on him: I must instantly catch up with those enormous expanses of silence in which my history has gone astray" (IP 38). It is not enough to find a history, essentially that of the slave trade and the colonization of Martinique—two themes that Hegel does not so much as mention. This history must also be straightened out: it must be tackled not by the concept, but by the imaginary, and this history, "my" history, must be extracted from the provocative silence in which Hegel veiled it. The critique, it is important to emphasize, does not concern the ambition of Hegelian totalization in itself; on the contrary, Hegel is reproached for not having been sufficiently comprehensive or systematic *enough* precisely because he erased Africa: in the last analysis, he failed to arrive at absolute knowledge because he fell short of the Whole. From which we can infer, in Glissant, a hunger for totality, coherence, the absolute and the system even more intense than in Hegel. This demand for totality, however, differs from the Hegelian summa in two fundamental ways; first, it is always open, as histories begin and do not end. Then, poetry is his chosen means, while Hegel thought poetry was exhausted.

There is no trace in Glissant of the accusations of racism and totalitarianism directed at Hegel by Karl Popper and the French New Philosophers. In fact, scholars have long since shown that these attacks were unfair. First, Hegel unequivocally condemns slavery as an absolute evil in many passages of the *Principles of the Philosophy of Right*. He never said or thought that Africans were ultimately unable to join the historic movement that in his view came to its consummation in the West. On the contrary, as Susan Buck-Morss has shown,[13] Hegel saw the revolt of Toussaint Louverture as the enactment of his own ideas. Then, for Hegel, the perfect form of government was liberal parliamentarism, whether this was exercised in a monarchical state or a democracy, that is, a governmental regime the complete opposite of totalitarianism or authoritarianism; the difficulties he faced from the Prussian administration of Frederick William III are well known.[14] Glissant, of course, was never tempted by totalitarianism, except perhaps when it took a leftist turn: his admiration for Fidel Castro or Che Guevara,[15] in such an emancipated man, always surprised me, but this was an idiosyncrasy common to many French intellectuals of his generation. Be that as it may, one cannot argue against Glissant that, in the name of his fidelity to Hegel, he fell prey to any totalitarian temptation: this is mere fantasy, and it is quite untrue to both Hegel's vision and to Glissant's.

The Whole-World, creolization, Relation, wandering, may indeed be new, but they are never presented as ideological; this was not Glissant's field of struggle or of his dialectical approach. In one sense, for Glissant as for Hegel, the (French) Revolution has already happened—there is no need to return to it; his mistrust of the results of anticolonialist revolutions and struggles is a constant. They are, for the most part, necessary and legitimate; but often they bring back the master in a new and even fiercer form, and they trap communities in an infinite repetition that the dialectic should have overcome: "How many revolutions, rich with how many overcomings, have sunk into blind limitations and absurd principles, thus relapsing into precisely what they had fought against? The poetic perception of the chaos-world leads us to sense some of the lessons of so many failures" (PR 217). Here we are far from triumphalism, from the celebration of liberation, from a naively positive view of the postcolonial break (and, as a corollary, from an entirely negative and equally stupid vision of the West). Like Hegel, these negatives are for Glissant rich with a future that will turn them into positives.

The concept of "revolution" is not to be read only as a social and political movement. Glissant tends to a revolution in thought; but in his work a revolution is by no means a tabula rasa. The new names, which call forth worlds to be born, are at the same time old, sometimes very old names. Relation exists not only in extent, composing the moments of a contemporaneity or outlining the hopes for a happy future; it exists just as much in temporality, in relation to different pasts, histories, and traditions, albeit re-read in a completely fresh way. The radically new must be thought in the mulling over and displacement of the old. We need to construct the system (in structure, in extent) of the Whole-World, Relation, creation, genesis, and digenesis, as well as carrying out their archeology (the diachrony, in historical depth). Glissant's thought is always, like Janus, doubly oriented: the present of writing prophesies the past and mulls over the future.

Chapter 5

"Everything is in everything"

Today we live in the era of the non-Totality: "There is no All. Since there is no All, nothing is All," says Lacan,[1] taking note of the scientific revolution that separates the sciences from the arts (until Galileo, it was possible to conceive of knowledge as a Whole). Non-Totality, incompleteness, the impossibility of totalization can be conceived as the index of Western modernity. In contrast to the Whole-World, our world forces us to live where nothing is in anything: a reality divided into scattered subsets unconnected with each other. Separation and segregation are at the heart of this world of non-relation (not only sexual). The last moment of the dynamics of non-Totality is undoubtedly that of the discovery of the unconscious by Freud: human beings now know they are divided between a conscious part and a part they can neither access nor express.

Glissant is aware of the modern impossibility that dismisses the very idea of totality. This does not prevent him from proposing it, from the very start of his theoretical work, as a fundamental intuition: "I sense that maybe there will be no more culture without all cultures, no more single civilization that can be the metropolis of all others, no more poets unaware of the movement of history" (SC 11). Intuition is clarified in *L'Intention poétique*: "To consign the "planetarization" of thought is thus to confess that man is in a new situation: in touch with himself—with 'his totality' [. . .]." (IP 27) Intuition will find its assumption in the notion of the Whole-World, successively unfolded in a novel and in a treatise.

The question thus arises of how the West separated out from a cultural heritage that originally thought of itself as a totality. In philosophy, for Hegel as for Glissant, there is a break between Heraclitus and

Parmenides, and even more between the Pre-Socratics and the Sophists on one side, and Socrates and Plato on the other: when philosophy is called on to account for the coherence of its reasons, and thus fundamentally separates the thinking subject from the object of thought. The epistemological break produced by Socrates, which subjects thought to the evidence of reason and reasons, to the primacy of the concept, cuts man off from the world:

> The situation in which we find ourselves is the following: we have already passed through the concept: there has already been, from Plato onward, this separation between man and the world. [. . .] In my opinion, it is from Plato's idea that the Pre-Socratic principle of indissociated knowledge has been called into question. Plato thus rejects two principles of knowledge: *the indissociated principle of the Pre-Socratics, man and the world, and also the fusing principle of the Sophists, consummation by language.* He questions these two modes of relationship with the world in order to found what he considers to be the true relation, which is the relation in ideas. From such a magisterial masterful fantasy there proceeded the sureness of Aristotelian realism in its different forms. The relation in ideas necessarily led to the concept, which separated man from the world. (EBR 145, my emphasis)

With Socrates, thought *as thought* make immense progress, positing, as its desire and purpose, the coincidence of discourse with truth. But, at the same time, something essential is lost, repressed, forgotten: Pre-Socratics and Sophists are rejected as "heretics" according to the measure of rational thought. With them dies the totality, that is to say, an extended notion of rationality that includes poetry, the world, and nature (*physis*). The Pre-Socratics and Sophists are figures of the primordial poem that opens the *Philosophie de la Relation* and that our modernity must resuscitate while modifying it. This poem is buried, in Glissant's image, under thousands of years, superimposed layers of rocks and earth, successive strata of repression, exclusion, and oblivion.

Socrates makes the Sophist a merchant of words empty of meaning; the Sophist commercializes a knowledge that has no secure foundation. Thus, the Platonic dialogue entitled *The Sophist* is a polemical caricature that reduces true philosophers to mere traders in rhetoric. Socrates's attack extends to Heraclitus and Parmenides, who are, with the Sophists, the "masters of Greece," in Hegel's formula.[2] As early as Plato, Heraclitus is no longer understood as anything other than the proponent of the extreme mobility of becoming that Cratylus inherited from the Pre-Socratics. Aristotle rejects Heraclitus "the Obscure" in the name of transparency in his *Rhetoric* (Γ 5, 1407 b, 11); he strips him of his "right to opacity," dismissing him from philosophy properly speaking, understood as the clear light of reason and logic. Moreover, for Aristotle, Heraclitus is obscure because he is opaque to "himself": "And perhaps if we had questioned Heraclitus himself in this sense, we would have reduced him to confessing that it is never possible for contradictory propositions to be true at the same time for the same things; *indeed, it was because he did not understand what he wanted to say that Heraclitus professed this opinion*" (*Metaphysics*, K 5, 1062a, 31, my emphasis).[3] Glissant takes his stance in this thousand-year dispute, opting for Heraclitus's poetic opacity against the transparency of Aristotle's logico-philosophical system.

What the trio of the founders of philosophy buries, when they decide that the Sophists are "heretics," is in fact what Glissant intends to re-establish by mulling over it, that is to say by displacing it. First, the sovereignty of the art of poetic oratory over all others, as Gorgias had said to Socrates: "In the case of oratory, there is no such mechanical operation, but its activity, the sovereignty it possesses, is the word which is its instrument" (*Gorgias*, 450 a). Or again, as the Sophist Protagoras had said in his comments on a poem by Simonides: "I for my part, Socrates, think that for a man a very important part of culture consists in being versed in the art of poetry" (*Protagoras*, 339a). Next, there is the rejection of the breaking up of knowledge into specialized disciplines: discourse is transgeneric (*Protagoras*, 316d–317b) and transdisciplinary. Only the poetic is in a position to affirm the imaginary of total knowledge: before Socrates transformed the notion of Sophist into a consistently pejorative label, "sophist" (from "*sophia*," wisdom) meant one who is scholarly in all disciplines, in a notion of human knowledge as a totality.

From *L'Intention poétique* onward, Glissant categorically rejects the Platonic expulsion of poets from the utopia of the Rational City:[4]

Almost ever since the Platonic idea rose into the heavens of thought, the poets were banned—something with which they coped very well. Plato had banished them from the city; what did it matter? They reserved for themselves, in the company of the Muse, the domains (with no endangered borders) of sensibility, grace, and fiction, where no one sought to harm them (IP 59).

The Platonic break is a truncation of the whole. It annihilates the poetic to let the rational occupy the space of thought. Plato condemns Homer, and, through him, poetry, in the name of a mimetic conception of art. The art of *mimesis* is relegated to the third degree of truth, in a hierarchy that puts the idea first, then the thing that represents it, then the artist's imitation of this thing (*Republic*, X, 603 c): art is the degradation of the Idea, to which it should always be related. The subjectively knowing whole is atrophied.

However, everywhere and always, Glissant affirms or practices a poetics that does not fall under *mimesis*: he rejects the realism of representation and the exoticism of folklore—in his view these are passive representations that are only semblances of reality. The poet can resume his place in the *polis* only by refusing to bend to the Platonic edict: he does not have to produce a *mimesis*, but to bring together an imaginary and a utopia that arise from the negativities that the city generates.

In the "completion by language" that the Sophists bring about, Glissant allusively takes up a capital notion, that of *plasma*, advanced by Gorgias in the *Praise of Helen*. *Plasma* is the intuition that a poetic and rhetorical discourse can create, alongside the *pseudos* (a fiction unrelated to the true or the false), a fictional and poetic world that can be true. In this sense, the Whole-World to come is an effect of *plasma* (of the discourse that can create figures) produced by Glissant, who rejects the condemnation of the sophist's art by Socrates ("But I refuse the name of art to what is an irrational mode of activity," *Gorgias* 464 a).[5] It is not surprising, therefore, that he should be so attached to the Sophists, those rebels of philosophy: they are a capital source of his thought. However, while the Sophist's *plasma* applies only to the city-state where he practices his art (an essentially political art), Glissant's *plasma* has such breadth that it extends to all the figures of the world.

The affinity of Glissant's thought with Sophistry and the Pre-Socratics is made clear everywhere: Gorgias, like Glissant, has challenged the knowledge of Being;[6] Parmenides, like Glissant, and against Aristotle who criticized him, questioned the determinations of the One: "The One which is not has no determination in any respect" (*Parmenides*, 164b); Cratylus fused the name and the thing, the subject and the object, in an anticipation of Glissant's primordial poem. This premonition is all the more relevant as it is not linked to a language, nation, or ethnic group, but applies to all languages, those of the Greeks and those of the "others": "A certain correctness of denomination exists originally for Greeks and Barbarians, and it is the same for all, indistinctly" (*Cratylus*, 383 a–b). It is these primordial and poetic thoughts from before the Socratic break that Glissant endeavors to disinter, in a mulling over that is not a repetition: "Repetition is not an unnecessary duplication" (PhR 62).

It is clear that Glissant wants to "recompose" (that is, reinvent) the uncreated world of antiquity. The primordial poem is pagan or polytheistic, in the sense of Heraclitus, who criticizes myths and religious rites, but also sees them as embodying the union of the divine and the human,[7] fusion and totality. "The gods exploded, we recomposed them" (S 95), say the Batoutos in *Sartorius*. In this sense, recomposition is synonymous with mulling over. Polytheism returns, moving beyond the monotheistic break that caused it to disintegrate: the very title of the collection of Glissant's first plays, *Le Monde incréé*, indicates this; but the uncreated world is not merely a reappearance of the origin, it is also the world to come, the world still to be created. The return of the old gods is not a regression, but a reconstruction: "The poem buried in epochs outside humanity will not sound the same way for us today" (PhR 37). Repetition is never passive redundancy, and the rediscovery of the multiple nature of divinity in modernity modifies the place and status of the divine: gods who no longer reside in some Empyrean, but in the world. More than a regression to paganism, this return to the dawn of the poetic traces the path of an opening up of possibilities against a background of recomposition:

> Elevation had led to the word spontaneously taking off at the same time as it was erased from every possible place, like a numberless bird; this happened before races and languages and postures had become differentiated and then opposed, and the poem had disappeared into gulfs where the earth had collapsed, into unknown obscurities, and with the poem all the possibilities of different languages, which now needed to be *recomposed* as broken roots. (PhR 13, my emphasis)

Contrary to the Platonic fragmentation that separates the idea from the concrete, it is possible to maintain, as does Hegel, and Glissant in his wake, that the history of human thought begins in the poetic imagination of a totality:

> We are in the presence of a first unitary phase which does
> not involve any difference between soul and body, concept
> and reality; the corporeal and the sensible, the natural and
> the human are not only the expression of a meaning distinct
> from them; rather, the external manifestations themselves are
> considered as implying the reality and the immediate presence
> of the Absolute . . .[8]

At the end of history, humanity will rediscover, in a circular way, this paradise of unity and totality.

Glissant was always worried about the way his readers might amalgamate the figures of totality that he proposed with some form of totalitarianism, either of thought or of (political) fact. But such an amalgam has no place: since Relation cannot be figured, as it is still to come, no one, starting with Glissant, can go round it and propose a summa of it, figuring it as an irrevocable form that would close down all challenge and all discussion. Relation is the objection against the totality of totalitarianism, and the supposed totality of the universal. The very notion of Whole-World, in the infinity of its detail and its differences, presupposes its incompleteness: "The Whole-World is total to the extent that we all dream of it as such, and its difference from the totality remains that its All is a becoming" (TFEV 19).

Thus "Everything is in everything" (NRM 102) or everything *can be* in everything—provided that a part of this tautology remains in the state of incompleteness, of the virtual, or of a reality that is solely poetic. In our world of distinctions and segregations, only the poetic, strictly speaking, can make a totalizing fusion possible.

The thought of Glissant is a return to a golden age of fusion, a return that constructs an incalculable future. It is a return to an old ideal, one that modernity considers outdated. The primary elements of matter lay at the center of the Pre-Socratics' mediation on *physis*. For Thales, it was water that was fundamental, for Anaximenes, air, for Empedocles, the four fused elements, and finally, for Heraclitus, fire, as a quotation in the anthology of the Whole-World does not fail to point out: "Fire rules everything"[9] (TEFV 68). Chemistry after Antoine Lavoisier, and the physics of the atom after John Dalton, broke apart the first elements (*stoicheia* in Greek) of matter that had dominated the thought of *physis* until the end of the eighteenth century. The four elements took refuge in the imaginary, the primordial place of knowledge for Glissant. Thus, the program of research on the imaginary launched by Gaston Bachelard drew on the Pre-Socratics: it was an elemental[10] reverie the importance of which Glissant, a student of Bachelard, could not fail to see. The two fragments from Bachelard, excerpted from *La Poétique de la Rêverie* (*The Poetics of Reverie*) and *La Terre et les Rêveries de la volonté* (*The Earth and the Dreams of the Will*) that Glissant includes in the anthology of the Whole-World, unequivocally bear witness to this; in them we find many of Glissant's themes: the primordial poem buried in the earth, the poetry of matter, the fusion of man and nature, the detour, the realm of the living that extends throughout the whole of the cosmos and thought:

> Anyone who goes to the heart of reverie rediscovers natural reverie, a reverie of the first cosmos and the first dreamer. So the world is no longer silent. Poetic reverie revives the world of the first words. [. . .] Only the detour of dreams that bring the earth to life can give an activity to the depths. So we must meditate not on *sediments*, but on beings arising, on the living mineral, on the mineral with active roots that seek in the center of the earth the secret of vertical life. (TEFV 103–107)

Right from the start, Glissant's intention is to update the elemental poetics of the Pre-Socratics. In *Soleil de la conscience*, there is a 1949 text from *Le Sang rivé*, entitled "Élément," that is introduced as follows: "And I abandoned myself to the elemental [. . .]." (SC 35) In this beautiful poem, where "the word joins the materiality of the world" (PR 219), the four elements play a fundamental role:

> O extinguished suns! I will find a health of fruits in *flames!* [. . .] How, without a renown unravelling from unheard-of tropical levels, the black flame licks under the *wind!* [. . .] You have slid into the *water* the panting of your silhouette broken with glass. [. . .] the *lightning* of you, air and love intertwined. [. . .] O suffering, this beating of the *wind* in the streets. And poverty is ignorance of the *earth*, imagination is passion. [. . .] Storm stained [. . .]. The *fire* chose this *wave* that I thought the last, to surround me in its turn. (my emphasis)

There is something like a Saussurian anagram here, simultaneously an interpretative key of the poem, and, beyond that, of Glissant's work.

We must also see it as the fertile seed of *La Terre le Feu l'Eau et les Vents*, which thus returns to the very origin of the poetic writing of the Greeks:

> You enter by knowledge and experience into the elements and you share them, divide them, reveal them also, in nuclei and particles: one must nevertheless ask where and in what their thought holds together, and holds us. All in one piece? Water, fire? How do they persist, beyond any analysis, molecular or symbolic, in this mysterious unity that commits them as they are to our imaginary, to our realities? Even if they ravage our lives, borne here by tremors and swollen by the winds, we invoke them anyway and live on them. (TFEV 18)

It is worth emphasizing: the return to the elemental is not a regression, when it occurs after the history of thought and literature; on the contrary, it is revision and project: "The elemental recomposes itself absolutely" (PR 55).

The "first braziers of the earth" give birth to the poem of fusion, whose traces are for Glissant buried in the caves painted by the human beings of prehistory: "Eternities further along, what arose on the darkened walls of the cave was not the deceitful shadow of a reality outside, but the very sign of the fusion of everything with everything: the humanities had not yet cut off their differences by amputation" (PhR 12).

Two and a half centuries before the Pre-Socratics, Greek thought had begun in myth, especially in Hesiod's *Theogony* from the eighth century BC (the name means "the origin of the gods"), in which the elements were deified: Chaos, Eros, Gaia (Earth), Ouranos (Heaven), Erebus (Darkness), Nyx (Night), Aether (Day).[11] This was a sexual myth, in which the entire cosmos was born from the founding mating of Gaia and Ouranos. When the Pre-Socratics replaced these first gods with the elements of matter, their aim was to get rid of religious thinking and move from a cosmogony to materialism.

In this break, however, the ideas of totality and fusion are preserved; thus Heraclitus: "Join what is complete and what is not, what is concord and what is discord, what is in harmony and in disharmony; and from Totality is born unity and from the one, Totality" (D 10). This idea is found in the phrase *Panta rhei* ("Everything flows"), where totality and unity are presented as an unlimited and perpetual becoming. Édouard Glissant shows a profound affinity with this way of thinking: Heraclitus's

Panta rhei figures prominently among the quotations from Heraclitus chosen for the Whole-World anthology (TEFV 68). On the other hand, the Heraclitean fragment was also echoed in the philosophical tradition: in Jena, around 1800, the young Hölderlin, Schelling, and Hegel had chosen for themselves a slogan spelled out in Greek:[12] *Hen kai pan*, the "One that is all." Was Glissant a "pantheist," of either an Eastern or Western kind? No: Glissant's *pan* has no God and is not a god, and it is not One: in the place of all divinity stands Relation, a worldly immanence freed from religious transcendence.

Heraclitus makes the union of opposites (subject/object, cosmos/humanity, etc.) a synthesis in the making, that is to say a historical dynamic.[13] In this, he is indeed the source of Hegelian and Glissantian dialectics. The Totality or Whole of Hegel (*das Ganze*) is the result of the sublation of thesis and the antithesis into their synthesis, a process that leads historically and dynamically to the truth, as in Heraclitus; the totality is thus the culmination of a dynamic that is by definition digenetic, composite, or crossbred, as Glissant desires.

However, he distanced himself from the Heraclitean totality, an ontological union of opposites, to which Kostas Axelos remained faithful in *Le Jeu deu Monde*:

> Similarly, Kostas Axelos proposes a totality that is not "the sum or synthesis of all that is [. . .]." It is *the* "totality," in which one can emphasize "the same in the other, the other in the same." However exciting this game may appear, we cannot ignore the way it involves an element of generalization that undifferentiates the other from the same, going beyond them while maintaining them. For all peoples threatened with indistinction, such a game seems deadly. The non-exclusive series, the non-transcendental differentiations proposed by a science of Relation would constitute the necessary logistical base, going beyond itself in an open dynamics, for all the totality of the world. Even hypothesized, totality easily becomes totalitarian when it exempts itself from surveying *beings*. (DA 196)[14]

Or again, a little later: "The totality is not what has been called the universal. It is the finite and realized quantity of the infinite detail of the real. And, being a matter of detail, it is not totalitarian" (TTM 192). If Glissant's thinking is, in all its aspects, absolutely systematic, in its attention to detail, to particularity, to the different, to the inextricable, it abandons any ambition to constitute itself as a metaphysical system. Against this background, the dream of the Whole-World appears, not as a law of generalities, but as a dynamic (a bringing into relation) of specificities; that is why "the Whole-World, which is totalizing, is not (for us) total" (TTM 22).

Totality escapes the totalitarian by refusing the abstract and universal idealism of the "idea" of totality, which withdraws from the Whole by placing itself outside the world: "Let us say it again, opaquely: The idea of totality alone is an obstacle to totality" (PR 206). In the last analysis, Glissant's totality is the equivalent, irreducible to any summa, of the future of Relation: "The world as totality, which is so dangerously close to the totalitarian. No science gives us a truly overall opinion of it, or allows us to appreciate its unprecedented crossbreeding, or allows us to know how we are changed by frequenting it" (TTM 119).

We can see the precision with which Glissant, via Axelos, simultaneously recognizes his due to Heraclitus and the movement by which he seeks to go beyond the latter. The Heraclitean totality, in Axelos's interpretation, leads to a synthesis that resolves and dissolves, by the Logos, the differences in the fundamental and undifferentiated One, which belongs to defined Being. On the contrary, Glissant's totality is a preserved multiplicity and diversity that takes into account not Being, but beings; we thus return to Heraclitus, but the Logos and the One are dismissed from the totality as Heraclitus conceived it:

> It is the idea of totality itself, such as Western thought has superbly expressed it, which is threatened with immobility. We have argued that Relation is an open totality, in motion on itself. That is, what we subtract from this idea, as it was thus forged, is the principle of unity. Here, Totality is not the final goal of the parts, for multiplicity in totality is totally a diversity. (PR 206)

Glissant transmutes a totality of Being, conceptually unified and thereby frozen, into a totality of beings in perpetual becoming, never fixed in the gathering of the one or of Being.

Like Glissant, Hegel returned to the Pre-Socratics, who had folded thought onto itself and removed it from history.[15] Like Glissant, Hegel reactivates (by returning, mulling over), in a circular motion, the inaugural moment of totality, the moment of Heraclitus. In so doing, he becomes the last philosopher of the Western tradition to explicitly propose his philosophical trajectory as all-encompassing: he is the last thinker of Totality, with the major exception of Édouard Glissant. Christian Godin, in *La Totalité*, shows how, for the philosophers who follow him, Hegel is the "philosopher to be defeated":[16] for a contemporary thinking that has become powerless to meditate in overall terms, which can grasp totality only as totalitarianism, which considers everything solely from the angle of the categories and distinctions of the fragment, the angle of the partial, particularity and singularity, Hegel is the chosen enemy.

The Hegelian totality is expressed in the form of "absolute knowledge" (*Absolutes Wissen*), which concludes not only his journey as a thinker, but human history as a whole. It is important to specify here what Hegel means by "objective knowing" (*savoir*), so as to contrast it with the subjective "knowledge" (*connaissance*) that Glissant pursues. Knowledge is a matter of concept and abstraction, so it has an entirely philosophical sense: it is the sum of the experiences of human consciousness, progressing from a first, poetic revelation to the self-knowledge of *Selbstbewusstsein*, total self-knowledge. Absolute knowledge is the unconditioned knowledge of Being in its totality and in its truth, which are synonymous in Hegel: "The True is the Whole."[17] As a result, Hegel's concept of "science" has nothing to do with modern (Galilean) science. *Wissen* (objective knowledge) and *Wissenschaft* (science) in his work need to be translated as the knowledge and science of human history, in pursuit of truth, and not as a science of matter, seeking accuracy (as opposed to the truth). Hegel could not be more peremptory on this subject: "The evidence of this flawed knowledge of which mathematics is proud, and of which it boasts in the face of philosophy, rests solely on the poverty of its purpose and on the defectiveness of its material: its obviousness is therefore of a kind that philosophy must disdain."[18] On the human level, the most important effect of modern science is undoubtedly the abolition of the subject: science is an expansionist machine that operates without regard to what we desire or find desirable. In this sense, we can agree with Hegel when he excludes science from his inquiry: as a science ("mathematics" in the *Phenomenology*), it does not concern itself with the states of human consciousness, which are the object of the Hegelian quest. For Hegel, man's destiny can be played out only in art and philosophy, not in science; we can say that absolute knowledge is truncated, as it is cut off from what is now seen as a crucial part of it, namely historical development.

But this is not what Glissant criticizes in absolute knowledge. His notion of totality differs profoundly from the Hegelian *summa*, although it is inspired by it. In the first place, very early on Glissant criticizes both Hegel's abstraction and his universalizing claim, while absolute knowledge is in fact localized, anchored in the Western tradition: "Thus the man of the West thought he was 'living' the life of the world" where in fact he often merely reduced the world and induced a general idea from it—an ideal generality that was certainly not the totality of the world. Poets nobly suffered and expressed this gap, which ideologies and systems tended to deny or to disguise" (IP 27). Hence this idea, stated at the very start: "No art [as much as poetry] needs to be so extremely vigilant about objective knowledge" (SC 41).

Glissant does not reject the idea of Hegelian totality: he denies only that it can claim universality and completion. There are other histories than History, and if we can consider with Hegel that the history of the West is complete, we cannot extend this closure to other histories that are being made in Africa, in Latin America, in the East. We must return to the Pre-Socratics as philosophers, but also as poets—while still being aware that the concept, the abstraction, this "magisterial fantasy" (EBR 145) of Socrates, Plato, Aristotle, and Galileo has triumphed: "And, for example, we come across, in the hacked, fragmentary texts of the Pre-Socratics, as if the fragment were the piece of an expired persistence, this feeling that our own time has renewed that Pre-Socratic era, where the crossbreeding of islands, archipelagic thoughts and reveries of the Great All had linked the human to the terrestrial, or to the cosmic" (TTM 165). It is a radical reversal that is being proposed here: the imaginary marks the philosophical, which thus becomes poetic, and the poetic is again charged with the responsibility for (and the possibility of) knowledge, in the concrete reality of the world, without the mediation of ideas. In other words, the return and mulling over of the origins of thought transform that thought by displacing it:

We are in a new situation where we must be ingenuous and naive, as we are knowing. And I say ingenuous and naive in the full sense of the word: we must be immediate, in contact with the world, and at the same time rational, and reflecting the world. In the history of the West, the poets had gradually freed themselves from the task of showmen or entertainers that Plato had assigned to them by driving them out of the city, and had gone back to a Pre-Socratic aspiration that would have fostered the ambition of a total poetic knowledge. (EBR 143–147)

Glissant's totality is a totality-world, a globality-world. It is worth returning to the etymological sources of the terms "Whole" and "World," first of all out of fidelity to the thought of Glissant that goes to origins, including linguistic origins, so as to recharge them, but also to determine precisely how very original is the coupling of Whole and World.

As early as Homer, the Greek word *kosmos* means "order"—hence "order of the universe" on a very large scale, but also, on a very small scale, the "order of toilette," hence "cosmetics," the art of adorning (oneself); the antonym of *kosmos* is *chaos*. The chaos-world of the *Traité*[19] applied to the cosmos would therefore be, for Greek thought, an oxymoron, an impossibility: the ancient cosmos is spherical, it is totalizable, it is the image of order, a vision of order as such; it leaves nothing outside of itself—it is, for its contemporaries, the Whole, but a predictable and non-opaque Whole. The only exception, and it is a huge exception, to this cosmic harmony is this world below, that of men and their history. This *chaosmos*, for the Greeks and the Romans, is in the thrall of perpetual contingency, mortality, disorder, and change.

Ultimately, the designation of "Whole-Universe" would have corresponded better to Glissant's thought than "Whole-World"; the modern world is limitless, whereas the ancient world was bounded by the sphere, the image of all perfection,[20] and was thus a closing off of possibilities, something that Glissant would inevitably reject. But the choice was made by Glissant himself, and we cannot change it, except to say that he saw in advance and even declared that the Whole-World should imply the universe; hence this statement in the *Traité*: "I call Whole-World our universe" (TTM 176). Be that as it may, more than the universe, it is the world of men that is the aim of his work, not interstellar space.

The term "All" covers two different notions, which were distinct in Antiquity, *holos* and *panta* in Greek, *totus* and *omnia* in Latin, the Whole as totality (holistic) or the Whole (Totality) as the set of all things in the world, as linguist and philosopher Viggo Brøndal points out:

"All" is sometimes:

1. The integral (*tōtus*, ὅλος, whole or entire);

2. The universal (*omnis*, πᾶς, all or every);

3. The distributive or iterative (*quisque*, ἕκαστος, every/each);

4. The general (*quisquam*, ὅστις, anyone, whoever).[21]

We can see that Glissant is using the equivocation or fusion of *all* these different meanings when he proposes the *Whole-World*: this is at once a future *wholeness* or *universality*, and it takes into account all *particularities*.

As for the coupling of the two notions, "All" and "World," it appears as such in the Latin of the Vulgate, in Saint John the Evangelist in the form *totus mundus*: "We know that we are of God, and that the whole world (*totus mundus*) is under the power of the evil one" (John 5: 19).[22]

But the "whole world" of the Bible, completely in thrall to evil, differs from Whole-World, which is a world of inclusion: Evil is part of Glissant's cosmos, as a (Hegelian) negativity indispensable to any affirmation of the positive: "Here we need to detect the angelism involved. It is mere vanity, one that is immediately drowned in the din of bombs and the echo of tortures, to posit relation as a substitute for the absolute (as an ideal perfection, in which man would be a lamb for a man); it implies that we dominate and weigh that part of everyday life that belongs to negation, to the horrible, to resignation" (IP 24). In this sense, Glissant's thought is as far as possible removed from an ideal of (moral) purity or (aesthetic) purism: it combines all the Good and Bad things of the world in its alchemy.

This (re)integration of the initial unity of knowledge is meaningful only if it is related to the poetic and the imaginary, not to the symbolic that differentiates, and not to the real that exists outside utterance. Only the imaginary can capture the totality, and paint it, precisely, as an image, beyond the distinction between subject and object: "But in truth, only the human imaginary is not contaminable by its objects. It alone diversifies them infinitely, while bringing them back to a glimmer of unity. *The last moment of subjective knowledge is always a poetics*" (PR 154, my emphasis.) The poetic becomes (yet again) the answer to the dereliction and atomization of the "Western" subject.

While Glissant's totality draws on a tradition going back several thousand years, it is still a new proposition. To bring back the Whole into a modernity that challenges it is not tantamount to abandoning itself to an obsolete reverie, as he remarks in parentheses: ("To dismiss the 'planetarization' of thought thus means to confess that man is in an unprecedented situation: in touch with himself—with his 'totality'—for the first time, aware of, and troubled by, the parts of himself that he had—if Western—hitherto misjudged, or even ignored, or—if not Western—ignored, or even suffered)" (IP 27).

The totality that appears in *L'Intention poétique* in 1969 is complemented later by the notion of the Whole-World, which has two fundamental aspects: a poetic aspect, represented by the "novel" *Tout-Monde* (1993), and a theoretical aspect, that of the *Traité du Tout-Monde* (1997): first of all the knowledge of the *inextricable* elements (places, landscapes, moments), which are brought into relation with one another, and then the reflection that extracts what can be *handled* in these inextricable elements. *Tout-Monde* (the "novel") puts these two stages into a chiasmic relation, announced by the subtle typography of an exclamation, which inverts and then unites ("ah ha" / "ah-ha"):

"But the world is not the Whole-World," says Longoué.

"Ah ha."

"Ah-ha. Because the Whole-World is the world that you have turned round and round in your thinking as it turns you round in its rolling" (TM 177).

The real Whole-World cannot be grasped by the "thought" of the Whole-World, but by the chiasm, where the moment of reflection and the moment of the imaginary end up, as always in Glissant, by merging: "The procession of *Theres* has risen up in a storm of *Heres*. The Whole-World is radiant with *Heres* that lead into each other" (TM 490).

As a result of the historical errors of the twentieth century, we have become incapable of understanding totality other than in terms of ideological, Stalinist, or Hitlerite totalitarianism. It is obvious, however, that Glissant's whole is not a political ideology. How does the Whole-World avoid being totalitarian? Glissant answers this question through what seems to be a pirouette, a pun based on an oxymoron: "The Whole-World, which is totalizing, is not (for us) total?" (TTM 22). Thinking the Whole-World is first and foremost thinking of a future: its figure cannot be the (political or symbolic) summation of all speaking beings—it is eternally open to what can happen:

> The circulation and the action of poetry no longer conjecture a
> given people, but the becoming of planet Earth. This is a com-
> monplace that bears repeating. Today, all expressions of humanity
> are opening up at once to the fluctuating complexity of the
> world. Poetic thought preserves the individual, since it is the
> totality of the truly safe individuals which alone can guarantee
> the energy of diversity. But this individual, each time, is one
> who puts himself in relation in an intransitive manner—with
> the finally realized totality of possible individuals. (DG 12)

We are here not in the closed totality of language (the sum of
signifiers), as this would be a formal and symbolic fixity (a structure),
but rather in the dynamic aggregation, the "energy" of the beings of the
world, which include diversity and particularity: a totality both "realized"
and virtual, thus open to all possibilities.

It is only between this realization and this virtuality that the
Whole is thinkable: "Now, what is this totality? Simply the meaning of
the Whole? Or the reality collected from the archipelagos? From seas,
from the whole earth? And finally, from the universe? From the universe
surrounded by nothingness, which terrifies us? From the universe enveloped by all knowingness, which petrifies us?" All of this, no doubt, but
considered from the angle of becoming, outside any fixity: "The totality
is the process, uninterrupted" (CL 139). The Whole is not eternally fixed
as transcendence and system, but the change immanent to all things.

The Whole-Book?

In the Judaeo-Christian West, the expression of the Whole is based on
the Book and the Word: *To Biblion* is the totalization of the world and of
God. Four writers in the French tradition, all four atheists or agnostics,
take up this idea of a total Book, an idea that is thus transposed from the
religious sphere to that of literature. First there is Mallarmé's project, one
that he will never realize: "The world is made to end up in a beautiful
book." Ethics has been subjected to aesthetics, the Western poet-subject
has passed through his "elocutionary disappearance," and produces an
"abolished trinket of sonorous inanity." The putative Book is both a sign
of the disappearance of the Western subject and a testamentary resumption that intends to compete with the biblical Book. It is undoubtedly

Mallarmé (as well as Hegel, Balzac, and Proust) whom Glissant has in mind when he writes in *Soleil de la conscience*: "Who has not dreamed of the poem which explains everything, the philosophy whose last word illuminates the universe, the novel which organizes *all* truths, all passions, and leads them and enlightens them?" (SC 60). Proust's project is the prose realization of the Mallarmean program. At the end of the fictional and autobiographical journey, the figures of desire are absorbed into the *Search for Lost Time*, which replaces them in their entirety. The world has thus really ended up in a beautiful book.

Surprisingly, we also find the Mallarmean program in a writer who seems prima facie to be the polar opposite of Mallarmé and Proust: Céline, who writes: "It takes something of everything to make a world . . . so, a book!"[23] Maurice Blanchot closes this quartet, with "the greatest, the most terrible and the most beautiful of possible worlds, alas, a book, nothing but a book." The Mallarmean program finds its end in the book yet to come, which "relates only itself,"[24] and there is no doubt that Blanchot also intends to compete with and suppress *To Biblion*.[25] It is a fundamentally "monotheistic" belief, one that Glissant criticizes in Proust and Balzac, this conviction "that we can express history, the world, that we are the only ones who can express it because we are the only ones able to control it" (IL 115). To ensure that *The* Book is the Whole of the World, to supplant the two Testaments, to transform ethics into aesthetics: such is the aim of a whole swath of modern French literature, including its epigones.

Glissant's ambition is different, whether considered in terms of project or realization. The Book will be multiple, not One, it will remain, for all eternity, virtual, not accomplished: reserving a future full of possibilities, in contrast to the finality that Mallarmé, as well as Proust and Blanchot, sought to impose. I remember a remark Glissant made at a conference: "Mallarmé wanted to make a single book, we [Caribbean writers, or those of the Whole-World], we want to write a lot of books!" For Glissant, the Mallarmean project is the figure of a totalization that would have killed all books; in this sense, we are lucky that Mallarmé's "poetic intention" did not find adequate fulfillment: "Now, if Mallarmé had realized his Book, which would have been the Book of the World, then all books would have disappeared from our horizons, both as project and as object" (TTM 159).[26]

But above all, future Books, the virtual summa of all books, have no ambition to replace the world, unlike the Mallarmean project, or to create it, as in the biblical project. Glissant's Whole-Book is All-the-Books, multiplied over and over. Moreover, it is not only bookish or textual, unlike that of Derrida, for whom "everything is text." While it expresses the Whole-World, it cannot exhaust it. The programs of Mallarmé, Proust, Céline, and Blanchot remain unfulfilled, or are content with an illusion of completion; the destruction of all measure (that of verse for Mallarmé; that of classical bourgeois prose for Céline) remains insufficient: "Let us open within ourselves this book of the world, typographic or informatic. It is the task of poets to invite us to do so. Not, however, Mallarmé's Book, absolute and improbable, not that measure of excess of which he so generously dreamed, but Excess itself, unpredictable and uncompleted" (TTM 168). The Whole-World can be glimpsed in two figures, namely Glissant's work itself and the way he adjusts different cultures in the collection *La Terre le Feu l'Eau et les Vents*: the Whole-World must end up in a multiple poetics—an infinity of books and poems. The Whole-World is an impossibility, an incompleteness (not a utopia, which is mostly realized in a disastrous form), one reabsorbed only into poetic utterance and whose realization is a matter of perpetual becoming.

But Glissant distances himself even further from the Mallarmean project: "We should be careful here to avoid nominalism. That is, we must not believe that revelation lies in the words or in the letter of the text or speech. I believe that what is in the letter of the text or speech is the possibility for the imaginary to form or to reform itself. That is what is in the text. But it is not reality, as was believed in the West" (EBR 101). The text is therefore not the revealed transparency of the Whole. From this anti-textualism it follows that the Book cannot be the Whole. The Whole-World brings all the books into relation with something that is not in the Library, the reality of the world: "Such a structure addresses readers who will no longer believe that they can verify merely a principle of reality in it, but who will think by this detour that they can really imagine a principle of relation. It is not the same thing. A literature of meaning is not always a literature of the real, and Relation is indifferent to the finality of a meaning; it is up to us to place it there" (EBR 103). Thus, literary realism is left behind: all subjective knowledge (and not "objective knowledge") that focuses on its object at the expense of its poetic forms is reductive; this is true of folklorism or exoticism: "What I call an exotic or folkloric literature is a literature which, in writing, concerns only its object, the object of the work" (EBR 63). This rush toward theme or content is also the hasty procedure of realism, here associated with Caribbean art:

In the exercise of prose, as far as our literatures are concerned, writers are too inclined to believe that the description of the real accounts for the real. It's a bit like artists who create depictions of customs and manners or genre paintings: a tropical market or Caribbean fishermen. They believe that they are accounting for reality. This is not true at all. They absolutely do not reflect reality; the reality is something other than this appearance. (IL 29)

Finally, the Whole-Book, dreamed of by Mallarmé and realized by Proust, is fundamentally conceived as a task that a singular subject imposes on himself, the ultimate expression of the "Western" individual who exhausts all possibilities of representation and, with the fixity of the masterpiece, brings to a close a very long process that he synthesizes. On the contrary, Édouard Glissant's total book is or will be the expression of a common will and desire; it is not limited to a single work, or to a single community, and does not aim at a goal that would fix its representation for all times; the focus is on a dynamic process:

Let us see that the *total* book [. . .] is at once *shared* (with a people: knitting this people together in their first unanimity). After that, the weakness of the *deliberate* "shared" work (as compared to that which was a synthesis) could, in the current times of split consciousness, become a force and an advantage. Finally, this advantage would have to extend from the work to the literature which it inaugurates, and which nevertheless brings it into being. (IP 37)

"A circle whose center is everywhere and circumference nowhere"

For Heraclitus, the end of the path of thought coincides with its dawn, and vice versa: "For the beginning and the end coincide in the circumference of the circle" (Fragment D 103). This Pre-Socratic figure of circularity inspired Hegel: as absolute knowledge unveils itself, it must then be applied, retrospectively, to what preceded it. The last moment of Being rejoins the origin, that primordial poem where, starting to speak, man composes a hymn, a poem to some god: "The true is the becoming of itself, the circle which presupposes and has in the beginning its own end as its goal, and which is actually real only by means of its developed actualization and by means of its end," writes Hegel.[27] Thus the circle is the fundamental figure of totality: "Philosophy, being a totality has, as such, its beginning everywhere. But essentially, this beginning is everywhere a result. Philosophy must be conceived of as a circle turning back on itself."[28] This circularity, on which Kojève placed great emphasis, is what guarantees the coherence of the totalizing operation that Hegel carries out on the history of Being in the West: it is therefore not solipsism or tautology, a passive repetition of the Origin: "science must be circular, and it is only circular Science that is completed or resolved Science."[29] In the *Science of Logic*, Hegel asserts that the circle is "enwrapped in itself, in the beginning of which the simple foundation [objective knowledge] of mediation enwraps in turn the end."[30] The Hegelian circle, in a surprising premonition, is a Moebius strip (the German mathematician Moebius created this topological figure in 1858).

Glissant, too, inscribes thought into a circle, which puts its seal on the totality: "A time of human memories and a time of cosmic look-outs. For the one who rises today, from wherever in the world it may be and for whatever reason he says it. *Every horizon is original*, opening another region in a new totality" (PhR 32, my emphasis.) This time it is not self-consciousness and absolute knowledge that are the point of departure and culmination—the circle is not closed but opens onto other past and future circles where the poetic as thought takes charge of meaning, in a Moebius strip as in Hegel, but without any finalizing linearity.

The circle is the very material form of Glissant's writing:

> Édouard often said that he wrote the first and the last word of his books together. His archives have demonstrated this to me. Some manuscript notebooks are annotated on their last page with the same ink and writing as on the first page. He himself explained that all the work of writing consisted in getting to the last word, which was actually also the first one, that is to say that all the labor of writing was an attempt to recover the original intention, or at least to get closer to it.[31]

The circle whose end and beginning overlap is perhaps a tautology; but Hegel remarks that tautology is dynamic, that repetition can produce, not the identical, but the unheard-of: "What is present [in tautology] is not just naked unity, so with no difference being posited; but what is posited is rather the movement by which a difference is certainly instituted, but by which also this difference, by not being one, is again suppressed."[32] In this sense, tautology is always a false tautology: repetition and mulling over produce the new in the same. Tautology displaces, as movement, differentiation, and becoming: the wandering philosophy of Relation is this very movement, "whose poles and points of exchange move incessantly" (PhR 62). The point here, following Montaigne, is not to paint a static and closed Being, but the unlimited passage and dynamic movement of beings—and not only to "paint" them, but to think them (philosophically), and construct them (poetically). Tautologies are part of the circle from poetry to poetry, where an immense expanse of time and space constantly produces a redefinition, a difference. The poetry of the origin is identical with, but at the same time differs from, the poetry of the end. In Hegel, art progresses in stages from the initial revelation to the philosophical end. In Glissant, this idea of progress in art is absurd; the poem is heard regardless of the time and place in which it originated—it returns to speak in our present: it is forever and simultaneously our past, our present and our future.

In Hegel's *Aesthetics*, as in his *Phenomenology*, poetry is originary: "The poet is then the first who, so to speak, makes his people open their mouths, who establishes the link between representation and language."[33] This poetry is also a relation that fuses generality and particularity: "As an art, poetry is older than prose. It expresses the spontaneous representation of the truth, a knowledge which does not as yet separate generality from its living particular manifestations, the law from its applications, the aim from the means, *but it conceives each of these terms only in and through the other*."[34] Compare the Hegelian imaginary of genesis with the opening of the *Philosophie de la Relation*; the similarity is manifest: "To write a poem, or to sing it, or to dream it, was to consent to this unverifiable truth, that the poem in itself is contemporary with the first blazes of the earth" (PhR 11).

The fundamental difference between the Hegelian and Glissantian imaginaries is that the first posits an evolution that leads to a philosophical fulfillment: once absolute knowledge is reached, the philosopher has nothing more to think about—he can become absorbed in a serene meditation. On the other hand, for Glissant, the origin, the primordial poem, is also the term; and it is an endless finality, one that remains open to the unpredictable surprise of becoming: "Thus we travel along the open circle of our relayed aesthetics, our tireless politics" (PR 220). As a result, the ecstasies of meditation can no longer exist: becoming demands the constant flow of the poetic act in harmony with eternal change.

It would be to force our interpretation of Hegel to assume that absolute knowledge is necessarily an insurmountable closure, which in its completion petrifies all the parts of the system. The circle can be dynamic, since one can go backward by creating a refiguring (*Umgestaltung*) of the past and conceiving the Other of the present and the future. "Refiguring" is exactly the term Hegel uses at the start of his *Phenomenology*: "The spirit has broken with the world of its being-there and the representation that has lasted until now; it is about to bury this world in the past, and it is involved in the process of refiguring it."[35]

This refiguration will then also be a prefiguration. To all such ideas Glissant would subscribe without reservation: his circularity is open to the future and rewrites the past as a Moebius strip. But Glissant's thought, which like Hegel's originates in the poem, does not have philosophy as its final goal, but the poetic, and it remains open to multiple and various poetics still to come, whereas in Hegel philosophy finds its closure in absolute knowledge. The work of Glissant, made up of circles that are ceaselessly becoming ex-centric, is a dynamic where shapes are untiringly made and unmade.

In the twelfth century, Alain de Lille and, after him, three centuries later, Nicolas of Cusa, gave a paradoxical definition of the circle, applying it to God, "a circle whose center is everywhere and circumference nowhere": an impossible circle as far as geometric knowledge is concerned, but one whose open character is a good definition of the poetics of Édouard Glissant, who writes: "Then you will reach this, which is a very powerful subjective knowledge: *the place grows from its irreducible center, as much as from its incalculable borders*" (TTM 60). Each particular place is a center (the place is also, here, the common place of poetics, which thus occupies the centrality that theologians conferred on God): there is thus no longer a single Center, but a multiplicity of different mid-points, spreading out everywhere, in what Glissant has called "archipelagic thought." Circumference is no longer limited—it becomes incommensurable, open to an infinity that belies the closed circularity peculiar to the Hegelian system; it is the place one cannot get round, since one cannot draw its outline: "[subjective] knowledge is wandering much more than it is universal, as it proceeds literally from place to place [. . .] subjective knowledge is reinforced and released (intensively diversified) by this path" (PhR 62).

As soon as the circle seems to close into a circumference, becoming organized into a geometric, general system of ideas, Glissant breaks it open by means of the singularity that has escaped it and the unpredictable flow that gives it life:

> The circle opens again, at the same time as it takes the shape of a volume. Thus, relation is at each moment completed, but also destroyed in its generality, by the very thing that we bring into action at a particular place and time. At every moment and in every circumstance, this Relation is destroyed by this particularity which signifies our opacities, by this singularity, and again becomes a lived relation. Its death in general is what makes its life a shared one. (PR 219)

The circle, then, is not a line that returns to its starting point by curving itself into a two-dimensional linear space: "When we say that this poetics of Relation is now being woven, that it is no longer project but part of a circularity, we are not referring to a circuit, to a line of energy curved back on itself [author's note: in the guise of the Heraclitean or Hegelian circularity]. In truth, the trajectory, even when inflected, has lost its value" (PR 45). Glissant's circle is four-dimensional; in volume and temporality (through becoming): "We can thus imagine, in a circular volume, an aesthetics arising from Chaos, one which is not reducible to any simplicity of norm and whose every detail is just as complex as the whole" (PR 45).

Chapter 6

"Universality has no language"

From Heraclitus onward, the question of the Whole has been inseparable from that of the one and the universal; like the Greek philosopher, Glissant never ceased to associate the thought of the Whole-World with his reflection on universality, but also with his consideration of multiplicity, diversity, and particularity. However, this reflection must be carried out not in an abstract and conceptual language but on the basis of the existing multiplicity of the world's languages:

> If we consider that there is mainly Being, language is what gives structure, and this is obvious when we examine what happened over the histories of Western cultures. But if we consider that Being is not, as Being, and that what is constitutive (to put is simply) is not Being, but Relation, then language will no longer be constitutive in itself. [. . .] Thus language is no longer constitutive apart from in its relation to other languages. (EBR 93–94)

We will not need to consider universality in itself, within the context of a single language, or even abstractly, as if the universal word had a stable value, everywhere and always in all the languages of the world, as if it could be infinitely translatable without its meaning and value being affected. We will need to bring universality into the dialogue of languages. This is what the aphorism of the *Entretiens* insists on: "The universal has no language" (EBR 17); it is precisely by following a "creole" path, with several languages being brought together, that this proposition can be rigorously verified. The corollary of Édouard Glissant's proposition is that every language thinks, and thinks universality, but in diverse ways: universality must be translated from one language to another. To address this problem, we must undertake an etymological and linguistic investigation: we must, as Glissant likes to do, sail up the river of time and names, considering the multiplicity and totality of languages: "What every translation now suggests in its principle, by the very passage it enacts from one language to another, is the sovereignty of all the languages of the world. And translation for this same reason is the obvious sign that we have to conceive in our imaginary this totality of languages"[1] (IPD 45). There is a vast research program there, which I leave to others more competent than myself: how are the universal and the Whole, particularity and diversity, expressed in Urdu, in Bambara, in Persian, in Hindi, in Inuit?

In philosophy, it is obviously among the Greeks and in the Greek language that we must seek the European origin of the universal. Greek gives the universal a particular semantic field: it is expressed as *katholou*, which must be broken down into *kata*, "from the point of view of," and *holon*, "the Whole." Universality is posited as a point of view that founds it—if the subject, in its singularity, plays no part in it, yet the Whole is stated in the singular, as one category, or a category that depends on the One. As for multiplicity and diversity, their grasp occurs *after* this founding moment. The word *katholou* (the Whole) has its reverse, the not-Whole, but it is not linguistically correlated with *katholou*; the opposite in Greek is either *to hen*, "the one," "the individual"—that which cannot be divided into smaller elements—or *idios*, the singular, that which cannot be assimilated to any general category. This non-correlation reveals, in Greek, singularity and particularity as not belonging to the notional sphere of the universal: there is no possible dialectic between singularity and universality.

In Aristotelian philosophy, the universal appears in the form of a syllogism *in the singular*—which founds formal logic (Aristotle, *First Analytics*); the translation as a plural form of "all men" is erroneous:

> Every man is mortal;
> Socrates is a man;
> Therefore Socrates is mortal.

Commenting on Claudel, Glissant notes that this, in his view, obeys neither the scientific definition nor the philosophical logic based on the Aristotelian syllogism: "Such a logic displaces the 'old' version, based on the syllogism, and its organ is metaphor. [. . .] Thus poetry, the domain of metaphor, will be installed at the heart of subjective knowledge. The logic of what is born is ultimately an Art of Poetry" (IP 106). Aristotelian logic is replaced by a poetic logic of the living, which will be found at the end of Glissant's journey. It is not a question of suppressing reason, but of submitting it to a thought (de)centered by metaphor, and thus passing from objective knowledge [*savoir*] to subjective knowledge [*connaissance*]. This return to a form of philosophy practiced before Socrates invented maieutics and Aristotle invented logic and the syllogism reflects many of the characteristics of Glissant's style and thought: he dispenses with philosophical and academic forms, which are replaced by abrupt statements, and goes directly to the conclusion, without indexing the intermediate stages of reasoning. It is for the attentive reader to restore what Glissant has intentionally omitted. Here Heraclitus and Parmenides inspire him: poetry makes thought manifest, and works in place of any logical demonstration. I remember a remark that Édouard made on the style of *Fiction et Incarnation*: "But delete such words as 'thus,' 'though,' 'accordingly,' and leave the reader to do the work!" In fact, he was simply describing his own language.

For the Greeks, the presence of universality is not limited to philosophy: it also appears in the *Poetics* of Aristotle (9, 3), which contrasts the chronicle, a field that considers historical facts from the point of view of particularity (*kath'ekaston*), with poetry which, by creating the type (*paradigma*), takes things from the point of view of generality (*katholou*). Thus, unlike Plato and his ban on poets in *The Republic*, poetry can attain a more philosophical dignity than a historical chronicle.[2] It is not certain that Glissant was inspired by Aristotle to restore to the poetic domain the badge of nobility that Plato had stripped from it, but the convergence of Glissant's point of view with the Aristotle of the *Poetics* is obvious. If "philosophy is an art" (NRM 128), then as a corollary art and poetry are places of thought: they are philosophical. In this respect, Glissant separates himself from Hegel, for whom art and philosophy are radically distinct domains. In Glissant, this segregation of the fields of objective knowledge is reduced to a chiasm: poetry is philosophy and the latter is an art.

Latin culture does not use the Greek *katholou* to express universality. This category is expressed quite differently, as *universalis*, and appears late, in Quintilian, in the first century AD, which is the first century of the Empire—and this is no coincidence. A seemingly identical concept, by moving from one language to another, thus takes on a very different accent. There is something universal, but it is translated from one language to another, from one community to another, and thus begins to differ from oneself: to be creolized. Remember, "the West is contradictory to itself" (PR 205), subject to one or more digeneses.

In Latin, if we analyze *universum* and *universitas*, we see two elements appearing: *unus* ("one") and *versus* ("in the direction of," "toward"). Unlike in Greek, in Latin it is the singularity, not the totality (*to holon*) that is posited first, and moves dynamically toward a totality not included in the term that designates it. Everything happens as if the universal had to be considered from the point of view of the singular, and as if what effected the sum of singularities was outside of words, outside of language, unspeakable. The antonym of the *universum* is the *diversum*, the *diversitas*: *di-* (the "division," the "separation," the "distinction," the "negation," and, by reversal, the fulfillment, as in *di-lucidere*, "to shed light"), and *versus*, yet again; diversity is "what goes toward scattering." From Greek to Latin, the way universality is thought of is radically reversed. One might argue that the notion of universal in Latin is perfectly suited, by its openness, to Glissant's project, but that would be at the very least premature and perhaps even wrong. As we have just seen, the Roman universal, entirely subject to the Empire (and the mastery of a single language), is not inclusive. Against the contamination of the Barbarians, this universal builds immense ramparts running from one end of Europe to the other (Hadrian's wall in Great Britain, the *limes*—the limits and borders—of Germania, Dacia, Moesia, Cappadocia, Armenia, Mesopotamia, Arabia: the Romans were obsessed by Latin purity).

Édouard Glissant writes "in the presence of all the languages of the world" (IPD 39), without privileging any of them, including his own: the cultural fusion he proposes is not organized by the structuring principle of a single language—all are invited to participate. The concrete presence of "all the languages of the world" or of the Whole-World of Languages, in Relation and in extent, is contrasted with the abstract universal of *the* language (structure or nation) and the notional absence imposed, in depth and verticality, by any one language: here, for example, the conceptuality and uniqueness of Greek. From then on, the curse of the Tower of Babel, far from being the catastrophe that destroyed the closed and ideal uniqueness of humanity, becomes an opportunity to be grasped: "Beyond the acute struggles against different forms of domination and for the liberation of the imaginary, there opens up a multiplied field where we are overcome by giddiness. But it is not the giddiness that precedes the apocalypse and the fall of Babel. It is the initiating tremor in the face of this possibility. In all languages, the possibility of building the Tower is granted" (PR 123).

Glissant thought the limit and the border in such a way as to make them the exact reverse of the Roman *limes* and, beyond that, the lines of demarcation of our present: "The temptation of the wall is not new. Whenever a culture or a civilization has failed to think the other, to think itself with the other, to think the other in itself, those looming reservations made of stones, iron, barbed wire, electrified fences or closed ideologies have risen up, collapsed, and are returning to us with a new stridency" (QLMT 6).

The border belies the claim to universality; it must therefore be reevaluated by "the new thinking of borders," a place of passage, exchange and Relation, as well as the naming of inextricable places, irreducible in their singularity. This new *limes* appears in *Une nouvelle région du monde*; the wall gives way to the exchange of time and geography, "a new region which is an era, mixing all times and all periods, an era which is also an inexhaustible country, accumulating expanses which seek out other limits, incalculable but always finite in number, as has been said of atoms. [. . .] The humanities do not fully measure these geographies of today and we are more prepared to be limited by borders which stretch into the immeasurable" (NRM 23–25). The border is no longer the separation and measure of a territory, it is an infinite and universal opening to all other regions, regions that are innumerable, in excess of all territorial measure: "The idea of the border now helps us to support and appreciate the flavor of different things when they are appended to each other. To cross the border would be to freely connect one vivacity of the real to another" (PhR 57). Thus the wall is scorned, as there is no longer any need for it: to reach the universal, we must move from one "new region of the world" to another, and these regions are delimited only by the inextricable nature of a place; for the rest, they can participate in the universality of Relation and the Whole-World.

Roman universality changes once again when it merges with the universality of the Church. In what is hailed by those obsessed with homogeneity, but is a catastrophe for the lovers of diversity, the new union of Church and State forges an indissoluble link between the political realm and the spiritual. Note that this is only a renewal of the pact that bound the Empire to Roman religious rites: Julius Caesar and Augustus claimed a divine ancestry; the dead emperor was deified and had to be worshiped as the guarantor of the unity of the citizens. The Catholic universal replaced devotions to the emperor and the state religion in 380 (the Edict of Theodosius in Thessalonica). The situation was reversed: the former persecuted became the new persecutors, and paganism was driven out across the Empire. At the same time, in 381, the Nicene dogma (325) was reaffirmed by the Council of Constantinople (381), which excluded those who challenged the Nicene Creed and labeled them as heretics. The Catholic universal was now a unity; but this came at the price of a series of exclusions.

When Édouard Glissant re-reads this history, and all other histories, it is not to deduce from the fait accompli some absolute and unchangeable determinism, but to dream of the possibilities on which the universal of exclusion has slammed the door shut: "But what if it had been the thought of Ramon Llull who had led or directed the history of the West, and not the thought of Saint Thomas? What would have happened?" (EBR 25) Glissant knows that these questions are idle from the point of view of historical knowledge. But they have all their relevance for the possibilities latent in our contemporary situation. Again and again, in prophesying the past, it is a question of preserving in our present the possibilities of a becoming that never accepts the determination fixed by the status quo: "Is the thought of the universal, which is so magnificently and sumptuously realized in the history of the West—is that thought still capable, in itself, and in its system, of opening up new horizons for us, for the world we live in now?" (EBR 25).

"Catholic" is a direct calque on the Greek *katholou*. The word does not appear in the New Testament, but, for the first time, in the letters of Ignatius of Antioch written in Greek (d. 107). Toward the end of the second century, when the notion of the universal appears in the Latin of the Church, it is not expressed in terms of the Latin *universalitas*, but with a neologism imported directly from the Greek, *catholicus*, used to designate to the set of local churches, and also to theologically define those who are not part of them, namely the heretics.[3] In short, catholicity eliminates the tension of a universality open to the possibilities it leaves unnamed, closing the door on this uncertainty and constituting the monolithic homogeneity of the community of believers. The universal of the Church becomes political, an aggregation of everything and everyone. In the Roman Empire, the aggregation of the religious sphere with the domain of the polis later produces, in the fifth century, the notion of *catholicitas* (in Boethius's work *In topica Ciceronis commentaria*).

Glissant emphasizes that, little by little, Latin, after the dissolution of the Roman Empire, loses its universal privilege in favor of the vernacular languages: "Oho! The universal which triumphs as a system is not able to preserve Latin as one of the languages of the universal: it is obliged to compose (and compromise with) regional languages. Universality composes diversity! The universal, we need to be clear, has no language" (EBR 26). The universal thus differs in each language taken one by one. The linguistic and anthropological history of universality does not make it possible to affirm that it is One. On the contrary, the Whole-World and the Relation will be universals only if they reserve a place not only for languages but also for the multiplied languages of poets, all differing in their opacity.

Recognizing the origin of individuation in the figure of Christ, Édouard Glissant, far from seeing in this point of origin the antinomian pole of universality, sees it as its very source: "If the whole man, at once flesh, soul and spirit, is in Christ, then the universal can take wing" (TTM 97).

When he comments on Paul Claudel, Glissant emphasizes the contradictory relativity of the "catholic" universal and, in *L'Intention poétique*, brings it into diversity and relation: "If we now assume that there is diversity in the nature of man, we will need to accept it in the relation with God. [. . .] The created world includes the different, but as a variety of its total, not as a modality of Being which opposes and proposes itself to its difference" (IP 114).

Christianity can impose a totalization only by going against its own structure of knowledge, a "schizophrenic" structure or, at the very least, a structure divided by a radical antinomy between the universal and the catholic. The origin of the West is therefore impure, because it is essentially hybrid, torn apart by an antinomy between Greco-Roman thought and Judeo-Christianity: to declare that the West is homogeneous, and has issued from a single stock, is to force things into a conceptual pattern that does not correspond to historical facts. It should be noted that the first people to fabricate this uniqueness were certain "Westerners" themselves—and indeed this label ought always to be put in quotation marks, as a precautionary measure; the monolith is still just as imaginary (which does not mean ineffectual). There is thus an unstoppable logic to Glissant's call for an "other" imaginary (one that is relational, open, diverse, and poetic) to counter the often harmful effects of the universal imaginary. Glissant's interpretation chooses the right ground: it corrects the imaginary of the monolith by the imaginary as well as by the reality of the multiplicity of diversity and digenesis.

By rereading history in line with Glissant's vision, the universal as captured in languages appears in a multiplicity that is its own contradiction. There is no monolithic, universal, fixed, or unique thought in the history of the West, but only a "claim" to universality grounded solely in the imaginary. Glissant saw this clearly, stressing, however, the need for a tête-à-tête with the West: "We must indeed dialogue with the West, which is also *in contradiction with itself* [. . .]. Consider, too, that from the West itself are derived the variables that have on each occasion contradicted its impressive itinerary. That is why it is not monolithic, and that is why it certainly must involve entanglement" (PR 205).

The notion of digenesis appears in *Faulkner, Mississippi* in 1996 as a challenge to the myths of creation: "This 'origin' of a new kind is what I call a digenesis" (FM 267). It is repeated in 1997, in the *Traité du Tout-Monde*. At first sight, it contrasts the atavistic genesis that bases its legitimacy on a creation myth with the composite that marks the origin of colonial and slave-owning societies: "The genesis of the Creole societies of the Americas is based on another darkness, that of the belly of the slave ship. That is what I call a digenesis. Adapt the idea of digenesis, become accustomed to its example, and you will leave the impenetrable demand of an exclusive uniqueness" (TTM 36).

Digenesis is opposed to myths of origin insofar as it is historical. Thus, the African displaced by slavery no longer has the original stories circulating in his community at his disposal: he is forced to invent an origin with a double face, a crossbreed of historical condition and lost genesis. Digenesis therefore applies to Glissant himself, an Antillean-French cultural composite.

We can also extend digenesis radically to all cultures, because none of them has a single root, that root that epics (*The Iliad, The Aeneid, The Song of Roland*) seek to found in order to ward off the composite.

Édouard Glissant thus defines a program of research into the history of cultures and ideas that is completely original, fitting both the Whole-World and Relation: nothing is excluded, especially not the West; it is a question of discovering in it the traces of "variables" rich in potentialities, not the absolute fixity of that which has been and has vanquished the heretical and ex-centricity. For example, the Middle Ages, in this new story, appear as fundamentally divided: "Two ways of proceeding, two opposite givens, two extremes in the search for subjective knowledge: the Middle Ages will be the scene of their opposition and, when systematic thought has vanquished, the universal, at first Christian and then rationalistic, will be spread as the specific work of the West, even after the latter has prepared what Nietzsche called the death of God" (TTM 96).

To grasp the West as a monolith, and then by reaction against it to hunker down in the soil, the local, the identitarian, is radically to block Relation. On the contrary, it is a question of identifying, in the West itself, what allows us to criticize it—the tremors of wandering, digenesis, and creolization that it has known. Relation is a vast enterprise of reconciliation of opposites, including those that divide a civilization against itself. In other words, in spite of Glissant's denunciation of unity, of the one, his thought prepares the advent of a unity that would no longer be, this time, exclusive.

Nevertheless, Glissant quite knowingly adopts the position of the heretic, for two reasons: by re-reading the West in line with its lost possibilities, and by rejecting in advance any approach that would close down access to "Western" thought in its totality. Among the Greeks, he prefers the Pre-Socratics and the Sophists to Socrates, Plato, and Aristotle, who draw inspiration from the former while rejecting them. In the Middle Ages and the Renaissance, it is Giordano Bruno and Ramon Llull rather than Saint Augustine, Saint Anselm, or Saint Thomas that Glissant prefers. This choice of ex-centricity extends even to the time of colonization, first as the forced imposition of a European and Western universal, but also as the possibility of positively questioning this universal from within; the reinterpreted past then becomes a vast reservoir of possibilities: "And it is then that the differences intervene: the immediate ex-centered thought, at this moment of colonization, is the thought marginalized in the very interior of the absolute center, the heir to the doomed thoughts of the Middle Ages" (EBR 53). In another area, modern poetry, Glissant's taste encompasses both canonical authors and marginal creators: "Maurice Roche, Henri Pichette and Roger Giroux are all marginal. Not in the antisocial or hippie sense, not at all: they are marginal in the sense that, being very diverse poets and writers, they can all conceive of poetry founding its own dimension and its own research, its demand, yes an absolute 'poemic' demand" (EBR 53). "In philosophy and literature, let us add, to the long line of heretics that began with the Pre-Socratics and Sophists, the names of Rimbaud, Nietzsche and Artaud" (EBR 147).

This overt favoring of heresy is not reactive: it does not simply fly in the face of the conventional, thus trapping itself in a subversion that would be the reiteration of norms and conventions. The rejection of the catholic as the universal does not result in the death of God, but in the birth of ex-centered thoughts: "There are no atheists, there are heretics" (TTM 96). The doctrinal model (or the universal), from which the heretic derives, is defined in the *Traité du Tout-Monde* by Saint Anselm, seeking to reconcile religious faith and philosophical reason, and by the summae of Saint Albert the Great and Saint Thomas Aquinas. Glissant interprets them as paths to knowledge (*connaissance*), whether of God or the world. But these paths are not unique: "If unbelievers are rare, the mode of accession by faith remains posited. To the luminous mysteries of the intelligible, the ineffable experience of mystical intuition may be preferred, for example. Or the rough-hewn thinking that refuses to 'understand' the unknowable in a system of transparencies, and prefers to confront the impossible" (TTM 95)

The meditation on the medieval history of thought describes the internal division of this civilization, but also Glissant's approach to knowledge [*connaissance*] itself, always caught in the digenetic separation of the system and ex-centricity, without this undermining his faith in his own thought. Anyone who has heard him speak knows what I mean: the quiet certainty that he showed in the development of his ideas, the charism that carried his listeners along and won their support, all came from an unshakable faith in the validity of his propositions. His only uncertainty focused on the real understanding of his audience. There is no doubt that he was particularly fond of mystics, saints, and heretics, who roamed along a path of subjective knowledge [*connaissance*] free of doctrinal constrictions. Heresy is close to Glissant's heart; he identifies with it not as an individual (which would have been an absurd pretense for him) but through means of a knowledge [*connaissance*] that goes beyond the "catholic"[4] and systematic universals:

> The cultures of rationalization have not exported to the world
> the thought of heresy. That's the main question: if you want
> to try to penetrate this thought of the apart, this thought of
> the margin, this thought of the otherwise, thoughts to which

these [Western] cultures have themselves given birth, but in reaction to their own universalizing vocation, and thoughts which other cultures have perhaps generated quite naturally, you just have to delve for these thoughts yourselves in the very margins, or in heresy; and you will first find these latter, if they exist, in many of those decentered cultures that were colonized. (EBR 29)

The Relation to come presupposes more than a will, more than a belief in its advent: it requires a true faith, one that runs across the whole of Glissant's thought. A path to subjective knowledge [*connaissance*] that passes through faith immediately raises the question of the sacred.[5] The sacred is at first separation: in Latin, *sacer* means, on the one hand, the separate space dedicated to the divinity and, on the other hand, the propitiatory victim who is destined for it. Thus, *sacer* also refers to the abject person, the one cast out of the community to be offered as a sacrifice. René Girard has repeatedly alerted us, throughout his work, to the violence that is the backbone of the scapegoating process, a resolution that connects individuals succumbing to the process of atomization so as to bind them together in community. Glissant takes care to demarcate his notion of the sacred from the bloody, immemorial heritage still alive in the contemporary world: "In such a mesh, the ancient sacred force of filiation would no longer play its game of exclusion, the resolution of the dissolute would be relayed by the aggregation of those who have been scattered. [. . .] There would be no more need for the sacrifice of a propitiatory or victimized hero: for we can unravel this plot, meditate on it together, recognize ourselves in it at each other's side" (PR 68). Glissant's sacred is entirely purified of all transcendence, anthropomorphized through and through; it unfolds in this world, also distinguished from the chorus of Greek tragedy, which was the voice of the gods themselves—it is the very order of Chaos, fixing the nodal points of Relation without, however, determining its future: "We will fix the sacred, the order pre-supposed in the disorder of Relation, without being stupefied. We will discuss it without being imbued by the solemn melopoeia of the Greek chorus alone. We will imagine it without perforce becoming the hand of a god. To imagine the transparency of Relation is also to found the opacity of what animates it. The sacred comes from us, from this plot, from our wandering" (PR 68). The sacred comes not only from the past, but from the future, as an "unsuspected appetite for the unforeseeable"

(TM 510). The writer (the unspeaker [*déparleur*]), is the one with the task of identifying those points where disorder hangs suspended, without any tremolos drenched in religiosity: "Any unspeaker [*déparleur*] is more gifted than anyone else for the search of the Sacred precisely because he unspeaks—in other words he is kidding, he is transported into exaggerations. Miseries confide in him without his seeing this as a priesthood. The unspeaker is the layman of the sacred" (TM 345).[6] Therefore, the sacred is not a cause, but a consequence of Relation: "The sacred proceeds perhaps, for us, from this Relation, and no longer from a Revelation or a Law" (TTM 113). Relation puts Re(ve)lation in brackets. But it is mainly the opening of the *Philosophie de la Relation* that has attracted the attention of commentators[7] to this "secular sacred" (still an oxymoron and indeed a joke) that Glissant proposes: "There was that which arose, a sacred word. And the poem, then the poem, of itself begotten, started to be recognized" (PhR 11). Let us emphasize that this genesis is indeed a hypothesis, "this myth, or this legend or this dream" (PhR 12). "Thus should have been pronounced, in the prehistories of all the literatures of the world, this same beginning" (PhR 11), an original integration, *one* genesis that opposes and is appended to any digenesis, "the very sign of the fusion of the whole with the whole" (PhR 12). The primordial poem has no speaker—it arises from itself, it holds no commerce with anything else (sex, God the Creator): "It was before all else humanity" (PhR 11), a "sacred word, born already from all things in the world" (PhR 12): before the *Enumah Elish*, before *Gilgamesh*, before *The Odyssey* and Heraclitus. The poem is therefore without words, inarticulate, and inarticulable, a "song of the world" (as Bernadette Cailler puts it) that precedes the divisions and distinctions necessarily implied in any act of speaking, right from the very earliest times:

> What did this word of the sacred seek (it is the entirety of the world I am talking about), if not to confirm so many unavoidable obscurities? It had supposed, first and foremost, that it could forestall (or struggle against) the partitioning of differences, a partitioning which seemed inevitable, and then, when the paths and inspirations of the world were indeed divided, this word took care to gather these differences together again, panting in the same, ever-same way, so that the divergent sound emerging from it and echoing to the horizons would appear calm and reassuring. (PhR 14)

The sacred word is therefore an oxymoron, since it is outside of language: in this sense it is literally inconceivable, inextricable, unavoidable. Believing in its existence is a matter of faith: the primordial poem is the "*credo quia absurdum*" that Glissant takes from Tertullian,[8] applied to a completely different object than the glorious Body, albeit with some striking analogies. The sacred word has been buried, lost, repressed, like Christ: "Let us remember well: the poem was buried in a collapse of the earth" (PhR 15). The primordial poem is the obscure object that poets seek, their original horizon: "and this poem comes back each time to what was an episode or a need of the prescience of the humanities, and it renews, with the most unexpected poets, in their need for speech, this journey that led from the original obscurity of the song to its trembling appearance" (PhR 12–13). The sacred word (of which Lascaux provides the buried image; PhR 12) is the horizon of all literature: "I think that in the history of all arts and all cultures there is a nostalgia for that primordial—and not primitive—moment when the same was related to the other. The same who was the cave dweller had, as his other, not another person; his other was the animal and his surroundings [. . .]. And I think that we have tried by dint of regulating the beautiful to forget this moment" (IL 93–94).

But the analogy with Christ does not stop there: the sacred word says that we must also resurrect, to build the future: "We can then understand that what distracts us from the 'essence' of a sacred, from the reading of the primordial poem, is not the banalization or the unstoppable technicization or the legislated secularism of our forms of objective knowledge [*savoirs*] and our current mode of life, but this fact: the poetics of Relation has projected before us this poem in extent that we deem to have been born from primordial lavas" (PhR 148). The sacred word is origin and goal; a circular fusion of everything, it is the One, even though Glissant rejects elsewhere the philosophers' obsession with it. For two reasons, the sacred word is Faith, past and future, a dual "*credo quia absurdum*" clearly opposed to the rationalization of the "*credo ut intelligam*" ("I believe in order to understand") of Saint Anselm, which is completed by Saint Albert the Great and Saint Thomas Aquinas in the systematization of the *Summae*. This "believe in order to understand" aims to block the "temptations of the thought of the Infinite and the Cosmos, a thought which will at the same time follow more obscure paths, byways that are usually prohibited" (TTM 95).

The new gods, recomposed from the old, are therefore secular, and the sacred word is a path to subjective knowledge (*connaissance*) that goes beyond the paths of rationality. Art is not reduced to the mere accumulation of the facts of its history and its achievements, true (subjective) knowledge (*connaissance*) is reducible neither to the aggregate of forms of (objective) knowledge (*saviors*) or to subjective and impressionistic evaluation.

The language we speak has always been used to anchor identity and connection to a community (tribe, ethnic group, nation, empire); for the Hellenes, the one who speaks Greek badly is a *barbaros*, an allogeneic element that cannot be assimilated to the city. For the Romans, *latinitas* is what defines being part of the Republic, then the Empire. Among the Jews at the time of Jesus Christ, Biblical Hebrew, the sacred language entrusted to the custody of the Levites and the Kohanim, defines the very purity of belonging to the nation.

But here again, there is digenesis or multigenesis. Indeed, the Hebrew of the Torah is doubled by a vehicular Hebrew called Mishnaic (from the *Mishna*, "repetition," a compilation of rabbinical laws),[9] and Ancient Palestine used another lingua franca, Aramaic, the language in which Jesus preached. Jesus himself was certainly bilingual, probably multilingual: he spoke Aramaic, knew the sacred Hebrew of the Torah (evidenced by his frequent quotations from the Old Testament in the Gospels and his polemics with rabbinical doctors), probably understood and could speak Mishnaic Hebrew, and may have conversed in Greek with Pontius Pilate. What a scumble of languages at the origins of Christianity! And this cultural exchange will become the rule with the second book of the Acts of the Apostles and Pentecost. If any speaker can understand preaching in any language, then there is no sacred language.[10] The glossolalia of the book of Acts is "the sign that every tongue [or language, *langue*] will confess" (Rupert de Deutz, *Les Œuvres du Saint-Esprit*). At the same time, what a hubbub in the development of the New Testament! In the second century, Greek-speaking Jews living in the diaspora, in Alexandria, translated Aramaic and Hebrew and produced the first version of the New Testament together with the Old Testament, translated into Greek from Biblical Hebrew. This was the Septuagint: it was then translated into Latin by Saint Jerome, and triggered a boundless dynamic process: Testaments exist today in three hundred languages; one thousand eight hundred and forty-eight languages include the translation of at least one book of the Bible.[11] This spirit of Pentecost is summed up by Saint Augustine in a pithy phrase: "The truth is neither Hebrew, nor Greek, nor Latin, nor barbaric" (*Confessions* XI, III, 5). It does not need to be articulated in a specific language: all the idioms of the world revolve around a truth without language: "[The truth] would say to me, without needing a mouth or a language, without making any syllables sound out: 'Moses speaks the truth!'" (Ibid.).[12]

The spirit of Pentecost reigns throughout the work of Édouard Glissant: in particular, the concept of Whole-World requires that we take into consideration all the languages in the world, without exception. Remember: "I write in the presence of all the languages of the world" (TTM 26).[13] The meaning of this proposition is developed in *L'Imaginaire des langues*:

> What I want to express when I say that we write in the presence of all the languages of the world is that there is a new condition for the existence and function of the writer: it is not only that we know all languages or a great number of languages, it is that we become aware in the totality-world that languages disappear and that with them it is a part of the imaginary of humanity which disappears. Our way of defending languages must be a multilingual way. It is in the name of multilingualism that we must defend our languages and not in the name of intolerant monolingualism. (IL 53)

Pentecost, where all languages are given the privilege of expressing a truth that is one and, in the last analysis, empty, blank (for God is ineffable), leads to what Glissant calls a "Catholic unanimism" (NRM 178) that he identifies, among others, in the work of Claudel. Pentecost is centered on God and the Holy Spirit, these empty categories that organize the movement of translation and the poetic interpenetration of languages. In contrast, Glissant proposes a new ex-centered Pentecost, with no fixed point of reference.

Pentecost collapses all notions of sacred language, thereby legitimizing the translation of the Gospel message into all languages. This universal, however, is the privilege only of believers. Glissant's reflection on translation in the *Introduction à une poétique du divers*, on the contrary, manages without transcendence: "the translator invents a necessary language from one language to another, just as the poet invents a language in his own language. A language necessary from one language to another, a language common to both languages, but somehow unpredictable in relation to each of them individually" (IPD 45). The translation of the Bible was based on a vanishing point that remained stable in all languages. In contrast, Glissant's art of translation first opens with poetics (the *idiomatic language* of the translator). Furthermore, it is a portal of the unpredictable, without the closure of a Last Judgment, that limit of Christian Being shaped by exclusion (the exclusion of unbelievers): "Translation, an art of the fleeting touch and the indirect approach, is a practice of the trace. Against the absolute limitation of Being, the art of translation contributes to massing the expanse of all the beings and all the existing things in the world. To trace in languages is to make traces in the unpredictability of our now common condition" (IPD 39–40).

Now, translation is organically linked to the notion of universality: if a concept is universal, it *must* be translatable into any language. Witness the translations of the Bible, where any language can translate the dogma and creed set down by the Council of Nicaea in 325 AD—witness, too, scientific theories and their applications, which can be grasped by an Indian person, an American person, a French person. . . . Modern science responds in its own way to the question of universality, since any of its axioms can be translated into any language. But in so doing it leaves intact the problem of the translation of the relations between human cultures, which lie outside its scope.

In both cases, translation can exist because it conveys a stable and fixed sense. But they are false universals: not everyone is Catholic, and every scientific statement is local, subject to revision, unlike dogma. Except for the statements of modern science (when it comes to human exactitude) and the prohibition of incest (when it comes to human truth), there is no universal that transcends all languages: the universal is always composed and crossbred by the imaginary of a specific idiom. Thus Hegel's universal obeys not only the requirements of the German language but is also shaped in the singular language that he had to invent to communicate his thought. The same goes for Édouard Glissant, because he explicitly aims to construct a universal—one that, in its expression, is based on the singular vision built up by the hybrid stylistics of his work, between Creole, French, and English.[14] To transcend the closure of languages, which often makes them untranslatable from one to the other, Glissant proposes the poetic and imaginary co-presence of all the earth's idioms: "Creolization is a perpetual movement of cultural and linguistic interpenetration—one that does not lead to any definition of Being. This copresence works only to remove the fixity, and to reject the ontological definition that all language imposes on the beings speaking it: "And we have gradually become accustomed to saying that language is Being. (But in accordance with the common meaning, and not that of the Sophists' thinking)" (EBR 70). Here again, Glissant makes use of the philosophical tradition preceding Socrates to dismiss language as a way of defining Being.[15]

The transformation Glissant seeks to bring to the Christian bedrock that is one of the major genealogies of his thought lies in replacing the god who is all, and yet unknowable, with a fully human opacity and unpredictability, an anthropologized unknowable, which is named Relationship, Whole-World, diversity. This unknowable merges into an unpredictable future (which can neither be said nor written), which is not finalized by an Apocalypse or Last Judgment: "the wanderer, who is no longer the traveler or the discoverer or the conqueror, seeks to know the totality of the world and already knows that he will never accomplish this task—and here lies the imperiled beauty of the world" (PR 33). The same goes for creolization: "Creolization is crossbreeding with the added value of unpredictability." The *Summa*, totalization, synthesis, and finalism, whether Christian or philosophical, are antithetical to the unpredictable: "Creolization is the bringing together of several cultures or at least several elements of distinct cultures, in a place of the world, that results in a new datum, *totally unpredictable relative to the sum or the simple synthesis of these elements*" (TTM 37). To go beyond the singular element is to fall into the abstraction of categories, the foundations of the Aristotelian universal, and to enclose becoming in predictability. Against the universal and thus necessarily abstract synthesis, against the Aristotelian categories of Being, there stands the concrete imaginary:

> We can conceive a totality of the object of the imaginary, but we cannot conceive the pure object of the imaginary as an abstraction: we cannot conceptualize the imaginary in any way. So it is absolutely not a category. We can accept the imaginary as a totalizing dimension of the world. But we cannot accept it or consider it as a concept, precisely because the imaginary completely eludes any forecast: but one of the founding claims of the concept is that it can include all that is possible and therefore allows us to make forecasts. The true languages of intuition do not forecast anything (at all) on the basis of the All. (EBR 149)[16]

In other words, the real of the category is always still to come, unpredictably, outside of the conceptual contrast between nominalism and realism and its ability to make predictions: the realism of the real is always a future, or a future anterior, as when Glissant returns to Heraclitus and his eternal becoming of thought and the World.

Reinterpreting the medieval past, Glissant does not hesitate to see a first moment of creolization in it: "We have great pleasure in discovering, in *Les Cent Nouvelles nouvelles*, processes of forging words that are so suitable for all the creolizers of all countries" (NRM 141). In the sixteenth century, Montaigne testified to this in his baroque language, which he carefully distinguished from the French of the court as spoken in Paris, and brought him closer to the Gascon spoken "near Lahontan," that is to say, an Occitan quite distinct from the French of the sixteenth century. But this Middle Ages, or this creolistic Renaissance of the language, was to be lost, in parallel with the exclusion of that lateral thinking that produced heresies: French classicism would purge it.

In the final analysis, while some of the roots of Glissant's inspiration lie in Christianity, it is perhaps also Christianity that is Glissantian. This is not a joke: Glissant's thought does bring out the creolizing aspect of the Christian universal, as well as its limits of exclusion; this is an extension of the ideal of Pentecost beyond its ecclesial limits, and its attentive meditation gives meaning to the equality in principle of all languages outside the Christian faith and the importance of transfers from one language to another by translation as a creative and poetic act. It is the function of the great writer to show us what we are blind to.

The universals that I have briefly mentioned, stemming from various traditions, are supposed to set limits, to close down any further discussion, whether in logic, religion, or politics: the Aristotelian syllogism "Every man is mortal," for example, and "Every tongue will confess" in Acts.[17] All these universals are closed to any debate; this amounts to saying that they leave outside of their reach any future, unforeseen case, and that, in their essence, they are all based on a logic of exception and exclusion. In *Whole-World*, these universals take the form of a psalmody, a bleating, a form of stupidity propped up by a good conscience, whereas no one can give them concrete form: "Then our good conscience is total: ah, we affirm, but without embarking on any action, because we are now complete, we check in at the end of this whirlwind, we finish our wanderings, to the applause of all, in the great churn of humanism. The lukewarm comfort of renunciation" (TM 435).

There is no doubt that the Whole-World and Relation are, for Glissant, universals. But to define them as such, he invests them with philosophical precautions of a singular depth:

> Can we also assure ourselves that beings are a set of work
> clothes, perhaps even a trapping of Being, and appreciate them
> for what they are ceaselessly becoming, *the realized quantity of
> all the differences of the Whole-World, and of the world, without
> excepting a single one?* This is also the only meaning that we
> could grant to the idea of a universal. The potential quality of
> a universal would not escape this totality. (NRM 43)

By landing a blow on Heidegger (beings as a trapping of Being) and by paying tribute to Heraclitus (Being becoming beings), Being and its qualities are transformed into beings and their quantities.[18] In this way, we move from the abstract to the concrete, even to the historical concrete ("*realized* quantity"), from ontological root to ontic uprooting, from singularity to the imaginary link, from the impossibility of making a *summa* of Being (always taking flight into its depths), to the possibility of totalizing beings through Relation. Thus a universal can come into being, one that has nothing to do with the universals that philosophy, religion, and politics have proposed in the course of the history of thought. The characteristic of the latter is that they are all based on a logic of cultural, linguistic, religious, or philosophical exclusion—only the empire of Alexander the Great and his library can escape them. The Heraclitean universal (the Whole) was One, the *Logos* excluding multiplicity and diversity. The universal of Aristotle was above all logical and conceptual, marginalizing the imaginary and the intuitive. The Catholic universal embraced only the community of believers. The Hegelian universal came up against the wall of the end of history. The literary absolute, founded by the Romantics of the *Athenaeum* at Jena, and pursued in various forms by Mallarmé, Proust, Céline, and Blanchot, was the index of a twofold limit: the limit of the expressive exhaustion of the individual Western subject and the limit of the focus on the One of the Book, whose aim was not only to erase *To Biblion*, but also to finish with multiplicity and diversity of all the books yet to come.

In radical rethinking of all these propositions, Glissant offers a universal of absolute inclusion that knows no exception, and *which thus includes all the universals that preceded it*—what a crazy ambition, what a magnificent act of overreaching, is Glissant's project! "ONLY DIFFERENCE, THEN, CAN BE UNIVERSAL, AND IT IS ONLY THROUGH THE INTER-PLAY OF DIFFERENT THINGS, AND ANY IDENTITY AT FIRST WOULD BE SOLELY OF SUCH A KIND AS TO TEND TOWARD THE OTHER" (NMR 130). This universal logic of the inclusion of the different is open to the differences that will inevitably arise:

> What I consider as a conceivable universal is the realized quantity of all differences, and this alone. I do not postulate that this realized quantity would lead to a kind of unity that would abolish the peculiarity of each of the differences. And therefore this realized quantity is the opposite of a certain universal. The universal is the ideal that can be realized on the basis of several real givens. What I defend is that the idea of beauty springs from a quantity realized as and when. The ideal that lies in the notion of universal is abolished in the notion of realized quantity. (IL 91)

Thus, "the universal is a lure, a deceitful dream. We must conceive the totality-world as a totality, that is to say, as a realized quantity and not as a value sublimated from particular values" (IPD 136). The totality does not become absorbed in universality, it is not transcendence, but realized immanence, constantly becoming, unaffected by any sublimation.

We can see the precision of the philosophical shift that Glissant has brought about. He downgrades ontological universals, always defined by the language of the speaking subject and always having an intimate relation to Being, if only at the most formal level of linguistic and philosophical predication ("Socrates *is* a man"). In place of this ontology comes a universal ontics (against Socrates and Aristotle, and also against Heidegger) of all beings, taken one by one in their difference.[19] "If we accepted this so-marvelous revolution in thought, Being would be illumined by this realized quantity, and would henceforth represent the absolute subjective knowledge of that whose instant intensity has been incorporated into being" (NRM 43). Glissant's thought is nothing but an epistemological break from and in the history of philosophy; the word "revolution" is extracted from the political sphere, and reassumes its original meaning: a return to the initial position, but a return that changes everything.

In the Whole-World and through Relation, it is poetry that thought and will think, it is poetry that was and will become philosophy, it is poetry that is the ultimate mode of subjective knowledge. Thus, the construction of Glissant's universality is based on an opposition to all the universals we have cataloged. Universality in philosophy or in politics is always initially expressed in abstract or logical terms. Glissant's universality, on the other hand, springs from a concrete empiricism, be it that of the poetic sphere, the landscape, or the universal library, and not from any ideality: "Do not think the imaginary of the world, but express it. To express it, the writer needs to think about it, but it is not an informative thought, it is an intuitive thought" (IPD 133).

This extraordinary escape from the philosophical, religious, political, and juridical universal is produced by a reflexive meditation on the philosophical tradition; this confers on this tradition the validity of its surpassing. It moves beyond philosophy not by an outright dismissal of it, a rejection declaring it to be inadequate, but by taking it to its ultimate consequences. It must be emphasized that Being is not at all dismissed with a wave of the hand, crossed out by beings; Being is the origin of the latter's becoming, and is always part of subjective knowledge, but as an abstract quality modified by concrete quantity. The universal does not close down the argument, it does not describe Being, it does not take refuge in abstraction—it opens infinitely into and through poetic subjective knowledge.

We return to the dynamic becoming of Heraclitus, but freed from the "magisterial fantasy" of the One. Glissant's universal and its ontic foundation, beyond the fixity of a universalizing ontology, anticipates its challenge and its difference, ready to integrate them whenever their unpredictability springs into being.

Chapter 7

"Bounds, breaks and sudden leaps"

Édouard Glissant's thought and writing are first and foremost a form of dialectical continuity (the integration between man and his place, between thesis and antithesis, between the West and its Other, between the written history of the masters and the history, abolished and reinvented, of slaves, a fusional mixing of digeneses, peoples, literary genres, and their worlds, a union of the poetic and the cosmic). But it also breaks away from cultural affiliations, and the repeated affirmation of a "new region of the world." How are we to account for this apparent contradiction between the breakaway and the recovery?

This question involves epistemology in a broad sense, not only as a history or theory of science, but as an *episteme* of objective and subjective knowledge; it goes without saying that Glissant's thought is *also* an epistemology. But in what way, and seen from what angle?

For classical epistemology, as defined by Alexandre Koyré, Alexandre Kojève, Karl Popper, and Thomas Kuhn, the epistemological break of modern science (or Galilean science, i.e., the same thing) is an absolute universal, which nothing escapes: it affects all fields of objective knowledge; everything is radically new, and no notion from antiquity corresponds to the meaning it acquires in the modern universe. In fact, the continuity that is called the "Western tradition," and indeed the very notion of the "West," is emptied of all meaning, since it is only the chimera of an uninterrupted linear continuity between the ancient, post-Socratic Greeks and modernity. The epistemology of science renders any continuum with the Greeks a mere phantasm, the purpose of which is often to prop up the claim to a supposed superiority. Glissant's return to the Pre-Socratics and Sophists is not meant, of course, to enact a restoration of the West and its continuity; the resurrection of this past that has, as much as Plato, become a dead letter for science, aims to overflow the boundaries of this science so as to include it in a new epistemology of subjective knowledge of which the West and its avatars are only a part.

For Alexandre Koyré, between the finite cosmos of the ancients and the infinite universe of the moderns, there is no synonymy of notions, and it is this generalized homonymy that is the very index of the break: we live irrevocably in a world other than that of Greek antiquity. Thus the orb of Ptolemy of Alexandria is not at all the orb of Kepler, the movement of Aristotle is not the same as in Galileo, and so on.[1] Koyré's epistemology is based on the belief that Galilean science is a major epistemological break. It entails the fact that we must re-read the Greeks only so as to show that they are different from us: in themselves, they have become irrelevant to our modern condition, and in such a vision, there is no more cultural past—it is abolished.

But what if that were not the case? What if the Galilean break affected only the *episteme* of science as such, and not the other fields of objective and subjective knowledge? If Galilean science is a major break, there is no need to worry about the human sphere (of culture), because the subject has no place in it. It is the "abolished subject of science," frequently mentioned by Lacan. In this field, the subject is the return of the repressed of science, and nothing else. Michel Foucault's epistemology assumes its full meaning here: for him, there is no major epistemological break, as any break affects only a specific field of knowledge without spreading out into others. In other words, we need to re-read the Greeks (and others); there is a cultural past that matters because no abolition is complete and definitive.[2] Foucauldian epistemology formally contradicts the epistemology of science, in the sense that it restores the past of the human sphere. It may be lazy thinking, or the fundamental lack of a spirit of liberty, to conceive of the major epistemological breaks as absolutely decisive moments; it is perhaps, at the same time, difficult to believe that the deterministic effects of these breaks are irrevocable, that one can neither return to the past nor consider a future outside these determinations. In the final analysis, it is unimaginative to be convinced that nothing new can be created outside the break itself or that all that is created arises from the necessity of one break or another. The past appears to us fixed within the linearity of causes and consequences only when seen retrospectively: but this has never been the case, we forget that the process of becoming, at the very moment of fundamental breaks, has always left open the field of possibilities. Breaks in science and radically new forms of art are by no means the same; continuities and discontinuities in these two fields are asynchronous and heterogeneous: Michel Foucault is right.

The first moment in humanity, for Hegel, is a fusion where man is not yet an individual subject; he conceives himself as part of a community, and his consciousness has not yet separated out from its natural environment: "Poetic diction can be born among a people at a time when their language is not yet formed, but it is in poetry that it develops."[3] And this form is original: "As an art, poetry is older than prose. It expresses the spontaneous representation of the true, an objective knowledge that does not yet separate generality from its living particular manifestations, the law from its applications, the end from the means, but it conceives each of its terms only in and through the other."[4] Glissant could very nearly have written these lines; he calls this genesis the "primordial poem": "There was, arising, a sacred word. And the poem, then the self-generated poem, began to be recognized. [. . .] Eternities farther on, what sprang forth on the darkened slopes of the caverns was not the deceitful shadow of a reality from without, but the very sign of the fusion of everything with everything else: the humanities had not yet cut off their differences by carrying out amputations drenched with blood" (PhR 11–12). The poem of the origin is discussed in *L'Imaginaire des langues*: "I think that there is, in the history of all arts and cultures, a nostalgia for this primordial—and not primitive—moment when the same was in relation to the other. For the same who was the cave dweller, his other was not another person, his other was the animal and his own surroundings" (IL 93). In the beginning, for Hegel as for Glissant, came fusion: the fusion between the notion and the object, between man and his place, between all the places (not a primitive fusion that was to be surpassed, but a primordial fusion that was to be rediscovered). Plato's cave has not yet split the Heaven of Ideas from the world of the here and now:

The idea of fusion is expressed or revered or meditated on. It was argued over before becoming a form of ecstasy, with the one god or with the idea of the god, and so it turned to philosophy, to theosophy, traditionally speaking, which then inspired the mystics. By a primordial reversal, it initially rose to an ecstasy beyond any ordered knowledge, absolutely outside

of it, with the gods who were deemed to be obscure and/
or primitive, and so this fusion was said to be impure magic.
(PhR 99)

For Hegel, the Enlightenment of the seventeenth and eighteenth centuries (*Aufklärung*), the moment when Christianity became secularized and replaced faith with rational knowledge, is an offspring and a consequence of the Christian break; in other words, Christianity, and it alone, contained in itself the possibility of its own critique.[5] This fissure, potential and realized, exists only in the Christian West: only the West, of all civilizations, has given itself the "internal" possibility of criticizing itself, as opposed to all other civilizations in which critique comes from outside—by comparison and struggle with other cultures. In this respect, the thought of Glissant, a critic of the universal of the West, is indeed "Western" (but not only Western).

Glissant takes from Hegelian epistemology the return to the Pre-Socratics, in particular to Heraclitus, through whom Hegel recommences philosophy; after this, the Socratic–Platonic break was a hasty and negative flight into the abstract and the destruction of the original fusion. As in Hegel, it is not the heritage of the dominant Greek philosophy that returns, but the heritage of those poets/philosophers whom that philosophy condemned. This continuum, both old and new, certainly originates in the Greek "West," but brings back those "heretics," "as heretics," and not a source allowing a new atavistic filiation.

Apart from this mulling over, everything is different: Hegelian linearity, which supposes a historical end goal, is rejected. The break represented by the incarnation is an invention and imposition of linear time (homogeneous with the historical vision of Hegel): "Christic individuation did not result in an ebb of history, a cycle of re-beginning; instead, it generalized (by the universalism of linear time, *before and after Christ*) the chronology of the species and inaugurated a History of Humanity" (PR 61). The Incarnation then becomes a mistaken generalization: "In western thoughts, solicitous for human dignity and proceeding from an individual adventure, there is finally, and by another paradox, only generalization. History (natural history or that of humanity) is present in germ in the philosophies of the One" (PR 61). Christic individuation universalizes transcendence, that is to say, trivializes it. Anyone and everyone is then a philosopher, even without having to think of it: "What Christian thought adds here is a form of democratization, in that it trivializes this position [of the philosopher, hitherto reserved for the masters]. That is, it makes each individual a potential philosopher-king. Transcendence is thus shareable. [. . .] Common thought, admittedly of the non-scholarly kind, does not notice any leap of thought here" (EBR 151). Glissant, however, takes the precaution of specifying the level of his break with Hegel; we are in the doxa, in common opinion, not in learned discourse. Glissant is here not talking to academics, theologians, or scholarly epistemology (places of every clarity, but also of every blindness and every exclusion), but to "common" thought (the place of every confusion, but also an imaginary in which Relation can potentially shine dazzlingly forth). Christianity is then a way of extending philosophical activity, the privilege of slave-owning masters, to the slave. By this, philosophy loses its aristocratic character—it becomes the commonplace occupation of all.

Poétique de la Relation contradicts the Hegelian interpretation of the Incarnation and the death of God as the end of transcendental filiation: "Christ is above all the Son: he consecrates filiation, being a descendant of David and at the same time the Son-of-God who is God" (PR 60). The "son of Man"—that is to say, the death of God—coexists in the Gospels with "son of God" (the consecration of filiation). Glissant, from this digenesis with its impossible logic, resolutely chooses the Son of Man as against the Son of God—that is to say, against Hegel.[6] The *Traité du Tout-Monde* adds a new twist to the problem of the Incarnation; if the Incarnation is a flight from generality (the generality of a "bad" universal), it is also the foundation of human dignity. Glissant thus manifests the contradiction of the Judeo-Christian West with itself as well as its dialectical digenesis, which holds together the most general universal with the most individual singular: "If the whole man, at once flesh, soul and spirit, is in Christ, then the universal can take wing. Even today, Western cultures hold together the generality of the Universal and the dignity of the human person, despite all the many abuses, oppression and profiteering that their societies have inflicted on the world" (TTM 97–98).

In the history of human cultures, the Christian Middle Ages, born from the break of the Incarnation, is not universal in scope: "I see this European Middle Ages, it appears above all as European, does it not . . . ?" (EBR 147). He once, in conversation, gave me a striking and precise formulation of this, which was not repeated in the *Entretiens*: "Only the West had a Middle Ages." The exceptionality of the Western Middle Ages is developed in the *Traité du Tout-Monde*; the European medieval era was the space of the struggle between the uniqueness of the Faith and the multiplicity of heresies—these latter would eventually succumb to dogma: "The unique feature of that time was that it was the scene of such a long quarrel, and experienced the anguish of such a decisive dispute, of a suspense that made Being a torment, and that it first tried to propose a flamboyant response, solar and lunar, a totalizing response—that of the heresies—opposed to generalization, the summae, systematic thought" (TTM 96–97). Born from a dual and contradictory source, Judeo-Christianity and Greco-Roman Antiquity, the West appears in a digenesis.

From this dialectical struggle comes the possibility of critical and self-critical thought. All other civilizations have been continuous with themselves; the breaks appear only if introduced by other cultures, willingly or by force. Only the West involves breaks, including with itself, "contradictory to itself." It follows that to break with the "West" will always be to realize its deepest possibility: it is this virtuality that Glissant's "rethinking" realizes as it works through this tradition. He and I differed, not on the uniqueness of the Middle Ages in the history of cultures, but on their consequences; he saw that period as the closed nature of the theological summae, the pursuit of heretics, the exclusion of unbelievers. Without denying his negative reading of the consequences of the medieval era, I decipher in it the birth of the modern individual, the first fruits of the abolition of slavery, the creation of the novel as a genre, and an extraordinary artistic flowering in every domain.

The Hegelian end of Universal History is dismissed by Glissant, who prefers the beginning of "histories" in the plural, those histories that Hegel did not see or could not have foreseen. I had raised this problem with Glissant in the *Entretiens* (EBR 30); the reply is nuanced and oblique. Only the excluding universal was exported, "without all that wonderful blossoming of heresies that accompanied the birth of such conceptions *in the West itself*" (EBR 33). Not without devastating consequences: the rational critique of the Enlightenment, assimilated by the colonized, is transformed into rationalization—it is an "initiator of weakness or, at least, a carrier of uncertainty. Assimilation ravages Being, which then ratiocinates, even with reason. Then, I am no longer a fearless onlooker, but a whole mixed-land" (Ibid.). Therefore, following Hegel, the *Aufklärung* is grasped as a splitting (of self, of communities) and leaves a void. Hegel fills it with absolute knowledge, Glissant through a return to belief, not as a means of knowing God, but as a process essential to poetic subjective knowledge.[7]

All cultural Darwinism, insofar as it assumes an evolutionary continuum in the "progress" of civilizations, is flushed out and rejected by

Glissant. Determinisms and filiations represent the "bad" universals and "deceptive lures": "The generalization inspired by Christ was at that time taken up and continued by the generalization proposed by Darwin, with them initially being opposed to one another. In both cases, it was a question of transcending the old mythical lineage, linked to the becoming of a community, and transcending it in a generalizing conception that would have nevertheless retained the force of the principle of linearity, able to 'understand' and motivate History" (PR 61). The linearity of the past and the future is antithetical to all that Glissant hopes for and does. He recognized the breaks within it and confronted them, in order, ultimately, to reject all determinism: "Then the scientist or the historian or the man of action may be wrong, and in their systems Darwin may be wrong, and Hegel may be wrong, and Gibbon and Che Guevara may be wrong too, so all of them may be wrong, but their overall visions tremble and do not fail" (NRM 124). Instead of the continuum of determinism, Glissant proposes a cultural and poetic creationism that defines becoming as an infinite series of breaks: "In truth, the creation of the world is always beginning afresh. Our digeneses are inexhaustible" (CL 60). The rejection of linear fatalism is, in Glissant, universal: inter alia, this is a rejection of the folkloric continuity between the soil and its expression by the writer; a rejection of biology and confinement by one's skin color; a rejection of the classical normativity of French in grammar as in literature, and in the classification of genres. It is a rejection of philosophical and scientific universals, when they are not universal enough; of the globalized commodity culture; of totalities and units, when they are not open; of colonial and thus of postcolonial determinants; of the End of History, or any final or permanent revolution; of the atomization of the individual. Glissant is here inspired by Nietzsche, who had already criticized Hegelian historical determinism: "So much so that for Hegel the culminating point and end point of the world process coincided with his own life in Berlin. [. . .] But the man who began by bending down and bowing his head before the 'power of history' is the man who will eventually kowtow mechanically to any power"[8] So we must free ourselves from the determinisms of the "West," but also from those of all other cultures, without exception.

In the final analysis, for Glissant there is only one fundamental break in the history of thought; the continuum of the poetic was broken by Socrates, Plato, and Aristotle, against the Pre-Socratic and Sophist poet/philosophers: the Greek rational triad is above all a catastrophic parricide of the fundamental poem, a rent to be repaired. This casts light on a conflict that arises and is resolved in the *Entretiens*: as a good Lacanian, and therefore rationalist, I maintained that as soon as language arises in human evolution, the separation between culture and nature, man and woman, and intuition and concept takes place; the possibility of reason immediately arises. Glissant completely rejected my idea: "No, I do not believe that language first carries the concept or first goes through the concept. Languages of intensity and affectivity are formed, or contact languages, that do not go through the concept" (EBR 145). The ground on which the break takes place, each time independently, without any hierarchy being established between major breaks and minor breaks (the latter depending on the former), is none other than poetic writing, intense and passionate, in Relation, which restores, detail by detail, singularity by singularity, the continuity of everything with everything else.

The Socratic-Platonist break does not take the form of fate or irreversible determination (of a major epistemological break) unless one considers the history of thought as linear. The fatalism of this break can therefore be reversed by going back before Socrates to the philosopher-poets whom Plato excluded from the *polis*. In addition, this restored continuity shapes a future where literatures will henceforth contain many breaks. Instead of the great epistemological breaks proposed by both the history of science and the history of the episteme (especially in Michel Foucault), Glissant puts forward an infinity of micro-breaks, all assigned to the field of the poetic.

This refusal of determinism would be only intellectual chatter, if its negativity did not give rise, each time and systematically, to the affirmation of new poetic theories/practices. Thus, the rejection of universals leads to a broader universal, that of Relation; from the rejection of totalities springs the Whole-World, a more total totality; a rejected classicism generates a generalized "baroque," etcetera. This in the name of a claim to radical freedom, the poet's claim to be able to stand outside all fatalism, even those forms of fatalism that he has chosen for himself. This freedom is so radical and profound that it rejects even freely chosen constraints as much as those of any determinism, whether unconscious, social, political, or rhetorical:

> But it is evident that a poet does not obey or conform to general ideas which he has formulated, even those which he has formulated *for himself*. The general ideas and the project are there to highlight the trace. It is like marking a trail in

a forest. But we do not know where the trace leads. Plants that signal a spring are hidden, tracks that lead nowhere are too obvious. We have no determinants, nothing that points us toward the goal. Besides, history, as I understand it to be understood, has no ultimate point. [. . .] It is the innocence or the instinctive cunning of the poet that seems to prevent him from finally consenting, or sacrificing, to determinations that he himself has deemed to be quite obvious. (EBR 42)

The problematic of filiation, of relation to the root and patrilineage, is profoundly related to determinism and its dissolution in philosophy. This theme appears in Plato when he breaks away from Parmenides by committing a metaphorical murder of the father; filiation and break (philosophical and epistemological) are inextricably linked: "*The stranger:* Here is another prayer I must address to you. *Theaetetus:* Which prayer? *The stranger:* Not to regard me as a parricide. *Theaetetus:* Why is that? *The stranger:* To defend ourselves, we must put to the question the maxim of our father Parmenides, and by violence establish that non-Being in some sense exists, and also that Being is not" (*Sophist*, 241d). Platonic parricide is the emblem of the break that Plato, caught in his "ideomania, his almost religious madness for forms"[9] imposes on the evolution of thought by driving out the Sophists and the Pre-Socratics (or "Pre-Platonics," since many of them were contemporaries of Socrates) from the Heaven of Ideas where such things are debated in purity and serenity.

In Hegel, as in Glissant, parricide is not an absolute break, since the new (the synthesis) is also the preservation and revival of the old (the thesis denied): "According to the images which hover over the last lines of the *Phenomenology*, every birth of a new spirit (and especially the birth of the definitely *new* spirit) is a necessary *parricide* which re-invigorates the old spirit, which gives it its new truth and which finds its old truth in it."[10]

I remember that Édouard, who (almost) never spoke at random, mentioned to me one day something his own father had said to him, using the formal mode of address that Martinicans use when they are talking to their children about important business: "Remember: I like coffee, I like milk, but I do not like coffee with milk." Jérôme-Paul-Édouard Glissant pronounced this judgment on the day in 1946 when his son for the first time embarked on the ship to cross the Atlantic and study in Paris. The paternal law forbids the adolescent to indulge in crossbreeding: the black blood flowing in his and his father's veins must remain pure.

We are not here psychoanalyzing Édouard Glissant and thus reducing him to the status of a case history; but it is clear that, later on, in his work and in his life, Édouard Glissant deliberately broke with the law of his Father that imposed on him a unique root (whether white or black is in this case of no importance) excluding any crossbreeding, mixing, or fusion with the other. In every sense, Glissant lives and works exactly the opposite way to this proud exclusion: the vertical root-identity is erased by the extended rhizome-identity and its multiple and noncontradictory roots; the segregation of races and cultures is overcome by Relation; this implies of course that there is no absolute break with the place of origin, but rather the creolization of this very same place; the opposition between the "white" world and the "black" world will be transcended in the Whole-World; he will marry "milk" in the figure of Sylvie Glissant, a daughter of La Rochelle and the Pyrenees. There will be two unavoidable places, the Antilles and Paris, two cultures that will preside over digenesis, written philosophy and literature, and spoken oraliture. The exclusivity of the single root will be transcended by the invention of the Whole-World, which, in principle, is the crossbreeding of all cultures.[11]

Crossbreeding thus does not amount to the non-critical rejection of all tradition, but to its integration. The injunction of Jérôme-Paul-Édouard Glissant senior was indeed rejected, since pure "coffee" and pure "milk," Western philosophy and its other, classicism and baroque, etcetera will merge in the Relation, harmonious and dissonant at the same time: "I do not reject filiation as a principle in itself, I reject it as a sealed principle, that is to say, one that excludes the other" ("La Relation imprédictible et sans morale," p. 191).

Édouard Glissant's reservations about Aimé Césaire's negritude are consistent with the displacement and inversion of paternal control: the logic of identity, insofar as it is exclusion, has no place in the writer's thinking: "What I criticized in negritude was that it defined Being: Negro Being" The same applied to the Creolity proposed by Jean Barnabé, Patrick Chamoiseau and Raphaël Confiant: "Now this is what Creolity does: it defines a Creole Being" (IL 31).[12]

Seeking to merge science, via chaos theory, with his poetics, Glissant also rejects the Galilean break as a universal absolute. Now, it is possible to argue that the break in science defines what we might call modernity. The question then arises: Is Glissant a modern? Let us note, first of all, that *modernus* is both a very ancient and a quite recent word in the history of the Latin language: it appears in the works of the grammarian Priscian of Caesarea, in the sixth century AD, and means "that which is always present." In the field of art, Baudelaire proposed a definition that closely resembles Glissant's modernity. According to the etymology, what is modern is a work of art that comes to speak to us in our present, even if this work was written centuries ago. Thus Homer, Dante, *The Song of Roland*, and Glissant are modern to us; in contrast, what is ancient, or rather obsolete, is a work that does not speak to us (any more), even if it is hot off the press and its ink is contemporary with us. The Baudelairian criterion of the modern thus escapes from a flatly chronological conception and, consequently, from the enforcement of any epistemological breaks: modernity is the index of the living relevance of a work in our present, from whatever period it arises. This notion of the modern is perfectly well adapted to Glissant's idea of the history of the poetic, from the primordial poem to the knowledge of the Whole-World and Relation. In this "Baudelairian" vision, any work, whatever its date and place, is able to seek our attention in our present. The modern is both historical and ahistorical: historical because poetics are born and die in an unavoidable place and time, and ahistorical, because time can be poetically traveled downstream and upstream; to take one example, Heraclitus and Hegel return to speak to us in our present (they are modern), but not everything has been said (there are possible futures that they could not calculate).

Reinterpreting the notion of modernity, Glissant gives it a completely different meaning from that of common usage, which conceives of all modernity as a break with the past. Contrary to all the logic of incompleteness and non-Totality, a logic that has exclusively reigned since Galileo and is therefore an integral part of what defines modernity, Glissant sees totality as the very sign of the modern: "Perhaps modernity is the contradictory and reflective totality of cultures?" (PR 234) The word "cultures" is crucial here: knowing that the Whole is impossible in modernity, Glissant shows that it can be deployed only in a poetics, outside the systematics of non-Totality, whether this be theological, scientific, or psychoanalytic: the poet's privilege is to escape from the rigidity of the succession of historical epochs so as to express the achronism of the poetic domain, outside rational and linear temporality. Returning to the totality envisaged by Heraclitus and Hegel, and dialectically going beyond it, Glissant writes resolutely and systematically *against* the whole of the contemporary concept of modernity, in whatever field it is exercised. In this new sense, the Whole-World defines itself as modern, because it rejects what preceded it: the segregation of literary genres, national and regional traditions, the exclusiveness of purism, the Platonic delineation of philosophy, the separation of the arts and the sciences, etcetera.

Glissant emphasizes the violence of the process of modernization, in its current meaning, and not in that of the Whole-World:

> There may be modernity when a tradition, at work in a time and a place, no longer gradually assimilates the changes that are presented to it, from within or without, but adapts to it by violence. [. . .] It is because the violence of change has become widespread in our era, and is accelerating, that we call this era absolutely modern. Thus a whole series of modernities has paved the way for modernity—which, extravagant and endogenous, is consumed in its predicates. Its persistence lies in its extremity: the more modernity displays itself, the more derealized it becomes. In this way, we would calculate successive futures without modernity, or infinite modernities without a future. (PR 234)

The modern, in the common sense, is also a matter of display and publicity, a declaration of intent rather than a thought or notion. Instead of this notion that is exhausted in the declarative, Glissant proposes a different criterion of the modern: the totalization of the world of beings. This idea is at once very ancient (it was Heraclitus's project) and entirely new (homonymous) vis-à-vis current notions of modernity. Glissant's modernity comes about not as an overhanging abstraction, nor in the spectacle that displays it instead of questioning and understanding it, but by way of the concrete (of place, of beings), and the discretion of the trace, and the itinerary of thought. Moreover, modernity neither founds nor is confined to a specific culture or tradition anymore: it becomes a universal process.

In other words, modernity is nothing other than Relation, a counterpart of Glissant's practice as a writer and thinker; it therefore has the appearance (but only the appearance) of self-definition and tautology.

The notion of epistemological break appears for the first time in a note in *Poétique de la Relation* that echoes our conversations while it was being written. What is certain is that Glissant was already familiar with this notion through Gaston Bachelard, with whom, Édouard told me one day, "I had a fried egg every day for breakfast."[13] These breaks appear in a particular context: they have not yet happened—they will need to be enacted in the future; the disaffiliation of the Whole-World and Relation has not yet taken place. As a corollary: the Whole-World and Relation *are* epistemological breaks.

But this dialectic of continuity and discontinuity must be qualified. If, in my opinion, the West comprised by Europe embraces both filiation and disaffiliation (parricide, modern science), since alone of all cultures it has entailed the self-destruction of its continuity (through the Incarnation and Galileo), thereby generating its own self-contradiction, the same is not true of Glissant; the epistemological break expresses both a sentiment and a resentment, not an acting out that destroys the West's continuity: "At the moment, we cannot discern any appreciable beginning to these self-generated breaks. If only in the West, and as if by antiphrasis, the intellectual quest for an *epistemological break*, whatever form this may assume and wherever it may occur, testifies to the sentiment (but also to the resentment against it) of this need to break with its continuum" (PR 235). In Glissant's rethinking, there is a "good" and a "bad" continuity. The positive continuum is the Heraclitean flow of becoming, dismissed by Plato, a flow with which we must reconnect; the negative continuity is the way we become tied down to the reflex of filiation and the un-examined repetition of cultural traditions.

It is in *Une nouvelle région du monde* that the discourse of the break is most clearly developed (the epithet in the title clearly indicates this desire for radical change, for novelty). This book, in its subtitle, is a first approach to beauty (*Esthétique I*), which places it on the same poetic level as Glissant's reflections on philosophy (we will be examining the history of beauty, that counterpart to the history of literature, set out in *Une nouvelle région du monde*). In one sense, the title already announces the entire project: the novelty, the break, regionality—in other words the space in which the break is unfolded, not in ideal abstraction, but in the concreteness of an inextricable place, here the rock of Le Diamant, just off a beach in Martinique, which is the essay's poetic exordium; but also, the relation of this place irreducible in its difference to all the differences of the Whole-World (we are not talking about any regionalism of the soil): "It is a region in which we are led to enter all together. This is the sense in which this region is new. [. . .] That is why there is a Whole-World, a new region of the world, beside the world itself, in the world itself, beyond the world itself, before the world itself, and merged with the world itself" (IL 89–90).

"Time has changed and space has changed" (NRM 24). This transformation, both spatial and temporal, connects all the moments of the various Histories: every region, every inextricable place opens up to all the other places: "A brutal separation of time and space, each overwhelmed by the other. A new region which is an era, mixing all times and all durations, an era which is also an inexhaustible country, accumulating extensions that seek out other limits, incalculable but always finite in number, as has been said of atoms" (NRM 24). The break ("an era") is therefore the falsely tautological break of the Whole-World and the Relation, redefining outlines and borders as well as diachronies. This marks the return of Heraclitean mobilism and becoming which, however, by the very fact that we are returning to them from our modernity, are transformed into signs that announce something else, "the now completely total changing of the world" (NRM 25), "such a beautiful revolution in thought" (NRM 43). By the circulation of (and in) the most ancient thought and art, by their dialectical negation, by their juxtaposition in archipelagos and not in isolated "insular" islands or in unshakable continents, there arises something altogether new.

But where? In which field of knowledge does the break occur? In literature or, more generally, in art, not in science, not in philosophy, not in the philosophy of history or religion:

> [. . .] literatures do not flow uniformly, nor in a consecutive way, they are made of breaks, bubbling inspirations, disputes and inventions of a quite unpredictable kind—that is, their intentions diverge, and these divergences do not arise from the tensions of generalities (which would have led to the universal): but rather confirmations of a relational gap (leading to diversities) . . . (NRM 39)

"Literatures break *with*" (PhR 43): thus, the breaks are in relation, synchronous or achronous, and do not follow any consecutive linearity. From then on, the field of the break is absorbed in the field of Relation: "[Relation] is not a matter of elevation but of completeness. Its propositions would then involve it widening to absolutely quantify this totality of differences" (PhR 42). But, simultaneously, "literatures, therefore, break *against*" (PhR 42) the sacredness of the soil, of blood, of inheritance. Breaks are then the dialectical subsumings of the negativities they overcome: "Interrelations proceed mainly by fracture and breaks. They may even be fractal in nature: this is why our world is a chaos-world. Their general economy and their swing express the desire for creolization" (TTM 24).

In such a vision, the continuum must be defined by a new (but only apparent) oxymoron: the discontinuous continuity, which balances the "against" of the break and the "with" of the Relating of all cultures.

The primordial poem (that of Heraclitus, Parmenides, Thales) is thus reborn in statements that are not simply obsolete survivals. A revival can lead to a break in the future, after the Pre-Socratics. Glissant gives three examples; there is Rimbaud, and those *poètes maudits* or accursed poets Nietzsche and Artaud: they were accursed because, over two thousand years, Socratic reason had strengthened its grip: "Because, when they do this, it is rational knowledge that has triumphed already, and poetic knowledge appears as a kind of crazed demand" (EBR 147). The example of Nietzsche, a philosopher-poet with a "crazed demand," is eloquent: he is exemplary both in his resurrection of the Great Year of Greek mythology in the form of the eternal return, akin to the return of the primordial poem, and also in his return to the Pre-Socratics and the Sophists, these inaugural poets whom Glissant celebrates. Moreover, from one of his posthumous fragments, we can verify Nietzsche's congruence with Glissant's thought; there is not a word in this quotation to which Glissant could not subscribe:

> [. . .] the *fundamental prejudice* is that order, clarity, all that is systematic is necessarily inherent in the "true essence" of things and that, conversely, all that is disorderly, chaotic, unpredictable appears only in a world of falsehood or recognized as unfinished—in short, it is an error. All this testifies to a moral prejudice derived from the reality that a trustworthy and truth-loving man is a man of order and principle, in short, someone who strives to be something predictable and pedantic. Now, one can never demonstrate that the essence of things obeys this recipe for the model civil servant.[14]

It is not only Nietzsche as poet-philosopher who attracts Glissant, it is also Nietzsche's critique, including his philosophical method ("philosophizing with hammer blows"), that Glissant continues while "stirring up" (as he puts it) metaphysical filiation, albeit on the basis of a deep knowledge of this same filiation.

Glissant everywhere practices the very language of the break, especially in the many interviews he has granted. The meaning he gives to the break is at once general and concrete, and is repeated with remarkable stability. To take one example: "We are in a new situation, where we must be ingenuous and naive, while being learned. And I say ingenuous and naive in the full sense of the words: we must be immediate, in contact with the world, and at the same time rational, and reflecting the world" (EBR 146). It must be emphasized that the Whole-World, in the innocence of its origins, is not contradictory with rationality: on the contrary, rationality accompanies its birth and its budding. The content of the break is nothing but the Whole-World and Relation, notions that have never been thought of, in the history of philosophy, on such a broad scale: temporally and geographically, Whole-World and Relation are infinitely extensible—they touch the infinite and tend universally toward it. In his essays as well as in his interviews, there are many "todays," "and from now ons" or, in a more developed form: "There is a new condition for the writer's existence and function" (IL 53). Or again: "Renewed birth today is not so much a matter of communities as an unexpected call for other modes of relation between communities of people" (EBR 119).[15] The immediate present is the pivot of the break. On his assessment, a series of notions are condemned to decrepitude, as regional literatures: "It is a completely obsolete discourse" (IL 46). Obsolescence has befallen many traditions: rhetorical habits, national literatures, philosophies of the abstract and the closed system, "bad" universals, and so on. But the break is not a rejection of any past: it also takes the guise of a return to the resources of the past (the Pre-Socratics, the Moai of Easter Island, the frescoes of Lascaux). In addition, the hinge of the contemporary, its *krisis*, opens up onto a future: "I do not want to be a prophet, but I think that one day the human sensibility will move toward languages that will exceed natural languages, which will incorporate all kinds of dimensions, forms, silences, and representations, which will be so many new elements of the language" (IL 34).

The temporal markers are clues to the break created by Relation and the Whole-World; these markers are always connected to a present, to a contemporaneity in motion. We cannot fail to relate them, too, to the "opportune moment," the *kairos* of the Sophists, those heretics of philosophy. For both Empedocles and Gorgias, it is crucial that a discourse be delivered "at the right moment," in the presence of the present, if it is to be effective: everything is a matter of circumstances and opportunity, not of a truth or logic seen in the absence of the concrete and the temporal. For the Sophists, the opportune moment is a matter of external contingency, which in Glissant assumes the figure of the "new" situation of the world on the way to totalization. But the *kairos* is not only the time of opportunists, among the Sophists it designates the decisive moment, the point of inflection where everything changes, the *krisis*: it is especially in this way that Glissant's temporal markers operate.

The present, the contemporaneity of the break, is paradoxical: they have no Year Zero or Ground Zero, and Glissant's break is not taken up into any chronological linearity, nor is it the privilege of any elected place. The break of Relation can arise at any time of the world, and in multiple places. Thus, the Whole-World can be prefigured by the library of Alexandria, and simultaneously appear in our contemporaneity, just as it can also outline a figure to come. In spite of Glissant's wish not to be considered a seer, the temporal markers of the break could be considered as so many oracular redundancies, whose only reference is their utterance. In a sense, what determines the before and the after, obsolescence and modernity, is indeed nothing other than the very thought of Glissant as it is realized at once in his own work, with all genres combined. But this very concretization *is* the break—and therefore not a dream, an illusion, a fantasy, a vain prophecy, or an unlikely oracle. The materiality of so many accumulated books proves and demonstrates the notions at work.

In addition, Glissant has produced an "extra" demonstration: the texts of writers and poets gathered in *La Terre le Feu l'Eau et les Vents*. This collection brings together fragments of everything Glissant has read and thought about throughout his life. It has an essential function in the whole of his œuvre: it is a question of proving that others, in different times and under different skies, have thought and written about Relation and the Whole-World. *La Terre le Feu l'Eau et les Vents* is therefore the "external" proof of Glissant's break.

Ultimately, in the year 2000, Glissant would designate the break that he intended to produce by resorting to a neologism, one that appears in *Le Monde incréé*: *poétrie*, the subtitle of the collection. When there is no word to express what we are doing, we need to invent one. The old names, especially the name "poetry," a name of such great antiquity, are no longer sufficient to designate the radically new vision that Édouard Glissant has produced in his work. The collection, which brings together three plays, circles back and returns to ancient manuscripts as well as prefiguring a book to come: "The three pieces here, composed, in the order of their current presentation, at distant times (1963, 1975, 1987), weave together a hypothetical novel." They also testify to the jamming of literary genres, as the plot of a "novel," a quasi-novel. In *L'Imaginaire des langues*, Glissant clarified the relationship of *poétrie* to classical literary genres, while emphasizing the "Creole" origin of the term; at first sight, it is a question of constituting a new literary genre, one that would be *transgeneric* and *translinguistic*, including many genres and traditional categories:

> It is an ambiguous word because it is a French word, *poétrie*, which refers to an English word. There is therefore a deliberate desire for confusion, or rather a mixture in origin, a deliberate desire to show that it is not a distinct literary genre, but a mixture of narrative, theatrical dialogue, poetry, reflection, etcetera. This is a first approximation of what could be a "destructuring" of genres. (IL 60)

The assembly of the three plays in a single volume is also a mark of the mulling over which produces the altogether new: "These plays did not suffer me, nor did they nag at me, to be packed at the bottom of a pile of papers, even though I had not forgotten them. As if they had waited for the last of them to complete their common curve and their trace. I have gone over some of these traces in earlier poems and stories—you have to keep starting over." Glissant always writes in the future anterior, to find the primordial poem and, circularly, open it up to the improbability of the radically new. The very title (*Le Monde incréé* or "uncreated" world) points both to an ancient world, not yet marked by the Creator of monotheism (uncreated: such was the cosmos, the Gods and mankind for the Greeks) and to a world that has not yet been created, which is still to be created, the world of Relation and the Whole-World: "It is a world which proceeds from historical events [. . .]. It is the composite world [. . .]. The set of three plays tries to show that there is a sacred of this world, that it is not the sacred of Genesis, but the sacred of what I call digenesis, that is to say a conjunction of stories that at a certain time meet" (IL 62). The new, the discontinuity, will be born from repetition: "It is a world that is to be created but is already there, and of which we do not yet have any obvious subjective knowledge. Therefore, it is a world that can be approached only with the powers of imagination and poetic intuition" (IL 63). This is *poétrie*, "already there" since the earliest times, and "to come" in the poetic domain, a "re-juvenation," and not an innovation separated from any history of thought and poetry, by which it produces a break: "Perhaps by their different and so very discontinuous ways, such words keep in reserve the sole secret of an underground road, of a wandering of the person or people which these words concern, a wandering shared but unknown, a matter of nothing but fractures and sudden leaps" (MI 7).

Glissant has, perhaps unconsciously, gone back further than to an English-speaking present: back to *poétrie* (or *poeterie*), also a word widely used in ancient French literature. The word "poetry" is in fact an English borrowing from Old French, which Glissant returns in his turn by readapting it to French. And for the medievals, poetry was equal with philosophy, it was a legitimate path to subjective knowledge of the world: "For this have the great clerics and people of great understanding yearned to learn science and to know the truth of things, some through philosophy, others through poetry."[16]

But the strongest sense of *poétrie* is found in medieval Latin literature, more specifically the *Poetria Nova* by Geoffroi von Vinsauf.[17] Geoffrey of Vinsauf insists on the joyous *rejuvenatio* that his poetics produces, which is modeled on the radical innovation that he finds in the Incarnation.[18] We find in Glissant the same optimism, the same jubilation of the unheard: "We are all young in the Whole-World" (NRM 81). Hegel's dialectical negativity is at work here, as "the faculty of turning into places of promise our places of suffering or defeat" (NRM 122).

Stated in the present, but unrepresentable, or representable only in the future ("*Poétries* of this kind are not representable," MI 8), *poétrie* is the radical homonym that designates the essential break, the break brought about by Glissant. We then remember the quotation from René Char that Michel Foucault eventually placed on the back cover of his books: "The history of men is the long succession of synonyms of the same term. To contradict it is a duty."[19] This imperative is overthrown by Glissant: it becomes the demand to create a fusion and a mixture that rules out any obligation to draw distinctions; the Whole enters into Relation, time and space go crazy: "These dates and these countries mixed together make *poétrie*" (MI 9).

Ultimately, Relation "is not uttered on the basis of any break" (PR 201). What does this mean? In its immanence, Relation and its *poétrie* do not depend on any temporal or spatial determination, on any epistemological fatalism: Relation opens every place and every time to an unlimited freedom. Relation has always been present from the first moments of thought, or of the world; it has always been absent because it projects into an unpredictable future. Its continuum thus escapes any epistemology of the break, any historical succession or break that would constrain it.

The challenge, fundamental and ambitious, is none other than to reopen, after Socrates, after Hegel, after Galileo, human histories, bring them back to the life of the poetic, without which they will irreparably have been consigned to the waste land.

Chapter 8

"Only the poets"

There is indeed a Glissant canon, which develops in two principal phases, first in *L'Intention poétique*, and then in *La Terre le Feu l'Eau et les Vents*, where it finds its definitive form. There are very few novelists in *L'Intention poétique*: Alejo Carpentier, Faulkner, and Victor Segalen—in other words, people who have been marginalized or excluded by the rules of a French-speaking canon; on the other hand, there are many poets: Claudel, Mallarmé, Rimbaud, Césaire, Miłosz, Char, Pierre Reverdy, Valéry, Homer, Dante, and Virgil: "Only the poets here were listening to the world, fertilized it in advance. We know the time it takes for their voices to be heard. Only the poets" (IP 42).

This first canon sets up many notions and oppositions that will be explored more deeply later. Thus Hegel is appended to Michel de Montaigne, and the antinomy between system and detail is underlined: "The Hegelian investigation, so finely systematic and so profitable to Western methodologies, often stumbles over the details where Montaigne's interest is at its keenest" (IP 37). It also sets up a surreptitious contrast between Hegelian aesthetic classicism and the baroque of Montaigne. As early as 1969, the purism and uniqueness of the classical era was questioned, not in a spirit of revolt, revenge, or irony, but in relation to a literary project whose purpose was not the obliteration of the detail by the system, but a system that started out from the detail and returned to it. Moreover, Glissant questions the coincidence of the aesthetic ideal and the nation united by its language; a canon cannot be national: "Being can no longer be elected in the solitary resonance of a language" (IP 45). Already, writers have the task of recomposing a totality, beyond and within the chaos of the world. "The era of languages proud of their purity must end for man: the adventure of languages (the various poetics of a world that is diffracted but recomposed) begins" (IP 47). We must break with the filiation of cultural heritages, while recognizing them: "I have to prove neither fidelity nor continuity [to the law, to the cultural whole], but to *stir it up*, tug it my way: this is how I recognize it (IP 45, my emphasis). Glissant's "stirring up" describes the reinterpretation of cultures and philosophy, a unique way of both affirming and challenging them by what they have given birth to but left fallow: the other, heresy, the margin, the detail, the inextricable.

La Terre le Feu l'Eau et les Vents, the repertoire of all the writers, poets, and philosophers with and through whom Glissant has thought and written, sets out the second, infinitely more populous canon, and brings out the characteristic features of the first. With its philosophical fragments, it is not only literary or poetic; unlike all other canons, it is potentially infinite, since it relies on the Whole-World of which it is the anthology. There are, however, revealing exclusions: Kant, Schelling, Heidegger, Plato, Spinoza, Proust, Christian mysticism . . . the canon does not include "everything." Some of these omissions are deliberate—especially Plato, Heidegger, and Proust. Others are due to the organically unfinished nature of the company: in Glissant, nothing comes to a final conclusion, anything that could block the future, including the canon.

Glissant's canon is not built according to the chronology of literary or philosophical history: "Then the baroque sometimes precedes the periods of classicism, far from needing to reform them . . . Later, the Baroque *is* a classicism" (TEFV 17). It is a canon of extent and surface, not of any depth of filiation or linear temporality: "No anthropology is organized according to the system of a rule of succession or in the light of any law of evolution. Multiplicity is always a matter of the here-and-now, even when it calls on the past. It is this fate and this chance which, in this place of poetry, are assembled" (TEFV 17). The poetic is what organizes contingency and generates encounters, apart from filiations and sources.

The anthology of the poetry of the Whole-World elects those who sense and write Relation, whether they are the "apocryphal" heretics of any canon, or canonically recognized authors. This means that the canon is neither oriented by the transmission of a legacy nor subject to the requirements of an exclusion, but open to a future; at the same time, it is rebuilding an unseen past that foreshadows an improbable future.

In *La Terre le Feu l'Eau et les Vents*, the concept and the philosophical final purpose that gave unity to Hegel's *Aesthetics* disappear: the concept is erased by the fragment; chronology, logic, and geography (the place of origin of various expressions) are jostled; the final purpose circles from poetry to poetry: "But the poem is indeed the only dimension of truth or permanence or deviance that links the presences of the world" (PhR 19). Hegelian in its ambition and inspiration, the anthology of the Whole-World is turned against Hegel. Glissant's gesture, a fragmentation of expression, outlines the unexpected face of encounter, another name of Relation:

> What disorders, however, caesurae, things taken by their small ends and laid head to tail: would you say that a poem can be broken, interrupted, that we could give some excerpts of it, choice morsels decided by the action of malignant winds? Yes, when the morsels are lucky enough, that is, are graced by so many encounters, when they agree among themselves, one part of a poem that fits another poem, with this new part, and becomes in turn an entire poem in the total poem which is sung all at once. (TFEV 15)

The canon, religious or literary, was at all times a matter of measure and regulation, as indicated by its etymology (from the Greek *kanon*, "measure" or "rule"). Its final purpose is none other than to frame a textual past to master any future dynamic. Now, throughout his œuvre, Glissant has balanced out the notion of measure, so as to challenge it.

To "stir up" the imposition of a canon, Glissant proposes a chiasm (TFEV 16):[1]

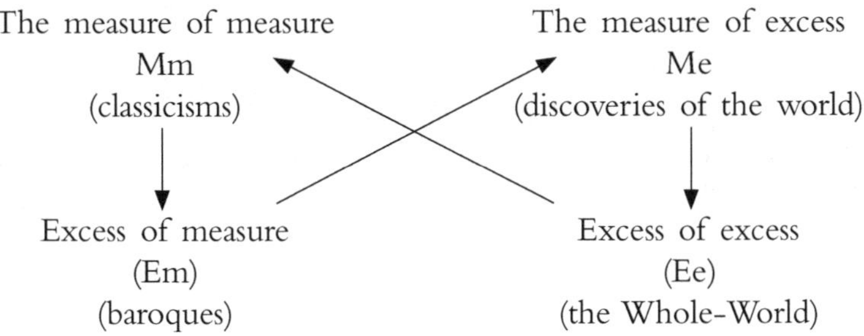

The chiasm, originally a cross, an X placed in the margin of manuscripts to indicate a passage disapproved of, is here a diagram in which the distinctions of literary genres and their canons permute, with arrows indicating the (not necessarily chronological) dynamics of a dialectic: the classicisms (still just as sociopolitical, the word "classic" itself coming from the five classes of Roman citizenship) trigger the baroques, the baroques join the time of the great discoveries (see once again Montaigne's essay, "On Cannibals"), the European explorations of the world prepare the way for the Whole-World. Each time, the measure is "de-measured" or excessive, and the excess is transformed into a measure, a new classicism which, modified by its commutation, opens up onto the totality, without affirming anything exclusive. Classicism is not only the classicism of the French seventeenth century, but also the norm of the "correct" language that Glissant learned in high school. But in linguistic perfection another ambition is revealed: "Classicism, for a culture, is the moment when this culture is sufficiently sure of its own values to include them in this measure of the measure and to propose them to the world as universal values" (IPD 93).

Now the critical rereading of classical formalism is already found in *Soleil de la conscience*. Its paradigm is the alexandrine, a formal constraint that has a very long history in French literature: born in the twelfth century in the *Roman d'Alexandre* (hence its name), popularized by the Pléiade group of poets in the sixteenth century, triumphant among the classics and Victor Hugo, this defining mark, put to death by Mallarmé, runs the risk of believing that truth lies in form alone: "Such is this tension of language that sometimes it becomes confused with the truth of its deep order. Thus can we believe that the alexandrine is only a line of verse of twelve syllables, balanced on a rhyme; but its true meaning is found beyond its number or the vocal exercises of its final syllable. When we use the material of the alexandrine (twelve syllables, a rhyme) as the measure of this verse, then we betray it" (SC 40). The alexandrine must open up to excess to be truly itself: Victor Hugo testifies to this, and his fragments of *La Pitié suprême* and *La Légende des siècles* (whole sections of which Édouard could recite) figure prominently in *La Terre le Feu l'Eau et les Vents:*

> *I weighed everything, I saw the bottom, I did the sum,*
> *And I did not subtract a single figure from the total . . .*
> *(La Pitié suprême)*

There, no more banks, edges, or horizons.
In the expanse, where nothing marks the seasons,
Where there are azure gleams, where the chaos sobs,
Millions of hells and paradises float,
Bringing light, with their mournful or enchanting fires,
To other humanities under other firmaments. (La Légende des siècles)

Classicism, respected in the form of the Alexandrine, can also open itself to the excess of excess, to the totality of the chaos-world; Glissant's aesthetic is not an aestheticism fixed by its purely formal identity.

The various forms of the baroque take the opposite route to the classical claim to depth, replacing it with expanse, producing an excess, a denial of metric measure: "For baroque art, subjective knowledge grows by extent, accumulation, proliferation, and above all not primarily by its depths and its dazzling revelation" (TTM 116). Baroque is a positive reaction, in extension, against a conceptual analysis that focuses more on depth: "Baroque art was a reaction against the rationalist pretension to penetrate with a uniform and decisive movement the mysteries of the known. The baroque frisson aims to show thereby that all knowledge is still to come, and that this is the source of its value" (PR 91). Science is no exception to this tearing open of surface expanse in favor of verticality: "Certainly, science postulates that the real is not definable from its appearance, that it needs to be penetrated it in its 'depths.' " In addition, the baroque overturns the claim to the universality of classicism, replacing it with the universal "good" of Relation: "What [the baroque] now expresses about the world is the proliferating contact of diversified 'natures.' It 'understands' (or 'includes'—*comprend*), or rather goes along with this movement of the world. It is not a reaction, but the resultant of all aesthetics, of all philosophies. So, it does not only affirm an art or a style, but goes further and provokes a being-in-the-world" (PR 92–93). The baroque is the very style, past and future, of the Whole-World and Relation; that is why, logically, it must extend to the whole earth ("D'un baroque mondialisé"; PR 91).

Glissant illustrates the measure of excess by three eponyms, which put into words "the claim to render by the original breath of life the excess of the world—namely Claudel, Saint-John Perse, and, long before them, Segalen" (IPD 94). But this excess, for Glissant, is still centered: "The original breath comes from a center and extends to the peripheries" (IPD 94). This concentration triggers and makes necessary a final reversal, an excess of excess, and this will be the diversity of the Whole-World, a diversity embodied in Glissant's literary work and in *La Terre le Feu l'Eau et les Vents*: "The anthology of the Whole-World, which is a changing and permanent anthropology, accommodates, to the point of vertigo, these measures to these excesses" (TEFV 16). The excess of excess, in any case, does not wipe the slate clean of past measures or excesses—it blends together what appeared to be antithetical. Moreover, it aspires with all its strength to become a new classicism, as indicated by the vector which commutes it into first position. Just as it was necessary, in philosophy, to return to Heraclitus so as to turn him into the future of thought and, in literature, to the primordial poem as a prefiguration of the Whole-World and Relation, the excess of excess aims to stir up measure and to take its place. It is thus not a rejection of measure, but its integration, one that anamorphoses it. The canon, by the same token, becomes paradoxical, or if you will, oxymoronic (a canonization of the noncanonical, and vice versa, *in a chiasm*), since it postulates a radically inclusive totality, capable of extension to the infinite.

Although not included in the anthology of the Whole-World, the example of Evariste Suffrin illustrates the radical inclusivity[2] of Glissant's canon. Suffrin was the founder, in Lamentin (Martinique), of a mystico-religious sect, the dogma of Cham. Between 1961 and 1969 he produced a series of proclamations that *Le Discours antillais* discusses (DA 381–389) and collates in its conclusion (DA 481–492). This discourse, an example of the verbal delirium produced by the Martinican context, is nonetheless treated with respect and seriousness by Édouard Glissant. These leaflets lie resolutely outside the ordinary norms of purism, of orthographic and grammatical correctness; nor do they obey the established rules of rationality, being part of the psychotic response made by Martinicans to their existential situation.[3] There is no attempt, in *Le Discours antillais*, to folklorize, to reduce "mistakes," to correct Suffrin's cry in any normative sense. On the contrary, his discourse is accepted as it is, in its barbarolexy: "I had observed that the printers who were responsible for the technical realization of these proclamations, and who were probably sneering quietly at so many blunders, had not given themselves the trouble to correct the most glaring 'faults'" (DA 485). On the contrary, the incorporation of Evariste Suffrin into the canon presupposes precisely that he not be "corrected," straightened out by the rules of good usage. The blunders are irresistible proof of a style that must be fully preserved. The details, the "mistakes" are the traces of Suffrin's cry of suffering; he translates this by an adequate expression: "From the conjunction of these cries there arises the proof that it is not necessary to "possess" a language, that is, to pretend to direct its perfections, in order to create a language for oneself within it. What M. Suffrin says, in a mixture of displaced Creole and French, has the very color of our mistakes. When I see him pass by, irreducible amidst our supermarkets, our absurd pretensions, our carnivals, I think that this is what a style is: an infallible fixity, able to articulate a voice" (DA 485). Évariste Suffrin, by practicing creolization, gives writing to his voice and his cry, turns negativity into a poetics, and stirs up literary and formal conventions, as well as any logic of meaning. He resembles a double of Édouard Glissant, but only to a certain extent: at a certain moment, the identificatory sympathy is replaced by Glissant's analysis of the Suffrin case, which grafts onto it a rationality outside of psychosis. The pages of *Le Discours antillais* devoted to Suffrin ("Sur une pré-enquête: le cas Suffrin") are the very expression of this distance from what becomes a "case," that is, a singularity that illustrates a clinical classification (DA 381ff). The verbal delusion of Évariste Suffrin, a symptom of psychosis, is replaced by the excessive baroque of Glissant's writing, which includes, literally, certain safeguards (*garde-fous* [translator's note: the French implies something that guards (against) mad people]): not only the dazzling stylistic virtuosity, not only the always verified accuracy of the writing, but also the notional frame of a solidity that can withstand all pressures.

La Terre le Feu l'Eau et les Vents shares with Hegel's *Aesthetics* the same ambition of totalization, but the two works have different aims. Hegel sees in the novel a "modern bourgeois epic": the ultimate form where art in general expresses the exhaustion of all its possibilities of expression. The novel brings to a close a linear generic evolution that begins with the epic, passes through lyric poetry, and then evolves into dramatic poetry. Even if he follows these steps, Glissant challenges both the linearity and the finalism of Hegelian literary history. For example, the epic is not an obsolete archaic genre; it is in full accord with our contemporary world, which for Glissant is the chaotic moment of all (re)beginnings; the epic was foundational—today it must lay down new foundations: "This means that poetry begins again in the fields of the epic. In our anarchic universe, such a way of poetry ceases to be accidental, and imposes itself as the imperious Harvest. It names the Drama which is ours: the fire of diversity, the fight of the Disparate, the wish of the Other" (IP 222–223).

After *L'Intention poétique*, Glissant continually returns to the *epos* as the foundation of the social bond of a nascent community (this is the classic definition of gender):

> We still have this: on the one hand, the work of literature is
> unequivocal and diversified, and on the other hand, before the
> appearance of genres there was, there existed, a genre, a com-
> mon trunk which in my view figured the literature that, it has
> been said, has an epic vocation. I characterize this literature as
> being, in Hegel's manner, the exhibition of a nascent commu-
> nity, not yet sure of its very existence, which feels threatened.
> The epic genre (*I am Hegelian on this point*), is the expression
> of the common consciousness at the moment when it is not
> yet political consciousness . . . (EBR 118, my emphasis)

Indeed, Glissant's notion of epic is very close to Hegel's, and Glissant
could not miss the affinity: "What forms the content of the epic work
is the *Whole* of a *world* in which an individual action is performed. This
content therefore comprises the most varied objects, in relation to the
conceptions, acts and states of a world. [. . .] So that we can say that epic
poetry understands the *totality* of what constitutes *the poetic life* of men."[4]

For Hegel, the *Iliad*, the *Aeneid*, *The Divine Comedy* are stages that
the following genres (lyrical poetry and dramatic poetry) supplant: they
subsume epic objectivity by leading to their final purpose: the expression
of individual subjectivity that blends into the totality of absolute knowledge. For Glissant, the era of the epic defines a series of enclosures and
fences. The *Aeneid* walls itself into the imperialist totalization of Rome;
Dante encloses himself into "his desire to universalize, to totalize, to
systematize" (IP 36). Homer is an exception to the ambition of systematization, as he gathers the Greek spirit without summing it all up, and
it is no coincidence that he is the first, the founder, the original moment
of the Western epic tradition: "The man known as Homer is a receiver
as collective, someone who *picks up*." Glissant adheres to the classic thesis
of the Hellenists, which makes Homer a fictitious name, designating in
fact a collectivity of different poets. After Homer, the epic tradition loses
its character of pooling diverse voices. The totalizing synthesis of the
community will no longer be its own work, but the individual creation
of a single writer: Virgil, Dante.

In *Faulkner, Mississippi*, as in *Les Entretiens*, Glissant always insists that
the epic describes a defeat or, at the very least, an ambiguous victory;
this is the case with the *Iliad*, where the victory of the Greeks is not

celebrated, since it ends with Hector's funeral. This is the case in the *Aeneid*, where Rome begins with the crushing of the Trojans, the original Romans. This is the case in *The Song of Roland*, the first text where the name of France is written in the vernacular, where the nation-state arises from the massacre of feudalism at Roncesvalles. This is the case, finally, in Faulkner, building the epic of his work from the defeat of the South in the American Civil War. In passing, note how bold Glissant is: he does not hesitate to turn what is without any doubt a positive event, the abolition of slavery, into a dissolving negativity from which will emerge, by Hegelian dialectic, Faulkner's epic Song.[5]

This insistence on epic defeat is a sign: it is none other than the diffracted symbol of the initial defeat that constitutes the "birth," the "filiation" of Glissant's discourse, namely the slave trade. Aside from the Holocaust, history has seen no disaster more radical than human trafficking—African community histories are erased, subjects reduced to the state of commodity objects; human beings, their legs in chains, are thrown overboard from the schooner when the Royal Navy's coastguard sailboat approaches the African coasts to carry out a check: "The second unknown is the marine abyss. When the frigates give chase to the slave ship in violation of the rules, the easiest way is to lighten the boat by throwing overboard the cargo, laden with chains" (M 216).[6] Hence, in the first place, a duty of remembrance, a necessity which for Édouard Glissant far exceeds the reiteration of an immense and justified grievance or of a demand for compensation:

> [. . .] This question of slavery is not an idle question, a question of rhetoric, a question of petty-minded people out for revenge or seeking compensation [. . .]. The memory of the thing has been obliterated and, even for a people who have lived through slavery, it is somewhat difficult to get into this period of their past. For us Antilleans it is all the more difficult because not only have we not mastered the memory, but neither have we—and this is a consequence—mastered history.[7]

This duty of memory is paradoxical, because the archive has either disappeared,[8] or been counterfeited, at the time of the abolition of slavery, by the bureaucracy of the colonizers. Hence the need for an ancestral myth, a fictitious filiation that will fill this abyss in memory and make up for the painful initial gap. Thus, in *La Case du commandeur*, the slave Aa self-identifies as the First Man, and chooses for himself "the first name by order of rank in the language of the deporters" (CC 167). Aa is the figure of a radical (re)beginning, a new history: he erases the Hegelian Last Man, renewing the language of the slave-owning de-porters as a de-speaker of the primordial cry. The repetition of the first letter of the alphabet indicates the digenesis of the tutelary ancestor. After the fictitious origin, which resorts to myth to fill the hole in the archives, comes the tragedy, which brings myth into history (the history of enslavement, exploitation, and dehumanization), but also into the new beginning of histories on the basis of negativity. The relationship with Faulkner is obvious—witness the fictional chronologies that end *Absalom, Absalom!* or the *Compson Appendix* in *The Sound and the Fury*, which sets out the invented history of this family cursed by defeat. Glissant makes much of this: "Then the marvel occurs, torn out of Faulkner like the exercise of an author summoned to provide explanations, the *Compson Appendix*, a dazzling genealogy with dizzying contractions and shortcuts [. . .]: drawing on the legends of the mountains of Scotland and finishing with a close-up of the face of Dilsey, the Compsons' black servant: They endured" (FM 64). Restoring duration (or enduration, or endurance), reconstructing the origin: this is the function of modern myth in Faulkner, as in Glissant: here we can refer to the chronology concluding *Le Quatrième Siècle*, which constructs the myth of the beginning of two families, the Longoués and the Béluses, dating it back to 1788. These are retrospective namings, myths, or epics after History, which initiate the plurality of the Histories and which are related, at the same time, to the *Popol Vuh*, to the *Chilam Balam* and to Faulkner: there is compensation for defeat in the form of a fiction of origins that produces endurance.

The succession and generic diversification we find in Hegel (hymn, myth, epic, novel, philosophy) is ultimately more deeply subverted than by any ideological or philosophical challenge. Subversion in Glissant is a subversion of thought and language; a content or a form is not revolutionary in itself, unless it makes everything return to its place, in accordance with the word's etymology (*revolvere*, to make something turn round in circles). Grasped from the angle of literary figurations or ideologies alone, "subversions" of content and form run the risk of being merely literary; that is to say, in the eyes of Hegel, as of Glissant, they in no way change the world, but fall into the category of the chatter of the Intellectual: "One must be both oneself, the other, and *an other*. And this also applies to language. To brutally change the language is the task of the rebel; to orchestrate this change seems revolutionary" (EBR 96). Relation, the Whole-World and creolization are never at the service of a "liberation," a "subversion," even a poetic one, or of a revolution, even if it is popular. These figures "are" the revolution, the revolutionary "orchestration" of the change that is already present, and which is pregnant with an unpredictable future; so Glissant replies to Lise Gauvin's question "What does it mean for you, 'to subvert the language'?" by saying "subversion comes from creolization (here, linguistic in nature) and not from creolisms" (IL 25).

From *L'Intention poétique* onward ("Luttes tragiques, libertés épiques," IP 201–206), Hegel's generic categories (fusional poetry, mythology, tragedy, epic, drama, comedy, and novel) are repeated in their distinctions and their historical succession: "Hegel analyzed these categories of the *Epos* at length" (IP 37). On the other hand, these Hegelian categories are far from exhausted, if not in the West (thus the judgment on the End of History thesis in Hegel is both verified and *restricted* to a specific history and region); they have a future, which is both elsewhere and differs in its content. Tragedy and *Epos* are already part of Relation and Whole-World:

> Modern Tragedy, in this view, sings the liberties of men; the modern *Epos*, their shared agreement. The *Epos*, in the past, was "concrete" where tragedy could go further, be "abstract," "universal'; today it is tragedy that seems to be concrete—it is the struggle of peoples, signaling those dark forces, knotted together, that can deliver us, and it is the *Epos* that can, as from the most distant planet, circulate through the human wish to connect, to relate. Tragedy is of men and the earth; the *Epos* will soon be part of the One (yet again the One, while waiting for it to crack and diversify again), the interplanetary One. (IP 205–206)

Glissant recognizes the Hegelian stages of art by stirring them up: imagining a future for epic, tragedy, drama (poetry), he challenges the closed final purpose imposed on them by Hegel.

Following Hegel, however, Glissant signs the death warrant of the "Western" novel. First of all, by his own practice as a writer, after *La Lézarde*; thus *Tout-Monde* is subtitled *Roman* (*Novel*), but this was the publishers' doing: "I do not see how a book with the title *Tout-Monde* [*Whole-World*] could be linear and conventional like the novels of the beginning of this century. [. . .] It is also a work that ventures beyond established literary genres" (IL 37). But this rejection of the generic category of the novel goes far beyond the borders of Glissant's work. The literary history of the novel (in the modern sense of the term, not in the sense of the Middle Ages, which created the notion and the genre),[9] born in England and France, is for Glissant an ideological colonization gradually extended to the whole world. "The novel is not a religious (hi)story, it is not a legendary (hi)story, it is not a mythical (hi)story, it is a political (hi)story, to do with the organization of the city. When the same Western communities colonized the world, the novel gradually and unconsciously became the art of those who, having conquered the world, had the right to say so" (IL 114). The genre of the novel then became the basis for a belief and a pretense, a "bad" universal:

> The Western novel is not so much a technique—there are many techniques—as a pretense, a belief. It is the belief that we can write history because we are the only ones to control it. [. . .] That is why the novel had become unconsciously and automatically the fundamental element of literature. Which it absolutely is not. (IL 115)

By an apparent paradox, it is the universal proliferation of the novel as an object of universal consumption that signs the death sentence of its expressive virtualities:

> Lise Gauvin—*So there is no future for stories, you think?*
>
> Édouard Glissant—No, none. It's over. The story will become a folkloric mode of the existence of literatures. I'm sure of this. The future of literatures is the inextricable, the incomprehensible, the obscure and the too vast, the too bright, the too illuminated . . . There is excess in the future of literatures, and the novel is a wicked art of making literary and commercial profits. (IL 116–117)

Now this end of the novel is perhaps also the end of the writer, the End of Literature (Glissant's diagnosis is reminiscent of that of Maurice Blanchot, announcing, in *Le livre à venir* [*The Book to Come*], the "Death of the last writer" submerged by the incessant murmur of everyday words).[10]

In any case, literature is threatened with extinction by the very fact that it is multiplying and becoming quantified to an amazing extent. It is literally becoming an image of the confusion of the world, of its inexplicable and unpredictable aspects. As a result, it is rapidly becoming commonplace. All consumable literature today is a literature rendered commonplace. [. . .] It is becoming a surface object, whereas literature, traditionally, is an object of depth (IL 71–72).

Entirely defined as an object of common consumption, the novel becomes the whole of literature and exhausts it in nonsense, reflecting the nonsense of the world, instead of finding the opportunity for a new production of full-sense (*plein-sens*). Literature is thus, within a globalized "Western" model, an additional sign of the End of History. If the history of genres is over, if literature is exhausted in and by the novel, Glissant intimates that we must leave behind the concept of literature as defined by Belles-Lettres; the creative practice of writing and poetry leads to a beyond of literature, something that comes into being in the concrete, in the community, discarding all formal and conceptual constraints while incorporating them.

In Glissant, the End is never final, it is always the offered possibility of a renewal: there is no Last Word, any more than there is a Last Man, . Thus, there are "novelists" who escape the implosion of the novelistic genre: among them, emblematic, the figure of William Faulkner, who escapes the novel by the novel and re-establishes in prose the primacy of the poetic, on the basis of a double negativity: he is thus incorporated into Glissant's canon as a principal figure.

"I am a failed poet," said Faulkner, a phrase duly repeated in the anthology of the Whole-World. These words first indicate a negativity, but immediately turn into a triumphant affirmation. The bankruptcy is not only that of a single individual who seeks in the existing forms of literature the means of his expression. It is the death sentence of the community of Belles-Lettres, but it is immediately redeemed by the invention of a new form. From failure, Faulkner moves beyond the Hegelian impasse, which saw the End of History as equivalent to the End of Art: he thus becomes a figure of Glissant himself, escaping the circle of final purposes in Hegel by reestablishing the open circle, a spiral or paradoxical circle, that moves from the hymn to the unpredictable poetics of the Whole-World: "Every important novel in literature is a poetics, above all a poetics." That's why I think it is wonderful that Faulkner said, "I am a failed poet." He meant by that: "I cannot say what I have to say by means of poetry, but I will say it by the means of a poetics which goes beyond all the given forms of literature" (IL 115).

Faulkner is therefore a double of Glissant: *Sartorius*, in 1999, is an open statement of this identification: Faulkner's novel, *Sartoris*, becomes Glissantian (and vice versa, Glissant's "novel," in a chiasm, becomes Faulknerian) by the mere addition of the letter *u*. The *u* was also the letter that the American writer added to his surname, marking both a distancing from his genealogical filiation and his entry into literature; this addition anticipates in reverse form the Senglis-Glissant anagram.[11]

The Faulknerian negativity is also historical: it is the negativity of the slave-owning South, defeated in the American Civil War. This is the opportunity not for a revanchist and backward-looking elegy but for a revival that opens the door to the future: "the epic has dried up, and yet from this drought has sprung the work of art" (FM 71). In Glissant's interpretation, Faulkner's situation is the opposite of that experienced by the descendants of slaves, in the Antilles and the Deep South—opposite, but still a reflection, since the defeat of the South repeats, by turning it over, the defeat of the slave trade, that radical negativity whose epic must be written and that makes the poetic reconstruction of the Antillean past necessary. When the slave system crumbles in America, it is the masters' turn to be defeated; all, masters and slaves, Blacks and Whites, must then remake their stories and reconstruct their poetics. Slavery, which imposed servitude and extermination, universally defiles the perpetrators with an ineffaceable stain: "It is just as if, for [Faulkner], the blemish of slavery were a moral suffering of Being, let us say, an indelible failing (absence from history), a much crazier burden to bear than the physical suffering of oppression and misery. But also, for the slave owner, an irremediable lack" (FM 99).

Faulkner, Mississippi contradicts the chapter devoted to Faulkner in *L'Intention poétique*, which concluded: "settled in his solitude, the Faulknerian hero (witness and victim) is cut off from the world" (IP 181). On the contrary, throughout *Faulkner, Mississippi* we see Glissant's affinities with his American double in evidence everywhere—that double who, in this second reading, has moved from a closed world to the Whole-World. Everything that Glissant says about Faulkner's recourse to accumulation, listing, mulling over, circularity, the spiral, can be applied to his own work (FM 265ff.). Moreover, in spite of appearances, Faulkner becomes an eminent and poetic moment in creolization (for Glissant, this is the only way to be Creole), as it is defined in *L'Imaginaire des Langues*: "Creolization is something else. It is the entry of systems of poetic images from one language into another" (IL 112). The translations of Faulkner indicate that a poetics is not unilingual or national, that it can migrate and merge into and with other languages:

> With regard to Faulkner, it must be remembered that in his text the web of what is different is translinguistic. The more we translate this work, the more we "understand" it. A poetics can "pass" from one language to another, henceforth, for the sumptuous and inextricable reason that nowadays we can consider all the poetics of all the languages of the world. We think and write in the presence of all the languages of the world. (FM 142)

Faulkner, Mississippi leads to the exact opposite conclusion to that given in *L'Intention poétique*: the American writer makes his sensational entrance into the Whole-World, while one might have thought that everything—themes, origin, filiation, language, and metaphors—restricted him to a single county in Mississippi: "Yes, Faulkner is a moment of world thought" (FM 143).

Faulkner thus escapes prose: in *Faulkner, Mississippi*, he is not related to the genre of the novel but to those whom Hegel and Glissant consider, apart from poetry, as capable of the absolute: "We can conclude that he has renewed, from bottom to top, from the Shack to the Big House, the principles of the epic and the tragic" (FM 137). The new epic is a response to the bankruptcy of the old: "The failure of traditional epic has engendered, before the final prosification, this new form of a properly Faulknerian epic" (FM 140). The prose of Faulkner and Glissant is not prosaic, it does not belong to the genre of the novel.

The collapse of the epic and the tragic into the prosaic abyss, that is, into the End of Literature, is a major theme in Faulkner's work: the Snopes trilogy—*The Hamlet, The Town, The Mansion*—stages this decay on the one hand in terms of content and on the other in terms of style: "Faulkner was reproached for the 'prosaicism' of the last books. But how could he have "forced" his imagination with regard to a reality he only felt obliged to report?" (FM 140) The Snopes family is the paradigmatic figure of the "modern bourgeois epic," utilitarian and materialistic, which ends up invading the space of literature at the expense of tragic or epic heroes: "The Snopes are not responsible, they are too mediocre for that.

They have not lived in the big Woods, they have not signed any pacts, they have not fallen from any high condition" (FM 85). They mark the end of the golden age of poetry, or epic, or tragic: "The county before the Snopes: the golden age that each time we can guess at or dream of" (FM 291). The Snopes are the triumph of prose, imposing on all, aristocrats and slaves, their universe "of the racket, skillfully conducted, with an instinct and a precision of adaptation of which patience is the main asset" (FM 72). They thus represent the dissolution of the Faulknerian epic, and more fully the End of the Literature anticipated by Hegel in his *Aesthetics*: "The entire work is ultimately made prosaic in this Snopian proliferation, which lies at the consummation of the epic and questioning" (FM 85).

The critique of bourgeois prose in Glissant and Faulkner is not only the product of fundamentally aristocratic minds, a product which, in Édouard Glissant, manifests itself everywhere in aesthetic tastes and choices, and which struck me from our first meeting, near the Place Fürstenberg in Paris. This was an aristocratism without hauteur, as it was corrected by an unlimited welcome to all the œuvres and works of art in the world, that is to say by a radical democratism. This welcome to everything and everyone defines Glissant's ethics: "You could not and would not want to erase anyone" (NRM 40).

The rejection of prosaicism is consistent with Glissant's oft-repeated condemnation of realistic literature and the novel, which have become insignificant by their very proliferation. Faulkner's poetic epic represents a fusion of genres that is Glissant's very project. Poetry is bumpy and chaotic, and prose "can be dreamy and tend toward a kind of torment, tournament or drunkenness, without ceasing to be significant. I believe we will invent new genres of which we at present have no idea" (IL 30).[12]

To return to the "failed poet," as Faulkner claimed to be, is also to return the epic and the poetic *after* prose: that is, to reject the fatalism of the end of art and literature. The fictitious county of Yoknapatawpha, which has become prosaic and flat, is nevertheless marked, under the surface and forever, by Faulkner's music. From the double defeat, that of the epic of the South, and that of literature, there arise the unvanquished many (or the single unvanquished spirit of Faulkner himself), reflected in the title of his novel *The Unvanquished*, in English both singular and plural, the unvanquished loner, namely the writer, and the solidary unvanquished, namely the community: "From the defeat raise another victory, called forth by Song" (FM 68). Thus, Faulkner's inextricable place, sited both in the real county of Lafayette where his Rowan Oak residence is located, and in his fictional county, Yoknapatawpha, opens his writing to the breath of the Whole-World, to escape the Hegelian curse of the dissolution of literature and art into prose.

Chapter 9

"The beauty of beauty"

Édouard Glissant was always interested in the visual arts. Painters (and they included several greats: Wolfgang Paalen, Wilfredo Lam, Enrique Zañartu, Matta and Augustin Cárdenas, among others) illustrated his collections of poetry; in turn, he commented on many artists.[1] The field of aesthetics is directly addressed in *Une nouvelle région du monde*, which answers the question: "Are the effusions of art, like that of poetry, the most important?" (NRM 41) For Glissant, art functions in homology with *poétrie*. His reflections about art can be applied to his own work, but also move from art to poetic text and vice versa.

Just as traces of the "primordial poem" appear in Heraclitus or the Sophists, we are familiar with the first drafts of the earliest art: they are buried in the caves of Pech-Merle and Altamira; and in Lascaux, where Glissant had the privilege of contemplating them in the original, despite the closure of the cavern and its reproduction for the commercial use of tourists (NRM 48; his emotion at these images was so powerful that it made him feel ill). In passing, we should note that the modern duplication of the paleolithic image of the cave is the very example of the passage imposed by modernity, from intuitive poetic knowledge to the commercial entertainment produced by the society of the Spectacle and its agents-of-fragmentation. Torn from its place of origin, mechanically reproduced, turned into merchandise, the work of art de-signifies itself, like the novel when it yields to the vice of commercialization.

Lascaux is the very moment of an original fusion: "From this beginning, art would not be an exorcism, would not be a field of recipes, it would be (in each of these works that did not know themselves as works), this joint effort, this tension of differences, insofar as they all hold to the same, and also connect to each other, when the same and the other were not known as given separately" (NRM 48). Lascaux is the first moment of Relation, in which art is not known as art, that is, as a representation separated from its object, but as an integral part of the world, in continuity with it. The (human) Other is not yet separated from the Same; it is the surroundings and the animal: "But let us see that, here, the other, relatable to itself in a transport whose evidence is marked by fusion, was the animal, it was the surroundings, here represented by elected species; it was not those specimens of the same kind as oneself, these similar to oneself, natural rivals, not representable" (NRM 48). Note that Lascaux is not an anticipation of the Whole-World. The prehistoric artist, in solidarity with his one and only tiny community, has no connection with the other tribes dispersed across an immense world.[2] As soon as a relationship is established with another tribe, the need for differentiation arises and everything is spoiled, as everything had been spoiled between Heraclitus and the Sophists, after Socrates. Then arise the desires for possession and domination, as, with Plato, was born the ideomania that wanted to territorialize the world by the depth of the Idea and the True.

After this primordial springing forth comes the fall. What the tribe must renounce is evoked by Glissant in these terms:

> this act of appropriation by the fusion constituted by the first artistic gesture, a divinatory act—that is, accomplished by one sole person, albeit recognized as such by all, an act which was no longer enough to sustain any connivance with the surroundings, an act which made it a matter of urgency to replace it with another act, a very realistic act—that of taking possession. Possession is here imposed and realized not on the basis of the nature of the thing possessed, but in accordance with the mere threatening presence of another possessor. This will be the principle of all utilitarian art. The humanities found themselves, as they emerged from this process, exhorted to dominate the world . . . (NRM 69)

The primordial poem, the first thought, the preliminary painting were thus all buried, some by Plato, some by forgetfulness (it took the contingency of the discovery of Lascaux for this anti-Platonic cave to see the light of day of the consciousness of humanity); literally and symbolically, the original moment is always repressed and forgotten. The painters and sculptors whom Glissant prefers are those who disinter the original moment of art, which is a moment of fusion. One such is Matta: "Thus is the organic unity of Being consolidated: space and thought, communion and otherness, suffering and dawn. Then Matta, with another push, tries to root the human in the Creative Nature where our gaze poses, beyond the given, the various forms of efflorescence" (IP 165). Another is Cárdenas: "The world of Cárdenas is radiant with its particular sun, evokes for us, already, here, centuries and centuries. It is a phenomenon in the world of invented forms, a universe that from its very beginning reveals the organic, the shadow and brightness united, the patience working through the material, the inexhaustible alliance of what is torrid and what is nocturnal" (IP 171). And another is Wilfredo Lam, the painter of an original digenesis that merges differences, the manufacturer of a composite that is an aesthetic creolization:

> From the formation of his universe, Wilfredo Lam tells us that this universe will not be the triumphant place of a uniqueness closed in on itself. It is a Genesis, the birth of an aesthetic world, but this world is already organically composite, and it moves away from the sectarian identities of any absolute. This genesis is a digenesis, a collection of several series of constituents heterogeneous with respect to each other, but the synthesis of which produces the unexpected. (CL 179)

Between the first, unified moment of the artist of Lascaux and that of our contemporary painters, the history (of art) and the process of becoming introduce diversity, the different, the multiplicity of the origins: the Genesis of Lascaux becomes the digenesis of Lam, who finds the primordial poem, but in a new form engendered by the passage of time.

The burial of this truly primal art, namely cave art, works exactly the same way as the burial of the primordial poem with which *La Philosophie de la Relation* opens: "Let us remember: *the poem was buried in a collapse of the earth*" (PhR 15). But this burial is not just an image—in Glissant, metaphors are never just metaphors. In 2008, Glissant returned to the Morne de Bezaudin, which had collapsed and buried the shack where he was born: "Where is this primordial house, our *caye*, whose earthen and wickerwork walls had in the meantime given way to rusty sheet metal, so that it finally did not even look like a dingy storeroom? [. . .] You will not find the shack, this time, among the shoots and the hulls of new cement, already broken, like those skewed tugs that are rowed along. You will never find it again" (PhR 17–18). The initial burial repeats Lascaux: "and at midnight the shack disappeared in this collapse of the earth, like a poem of the first days" (PhR 19). Further on, Glissant returns to this engulfment: "This cabin was finally engulfed in a sinking of the earth. As if all the births to which it had given rise, and mine as a consequence, had returned to a primordial abyss, immediately covered with vegetable banalities organized into a chaos" (PhR 117).

Is this memory of which all material trace has disappeared? Not at all: already on the ruins grows a new vegetation, a bearer of hope—life begins again, negativity is reversed: "The (large) blue caïmatiers and apricots whose skin can be scraped like a softened cork and the unassailable chadecks have mingled in a new beginning of time and earth" (PhR 19). Loss is redeemed into a poetics, life and images intertwine inextricably, everything is caught up in a Moebius strip in which the end coincides with the origin: "The shack of birth is one of the poetics of the place, even if you are still looking for it under the landslides into which it has disappeared. Poetry reveals, in the appearance of the real, what has been buried, what has disappeared, what has dried up" (PhR 102). Collapse and burial are not a death, but a return to the possibilities of the living; the only duty, the only necessity, is to excavate the buried origin, to open it up to the chances of the possible.

The rock in front of the Plague du Diamant bears witness to the same imaginary of collapse and renewal: "We believe that the rock is a point of recovery or rallying, and that it survived the brutal collapse of the ridge that in olden days advanced into the water like the pole of a tiller" (NRM 11). The same rock rises at the very end of *Une nouvelle région du monde*, concluding the treatise with an "open" circularity: "Different aesthetics move toward the Whole-World, and even if they stick together for each one of us, it is the wondrous island, to the *cohée* which that world opened up in its sea and which, one day, it travelled around. We, we, extreme density, multiple meaning, unavoidable extension, bowed to all the winds that keep us upright" (NRM 217). And yet the place, inextricable in its singularity, opens up in an extension that prohibits us from determining and defining its outline.

The cave of Lascaux, the shack buried in the landslide of Morne de Bezaudin, is the living contradiction of the cave of Plato, where man sees only the shadow of the ideas that reside in their Heaven, an Empyrean from which he is separated. For Lascaux is by no means a shadow, or a separation (between the idea and the concrete). The cave is the original moment when art brings about a fusion between man and nature, an appropriation by the hunter of the prey that is not a possession, but a fusion: "These first paintings were *magnetic bonds*" (NRM 48), the very time when the bond of Relation is initiated.[3]

In sculpture, the equivalent of cave art is the art of Easter Island, where Glissant, no longer able to travel by plane, delegated Sylvie Séma to act as his eyes. As the second origin of Relation, of the fusion of Everything with Everything (man, nature, art), the Moai of Easter Island, statues three-quarters buried (the visitor sees only the part that emerges from the earth), testify to the primordial poem: "And this other people of Rapa Nui has gifted us with so many mysterious signs; this people at this moment speak and signify for us, and so many sacred existences, as of that which formerly *marked*, truly, and so secretly, the word, which gathers our quests and our accumulations" (TM 19). The Moai and the petroglyphs are not just a prophecy of the past, but the opening of a possible horizon.

Obviously, once the first moment has been forgotten, art becomes utilitarian and representational, it works, like the epic, as an agent of separation of cultures. The Rousseau of the *Discours sur les Arts et les Sciences* and the Freud of *Civilization and its Discontents* emerge opportunely at this juncture, two crucial figures who in the last analysis are anti-Hegelian in the sense that, for Rousseau, progress is a loss of the state of nature, and for Freud, a constant consolidation of the demands of the superego that leads to ever more apocalyptic returns of the repressed: "Rousseau was right, and Freud also from the point of view of what he in turn calls civilization, and of course the advent of so-called realistic art will begin here, and by a veritable act of possession" (NRM 50). Jean-Jacques and Sigmund are right against Hegel, a man of the Enlightenment, for whom the notion of progress, in art as in human history (but these are for him the same thing), remains intact; and thus the primordial moment of fusion is buried in an almost irremissible oblivion to make room for distinctions of all kinds.

Schematically, ever since Plato, classical aesthetics has identified the True with the Beautiful. Both are reached through the abstraction and purification of appearances and matter. The perfection of the Idea is achieved by a progressive disembodiment of the body and of substance.

Glissant's rejection of Plato's split extends logically to the concordance of the Beautiful and the True: both flee the senses and matter in order to dissipate, moving from the sensible to the intelligible, into a conceptual ideal. The world, contrary to what it is in Plato's cave, is not the deceptive shadow of truth—it is a symbolic and real matter.

Glissant's beauty, like his poetics, is a return to before Socrates. As far as one can draw an aesthetic from the fragments of Heraclitus, his notion of the beautiful is the opposite of the aestheticizing irenicism that characterizes Plato's Beauty. The plastic harmony of Heraclitus is produced by the struggle of opposites: "The opposite is useful, and of all things different is born the most beautiful harmony [and all things are generated by discord]" (D VIII). The same idea, that of a beauty created by the tension of opposites, occurs in fragment D LI: "They do not know how the different concords with itself, it is a harmony against, tensed as for the bow and the lyre." From the contradictory tension of the bow and the lyre and their strings results harmony,[4] whether murderous or musical. But Glissant says exactly the same:

> For we have the intuition of beauty whenever we guess or feel, in an object or an idea or a work of art or a passion, not simply the meeting of the same and the other (this would be a good common place) neither the so-called perfection of forms (this would be a tautology), but the tension of a difference in itself which provides itself with other differences to know and to encounter. And this tension therefore intervenes, in the object or in the work of art, between differences which guess at themselves and differences which will be added later, and then the tension signals the possibility of their meeting. (NRM 45)

What Glissant says is precisely the same, but with one fundamental exception: the contradictory of Heraclitus is not the difference of Glissant; the dialectic at work for Glissant does not draw a contrast between the Same and the Other, but between a *full* difference and other, equally "full" differences. If there is a Glissantian aesthetic, it is not that of an aesthete, that is, someone who forgets the world and its conflicts and chaos to take refuge in the ecstatic raptures of contemplation, as does the romantic artist according to Hegel's critique.

In his *Aesthetics*, Hegel takes into account all the arts, including poetry and literature. Like Glissant, the work of art is for the philosopher a primordial index of thought and the history of consciousness. But Hegel's history of the arts has a final purpose; it begins with the fusional poem and follows an evolution to its end, the free and objective expression of the philosophical subjectivity that is the death sentence of all art. Once this goal is achieved, art is exhausted, and philosophy must take over: ". . . art [that is to say, both painting and literature] remains for us, as far as its ultimate destination is concerned, a thing of the past. *As a result, it has lost for us everything that was authentically true and alive in it, its reality and its necessity as in the past, and is now relegated to its representation.*"[5] This "death of art" opens up the space of infinite commentary, where one no longer creates but merely interprets representations that are in the final analysis so many objects held at a distance, dead and inert:

> For our spiritual needs, art no longer provides the satisfaction that other peoples have sought and found. Our needs and interests have moved into the sphere of representation and to satisfy them, we must call to our aid reflection, thoughts, abstractions, abstract and general representations [. . .]. That is why we are nowadays engaged in *reflections and thoughts about art.*[6]

Just as Western literature found its twilight in the book about the book, art dissolves into the abstract discourse of an aestheticization that comments, but no longer creates (entire swathes of what is called contemporary art verify the accuracy of Hegel's diagnosis).

This condemnation of the reflection in ideas on art (or the book), the art of art or the book about the book, which begins with Sterne and Diderot, and ends in a dazzling firework display (quite literally) in Proust is the very sign of a exhaustion of the possibilities of representation in Europe. In Glissant, like the novel, art leads, through the very development of its techniques, to a representation that is a forgetting of the first, fusional Eden:

> Hence it emerges from the histories of these civilizations that art was widely regarded as an indefatigable enterprise for developing all the various techniques, those for inventing and improving the means and modes of expression; as a result, the history of this art, i.e. of these illustrated techniques, almost ended up becoming the principal occasion of artistic emotion, and works of art have most often contributed (for

example) to perfecting the possibilities of the expression of the
instruments as well as the mastery of them; then the notion
of performance was gradually generalized, and eventually the
rules aimed mainly at facilitating their own, highly polished
adaptation to new intentions or obligations. (NRM 52–53)

Thus, art and literature exhaust their creative possibilities by the representation of their techniques of fabrication. On the other hand, I have
already pointed out how much Édouard Glissant rarely drew attention
to his own technique or literary style, however refined these were. This
refusal of the "book about the book" and of "art on art" is an outright
rejection of Hegel's thesis about the End of Art. The poetic, in art as in
literature, must be reborn after the closure of absolute knowledge, the
Last Man and the End of History. Hegel is rarely wrong, which of course
means that he is very often right; but he does sometimes err: "*Hegel can
be mistaken . . .* [He] raised beauty, she was without vision and without
Relation. He knew history, he recognized it, it remained infirm, without
the memory of any distance that might be close" (NRM 150). On the
contrary, Glissant's open aesthetics heralds a multiplicity of imponderable
futures, born of the very exhaustion of art: "At the end of all, fiction and
narrative will have the opportunity to parade their now commonplace
versions, and their denials of poetry, and will release every one of their
detestations. We find ourselves, perhaps, not far from the time when inconceivable forms and new genres of art, today unsuspected, will disclose
to us the rendezvous of differences and the other secrets of magnetic
bonds" (NRM 103).

For Hegel, the history of art was concomitant with a history of
nations or civilizations, impervious to each other were it not for the
dialectic that means that every stage of consciousness follows on linearly
from an earlier stage; Glissant summarizes the process as follows: "The
harmony of similar things reigned over people's sensibilities, works of
art depart from the revelation of differences, fail to recognize the impact
of conflicts and the overcoming of these differences; these works of art
become the explicit ornaments of the new identities of the peoples and
states and their closed places, and the ceremonial dress of their expan-
sions and their exactions across the world" (NRM 53). Great art is not
a confinement within a certain technique or an art of ornament—these
may have been formerly tribal, ethnic, or (from the seventeenth century,
let us say) "national," but the tension between these differences, what

Glissant calls the "energies of the world"; so there is no moralization of technical virtuosity seen as bad in itself, only the refusal of its self-enclosed obsession: "Artists, to begin with, out of the pleasure of complying with the rules, have never renounced the secret ambition of renewing their link with the energies of the world, and of considering and daring the old original attempt at subjective knowledge by fusion and collusion" (NRM 53). Back to *before* Plato, not via philosophy but by way of art and poetry. And mulling this over is our future.

During our aforementioned stay in Martinique, Glissant had disappeared all day with two of his dearest friends, Prisca Jean-Marie and Georges Guannel, nicknamed Apocal,[7] who were initiates of the virtues of mangrove plants. He came back proud of having somehow taken an exam with them, an exam he had passed, having remembered the names of the plants preserved in the shreds of tropical forest that still strew the island. The episode highlights a feature of Glissant's aesthetic that I would call *ecological*, because nature in all its aspects is a full and integral part of beauty. This ecological aesthetic is radically opposed to that of Hegel, who affirms (against Rousseau and the Romantics) the supremacy of artificial beauty over that of nature: "artistic beauty is superior to natural beauty, because it is a product of the mind. The mind being superior to nature, its superiority is also communicated to its products, and, consequently, to art."[8]

The "inextricable" and "unavoidable" place, and an "intractable" beauty, mean that Glissant's aesthetic never takes refuge in an idealistic sublimation, and has nothing to do with any form of aestheticism:[9] thanks to its ecological side, where the raw and natural beauty of places and elements is taken into account, it is equally anti-Platonic, anti-Hegelian, and anti-Kantian.[10] It is an aesthetic of matter and ancient elements, as well as volcanoes, rocks, landscapes, trees and birds, and rivers and seas. Very rarely does Glissant refer to the beauty of human bodies, that obsession with contemporary mass aesthetics that commercializes sexuality. These first elements, always fused within a singular place, are indeed *stoicheia* from which we can neither extricate ourselves, nor can we trace their outlines or treat them in any representation distanced from its object: the "beauty of the world" is never, in Glissant, the object of an idealistic negotiation or a cult of beauty for beauty's sake. The sublation of Hegelian aesthetic discourse is indicated by the title itself, *Une nouvelle région du monde*: the world, its landscapes, its places possess a beauty of their own, whereas Hegel recognizes beauty only when it bears witness to human action.

Moreover, the region is not what distinguishes between things, but what brings them together; the region mixes up all chronology and all space, whereas in Hegel all art is distinguished by a specific time and place: "a new region which is an era, mixing all times and all periods, an era which is also an inexhaustible country, accumulating expanses" (NRM 24). Hegel would not have accepted this disconnection of art from the chronology and geography and borders of nations, nor the fusion that Glissant brings about through the construction of an immanent region that gathers everything together.

It goes without saying that contemporary art is completely at odds with Glissant's aesthetic conceptions; the body of contemporary painters he loved is situated in the camp of figurative painting, or, like Matta, on the borders of the figurative and the abstract. Valerio Adami, Wilfredo Lam, Victor Anicet, Vincent Van Gogh, and Michel Rovelas, to name but a few, are either explicitly figurative or work with a very thick impasto to create objects that come close to the figurative; they link abstract and concrete, materials and forms, or even link to some reality: that is to say, they reject the abstract separation from place and body that are generally imposed, by fiat as it were, by abstract art, minimal art, and performance art; these are for Glissant another symptom of a modernity that has buried the earliest art.[11]

This view that art has decayed ever since its original paradise was lost could be mistakenly seen as backward-looking. But this is not the case; the negativity of evolution, of the history of art, paves the way for the affirmation of a new positivity, the coming birth of an art of relation which, at the same time, repeats the first moment and opens it up to an unpredictable future. This positivity is yet to come, just like Relation and the Whole-World; it is future as well as past: "And the beauty of beauty rested in this: right from the start, it presents intuition with one of the dimensions of the improbable, rather than already ratifying all truth in some obvious but hitherto concealed form" (NRM 46). Glissant returns to this in *L'Imaginaire des langues*: "The beautiful is a social product. Beauty is an aspiration for everyone. This is the big difference. We do not aspire to the beautiful, we conceive and manufacture it. Aesthetics in the traditional sense is the science of this manufacture. But aesthetics, for me, is the divination of this relation of complicity of which I have spoken" (IL 95). The original divination, complicity, and fusion are repressed, but they must and will return. The beautiful and the true, in Hegel, were the very place, the transcendent place, where author and reader could arrange a meeting; in Glissant, this transcendence has been stirred up, both in the past and in the future, in a first poem and an original art that have brought about (and will do so again) the fusion not only of matter and representation, but of painting and sculpture with the person who looks at them and meditates on them.

Now in literature, as in painting, everything happens as if the history of the arts were doubled in a Moebius strip: in the exhaustion of the novel, that negativity that is now finished, Glissant discerns the coming inspiration and the need for a poetics both very ancient and fully present: a poetics that is inaugural twice over (digenesis is not only the duplication of origin, it is the omnipresence of all times). In the history of art, technical improvement, and the representation that appropriates its object, awakens their converse: the excavations of Lascaux, Easter Island, and the demand for a new art, one that would be fusion and "magnetic bond": "It seems to me that there, in these vicissitudes that spread so widely across the world, a twofold history was woven, the history of civilizations and their tormented dark side, a history which has not yet come to itself, and has not yet caught up with what has happened in the Africas or the isolated Oceanias" (NRM 55).

In the final analysis, Glissant's aesthetic is closer to that of Friedrich Nietzsche: it is an affirmation of the living against Plato's disembodied ideal and against Hegel's materialized Ideal ("art as manifestation of spirit").[12] Neither Nietzsche nor Glissant accept Hegel's view of the End of Art. However, in Nietzsche, the Last Man must be overcome by the super-man, and the latter is above all an artist who brings the joyful vitality of the Pre-Socratics into the present: "History and the sciences of nature were necessary against the Middle Ages: knowledge against belief. Against knowledge, we are now directing art: back to life! Mastery of the instinct of knowledge! The strengthening of moral and aesthetic instincts!"[13] In Glissant, we have no superman, but an eternal return of the same that brings back to life the oldest things—Heraclitean aesthetics, the magnetic bonds of Easter Island, the caves of Lascaux—erasing the art that merely glosses other art instead of truly creating and growing organically. Thus the linearity of history is duplicated by what it has denied and therefore *produced*: the revival of classicism through the Baroque, of the Platonic cave through Lascaux, of theology by heretics, of globalization by global worldliness, of the bourgeois novel by the primordial and future poem, of the slave trade by new landscapes and languages, of philosophy by poetry, of Plato and Hegel by Glissant. The poetic, whether of the Word or of color, is therefore resolutely transhistorical: the oldest past returns to speak to us in our present, and the future performs the divination of the contemporary. Relation is in extent, not in verticality: it makes everything coincide in a radical simultaneity.

Chapter 10

"The dispute, one of the safest
and oldest reinforcements of thought"

Édouard and I often disputed with a passion and vehemence that sometimes went too far; Sylvie Glissant would then come running up to tell me, "You know, that's how Édouard is with his best friends!" And everything calmed down—dialogue and conversation were struck up again. A passage from *La Cohée du Lamentin* illuminated for me, twenty years later—twenty years too late—the meaning of these frequent clashes; for Édouard Glissant, disputation was an essential moment, and not only in his relation to the Other: it was also the very tempo of thought, an exchange in which the quibble-mongers both found themselves enriched; but the dialectic is never purely conceptual, it overlaps with the concrete of the imaginary that connects it to the life of historical and other figures. It should be emphasized that, rather than the Greek word (*Dia-logos*: the moment when the *Logos* displays the digenesis of its origin) or its Latin calque *Dialectica*, the origin of our "dialectic," Glissant prefers the Latin word *disputatio*, a pedagogical medium favored by the theologians and philosophers of the Middle Ages. In Latin, the prefix *dis-* indicates the contradiction, the doubling (and perhaps the *di*-genesis) that marks the threshold of thought (*putare*: to think, to believe, to suppose, that is, something that in itself is ambiguous, not only an affirmation without a reply, but a hypothesis and a tremor).

Dialectica—the third discipline of the Septennium—ends up merging into *Philosophia*; *disputatio* was one of the essential processes for entering into philosophy. *Dialectica* trained students in the finer points of argument; its highest form was the examination of quodlibetal questions, which could be freely proposed either by the master or by the student, and were debated in public before the faculty as a whole. *Disputatio* was oral and shared by the community of scholars; it was akin to Glissant's thought, which involves living presence and sharing, between masters and disciples alike, and solidarity with the *quodlibet*—any question was permitted—which presupposed a fundamental freedom of thought (the *disputatio* would gradually be replaced by the written exam, which privatized debate by restricting it to the student and the professor, whose power became absolute, no longer limited by the public). The dispute, in every sense, is thus perfectly suited to Glissant's thought: "Disputation, *disputatio*, is one of the surest and oldest reinforcements of thought, when thought becomes entangled with the imaginary. This sovereign dispute means that mutual fertilization, as well as fertilization by the other, can occur between elements that otherwise would have remained silent, in their desolate architecture" (CL 66).

The *disputatio* begins, according to Glissant, with oneself:

> I have already spoken of the kind of dispute that there was in my life between this frequentation and my organic relationship with my Antillean brothers. For example, when I was active in the Antillean-Guyanese Front in Paris, well, my French friends did not know anything about this aspect of my life, just as the Antilleans did not know anything about what I was discussing with the poets there. In other words, there was still some sort of established division. (EBR 57)

Thus the double origin, the Antilles and Paris, is right from the start a dialectic—and this can be extended to every digenesis, that is, to all origins: these are never one and pure: the beginning is always a dialectical dispute between antitheses. The points of origin have no fixity or uniqueness; they intermingle in a dynamic conflict (purity and unity always arrive after the fact, when the processes of exclusion of opposites have started to operate). The dialectic of *disputatio* is fruitful; when taken up and mulled over, it always generates a new synthesis: "But as I have already affirmed, and I would like to reiterate it, this established division was not a division: what I was looking for in both cases was this ec-centric discourse and, in both cases, I found resources, help that was of use to this very search. I say this again, because repetition and mulling over help me to dig deep" (EBR 57). The *disputatio* is a dialectical ferment, infinitely open between the *here* of the same and the *there* of elsewhere, of an infinity of creative processes: "Soon, what had been quarrel, dispute or challenge, debate and divagation—you have identified them in the book, but countless other processes could arise—gathers itself boundlessly together and breaks away from the violence, to gauge *here and there* its brilliance" (CL 239). If the dialectic "breaks away from the violence," it is distinguished from the Hegelian dialectic: the latter found serenity only with the advent of absolute knowledge; on the contrary, in Glissant, *disputatio* produces infinite stases, and is therefore endlessly relaunching the processes of history.

Very often, the dialectic of the *disputatio* is present as such in the essays, in the form of a "They say" (TTM 242), a "You say," a "I am often reproached for," a collective of frequently unidentified critics: "Often, when I speak of this expansion of the West, when I say that this sumptuous expansion was also deadly, everyone reprimands me: 'Ah! You are anti-Western!'" (EBR 29). The dialectical contradiction does not remain external to the work: it is an integral part of the theoretical development. Glissant thus recuperates his critics to make them part of his project, and not just as reductive and facile extras, but as active participants in the process of his thought, which thereby establishes its deeply dialectical nature. The work of Glissant is never a self-contained monologue: Europe, which invented the philosophical dialectic, never ceases to dialogue with its Other: they are engaged in *disputatio*.

There can be no question here of going over the whole history of dialectics (which would amount to the history of philosophy). I will therefore simply indicate the moments most relevant to Édouard Glissant's thinking. In Greece, dialogue, including and especially in the negation of the thesis, is the very birth of philosophical discourse. Heraclitus mocks religious practices to replace them with philosophical reflection; Heraclitus, Parmenides, and the Sophists give birth, by negative reaction, to Socratic maieutics; the Platonic rejection of poets establishes a separate autonomy for philosophy, and so on until Hegel. An "old reinforcement of thought," *disputatio*, in the form of dialogue, is indeed the origin of philosophy and perhaps its fulfillment, for example in the dialectic of Hegel.[1] Heraclitus lays its foundations, with his praise of struggle, of combat, of war: from the threshold of philosophy, negativity (the negation of the thesis) plays an essential role in becoming and thinking. And from the first moment, the philosophical voice is not One and transcendent, but bifid, quasi-digenetic, a Heraclitean *Dia-logos* split between negativity and positivity.

(Parmenides attempted to erase this dialectical moment by posing that Being is thought and that non-Being cannot be thought.)

Socrates breaks with the poetic dynamics of Heraclitean negativity, to subdue dialectic to reason by his maieutics. Thus, for Hegel as for Glissant, the dialectic is perverted, because it transfers becoming, the poetic and history into the field of the Ideas. Kojève, in his interpretation of Hegel, makes Socrates the anticipation of the post-revolutionary intellectual: "The Bourgeois [or citizen] seeks the truth; it is the dialectic of Socrates that destroys everything: relativism, critical irony, the use of empty ("abstract") notions of beauty and goodness."[2] We find the same emphasis in Nietzsche, who is here, for once, in agreement with Hegel: "This irreverence of considering the great sages as *types of decadence* was born in me precisely in a case where scholarly and unscholarly prejudice opposes it with the most force: I recognized in Socrates and Plato symptoms of decadence, instruments of Greek decomposition, pseudo-Greeks, anti-Greeks."[3]

Hegel rejects the Socratic break and returns to a dialectic inspired by Heraclitus, a dialectic that he taught:[4]

> Heraclitus is considered as the author of a dialectical philosophy which seizes by thought the incessant becoming of totality; negativity is the instigator of becoming, and the truth of the absolute and the infinite manifest themselves in the unity of opposites. Hegel is certainly a Heraclitean thinker, but he is so as a creator of his own philosophy who understands the march of the *Idea* toward *Nature* and the *History of the Spirit* in a way that could not be that of Heraclitus.[5]

Hegel never presents the dialectic in the ternary form of a Thesis-Antithesis-Synthesis. He attributes this terminology to Kant, and it was developed by Fichte. Hegel reproaches Kantian and Fichtean dialectics for being external to things, to history, to becoming, to beings. On the contrary, the dialectic that he proposes for the dynamics of historical becoming *is* this becoming itself. The Hegelian *disputatio* is no longer a verbal, conceptual, and abstract method for discovering a truth detached from its context; it is the notation of the very often bloody avatars of history: in this respect, the dialectic is simply a passive representation of the upheavals of world—it is content to spell out and understand its successive moments. In the *Encyclopedia*, Hegel defines the three moments of the ternary dialectic: Abstract–Negative–Concrete.[6] But these terms are by no means unique: Hegelian thought is not as rigid as it is sometimes said to be—it is much more flexible than people think, and obeys what Hegel himself called "fluidity" (*Flüssigkeit*).

The Hegelian ternary can take many forms; it just needs each of the three terms to play a part in a coherent set of contradictions. Thus:

Unity–Multiplicity–Totality;
Static (given)–Active–Effect;
Immediate–Suppression–Mediation;
Abstract Being (indistinguishable from nothingness)–Negativity–
Sublimation (surpassing, subsumption)
Identity–Otherness–Totality

In the *Phenomenology of Spirit*, which presupposes the completion of history in and through absolute knowledge, it takes the following form:

Abstract–Negation–Absolute knowledge (fusion of abstract and concrete, thought and history)

The first term, the Abstract, is a given (historical or conceptual), which remains empty as long as it has not been contradicted or denied; for example, the Self of the individual consciousness remains meaningless until it has been contradicted and denied by the Other. The second moment, that of Negation, therefore plays an essential role in the dialectical dynamic. The third moment, that of totalization, is at the same time the "suppression" of one of the first two moments, the "preservation" on the one hand of the first or the second moment, and finally the "sublimation, overcoming or uplift," or sublation, of the initial opposition; using the same example, the conflict between Self and Other is resolved in the community. The process of resolution is called *Aufhebung* by Hegel, a word endowed with a triple or quadruple meaning, as Jean Hyppolite remarks in his French translation of the *Phenomenology*:[7] in French, *Aufhebung* is untranslatable by a single expression. This impossibility of translation confirms Glissant's axiom that "the universal has no language," that it is a "lure"; a universal is in fact defined by its translatability into any language.[8] Hegelian dialectic depends on the Germanic lexicon. Placed "in the presence of all the languages of the world," it undergoes potentially infinite transformations.

We can give the process a penultimate form, one that I would call *structural*, before the name that Glissant confers on it (as we shall see below, he rejects structuralism, and this rejection is consistent with his overcoming of the Hegelian dialectic): Signifier (empty)—signified (the concretization of meaning, the negation of emptiness)—meaning (full).

Does language, as described by Saussure, obey Hegelian ontology, anthropology, and logic? These would then be universal, arising whenever a human being speaks. Every utterance begins from the degree zero of the signifier, a system of negative oppositions, which are filled by being negated first by a content (the signified), and then totalized by a meaning. The meaning sublates the signified, which in turn sublates the meaning. Glissant's anti-structuralism short-circuits the first two moments of the dialectic, signifier and signified, to bring them together in the sign. It retains only the sign and the meaning, in an apparent regression to pre-structuralism, but one that leads to a completely new grasp of the sign.

The Hegelian dialectic is dynamic movement, limitless becoming, although Hegel himself attempted to put it to death with absolute knowledge. The last stage, that of Totality, becomes, to infinity, a Given that a Negativity can challenge in its turn—and this is a perfect calque of Heraclitus's notion of becoming. I will need to come back to this in connection with the subject of the End of History, where Hegel may not be faithful to his own conception of historical dynamics. By translating Hegel's language into his own language, Glissant is on this point more Hegelian than Hegel, proposing a philosophy of wandering without borders. To put it mildly, while challenging ontology and its universality, Glissant is faithful to the Hegelian process of dialectics, from *Soleil de la conscience* onward;[9] he always follows it with great precision. But he retains its process and its dynamic, by changing its content and extending it to all histories, outside the West: "A.L. —It is language that moves in the shape of the master, toward the slave and the master is motionless: in Hegel, the slave is the active subject of history. É.G. —Yes, but if Hegel did consider the very structure of the process, he did not really look at its substance, its content" (EBR 72). In other words, Hegelian dialectics and logic are true; but their meanings are not fixed in absolute knowledge—they have their own dynamic that the philosopher could not or would not predict. Moreover, and this is essential in Glissant's dialectic, there is no longer any foundational and primary category, whereas for Hegel, the terms of the ternary dialectic are primordial and universal ontological categories (hence the need, for Glissant, to leave ontology behind): "In this problematic, no one knows how cultures will react to each other, nor which of their elements will be preponderant, or seen as such, beyond the determinations of power and domination. In this full-meaning (*plein-sens*), all cultures are equal in Relation. And, all together, they cannot be viewed as its primary elements"[10] (PR 177). The primary factors, lying outside the grasp of any concept or idea, are the elements of the ancient cosmos, the imaginary of which Glissant develops.

I will give a few essential examples of this substitution; by modifying the terms of the dialectical dynamics, Glissant retains its form (the "process"), but transforms its meaning entirely. Thus, the initial unity is questioned and replaced by diversity: the One, whether divine or not, is problematic: "The thought of the One, which has so magnified things, has distorted them too. How can we consent to this thought, which transfigures, without thereby offending or diverting diversity? For it is diversity that protects us and, if found, perpetuates us" (TTM 157). In parallel (and *logically*), primal Being is replaced by beings:

> Being is a great, noble and incommensurable invention of the West, and especially of Greek philosophy. The definition of Being very soon, in Western history, leads to lead to all kinds of sectarianism, of metaphysical absolutes, fundamentalisms whose catastrophic effects we are witnessing today. I think it must be said that, now, there are merely beings, that is, particulate existences that correspond or come into conflict, and we must abandon the claim to any definition of Being. (IPD 162)

Glissant is here being anti-Hegelian: for the German philosopher, the initial term is always empty of all (abstract) content, and the second term denies this abstraction. Starting from a fullness (of meaning), beings, difference, Glissant goes beyond Hegel's ontology and sets sail for an ontics.

The third and final example is that of the identity of the person. The first term, in Hegel, was the Self becoming aware of its identity in *Selbstbewusstsein*. Glissant replaces this with notions of community, people, nation. Identity in his work is shared, multiplied, and diversified, in contrast, first, with Hegel's Self, unified in his self-consciousness, and then with the self of Romanticism, the Intellectual, the beautiful soul. Identity-as-shared is the contrary of the atomization of human subjects that Hegel reabsorbs into the state and that for the romantic ends in self-contemplation and the ivory tower.

From then on, Glissant's relation to Hegel, and more generally to any culture that preceded Glissant's intervention, falls within *Aufhebung*: the dialectic is preserved, but its terms are sublated by a first substitution. The radical nature of this change must be emphasized: the attempt to understand the plurality of histories (of cultures, of arts) no longer has the truth of absolute knowledge as its destination, but aims rather to connect the full differences of the world (of beings). The Hegelian logic of contradiction is sublated by the connecting of differences, in a fundamental modification that turns the whole of Glissant's thought not into a contradiction of what preceded it in philosophy, but into an Other of thought that is not trapped in a surreptitious repetition of what it is supposed to be contradicting. The contradiction is sublated by the tension of the differences: "In the world, there is no opposite. I accept the dialectic of differences, not the dialectic of opposites, because the dialectic of opposites presupposes that there is a truth over there, and that its opposite is over there. Whereas I do not believe that there is a Truth . . ."[11] The differences here are not those between one being and another, or between one signifier and another (a negative difference, without substance, which is the negative of Saussure and the "differance" of Jacques Derrida), but between one being and the other, one thing and the other, from a specific place, inextricable from other places, inevitably interwoven with them: "The difference lies at the vital beginning of the movement, not the identical, or identity. [. . .] Thus, Relation weaves its relationship not only between two or more of these varieties (or identity), if there are any such, but more generally between everything and everything else, and in the domain of the unpredictable" (NRM 63). From this meditation arises a new definition of difference, an essential component of Relation, just as original as this latter, the primary element not of thought, but of the world: "The secret of difference is that it is the first to deal properly with the variations of identity, in other words the diversity of the living. It is certainly not the same and the other, or their accord, that weave relation, but rather the different, which drives the leaps and bounds of the Whole-World and allows same and other to be" (NRM 103).

At this point we can propose the content of Glissant's dialectic, which is at once a radicalization of Hegel's and a surpassing of it, beyond Being and absolute knowledge.

The Different Relation—The Whole-World

The first characteristic of this new ternary structure is that its terms can be commuted: there is neither temporal linearity nor any privileging of the prime element here, quite the opposite of the Hegelian dialectic. The first term has a series of synonyms: diversity, multiplicity, beings, places, people, cultures, etcetera. The second and third terms, though they can be permuted with the first and between themselves, do not, however, have synonyms: this indicates that they are the key words of the dynamics of this "wandering" dialectic, modifiable in content, but not in the way they operate. Finally, the totalization of the Whole-World is not a summa or a closed philosophical system: it remains open to unforeseeable development. Glissant's Relation, as a dialectic of differences, breaks with Hegel. Absolute Knowledge returned circularly to its point of departure, the simple, sensible certainty: from there, the history of metaphysics, ontology, philosophy, and history itself arrived at their coronation.[12] This point of arrival becomes the starting point for Glissant: ontology, the metaphysics of the One and of Being have exhausted their resources—we must revive the movement of thought and of becoming, starting from quantified differences and beings.

There is in Glissant a general refusal of any given, which is never a determination with an inevitable destiny: each time, the given must be denied, not for the passing pleasure of subversion, but to generate a new positivity. Being, the One, closed systems, universals, colonialism, the slave trade, empires, nations, the history of the West, *everything* must be reinterpreted, and then denied so as to find the resources of a different becoming. In other words, the first moment of the Hegelian dialectic is stripped of the privilege of priority: negativity can be commuted with the primal affirmation.

However, as in Hegel, active negativity always gives rise to an affirmative answer that sublates it. This is the case, for example, with colonization and its consequences (Glissant here undoes all the ideological apparatus of postcolonial studies, where the consequences of colonial intervention are always catastrophic and provide beautiful souls with an opportunity to intone the repetitive plaint of resentment, revenge, and lamentation): "The colonial intervention of the West, discoveries and conquests, has so obviously allowed and facilitated (in spite of the initial intention of its enterprise and despite its desire to separate, to set up borders) the rallying of the Whole-World, that we can suppose that it lies partly at the source of the appearance of the literatures of Relation" (PhR 43).

Glissant's negativity, however, differs from Hegel's; historical negation and its Hegelian totalization (its sublation) always bears on the One: "one" nation, "one" idea, "one" moment in History; this unification ensures the coherence of the linearity that the German philosopher assumes in the historical process. In Glissant, on the contrary, it is multiples and differences that are denied and surpassed by many diverse things. The historical moments are heterogeneous and numerous in their chronology and their geography, they lie outside any temporal or territorial homogeneity: the West is always doubled by its Other, universality breaks up in the sharing of languages, Being dissolves into beings, the root—identity is composed by the relation—identity, globalization gives birth to the possibility of its opposite (globality [or "worldification"—*mondialisation*]), epic defeat is the birth of the community, etcetera.

In truth, in the surpassing of Hegel's linearity-unity, there are the prolegomena of a fundamental revolution of thought: if we follow Glissant into the nonlinear, multiplicity, diversity, then there are, we understand, not only many different poetics, but also *philosophies* in the plural, and not just one Philosophy. For example, there is the philosophy of the fictitious Batoutos (because they are also thinkers, though invisible), which incorporates and transcends (the) Western Philosophy by Relation and the Whole-World: "This nation has, so evasively, proposed, we believe, that it verify the source of Time, the unhoped—for place from which the youth of the universe has grown" (S 30).

From the beginning, the dialectic always supposes a binary opposition, two positions, two philosophers dialoguing with and opposing each other; from the binary opposition there follows the synthesis that suppresses this first binary opposition by dissolving the antinomy. Just as the *disputatio* was mixed with the imaginary, the dialectical binaries abound in Glissant, but they are posed only in order for them to be surpassed:

> The imaginary first. It works in a spiral: from one circularity to another it encounters new spaces, which it does not transform into depths or conquests. Nor does it stop with those binaries that have seemed to occupy me so much throughout this book: extension–filiation, transparency–opacity . . . the imaginary is made complete in the margins of any new linear projection. It

> forms a network and constitutes a volume. Binaries are never anything but commodities from which to weave it. (PR 216)

In a note, *Poétique de la Relation* makes a partial listing of these antitheses, of which I here give some terms by way of an example: "Linearity–Circularity," "History–(hi)stories," "Totality: Relation," "meaning (linear), full-meaning (*plein-sens*) (in circularity)." These binaries are subject to three types of logical and grammatical connections: "In this litany, the comma (,) indicates a relation, the dash (–) an opposition, the colon (:) a consecution" (PR 236). Glissant's synthesis or totality is a leap ahead of and out of the dialectic, "Thought of the Other: –Other of thought" (PR 236), an epistemological break in the materialization of his poetics. On this point, Glissant could not be more precise: his dialectic is a sublation of all binaries, integrating them into the dynamics of a multiple real; in this way, dialectical binarism is subjected to a permanent reassessment and sublation: "The dialectic would have no occasion to enter into what we call the real, if it restricted itself to its constituent bifidities, for example the for and the against, the positive and the negative, the master and the slave, Being and nothingness. The humanities of today call on the unexpected (wild) dialectics of multiplicity" (PhR 67–68).

Hegel's *Aesthetics* ends with the dissolution of the transitional link between the author and his reader; their ephemeral union is replaced or sublated by an abstract communion; the philosopher and his reader are reabsorbed into the generality of the Beautiful and the True, posited as indestructible absolutes: "If, as regards this essential point [testing the fundamental concept of the beautiful and art by subjecting it to the scrutiny of thought], I have succeeded in satisfying my readers and the bond which was formed between them and myself must now dissolve, I will permit myself to express the hope that we will be more closely united by the far more indestructible link between the beautiful and the true."[13] These absolutes are a *transcendent third*, henceforth charged with connecting author to reader, where spirit ends in its simultaneously conceptual and concrete totality. Hegel is here closer to a Platonic idealism than perhaps he would like. This conclusion raises the question of sharing out (and therefore of Relation): do we always need to move into the abstract realm of transcendence in order to commune in truth or in beauty?

The transcendent third, the mediation between self and Other, authors and readers, peoples and other peoples, is a social and linguistic structure without which it seems impossible to live together, to communicate and to converse: for two (or more) singularities to talk to each other, for languages, communities and places to enter into relation (with a small "r"), mediation is necessary. Without it there reigns the law of the strongest where every Other disappears.

However, in accordance with his anti-Platonism, Glissant rejects any form of transcendence: "The only transcendence possible at present is that of Relation."[14]

There is a difficulty here, which I expressed in my first article on Glissant: "When there is no instance that transcends the old particularities, there immediately arise the murders provoked by the narcissism of the smallest difference, the genocides of classes, races [of ethnic groups and religions] in which the twentieth century has specialized: a historical avatar that is not specific to Westerners alone."[15]

In 1990, the transcendent third was the occasion of a dispute ("Homeric" as Patrick Chamoiseau, who often played an active part in the *disputations*, called it) between, on the one hand, Henri Meschonnic and myself, and, on the other, Édouard Glissant: Relation, he affirmed vehemently, as immanence and utopia, dispensed with all transcendence, against ontology and its absolute root, and for beings and their rhizomatic relationship.[16] Henri Meschonnic and I emphasized the need for a third party that allowed relations; with utmost vehemence, Édouard affirmed Relation as transcendence without mediation. He did this without any naivety: Glissant was very aware that, in historical reality, for example the bloody struggles that followed the decomposition of Yugoslavia, only a real force could prevent the bloody struggle of antagonisms: "If you take two communities that are fighting in the name of a single root and you put an army between them, of course they will stop fighting. But the day this army leaves, they will start fighting again in the name of the same principles" (IL 81).

The mediation of the transcendent third is therefore ephemeral: it is an ever-new task to protect the two parties from the violence to which they will, at the first opportunity (the absence of a law that will transcend their differences), resort again. If he proposes Relation as a remedy for violence, it is not in the present of our outbursts, but in the future; Relation can only replace transcendence if it is understood as utopia:

But if you manage to make ever more effective the maxim that
I can change by changing with the other, without destroying

or distorting myself, maybe at that moment you will manage to work on the subject of oppositions between unique roots and you will be able to persuade both sides to drop their weapons. This is what I call utopia and what I call the action of poetic thought on the world. I think that poetic thought today is as likely to succeed as political thought. (IL 81)

Relation is an optative in perpetual becoming; its destiny is to supplant, through a poetic imaginary, all the dialectics of contradiction, all the militant and aggressive ideologies and policies, so as to establish a world in which all differences would finally dialogue.

Chapter 11

"We do not name Relation"

There are two watchwords in Glissant's thought, the only ones that are, from a certain moment in the work onward,[1] capitalized, the only ones that do not have any plural: Relation and Whole-World, the process and its realization. These watchwords are true universals that aim to overturn the conceptual and linguistic limits of all the other universals whose illusory nature Glissant has endeavored to demonstrate. There is only one Relation as a principle and one Whole-World as the content of this principle. Glissant thus takes again the singular form of the universal Greek ("Every man is mortal'), to extend it to all places and all times.[2]

All the other notions, to take up the list in the *Philosophie de la Relation*,[3] can be correlated with the two key words: Relation and Whole-World are the *points de capiton* where the rhizomic fabric of thought is woven; the fact that they are not, in the *Philosophie de la Relation*, included in the listing shows that they are the organizing principle behind it. Relation is the only category in Glissant's thought (in the philosophical sense of the term), and this presupposes not only that it encompasses universally and totally any other category, but also that it is in its own right the very state of the world. As Jacques Coursil rightly says, "Relation has no outside."[4]

Of course, relation did not wait for Glissant to be practiced, then thought: it is the form of a fundamental syntax, present from the moment when man began to speak, the form of predication ('Socrates is a man"), which we use every minute, and without which it would be impossible for us to speak, to think, to communicate anything. Nor did it wait for Glissant to be thought: in philosophy, from Aristotle and his doctrine of the categories of Being,[5] up to Kant (and beyond) and his critique of the categories of judgment, it has played an essential role in predication, which correlates a subject to what it is. Kant modified this ontological aspect of relation and reduced it to a problem of logic, which Bertrand Russell and Alfred Tarski, among others, explored in logic and mathematics.

This very long and rich history of relation, which merges with the entire history of humanity, is submitted by Glissant to a fundamental shift, of which is important to take the measure, given the centrality of the keyword in his system.[6] Let us emphasize Édouard Glissant's originality: in the whole history of thought, *he is the only philosopher to have made Relation the unique notion that subsumes all others*, the thought that allows us to think everything and to think the Whole. In this he differs from all other philosophers, who differentiate the categories that are subordinate to Being or to beings and enumerating its or their qualities: in philosophy or logic, relation is never first, it is an addition to Being, its exteriority.

I will first highlight what I call Glissant's logion,[7] that is, a fundamental statement, which is mulled over, with many variations, but remains fundamentally stable. He says: "Relation is here understood as *the realized quantity of all the differences of the* world, without excepting a single one" (PhR 42).

One variant substitutes "beings" for "differences," reorienting (quite logically) the problem of quantity to the erasure of Being. The most significant (and most surprising) commutation, however, affects the very subject of predication: often, "Whole-World" replaces "Relation." Here is just one example of many: "The totality of the Whole-World is thus the realized quantity of all the differences of the world, without even the most uncertain of them being detachable from it" (TEFV 19).

Another interesting variant substitutes "globality" or "worldness" (*mondialité*) for Relation:

> F. N. –You write, in *Poétique de la relation*, that "globality is the finite and realized quantity of the infinite detail of the real."

> É. G.–Yes, that's against universality. In Western cultures, in general, the greatness of these cultures resides in trying to project a universalist image that surpasses all individuals. Now, what I'm saying is that in a system of relation, there is no need to surpass all individuals; it is necessary to bring them into contact under conditions of equality, justice and balance. And

consequently, as long as any detail of this relation is missing, this relation will not exist; on the contrary, we know that we can define universality without going through the details. For example, negritude is defined without going through the concrete situations of Negroes in the world, who are not the same, who are different. So, I think that the notion of universal, which was a generous notion, was also a deadly notion, because the detail, the infinite quantity of details, is what constitutes the Whole-World.[8]

We can then replace the realized quantity of differences or beings by the existing multiplicity of the "detail': "The detail is not a descriptive landmark, it is a depth of poetry" (PhR 28). "We are entering now, on the contrary, into an infinite detail, and first of all we conceive of its multiplicity everywhere" (PR 27).

Is this series of synonyms a negligence, a vagueness in thought? No: we have seen, repeatedly, how carefully Glissant weighed his language, even down to the smallest punctuation signs. Relation, Whole-World, differences, detail, globality—could they be homologous, and as such interchangeable? If they are not, what allows such a commutation? In short, I will say that at a certain moment, the realized quantity is considered from the dynamic angle of the process that produces it, namely Relation; when this is replaced by the Whole-World, the consideration becomes that of the outcome of the process; when the different or the detail intervenes, the angle is the angle of what exists before our eyes, of beings. There is only an apparent confusion: the process and its actual realization can and must be assimilated into a thought of fusion. Moreover, if we consider them from the point of view of their becoming, it is no longer paradoxical that process and result should be mixed: "The Whole-World is total in the sense that we all dream of it as such, and its difference from the totality still lies in the fact that its whole is a becoming" (TEFV 19). Thus, the realized quantity is the call for a *not yet realized* quantity that will befall it, where the former differs from itself in Time: "The difference of the Whole-World (from itself) is that it is a totality that is not realized but is visible in the future" (Ibid.).

Relation and/or the Whole-World, therefore, do not function according to the rules of a traditional philosophical predication that fixes a predicate to an attribute ("Socrates as man is mortal")—it is governed by a changing dynamic. A fragment from Gilles Deleuze in the anthology of the Whole-World sheds the most relevant light on the way in which Glissant thinks and practices predication (Relation, the Whole-World):

> Predication is not an attribution. The predicate is the "execution of the journey," an act, a movement, a change, and not the state of the traveler. The predicate is *the proposition itself*. And just as I cannot reduce "I travel" to "I am traveling," I cannot reduce "I think" to "I am thinking," thought not being a constant attribute, but a predicate as the incessant passage from one thought to another. (TEFV 24)[9]

In the predication "Relation is the realized quantity of all differences," each word is carefully weighed and supported by an immense philosophical and logical tradition, with the aim of reconstructing it from top to bottom. First, the notion of quantity: a category of Being according to Aristotle, it is contrasted with the notion of quality, as beings are contrasted with Being and essence with the accident. In "classical" philosophy, quality is the truth in ideas of quantity. To take Hegel's example: "The quantum [quantity] is no longer an external or indifferent determination; it is suppressed as such, and quality, by which a thing is what it is, constitutes the truth of the quantum, i.e. being a *measure*."[10] However, Glissant seeks to detach beings from their concept (of being). If quantity is no longer related to the being that measures it, then it opens up to excess (*démesure*) and to beings. Beings are "realized quantities of differences," not the "qualities" that founded the conceptual categories of predication in Aristotelian logic. Categories no longer qualify Being—they quantify beings. To take one example, Glissant's categories unfold to infinity the inextricable difference of places and their perception: "Landscapes as categories of beings. [. . .] But there are presciences that turn a landscape within us and without us, here and there, yesterday and now and tomorrow, in the likeness of this or that. It is then (within us) these categories of beings that unmake and remake the varieties of the real" (CL 92).

The word "differences" in the logion is laden with an immense genealogy. Let us first eliminate the false synonymies, and then follow the rhizomic tissue by which Glissant defines it. Difference is not structural difference (in the manner of Saussure and of Derrida, who proposes a kind of hyper-Saussureanism), that is, a purely negative difference (without substance or content) between one signifier and the next; it is not a difference of otherness that separates, individual by individual, the Same and the Other; it is not contradiction or Hegelian negativity, an antinomy of ideas, even if the latter are concrete; it is not a difference between being and being, or (as psychoanalysis would wish) between unconscious and unconscious.

Philosophy usually couples identity and difference in a dialectical opposition, where identity is a fixed point and a beginning that allows a differentiation that comes *next*, chronologically speaking. It is quite different in Glissant: identity (in the philosophical, psychological, political, or bureaucratic sense—the "identity card"), at first glance, differs from itself, it is a dynamic composite that from its very beginning is crossed by differences: "Identity is now not only permanence, it is a capacity for variation, yes, a variable, whether controlled or panicky" (PR 155–156).[11]

Relation and difference sustain the dynamics of change (of becoming) in predication, and precede or are simultaneous with identity:

> Most ways of thinking about difference have viewed it as just what separates, the gap, and what at first invites, a relationship or covenant, and perhaps what connects and links, too, Relation. This is so in Segalen, one of the most generous founders of difference, and in Deleuze, the imperceptible diffuser. [. . .] The differences [. . .] could not have played this game of negotiations (in French: *tractations*)/attractions, if they were not themselves and first of all living and changing realities preserved from the dismal ticking of the machine. (NRM 99–110)

Difference, before identity: that is what is constitutive and comes first. "In Diversity, too, difference constitutes, brings closer. But it does not govern, or governs only if the elements assembled are peculiar to themselves. The difficulty is that these elements are also all difference, and that nowhere do we find the absolute identical, which is sometimes separated within itself by blind bays of difference" (PhR 104). Difference is an ever-present tension between the Other and the Same, between distinction and fusion; the same applies, to take just one example, to the truly primordial art of Lascaux: it is "this joint effort, this tension of differences, insofar as they all hold to the same, and also connect to each other, when the same and the other were not known as given separately" (NRM 48).

The different becomes, in the literal sense, the very force of be-coming—it empties the immovable fullness of the Same and the Other: "The secret of difference is that it is the first to deal properly with the variations of identity, in other words the diversity of the living. It is not the same and the other, or their accord, that weave Relation, but rather the different, which drives the leaps and bounds of the Whole-World and allows same and other to be" (NRM 103–104). Difference "contributes to fusion as well as to distinction" (PhR 101).

In a vertiginous passage, "which marks the variegated complexity of the question" of *Une nouvelle région du monde*, Glissant redefines difference in its interplay with the Same and the Other, both of which are right from the start taken up in exchange and mingling; Relation, as a unique category, stirs up any other category; in it, same and other are permuted constantly without losing their irreducible character: "The different is not that which differs, or which has differed, but that which, added to the other, or proposed to the other, and coming from the same, being no longer the other nor the same, without ceasing to be the other, and consequently, and for itself, the same" (NRM 107).

Further, Glissant goes beyond the couple form/substance essential to Aristotle, and in the last analysis necessary to a whole swath of philosophy: "And what in the end realizes the quantity of these differences? Only this, it(self) alone, without any need to suppose in addition or to evaluate a form or a substance that would *create meaning*" (NRM 43). Substance, just like form, are variables (*pace* Aristotle); their coupling is not immo-bile: "substance varies, without ceasing to be itself. To be a self" (NRM 107). Hence, in the logion, the epithet that always accompanies quantity, namely *realized*: this nuance is necessary to avoid reducing quantity to the idea, and to suggest that the object of thought is no longer the Platonic Heaven of Ideas, but things, peoples, books, *objets d'art*, landscapes of the world as they exist. When the different replaces quantity, the same is true: beings are not defined in relation to any essence, but by their always permutable connections (Relation).

Thanks to its definition as the realized quantity of all differences without exception, Relation proposes a universal against the "bad" uni-versals, those that are "lures," which have only the appearance of the universality; it is a totality that erases and replaces them:

Relation is made up of all the differences in the world and
we should omit none, not even the smallest. If you forget the
smallest of the differences in the world, Relation is no longer

Relation. What do we do when we believe this? We formally question the idea of universality. The universal is a sublimation, an abstraction that allows us to forget small differences; we drift toward the universal and we forget these small differences, and Relation is magnificent because it does not allow us to do that. There is no relation made of big differences. Relation is total, otherwise it is not Relation. This is why I prefer the notion of Relation to that of the Universal.[12]

The logion can be applied to the work itself—we can elevate it to the rank of theory and method of interpretation of Glissant's text as a whole: bringing its aspects into relation through mulling over and amplification of the work as a whole, the differences (and mingling) of literary genres, the realized quantity of publications in their signifying materiality, the need to consider the work, always, as a whole: everything here points to a way of reading applicable to Glissant himself. The books in Glissant's œuvre are indeed the realized quantity of differences, perpetually and dynamically particularizing themselves through repetition. But this itself is just a moment that must be surpassed: the mulling over is wrapped around itself, sweeping the Whole-World up in its dynamics. Glissant is often reproached for not giving "examples" of his philosophy, which is seen as still just an abstraction; but the books themselves are the "examples" of thought, as well as being literally, everywhere and always, seeded with details that give concrete shape to the argument (the Rocher du Diamant, the caves of Lascaux, his birthplace shack, etc.).

Glissant's logion is remarkably stable, but it also generates a contradiction or an antinomy so inextricable that it seems impossible to reduce them:

Insofar as our consciousness of Relation is total, i.e. immediate and immediately bearing on the realizable totality of the world, we no longer need, when we refer to a poetics of relation, to add: the relation between what and what? That is why the French word "Relation," which works a little like an intransitive verb, cannot for example correspond to the English term "relationship." (PR 39–40)

Relation is full of all the differences and all the details (objects) of the world, but it is also intransitive, thus replacing the Being of metaphysics, and refusing its transcendence.

In *Les Entretiens*, Glissant intensifies the paradox in two stages; first, he proposes a radical absence of figure for Relation: "In this case, what is called 'Relation'? *We do not name Relation*, inextricably because it is unnameable. Why is it unnameable? It is unnameable because it is unpredictable. Nowhere could there be any question of arriving at the very principles of the reality of the World Relation, this would be a vain project" (EBR 102). This unrepresentability absolutely contradicts Glissant's logion that defines it: by definition, a "realized quantity" is represented or representable. Between the quantity of different things and the unnamable, there is a hiatus that no logic or representation can fill. Paradox or contradiction, Relation, if it is unfigurable, refutes the Whole at which all of Glissant's work aims.

But the antinomy can be resolved by what Glissant says of it: in the first place, if the relation is a future, a becoming or a utopia, it is logical not to capture it in some figure that would numb it: by definition the unpredictable has no visible figure, and the unpredictable is unnamable. Realized in the imaginary and the quantities of the world, Relation is at the same time an expectation that defers its advent. The relation is simultaneously a finite and real set, and an infinite without limit and without figure.

Relation is what takes the place of the Platonic and Hegelian transcendences, the True and the Beautiful that allowed the author and the reader to communicate. The sharing made possible by the transcendental third had a content: the abstract of the beautiful and the true in one case, the abstract of truth and absolute knowledge in the other.

Quite logically, Glissant frees Relation from the principles of truth and reality that govern fiction ("Western" fiction, he says, but we can generalize and add philosophy): "In Western literatures, writers always tried to proceed by diving deep down: to the real, to the truth of the real [. . .]. In the perspective of what I call the World Relation, this attitude, this option, this preoccupation fall away *because Relation has no reality principles of reality, it only has principles of relation*" (EBR 102: my emphasis). This relation to the real, whether through realism or symbolism, was already criticized in 2005, at the Carthage Symposium: "the practice of writing, from realism to romanticism, to symbolism, was a practice of direct relation to reality, whether this reality was imitated, as in realism, or symbolized, as in symbolism, as with Baudelaire, or else taken as the basis for the expression of feelings"[13]

At the same time, Relation knows no prime elements, no *stoicheia*, no atoms that, when assembled, would produce it: "No primary elements enter into Relation." A primordial principle would reduce it to an ontology: "Any primary element would summon the shadow of Being" (PR 175). It is therefore logical to affirm that, on its speculative side, Relation has no examples: "Relation cannot be 'proved' because its totality is not approachable—but imagined, conceivable by a shift of thought" (PR 188). From then on, the ordering of categories can be upset, displaced from any hierarchy, purified of any linearity, as from its anchoring in a particular filiation or nation: "Relation, as we have emphasized, does not play on the primary, separable or reducible elements—in which case it would have been reduced to a mechanism that could be dismantled or reproduced" (PR 186). Thus, Relation straddles the unfigurable and virtuality on the one hand, and the eminently figurable (beings, differences) on the other.

This falsely tautological refusal to define Relation by something other than itself is in line with the challenge to all philosophical effort since Plato. Something very ancient (from before Plato) returns, but transformed by this very return into our present. The True of ideas is reframed by intuition: "I believe that we need to return to the time of the Pre-Socratic philosopher poets: to multiply nuances and intuitions, to avoid the Truth that garrotes and that kills" (EBR 103).

From *L'Intention poétique* onward, the unnamable appears in the guise of the impossible, and we can recognize in these lines a first approach to the paradox of relation, here stated in the tension between the poetic absolute and the relative:

> The poet has legitimized his privilege of provoking the impossible (for example, the One). For, in its relation to the impossible, the poetic opens up to all possible relations: to an increasingly realized approach to man's condition in the world (for example, onto totality. Totality is possibilities relation to which, in the tortured gap of the world, the unfulfilled dream of the One is authorized). The poetic absolute is thus extended in the relative that is each time conquered anew. (IP 62–63)

This impossible figure can be compared to the Relation of the Unconscious: "The Real is impossible"—because it is not representable—says Lacan. This is no place to warble tremulous ditties on the unsayable, which does not interest Glissant, and which must be distinguished from the unspeakable. The unsayable is always the governance and the determining final purpose of the past that imposes itself on what we can do and say, while the unnamable is the without-figure of the future.

From *L'Intention poétique* onward, Glissant was attentive to psycho-analysis, the predominant field of the humanities in France. The European man knows, "with psychoanalysis, that he is in charge of a fallow 'slope'" (IP 27). Psychoanalysis occupies an important space in *Le Discours antillais*; but what Glissant focuses on is not the unconscious subject of psycho-analysis, a practice that takes individuals one by one in the treatment, and thereby fits into European individualism. Glissant is preoccupied above all with that which forms links, a community, a group: that is to say, always, with the imaginary, as opposed to the individual reality of the subjects and unconscious desire. For Freud and Lacan, the unconscious is what separates, and is unrelated to anything: "There is no (sexual) relationship," Lacan repeats, and I put the sexual in parentheses; for the unconscious, unfigurable, can only be the unrelated, absolutely. In this sense, Relation, which is entirely a link, is the logical and imaginary opposite of the notion of the unconscious. Hence Glissant's distance from Lacan: "Lacan places himself in the perspective of Being as Being. And it seems to me that this is a point to question" (EBR 99).[14]

A second plane of contrast is that of becoming. Destiny, in Freud and Lacan, takes a shape molded by the determinism of the signifier and its parades. Moreover, it is the future of individuals, not of groups, whatever they may be, that is at stake in the treatment: "*Wo Es war, soll Ich werden*," "Where it was, I must come to be" or "Where it was, where it is no longer because I know that I thought it, the subject must come to be."[15] In the final analysis, the purpose of the treatment is to accept that we cannot do anything about the lack of relationship; it is a question of learning to carry this cross with humor and a light heart, which is certainly not a negligible result. And always, the unconscious is the past that weighs on us, not the future that opens into the inspiring breath of Relation.

In Glissant, the unconscious emerges from the collective, from what says "no" to the atomization of the individual, without being confused with the Jungian archetypes; this shared dimension of instinctual drives is affirmed in *Le Discours antillais*: "We believe in the repercussion of socio-historical data not only on beliefs, morals, ideology (the so-called superstructures), but also, *in certain conditions*, on the formation of a field of 'common' instincts that could then be called the unconscious of a community" (DA 285). In addition, in Glissant's view the unconscious is linked to a place that specifies it: "Thus, what Freud has designated as It [Trans.: the Id] works in us [the Antilleans], like an It-There" (DA

291). In the final analysis, the place, by its *unavoidable, intractable, inextricable* character, being impossible to reduce by analysis, description, or formalization, replaces in Glissant the Freudian unconscious and the Lacanian Real. But the place, too, is cleaved by an oxymoron, since the landscape, the central motif of Glissant's poetics is, in addition to its irreducibility, just as much a thing, being, quantity (therefore calculable or "extricable"): "Places are repeated from one to the other, there is no limit to Relation, although it is above all a realized (finite) quantity of the different things in the world" (PR 46).

But the most salient feature of this difference from psychoanalysis is becoming: in Glissant, the return to or from the past is by no means the moment in which we abandon ourselves to all destinies, even those of the parades of the signifier. The past is the opportunity to seize the renewal and revival of poetics and the world through Relation. Here, Glissant is in opposition to Freud and Heidegger,[16] from whom Lacan borrowed in his notion of the parades of the signifier. Heideggerian man, "spoken by language," Lacanian man, almost entirely subject to the logical play of the symbolic, is the fixity of a destiny, where all the pathways to the future are already drawn out in advance. Glissant will have nothing to do with this fatalism.

Glissant anamorphose the Freudian unconscious and the Lacanian Real by opacity. This notion appears in *L'Intention poétique* in a study of William Faulkner, an author who "proves that opacity is fundamental to disclosure; that the opacity, the resistance of the other, is fundamental to his knowledge; that only in opacity (particularity) is the other knowable. Finally, unveiling is the very principle of the Tragic; and opacity subject to disclosure implies slowness, accumulation, and duration" (IP 182). Opacity is here again taken up in a lexicon (unveiling, resistance of the Other) that brings it closer to the unconscious. But just as Glissant will reassess the American author in *Faulkner, Mississippi*, the notion of opacity will later be subject to a complete overhaul. It intervenes first when we write: between the transparency of the poetic intention and its realization as a work, there inevitably slips a certain obscurity: for no text, as Glissant has been repeating since *L'Intention poétique*, can live up to the concept that the author has dreamed for it: "The text goes from the dreamt-of transparency to the opacity produced in the words" (PR 129). Then, when we read, in Glissant's transparency, there are always, at least, two or even three participants, in the triple shape of text, author and reader: "The practice of a literary text always represents a contrast between two opacities, the irreducible opacity of this text, even if it is the most benign little sonnet, and the ever-moving opacity of the author and the reader. Sometimes the latter becomes literally aware of this contrast, in which case the text is said to be difficult." Here we must distinguish between opacity and a hermeticism or an esotericism that are the choice of a small number of initiates, in which they can preserve their secrets; Glissant never wrote to found a sect or a cult: he aspires to generality, to a universal that preserves peculiarities; what makes his essays difficult is the breadth and depth of philosophical themes, not a vain desire for hermeticism. The principle in his work is always to enlighten thought to the maximum of the "sun of consciousness" (*Soleil de la conscience*).

Relation, the totality of the Whole-World, diversity, creolization find the limit of their extension in opacity. Without this boundary, these notions would lead to a pulverization, a dissolution that atomizes individuals. Opacity is what is at once irreducible to any system and any totalization, including that of the Whole-World, and the place of reunion for the inextricable: "The opaque is not the dark, but it can be accepted as such. It is the nonreducible, which is the most vivid guarantee of participation and confluence" (PR 205). The vocation of the opaque is to act as a contrast, no longer to the transparency in ideas of Being, but to the "sun of consciousness" of the imaginary: "We thus call opacity that which protects diversity. And now we call transparency the imaginary of relation" (PR 75). Homogeneity (of the world, of thought, of Being, of One, of the Same, and of the Other) is the enemy; opacity offers resistance to the self-sufficiency of any imposition: "Opacity favors no essence, as this would be withdrawn into its mere satisfaction" (PhR 70). Glissant clearly distinguishes between this resistance of thickness and of beings, which can in this sense be placed in Relation, and the resistance of the unspeakable, which remains insurmountable (the oxymoron of an opaque transparency will be noted): "Opacity is not a disturbance, it has its own transparency, not imposed, which we must be able to deserve we can feel. [. . .] The thick dimension is not an impenetrable darkness, and the philosophies of Relation are first distinguished by their multiplicity, so that we may as well speak of a philosophy or philosophies of Relation. Opacity is an attribute of Being-as-beings, which philosophy takes into account, without enlightening it" (PhR 70). Opacity thus opposes the transparency of any philosophical system, by challenging its claim to universality and its reduction of singularities. The multiplicity of opaque beings that Relation enables to communicate with one another therefore implies another sublation, another surpassing of (*the*) philosophy as, in its uniqueness, it has been conceived since the Greeks: to give an account of diversity and multiplicity, at the level of the ontic, and even more, to produce them—all this implies the proliferation of philosoph*ies* in the plural.

Where the Freudian (and Lacanian) unconscious dissolved all links (social, political, amorous) into an unspeakable singularity, Relation connects opacities: it is not the singular category of a single subject, it correlates the multiplicity of the individual: "To disindividuate Relation is to relate theory to the experience of the humanities, in their singularities. It is to return to opacities, fruitful with all exceptions, given momentum by all deviations; these opacities live by involving themselves not in projects, but in the reflected density of existences" (PR 211).

Glissant then advances the claim of a "right to opacity":

> I claim for all the right to opacity. I no longer need to "understand" the other, that is, to reduce him to the model of my own transparency, so as to live with that other or to build with him. The right to opacity would nowadays be the most obvious sign of non-barbarism. And I will say that the literatures rising up before us, and of which we can have foreknowledge, will be beautiful with all the lights and all the opacities of our totality-world. (IPD 71)

We thus see opacity, like all of Glissant's key concepts, joining the unpredictable future he grants them: and this means again that it is different from the Freudian unconscious, that past that returns to our present. This poetics-politics of opacity clearly replaces the right of the psychoanalytic subject, which Lacan states as follows: "Do not give up on your desire," singular and unspeakable. Opacity as a right takes into account the exhaustion of the "Western" subject, who by the same token is no longer able to claim any "right," despite all the "barbarities" he is threatened with today. In the final analysis, opacity subsumes the notion of a singular subject, dissolving it into the transparency of the chiaroscuro of beings, the inextricable places, the communities. Like the Antillean "It-There," opacity, if it is to found a right (that is, "its entry into the political dimension" [PR 208]), can do so only in relation to a specific place, time, community, and speaker, not as a universal right:

How can we reconcile the radicality inherent in all politics and the questioning necessary for any relation? Only by conceiving that it is impossible to reduce anyone to a truth that he has not generated of himself. That is, in the opacity of his time and place. Plato's City is for Plato, Hegel's vision for Hegel, the griot's town for the griot. It is not forbidden to see them in confluence, without melding them into a magma or reducing them to one another. And this same opacity animates all community: what would bring us together forever, singularizing us forever. (PR 208)

We are here at the polar opposite of identity politics and communitarianism. The obsession with identity, a cliché of a whole section of contemporary theory, is dismissed, starting with that of the author himself: "As far as my identity is concerned, I will settle the matter for myself" (PR 205). Conversely, the Other is requested in turn to settle the matter of his own identity by himself.

Glissant defines his relation to his work as a form of opacity, but also his relation to the texts of the innumerable others he has passed through, as well as the relation that the reader should have with his thought. Every grid or system or method of reading or theory produces an opaque residue, which is at once a resistance to all interpretation and the opportunity for an unlimited future commentary—one that cannot be resolved in any last word, because it leaves the door open to new relations.

Glissant therefore proposes an experience that liberates us from the psychoanalytical or philosophical determinism of the signifier: where the primordial poem was, the fusion of everything with everything, there we must together come to be, in the imaginary and the becoming of Relation. The primordial poem is then indeed a buried figure; it has become unconscious,[17] a forgotten thing, repressed since the beginnings of the world, and Relation has given itself the task of reviving it: "What I am is derived, without any fatalism, from what I will be. The poem too is always yet to come" (TEFV 19).

If Glissant's unconscious is homonymous with that of Freud or that of Lacan, it follows that the notion of the imaginary, so full of potential with Glissant, must differ from what it is in psychoanalysis. According to Lacan, the imaginary is a fundamental category of the subject, the set of projections and identifications that define the Self in relation to others; it is what makes (or unmakes) social connection, through which groups and communities are defined. Through the image, the imaginary bond acquires a newly concrete form: it is what consists. This social dimension is not at all absent from Édouard Glissant's construction, but it gives the notion of the imaginary a totally different nuance. First, the imaginary is "non-projecting" (PR 47); it evades the slide into identification-projection that defines it in Lacan. Then, the imaginary is not a category (again, this is the converse of the Lacanian system): "We cannot abstract the imaginary. Otherwise it would be a malleable object, which it is not [. . .]. We cannot in any way conceptualize the imaginary. So it is not a category [. . .]. We cannot accept it as a concept, precisely because the imaginary completely eludes any attempt to predict it" (EBR 148–149). The imaginary is almost synonymous with the poetic; just like the latter, it is a means of subjective knowledge indispensable to the inextricable complexity of the world. "We do not understand what happens in the world. The world escapes our comprehension, escapes us as a concept and escapes us because it has become so inextricable that we no longer have a system capable of bringing this inextricable under control. What is left to us is the imaginary."[18]

By its future and virtual aspect, the imaginary, like Relation and the Whole-World, escapes any conceptual fixity: it systematically lies outside any system. In contrast with the conceptual, the imaginary is the locus of the living, which prevails over the truth and the structure of the signifier. Glissant here proposes an alternative to the subjugation to the determinism implied by the parades of the signifier. Servitude is by no means automatic—*there is a choice*: we can decide on the imaginary at the expense of the Symbolic, beyond Lacan and Freud. Here lies the great distance between psychoanalysis and Édouard Glissant's philosophy: the rejection of all determinism, because what is without a figure is not the unconscious past, but the unpredictable future, where an individual and unshared destiny is surpassed in an opacity in Relation.

Relation connects surfaces, in extent ("poetry in extent" is the subtitle of *La Philosophie de la Relation*), not of depths and verticalities, for these are always suspected of imposing transcendences: "Against this reductive transparency [of 'the general truth of Man'], a force of opacity is at work. No longer that opacity which enveloped and reactivated the mystery of filiation, but another kind, sparing the threatened succulences which join together (without conjoining, that is, without melting) *in the extent* of Relation. This extent is not only spatial, but temporal; henceforth, the 'realized quantity' is not yet realized, the quantifiable, by oxymoron, is infinitized, the creolizations are yet to come: (Extension is woven. Leap and variance, in another poetics. Transversality. A quantifiable infinity. A quantity that is not realized. An entanglement that is not exhausted. Extent is not just space, it is also its own dreamed-of time" (PR 71).

The extent of Relation, rather than being a matter of the trees of objective and subjective knowledge, which always involve the constraints of cultural transcendences and genealogies, takes the figure of the rhizome: "The thought of the rhizome would be the principle of what I call a poetics of relation, in which all identity extends into a relation to the Other" (PR 35).[19]

Surface *below the surface*, rather than an area that appeals to a transcendence, a truth, a depth, a genealogy, or an idea of which it is merely a veil to be torn apart; the rhizome is simultaneously an image of thought and naturalness (a being) inspired by botany: ginger, the asparagus, the iris—all develop roots not in depth, but in extent. This fusion between a nature and a notion could not fail to inspire Glissant, but the poetic and philosophical rhizome has other claims on his preference: surface without depth, where every point connects with any other, it is multiple, and not One, as Deleuze and Guattari say: "The rhizome is an antigenealogy (TEFV 159). It is thus a non-hierarchical process rather than an ordering structure. "The rhizome is a network, an alchemy also" (CL 140), which transforms the lead of the true and the real into poetic and imaginary gold. Following Deleuze and Guattari, he relates diversity on the plane of the signifier, and on that of beings, "bringing into play very different regimes of signs and even states of non-signs" (TEFV 158). The rhizome is also the figure of a totality, it is homologous to the Whole-World: by linking each point of the network with all the others, it is opposed to any fragmentation and any conceptual differentiation. In Glissant, totality and unity must therefore be understood as rhizomic, where things and words all correspond together.

In contrast to the spherical ancient cosmos, closed in on itself in an image of its perfection, and in contrast with the linearity of a thought with a beginning and an ending (like Hegel's), the rhizome is open, susceptible to a becoming in which it grows and extends, as Deleuze and Guattari say: "It has no beginning and no end, but always a middle through which it pushes and overflows."[20] Relation is the authentic, concrete figure, at once anticipatory and poetically realized, of the rhizome. Note that the rhizome *is*, simply, elementarily; in Glissant, it does not have the revolutionary role (of thought) conferred on it by Deleuze and Guattari: "We cannot infer [from the rhizome] any function of subversion, any capacity of rhizomatic thought to upset the order of the world, for this would mean a return to the pretension of ideology that this thought is supposed to challenge" (PR 24). In this sense, Glissant marks his distance and his originality vis-à-vis his two philosophical friends.

It is therefore legitimate to raise here the question of reciprocal influences. Let us propose that Glissant's Relation is, as soon as it is formulated, rhizomic: it thus precedes, by a long way, the Deleuzian rhizome, since it appears in 1969 in *L'Intention poétique*: "Intention is thus made perfect in Relation. In the related: the words devoted to the complex state, neither to reject it, nor to mask it, nor to blister it. In the relating: being-self so as to be the Other, forever, hopelessly. In the relative: the negation of a History and the open dawn of (hi)stories" (IP 217). The question (I will leave it to others to map it out) is not how much Deleuze influenced Glissant, but on the contrary, how much Deleuze (and Guattari) owe to Glissant (a great deal, in my opinion). The works written jointly by Deleuze and Guattari deliberately depart from traditional philosophical discourse and attempt an approach to the idea that might be called poetic: in this, they echo Glissant's conception of knowledge: "The alternative views and solutions they propose together are marginalized by the powers in office, but they build up the fluid body of new types of poetics. That is why they are so decried, alive or dead" (CL 139). It is quite possible that Glissant's poetic philosophy contributed to the writing of *A Thousand Plateaus*.

In *Les Entretiens*, Glissant declares: "Relation is a poetics of the inextricable, not a good-becoming" (EBR 94). The Good is not the final purpose of Relation: "It is then realized that Relation has no morality, it creates types of poetics and it generates magnetisms between different things" (PhR 73). The same rejection of an idealizing and moralizing final end also applies to creolization: "But creolization has no morality. [. . .]. Creolizations have always existed but have no morals. It is not a question of creolizations leading toward a more compassionate, more civilized, less barbarous humanity. [. . .] Creolization is not a panacea. It is not a means for solving the problems of politics and the economy" (IL 79–80). (There is no point, then, in recuperating Relation for ideological purposes.)

The ethic of Relation is thus freed from the traditional kinds of ethos put forward by philosophy, from Aristotle's *Nicomachean Ethics* to Kant and beyond, which always posit the Supreme Good as a shared good, an ideal, unique, universal, and abstract end (the "Good," the "Beautiful') that commits the whole community to regulating exchanges and reducing the possibilities of conflicts between individuals or groups. Glissant's ethic is a morality of negativity and concrete opacities, an ethic that is once again deeply rooted in Hegelian thought:[21]

> [. . .] it must be said that Relation has no morality, that is to say, it does not aim at the Good. Relation has no morality and it may undergo crises, outbreaks of violence. *It is a little Hegelian to say this, but we need to do so, from time to time* . . . In the Whole-World, two cosmic elements initially favored colonization, the discoveries of the colonizers, and then favored migrations, i.e. placing people in contact and relation. And these two elements are two violent elements.[22]

Relation is "without morality" because, following Hegel, it grasps the negativity of conflicts, as forces destined to transmute into positivity: "Relation is without morality. In other words, conflicts are not rejected into a politics (or poetics) of relation as negative sides. In Hegel, for example, there is the negative side."[23] Thus Relation includes violence and negativity: "Relation involves violence, marks its distance" (PR 202). If Relation is a dynamic process, it has an essential element of negativity and destruction (to be overcome, surpassed, taken up—*aufheben*): "Relation is destroyed, at every moment and in every circumstance, by this peculiarity which signifies our opacities, by this singularity, and becomes again a lived relation. Its death in general is what makes its life a shared life" (PR 219). As an example, the "chosen people" of the Batoutos have given themselves the task of a post-apocalypse reconstruction: "The gods have exploded, we have put them back together" (S 95). Without an explosion (without negativity), there can be no synthesis or totality, no recomposition that goes beyond the apocalypse.

Relation composes the Same and the Other, the self with the stranger, the inside and the outside, one culture with another. Its ethics has nothing to do with the imperative of "openness to others," one of the stupid trivialities of contemporary thought (it must be said that this thought is a cornucopia of platitudes). "Openness to the other" conjectures the entirely familiar inaugural and fixed point of a same and a self; or else, it supposes that the Same dissolves in the Other and vice versa; as we have seen, thanks to Relation, the Same and the Other have neither fixity nor purity but are always composite; on the other hand, Relation does not in the least require opacities to be drowned in one another: on the contrary. *L'Intention poétique* devotes two pages to this problem, under the revealing title of "sur un défaut de poésie" ("On a defect of poetry"): the link of a landscape or a being to its other will always pass through a poetics that respects their specificity while putting them in Relation. Glissant criticizes both the Westerner and his other, the non-Westerner:

> The pretension (an avatar) of the universal leads, here and there, without it becoming apparent, to an imbroglio, a sterile to-ing and fro-ing, in which the Westerner will seek to turn himself into what he is not, will seek to change land, when he does not have the heroic lucidity of Segalen (but it is not a matter of changing land, it is incumbent on everyone to change his land, to save it); and where the non-Westerner will want to become and remain everything (cultivated, open, conciliatory, learned, synthetic, humanistic: "free"), when he is only prolonging an alignment. And also going beyond the temptation of going beyond. (IP 151)

Note the suspicion vis-à-vis this "going beyond": it is mimicry, an extension of the same by the same; but in Glissant there is nothing radically new if not in a sublation of the past, whether this past be negative or positive. As early as 1969, as if in anticipation, the rhetoric of postcolonialism is refuted. Its ideological mechanism flattens and dissolves any difference, any specificity, in the self-effacement that supposes "openness to the other": in the former colonized as in the former colonizer, the identical is prolonged. Relation does not demand that we repudiate ourselves, either by withdrawing and abstaining, or by engaging in pantomime: "*If you stop being yourself, where will the relation be? If I freely (freely?) turn myself into you, in what idioms, in your language or mine, will we converse?*" (IP 151). To meld without dissolving, both parties must find, not a common language, but two poetic languages in which they can find themselves and at the same time open up to each other. In this respect, Relation is indeed an ethic, guided by "the maxim that I can change by changing with the other without destroying or distorting myself"; and this ethics is specified of poetry: "The other is not another person, but my consented difference. Otherness is solely moral: in the Other lies all poetics" (IP 84).

Relation is a pact of reciprocity: one consents to the opacity of the other, if he consents in parallel. Once one of the parties does not commit to reciprocity, Relation is destroyed. The ethics of Relation is an impossibility, if Relation is related to the world as it was and is today: what should I do if the Stranger threatens me in my very existence? What should he do if I want to put him to death? It is immediately apparent that the Stranger, with me, must submit to the same ethic of acceptance of the Other (a transcendent third). Alternatively, we can project ourselves into the immanence of Relation. Applied to human relations as they are today in the world, Relation appears as an angelism that ignores the real conditions, stamped with the seal of hatred, which underlie the relationship of humanities with each other: the narcissism of small differences reigns supreme at all levels, and the whole edifice of sociality has but one goal—to make that narcissism less harmful. This angelism is only an appearance: "Here we need to detect the angelism involved. It is mere vanity, one that is immediately drowned in the din of bombs and the echo of tortures, to posit relation as a substitute for the absolute (as an ideal perfection, in which man would be a lamb for a man); it implies that we dominate and weigh that part of everyday life that belongs to negation, to the horrible, to resignation" (IP 24).

That is why Glissant reaffirms, again and again, that Relation, despite its present appearance as the realized quantity of differences, is a utopia without a principle of reality, unnamable, generous projection toward a future of Edenic love. That is why, too, it only makes sense in the specific space of poetics, where literatures can fight dialectically ("Literatures, thus, break *against*," PhR 42), without causing too much damage: "So what is a philosophy of Relation? An impossibility, insofar as it is not a poetics" (PhR 2).

Glissant's program is more than a "research program": an art of living (together), an art of living the world and thinking about it. His "realization" supposes an Other world and an Other of thought, projected into the future, a totalizing and always unfinished potentiality, of which, however, the harbingers are already present, under our very eyes: "The power of the imaginary is that of a utopia in each day, it is realistic when it prefigures what for a long time will enable us to foster *actions that do not tremble*. Actions which tremble would remain sterile if the thought of the whole world, which is a trembling, did not support them. This is where philosophy exercises its activity, and also the thought of the poem" (PhR 56).

Relation is caught up in the tension of a silence, unnamable because it is still without a figure, and a poetic saying, a realized quantity, which tries to approach it without ever immobilizing it. So Relation is double-sided, but this surface is unilateral (Moebian); the place of a dialectic divided within itself between empty transcendence and realized immanence, of which it realizes the fusion (or the synthesis). If it is a mediating third, this is not by elevation, looking down fixedly from above (which would be the transcendence of Being or of language), but by the extension and the becoming-in-tension of all beings.

This is the deepest cunning of the Whole-World and Relation, as opposed to the Hegelian cunning of reason: as the poetic keystones of knowledge, the Whole-World and Relation embrace all beings, including those produced by rationality. Glissant proposes a logic of meaning that knows no exception and that can be read in the only form adequate to it: a philosophical rationality *and* poetic writing inextricably mixed together, as in Nietzsche, even more so than in Deleuze and Guattari.

Chapter 12

"Now there are only beings"

We cannot attribute to the realized quantity of the differences that are the content of Relation either Being or anything that has accompanied Being in the history of philosophy ever since Aristotle: categories, qualities or attributes, form or substance. The different and the realized quantity are beings or virtualities of beings, detached from the transcendence of Being by their rhizomic immanence. One cannot further reduce the relation to philosophical predication of the type "Socrates is a man": "Being is relation: but Relation is safe from the idea of Being" (PR 199). This is because (and the whole history of metaphysics tells us this), Being is self-sufficient: it is not, by definition, open to any relation whatsoever, since it itself establishes, in transcendence, all (non–Glissantian) relation: "(But if we tried to approach Being as simply self-evident, we would thereby adopt the indirect approach of thinking that no questioning is possible—because Being does not suffer any questioning whatsoever to be imposed on it. Being is sufficient, whereas any question is interactive.)" (PR 174). Thus, Relation and realized quantity have been infinitely distant from the entire history of metaphysics, "the science of Being as Being," ever since Plato and Aristotle: "*The thought of wandering* is not the distraught thought of dispersion, but the thought of our alliances not claimed in advance, by which we migrate from the absolutes of Being to the variations of Relation, where *Being-as-a-being* is revealed, as the indistinction of essence and substance, dwelling and movement" (PhR 61).

Glissant re-reads the history of Being in its depth and breadth, which again testifies to his strictly philosophical ambition. This tradition here requires various indispensable landmarks; we will see that the question of Being is far from being univocal. Glissant's program is announced as early as *Le Discours antillais* in a very precise form and with very specific philosophical references; and already, relation is contrasted with the depth of Being, and already beings are a totality: "Neither the Parmenidean text, 'Being is,' nor its opposite in Heraclitus, 'All changes,' by which the different forms of metaphysics in the West were conceived, but by a transphysics that could be summarized as follows: beings (what exists as a totality) relay one another. What exists by relativized totality" (DA 251; note the way that Heraclitean becoming is downplayed here, as it does not seem enough in itself for Glissant's project).

Originally, the word "metaphysics" was due to an editorial decision of Andronicos of Rhodes (c. 60 BC), who divided Aristotle's corpus into the writings that deal with physics and those that come "after" (*meta* in Greek) physics. This distinction shows that Andronicos perceived two branches of philosophy: that which deals with nature, such as the great inaugural poems of Heraclitus and Parmenides, and those thinkers who, after Plato, busied themselves defining thought and its modes in themselves. In c. 535 AD, Simplicius ratified the definitive separation between the objective knowledge of philosophy and the subjective knowledge of nature; the separation of the domains is thus of Neoplatonic origin: "The discipline which considers the realities completely separated from matter and the pure activity of the intellect in act and the intellect in potentiality, that which is raised to it by Activity, all this they call theology, the first and metaphysical philosophy, since it lies beyond physical realities" (*Commentary on the* Physics *of Aristotle*, I, 21).

The word "ontology" is even more recent: it appears in 1613 in the *Lexicon Philosophicum* of Rudolf Goclenius, as a composite of *onto-* and *-logia* (in Latin: *philosophia de ente*). As a discourse on (or of) beings, ontology would have been perfectly suited to Édouard Glissant's philosophical project, except that the discourse on *ta onta* was immediately attached to metaphysics as one of its branches, and is these days understood as the discourse on Being. In the final analysis, despite appearances, "metaphysics" and "ontology" are not Greek words; they are the late creations of Christian and Latin Neoplatonism and medieval scholasticism.

Henceforth, to distinguish between them, we need to say of Glissant's philosophy that it is an *ontics*, not only a discourse on beings, but a space where things themselves (beings) speak. Lava, rivers, rocks, birds, trees, elements, in Glissant, have meaning in that they whisper their subjective knowledge into our ears: the discursive (or logical) dimension of ontology merges, at the origin (Lascaux, the Pre-Socratics) and at the end term (the unnamable and unpredictable aspects of relation), with that of which it speaks, namely beings.

Be that as it may, the philosophical history of Being, and its dispute with relation, begins at Heraclitus and Parmenides, who both write poems *On Nature*, or *Poem*, the only titles attested by the scholiasts and commentators of Antiquity. In the case of Parmenides, the titles *On Nature or Being*, *On Nature or on Beings*, are modern creations. Philosophy is inaugurated in a poetic form, and poetry is the form of the philosophical, not the discursive and logical syntax of prose: this could not be perfectly adequate to the writing practiced by Glissant throughout his work. Moreover, before thinking itself in its method, philosophy begins with a reflection on the *physis*, on nature as the Greeks conceived it: "Yet already among the Pre-Socratics, the thought prevailed that Being is relation, in other words that Being is not an absolute, that Being is relation to the other, relation to the world, relation to the cosmos" (IPD 30).

Parmenides, to my knowledge, appears twice in Glissant's work: in the *Entretiens* where, as the initiator of the problem of Being, he is like an ancestor who does not have to bear the weight of the philosophical history of Being, since he inaugurates it: "We have to fight against something, namely the historical weight of the concept, which was not the case of the Pre-Socratics. Happy Parmenides, who did not know this fertile torment. For language did not produce the concept from the beginning, Aristotle brought us to that point" (EBR 146). The history of the interpretations that follow the dawning of the question of Being is a fruitful one—and this indicates that it must not be circumvented, and that any return to the Pre-Socratics cannot be a form of mimicry; if they return into our present, it will be in a way that transforms them.

The second mention of Parmenides appears in the anthology of the Whole-World (TFEV 163), where the fragment of the *Poem* is entitled exactly as in the title of Barbara Cassin's book: *Sur la nature ou sur l'étant. La langue de l'être? (On Nature or on Beings. The Language of Being?)*.[1] This title shows the switch between Being and beings, ontology and the ontic, which will mark all philosophy.

For Heidegger, who gives Parmenides's *Poem* a quasi-sacred status,[2] by a return to the Pre-Socratics that differs in emphasis from that of Glissant, the quarrel of Being with beings is in principle resolved. First of all, beings are always the way toward Being: "The understanding of Being is itself a possibility of Dasein's Being. The ontic privilege of Dasein is that it is ontological" (*Being and Time*). If ontology and metaphysics must be surpassed, this evolution depends on them and separates from them only by an evolution internal to themselves: "We cannot represent the surpassing of metaphysics if not from metaphysics itself, as if a new level were being added to it."[3]

In the second place, for Heidegger, there are only two languages of philosophy: Greek (albeit it not the Greek of Plato or Aristotle, but that of Heraclitus and Parmenides), and German: "This character of depth and philosophical creativity in the Greek language can also be found only in German." Two languages, two privileged places of the West that are the only ones to enter into relation, closed to all others, even to French and France: "When the French do philosophy, they think in German." This "ontological nationalism"[4] anchors and encloses the history of Being in two "nations," the only ones to enter into relation. Heidegger does not think in the presence of all the languages of the world: this is the absolute polar opposite to all that Glissant thought and wanted.

When Heidegger comments on the Heraclitean *Logos*, he says: "In the time of the Greeks, the Being of beings became the thing worthy of being thought; this fact is the beginning of the West, it is the hidden source of its destiny." If one thinks beings in their Fold with Being, in their "ontological relation" to Being, and thus in Heideggerian terms, then we are in Western thought. More than that: we are in the West, we are Western.

But this twofold Heideggerian and national *"Grund"* (both Greek and German), at once soil, territory, language, and the foundation of thought is, in Heidegger himself, insecure; as he notes in his *Introduction to Metaphysics*, the roots of the word "to be" are manifold:

1. From Sanskrit derives *esum*, and the Latin *esse* that designates "life, what is alive." Nietzsche emphasized the metaphorical aspect of this first principle, noting that *esse* means "to breathe."[5]

2. Moreover, the derivative of the first Sanskrit root *est* means "what is standing, what is there," hence the Greek *esti*, the Latin *est*, the German *ist*, the French *est*: there is a remarkable stability, in all these languages, to the founding principle of identity, which seems to pass, in the third-person singular, from one language to another losing nothing in translation.

3. The second Sanskrit root is *bhû*, "what shines, what manifests itself," that gives *phuein* in Greek and its derivative *physis*, nature. In Latin, *fui* gives the *je fus* ("I was") of the French preterite, and the German *ich bin, du bist*.

4. Finally, in German, *wesen* ("being") derives from a third Sanskrit root, *vasamin*, "to dwell."

Moreover, when the Greek says being, it states it in the third person of the singular, without a subject (the infinitive form, εἶναι = "is"): when it thinks beings in the singular (τὸ ὄν) or the plural (τὰ ὄντα) it uses a present participle, a verbal form also used in French (*l'étant* for the singular being, *les étants* for beings). Being "is-to-itself," alone, without qualities and without quantities, withdrawn from presence; beings, in presence, affirm the diversity of the world that exists, but are brought back to the ideal and transcendent world of Being. Jean Wahl, Édouard Glissant's teacher during his formative years, rightly remarks:

> Heidegger wants to return to Greek thought, especially to Pre-Socratic thought. But it has been rightly pointed out that the very question he poses (why is there Being rather than nothingness?) and even what he calls the pre-question (what is Being?) can hardly be formulated in Greek. First of all because Greek will in any case talk about beings and not of Being, and then because true being itself has, according to Heidegger's own observations, three different roots, the root *fu*, the root *wes* and the root *es*; which of the three will he choose? There will thus be great difficulties in the very formulation of the question.[6]

Being is therefore caught up, at the very origin of its question, in a multiple, diverse, creolizing trigenesis (three languages, Sanskrit, Greek, and German, are in play) which prevents us from thinking about it in a unity and a universality. In Greek, Latin, German, and French (in the European tradition), Being is a carrier, linguistically and philosophically, of a multigenesis of which it is the shadow. The very task of philosophy, since Socrates, has been to reduce this equivocation to a single, linear meaning. To the extent that to think philosophically, in the Western tradition, is to think "Greek" or in Greek, the linguistic multiplicity of Being strips Greek, and the other languages in its wake, of any pretension to universality. This multiplicity, we see, is also a question of translation from one language to another: in historical depth, from Sanskrit to the languages that derive from it; in extent, between Greek, German, French, and other languages. Being, from the beginning, is plurigenetic, diverse, multiple: creole. To reduce it to one (two, three languages) is to fix it in its immobility:

> And we have gradually become accustomed to saying it: language is Being. (But this in the common sense and not in the Sophists' thinking.) What is also important is that this process confirmed or reinforced the very idea that there is Being. [. . .] When people in the West said: "Tell me what language you speak, I'll tell you who you are," in the sense of [objective] knowing, what was understood was: "Tell me what language you speak, I will you in what way you participate in Being." (EBR 70)

Glissant summarizes in a dense formula the totality of Heidegger's thought ("language—Sanskrit, Greek, German or French—is Being"). At the same time, he points to another line of inquiry, that of the Sophists.

We must therefore re-read Parmenides and his first opponent, the "sophist" Gorgias, bearing in mind that, if a Greek philosopher entitled his treatise or poem *On Nature*, as did Heraclitus and Parmenides, his purpose is to talk about the *physis*, that is to say, about beings and living things, not about Being—hence Jean Wahl's remark and Barbara Cassin's unconventional translation:[7] we can here clearly see the reasons behind Glissant's affinity with the two Pre-Socratics. The living thing, in Greek cosmology, is that which grows and dies, and whose place is here below, a chaos or *chaosmos* delivered over to contingency and disorder: a world whose main characteristic is its mobility, its incessant alternation of destruction and renewal, to which the eternal laws of thought, in their fixity, can scarcely be applied. According to Barbara Cassin, Parmenides's *On Nature* is a path from Being to beings, a passage from ontology to the ontic.[8] Gorgias' *Treatise on Non-Beings* (in Cassin's nontraditional translation, *Traité du non-étant*) challenges Being as the first and founding principle of thought. The demonstration is based on a paradox, that of the liar, that Glissant will take up again in his "Nothing is true, everything is alive."[9]

To say that Being is not, Gorgias needs the principle of identity and predication without which all discourse is simply impossible, and a fortiori any logico-philosophical demonstration; it cannot be said that "Being is not" without ensuring that the verb "is" has a certain consistency. I will here summarize the three sections of the *Treatise*: (1) Being is not, nothing exists; (2) If Being exists, it cannot be thought; (3) If Being can be thought, it cannot be communicated. In his note, Jean-Louis Poirier comments: "An ontology without Being is not strictly speaking a negative ontology (that is to say, one whose object would be a being of which one could not say anything), but a non-theoretical ontology: the ontology of the practice of discourse. What is rejected is not Being—we know well, and the Sophists know well, that there are 'things'—but a philosophy of Being."[10] According to Gorgias, therefore, there is no possible metaphysics. Eugène Dupréel's interpretation of Gorgias can be applied almost word for word to Glissant:

> The art that should be cultivated is not the vain science of Being, that is, the effort to gain an adequate knowledge of a thoroughly objective idea, whether it be one, as those from Elea claim, or multiple, as those interested in phenomena see it. It is not this substance in itself to which we should turn, a substance with which our thought identifies by means of science and which it passes on to other people in words: we need to go straight to the science of discourse, which is built up on the perceptions and experiences common to the one who teaches and the one who learns.[11]

Moreover, according to Barbara Cassin: "Being is an effect of discourse."[12] Glissant says the same when he writes: "The thought of wandering is a poetics, one which implies that at a certain moment it utters itself. The utterance of wandering is that of relation" (PR 31). We can see then that Glissant's wandering is not only that of the journey, the migration, the exile and return of this or that explorer or this or that slave, but also a wandering outside of the fixity or fixation of metaphysics on Being, *a wandering that must be said.*

The Platonic dialogues dedicated to the technique of the Sophists, namely *Theaetetus, The Sophist,* and *Gorgias,* aim to destroy Gorgias's thesis, to discredit and exclude it from philosophical debate; Plato seeks to establish that Being and the True exist, and that discourse, by following certain rules, can reach them rationally. Then, Being becomes what withdraws from living things and beings (from appearance, things, contingency) in order to tell their truth. It will be the same with Aristotle, who also reproaches Gorgias with employing over-poetic figures in his philosophical prose. This critique is related to the conflict between Atticism, the rules of speaking well according to the classics of the region of Attica, and Asianism, the half-"barbaric" (baroque) discourse of the Greeks of Asia, or, in the case of Gorgias, of "Leonteanism," from the name of his city of origin, Leontium, located on the south coast of present-day Sicily. Between Gorgias and Socrates and, later on, Aristotle, there is a founding example of the war between the various forms of classicism and those of the baroque, or of measure and excess (*démesure*) in Glissant's terminology. In addition, philosophers expressing themselves in poetic figures could not fail to serve as models for Glissant. Thus the accusation laid by the philosophers against the art of the Sophists, of being a rhetoric empty of meaning, is reversed; yes, rhetoric thinks: "When we say: rhetoric, we do not mean a body of cleverly implemented precepts nor a cunning didactics but an adventurous dynamic of words, a wager that lays itself bare, in the relation inside-outside, self-world, existence-expression" (TTM 135).

For Parmenides, however, there is only one path for philosophy: that of Being (for him the universe, the *physis*). Being is thinkable, non-Being is not; the path of opinion (*doxa*) does not count for thought.[13] The rejection of non-Being as an object of thought traps philosophy in an impasse. Plato's *Parmenides*, which portrays Parmenides, his disciple Zeno of Elea, and Socrates, challenges the contrast between Being and non-Being and proposes a third way: "In all likelihood, whether there is the One or whether there is not, in any case, itself and all other things, respectively as well as reciprocally, with all attributes, in all respects, have Being and non-Being, appearance and non-appearance." I have no intention here of repeating the history of a controversy which, ever since the dawn of philosophy until today, has been investigated in all its details and in all its greatness: I am simply seeking to show that originally, if there is *one*, or *Being*, their others, their contra-dictions, are also constantly present. The word "Being" itself, in its history dating back to the beginning of humanity, testifies to this digenesis.

In pushing Heidegger to the ultimate consequences of his thought, while perhaps suggesting an implicit political critique of him,[14] Jean Wahl concludes that the question of Being has become insoluble: "Being is-to-itself, according to Heidegger himself. We see only beings, and the word "beings" now appears to us merely as a rather vague and empty word. Is not this our sober wisdom?"[15] This "sober wisdom" is also a circular return to the first Greek thinkers, especially the Sophist Gorgias and, a century before him, the Pre-Socratic Heraclitus. For Gorgias, the only Being is a Being of discourse and rhetoric. For Heraclitus, "every being goes toward another being; that is, becoming occurs in Being, *if we can indeed, it must be added, use the word "Being"*; it occurs in any case from one being into another being."[16] We are here in the becoming of appearances that do not refer to a being they conceal or reveal. Appearance is Being; if there are only appearances, there is no Being, and appearance is not an appearance, it is self-sufficient: this is what Nietzsche rediscovered: "Ah! those Greeks, they agreed to *live*: for that the important thing was to stay bravely on the surface, to stick to the epidermis, to adore appearance, to believe in form, sounds, words, the whole Olympus of appearance! Those Greeks were superficial—*out of depth*!"[17]

There is a similar move in Édouard Glissant, when he deletes the problematic of the Being of the history of philosophical thought (Greek, or Western): for him, the question is exhausted. One remembers the logion that defines Relation, whose content is "the realized quantity of all *beings* (*étants*)," and not of all beings-as-activities (*êtres*). On the basis of this obliteration of Being there arise beings, and all the motives of Glissant's thought are illuminated and become consistent, including with each other: extent (*étendue*) (one is tempted to write "being-due," "*étant-due*") against depth, poetic tremor against rational fixity, archipelago against continent, rhizome against root and identity, wandering against rootedness and dwelling (which is one of the important senses of the word "Being" in Heidegger), becoming (utopia) against immobility, phenomenon, perception, and beings against reason: all these choices stem from a thought that rejects the Socratic and Platonic curse, the separation between poetic knowledge and rational knowledge, anchored in the rationality of Being, the dismissal of beings as secondary to ("mere trappings" of) Being.

It is not merely a question of a return: just like Heraclitean or Nietzschean becoming, against Being and for beings, Relation is a strenuous urge toward an unpredictable future, this time as opposed to Parmenides, for whom non-Being was nothing, because it was unthinkable: "This is why Relation also disassembles the thought of non-Being. [. . .] The non-Being of relation would be its impossible fulfillment" (PR 201).

Non-Being here finds the essential function it had in the thought of Heraclitus, or (in the form of negativity) in Hegel; against Parmenides, it is not nonsense, it is not a radically unthinkable antinomy of Being, it is the becoming of beings, with this difference that for Heraclitus Being (and not beings) merges with becoming.[18]

Thus, Glissant returns to Heraclitus, overturning Aristotle's critique of the Ephesian: "It will no longer be the unity of Being that the discourse [of the Heracliteans] will focus, but on the nothingness of Being and the concepts of quantity and quality will be identical" (*Physics* I, II, 185b: remember the "realized quantity" of relation). But when beings return in modernity, the name to which he eagerly turns is no longer that of Heraclitus, but that of Faulkner the "failed poet," that is to say, not a philosopher in the post-Socratic fashion, but a writer. Faulkner, as well as his double Édouard Glissant, attempted "this effort, the most total that, since Nietzsche, any creator has undertaken to 'rethink' the ground (Being, and its derivatives in the real: identity, belonging) on which Western ontology had rested for so many centuries and with such profundity" (FM 181–182).

With Glissant, "disappearing" (*disparaître*) becomes a "disappearance" or "Being as disappearing" (*disparêtre*); in Relation, Being is dissolved and replaced by Relation, which proceeds only from beings:

> This is why [Relation] is not: (of) Being but: —(of) beings.
>
> Non-Being would exist only outside Relation.
>
> Non-Being does not precede Relation: the latter is not uttered on the basis of any break. (PR 201)[19]

The Being of beings does not precede Relation: right from the start, Relation is presence, in its future anterior. If Relation is not a break (as we have seen above, it is *poétrie* that causes a break in poetic practice), it is at once first and last, not only in the order of thought, but in that of beings, even unthought beings: "The idea of relation does not pre-exist (Relation)" (PR 199). As a category, it is similar to the a priori forms of the understanding in Kant, but it immediately differs from them: "[Relation] does not precede itself in its act, does not suppose any a priori. It is the limitless effort of the world: for it to be realized in totality, and thus to escape repose. We do not enter into relation, as we might have entered religion. We do not conceive it at first, as people sought to conceive

Being" (PR 186). This way of keeping Kant at a distance is underlined by a note from *Poétique de la Relation*.[20]

Glissant's Absolute is no longer in search of Being, but aims to take all beings into account. The two parts of *Poétique de la Relation* (whose titles perfectly condense the intention: "What what" and "What beings what are not," PR 173 and 199) dealing with this question are a suite (in the musical sense of the word) of aphorisms in which, each time, the Relation of plural beings contrasts with singular Being. Being is self-sufficient, it is self-sufficiency in all the senses of the term—at once pride, closure, and absolute autonomy of the science of Being, which is nothing but metaphysics in its entirety: "Being-as-Being is self-sufficiency" (PR 200). This (self-)sufficiency makes it impossible to question it or open it up. Relation opens up this presumption of self-sufficiency to beings: "Relation strives and is expressed in opacity. It defers self-sufficiency" (PR 200).

This contrast between Being and Relation (of beings) is radicalized in *L'Imaginaire des langues*, in a passage that must be quoted in full, in which Glissant distances himself from Césaire and Senghor, who are, he believes, still too stuck in ontology and in Being:

> What I criticized in the negritude [of Césaire and Senghor] was that they defined Being: Negro Being . . . I believe there is no longer Being [IL 31] . . . Being is a great, noble, and incommensurable invention of the West, and especially of Greek philosophy. The definition of Being very soon, in Western history, leads to lead to all kinds of sectarianism, of metaphysical absolutes, fundamentalisms whose catastrophic effects we are witnessing today. I think it must be said that, now, there are merely beings, that is, particulate existences that correspond or come into conflict, and we must abandon the claim to any definition of Being" (IPD 125).

Let us note in passing that Hegel also thinks of putting an end to ontology; when absolute knowledge is accomplished, all that is left is what he calls sensible perception, the very thing which, according to him, lay at the beginning of thought. Being has been liquidated by a return to its origin.

In Glissant's logion one can then replace the "realized quantity," the "detail," the "different" by beings, in the chiaroscuro of their opacity and their existence: "Do you mean that beings are a pure and simple quantity? Yes, a quantity, but neither pure nor simple" (NRM 58).

I think that in 1996, in the *Introduction à une Poétique du divers* and *L'Imaginaire des langues*, Glissant forces things (or prepares a new displacement of his thought) when he states that there are now only beings: when it comes to Being, "disappearance" (*disparêtre*) is neither his first nor his last word on the contrast between Being and Relation. Indeed, in 1990 (before the erasure), *Poétique de la Relation* placed the terms of the contradiction in a deeply dialectical relation, where Being-as-Being (metaphysics) was confronted (sublated, in Hegelian vocabulary) with and by Relation: "Thus [Relation] is an idea of Being, but one which de-parts from Being-as-Being and confronts presence" (PR 200). As a dialectic of risk and excess, Relation has the effect of replacing the Being of ontology with the Being of the world: "Relation is the subjective knowledge in movement of beings, which risks the Being of the world" (PR 201).

In 2006, in *Une nouvelle région du monde*, after the erasure of the *Introduction à une Poétique du divers* (1996), Glissant comes back, albeit without any palinode—like Montaigne, he never retracts or apologizes—to the history of Being, in a short narrative of its avatars: "For if beings (we will mark them thus, rather as Beings, with the capital letter which would be an idle mimicry of Being), are now devolved to the forms of chaos, the 'chaoses of Being,' does this mean or allow us to sense that in mythical ages, in another region of space and time of which we have never known anything or which we have completely forgotten, these beings would have been deemed to be vaguely in harmony with the very idea of their own existence, and thus as close to approaching the serenities of Being?" (NRM 42–43).

This history, like the history of poetry, supposes an original moment when Being and beings were united, merged by the primordial poem, where appearance and essence were inseparable, very similar to the Heraclitean river as evoked by Kostas Axelos: "There is here neither any supremacy of the sensible figurative (the river) nor of the abstract and non-figurative (the principle). Both are confounded, are not yet separated, and together form the attitude of the thinker who thinks the river and who lives the transformation."[21]

Being is the "exploded field" of works of art, and "Being their true denial as well as their recognition." (NRM 59) Being recognizes art and literature only at the cost of emptying them of content. Art as a manifestation of the spirit in Hegel, just as the Heideggerian bond (the Fold) that related beings, existence, and poetry back to "Western" Being, must then be rethought outside of metaphysics and ontology: "Thus we will have to designate Being and beings by other appellations and new meanings. [. . .] for example, they might be energetic Being and material beings, an energetic spirit and a material spirit" (NRM 59). There is a chiasm here, compared to the philosophical tradition; Being abandons its character "as absolute, as a transcendence or a sublimity" (NRM 178), its immobile uniqueness, so as to merge into the flow of becoming. It then approaches the variables of beings: "If it is difficult to speak of the qualities of Being, it is possible to do so for beings, but these qualities are not qualities of beings, but variables" (NRM 179). The realized quantities (of beings) permute in a chiasm, to infinity, with the becoming (of Being). In contrast to what happened in Hegel (*quantum*, measurement) and in Marx (the quantity that is transformed into quality), the qualities in Glissant's ontic always become quantities, and these are not reabsorbed into a measurable quantity, but vary in the movement of the different. Then the original fusion becomes the ultimate fusion, which reabsorbs into a Moebius strip the distinction between Being and beings, while maintaining their difference: "Being and beings, not universal or exclusive or transcendent, but both unanimous with each other" (NRM 44).

Drawing inspiration from Jean Wahl's *Vers la fin de l'ontologie* (*Toward the End of Ontology*), Glissant offers a subtle ontic poetics in which beings (art) and being (meaning) agree, without either of them having any privilege of transcendence or anteriority. Thus metaphysics will have been not subverted, reversed, or abolished but surpassed in a recovery that runs through all its stages: a daring journey built in a conscious and deliberate mulling over, both in relation to the "science of Being as being" and outside of it, both without a break and in a kind of relay: the Being of the things of the world, the non-Being of becoming become, chiasmatically and eternally, realized beings as well as the dawn that heralds radically new variations.

Philosophy is not linear, in the sense that it has an ancestor, then heirs, who develop it in a harmonious and non-problematic filiation going from its genesis to its final goal: the first word of philosophy is not taken up and then erased by the second, or the second by the third. Hence the first word (that of Heraclitus) can return and become the last word. The thirteenth thought comes back, and it is still the first: Glissant returns to the origin to produce the future.

Chapter 13

"The slave is the one who does not know, but who desires with all his strength to know"

Few explicit representations of sexuality appear in Glissant's work. Sexual acts in his novels are most often subject to ellipses or euphemisms; they are also set within a broader context, such as the reproduction of the slave labor force for the benefit of the master of the plantation, or in the poetic escape that sexuality can represent. Édouard once told me that he did not understand the contemporary obsession with sex, evident everywhere in our society. This remark was in no way a symptom of prudishness: as we shall see below, Glissant was quite capable of writing about sex without resorting to modest detours. Modern sexuality, however, must be seen within a framework that transcends it: it is part of the commercial world (that of the bourgeois prose that Hegel and Glissant reject); it is sold and bought, it is sold as an essential commodity of the society of the spectacle, entertainment, and its agents of fragmentation. In other words, sex has lost its dimension as an event, which has been dissolved into the pleasure of commodities.

In an exception to this muting of sexuality, Glissant speaks in quite direct terms of sex in Martinique. This is the third book of the *Discours antillais*, subtitled "Inconscients, Identité, Méthodes" ("Unconscious, Identity, Methods"), a revised version of a lecture given in 1973 at a symposium in Bloomington, Indiana (DA 275–311).

The evaluation of Martinican jouissance, postslavery and postcolonialism, is anchored both in Hegelian conceptuality and in its Marxist successor (i.e., commodity); but Glissant builds a specific framework that avoids the universalism of Hegel and Marx. Indeed, Martinican jouissance finds its background and its determinations in an abolished history: the slave trade erased all traces of an African past, destroyed traditional structures, and redefined the slave-as-a-being as a thing and a property. The slave is reduced to the status of commodity, whose value is his labor force. From then on, it is these new determinants that will characterize Martinican jouissance. Trafficking, in particular, has abolished all the traditional kinship structures that flourished in African societies. In the space of the plantation, the "elementary structures of kinship," the structuring role of the Name-of-the-Father, of the law (whatever their forms in the African tribe, now devastated and abolished), are usurped by the slave master alone. Thus the function, traditional or not, of desire, which depends on and is a response to the various forms taken by the Name-of-the-Father, is completely ravaged.

Freud has accustomed us to think of the structuring of desire in line with the triangulation of the Oedipus complex, an original (among the Greeks of the West) and universal phenomenon. But, in the case of the slave trade and the slave settlements in the Caribbean, the Oedipal triangle does not occur at the beginning of the story, but at its (provisional) end. Although it is possible to argue that there are African "Oedipus complexes" with their own forms, triangulation, like all memory, is erased by the slave trade; the Antillean Oedipus complex is born only belatedly, when it is reintroduced by the freeing of the slaves: "My suggestion, a controversial one, in a discussion on the Oedipus complex, was that the Oedipal relation to the mother did not here raise any problem (or, generally speaking, that the Oedipus complex as a problem is a creation of the West), as Martinican society has not been obliged to adopt the Western (triangular) model of family organization" (DA 286).

So the Oedipus complex is neither universal nor original.[1] Lacan draws the consequence: the Oedipus complex, "Freud's dream," is "strictly unusable,"[2] and by the same token, not generalizable.[3]

In the gallery of Oedipus complexes, let us not forget the Oedipus of the poet, that of Saint-John Perse, "undeniable and inseparable," that is, universal and totalizing:

> Uterine sea of our dreams and Haunted Sea of the true
> dream,
> O you who know and do not know, O you who say and
> do not say,

O Consanguine and very far away, O you incest and you
   the elder daughter,
Sea forever irreproachable, and sea finally inseparable!
Is it you, Nomad, who will ferry us tonight to the banks of
   the Real?[4]

There is thus a split between those for whom the myth has universal value (Freud, René Girard, and Saint-John Perse),[5] and those for whom it is a particular moment in a culture, even the "(hi)story" of a single individual (all other exegetes, including Levi-Strauss and Glissant). The very diversity of interpretations demonstrates that the Oedipus complex cannot be constituted as a universal structure.

In this critical constellation, we must give special importance to the *Anti-Oedipus* of Gilles Deleuze and Félix Guattari, an attempt to overcome the familialism that in their view affects Freud's theory; their book greatly inspired Édouard Glissant. It is the refusal of the determinism implied by the Oedipus complex that is highlighted, by Deleuze and Guattari as well as by Glissant; but the latter adds a particular nuance, by linking this rejected causality to the problematic of filiation: "In an exemplary case, that of Oedipus, the Freudian reinterpretation of the myth confirms the process of filiation which is being questioned, and tries to generalize it. But we will see that what contrasts this new kind of generalization is the extent, force and reality that we will define, and which presupposes the opposite of filiation" (PR 65). As against the depths of the father-mother-son triangle, Glissant sets up "the extended family" (which, it has to be said, is also a constraining myth, unless we consider it as a utopia freed from the impositions of the tribe); it is not African family structures that serve as an example here, but Faulkner:

The Oedipus complex is governed by the laws of filiation, when, on the contrary, the extended family is circular and meshed, as is the fabric of Faulkner's work. (And in parenthesis we can insert another: all the interpretations (of our societies) which are dominated by the themes of filiation—phallism, Oedipus complex, mother complex, etcetera, and you have to admit that there are more than we need—are basically ethnocentric, often naïve, projections of Western thought (PR 71; Faulkner) would then be, in a way, already outside the West and within creolization.)[6]

In every sense, we will need to free ourselves from ethnocentric projections:

> The Western work of "generalization" has, for centuries, introduced the equivalence of various communitarian times and tried to order (to prioritize) their flowering. Once the panorama has been resolved and the equidistances defined, perhaps there is reason to return to a no less necessary "degeneralisation"? Not to a renewed excess of specificities, but to a total (dreamed) freedom of their relations, whose path has been opened up in the very chaos of their confrontations. (PR 75)

In *Faulkner, Mississippi*, Oedipus becomes both the incarnation of legitimacy, the only heir to the throne of Thebes, and its opposite: by incest and the murder of the father, he at once establishes and destroys the system of differences comprised by filiation, by perverting legitimacy. He is a total sign: "That is why Oedipus is an absolute, which presupposes neither explanation nor gloss. He is self-sufficient, at once a criminal, a victim, a judge, and a sacrificer." As bringing together two radical and real opposites in his name, Oedipus is a *nefandum*, not that which should not be said, but that which cannot be said: "One can neither comment on nor explain the unspeakable. [. . .] More than will be determined by any usurpation, incest constitutes the absolute dereliction of the legitimate. Of Oedipus's incest, the only one to have been realized, one could say that it is that after which there is nothing" (FM 178). The black hole of culture, the Oedipus complex, which belongs to the *nefandum*, is to my knowledge the only moment where the unspeakable as such appears in Glissant's thought. In contrast, the unspeakable (that of Relation for example) calls for comments and explanations.

Against Freudian psychoanalysis, Oedipus is at once a beginning and an end, a First and Last Man, of whom nothing remains to be said. Outside the Western tradition, Oedipus would not produce the closed drama that Sophocles creates and that Faulkner reworks by turning it upside down. In *Absalom, Absalom!*, the attempt of the central figure, Sutpen, to found his lineage by committing incest with his own daughter in order to preserve the purity of his blood and his legitimacy makes explicit the absolute contradiction between incest and legitimacy. As the antinomy of Sophocles's Oedipus, this incest has the same effects: "savagely possessed, [Sutpen] does not know, does not want to know, that incest is the very, and irreparable, denial of legitimacy: that incest thus 'realized,' the inverse of that of Oedipus, will lead to the same cataclysmic consequences: either immediate (the death of all the protagonists), or postponed (the final fire of the Mansion)" (FM 186–187).

But the fictional county of Yoknapatawpha created by Faulkner has a deep connection to the Caribbean: like all the slave-holding South of America, it is part of what Glissant called the space of the plantations: "We already know that Louisiana is in many ways close to the Caribbean, and especially the Antilles: the system of plantations, the moving persistence of Creole languages, the background of the French language, and the most pressing element of all, one common to all slave countries, the suffering and the *marronage* [Translator's note: a word used to refer to escaping slaves] of the Negroes" (FM 46). However, Antillean space, with one massive exception,[7] lies outside of the drama of incest that marks *Absalom, Absalom!*

Since the uninterrupted process of filiation is the sole guarantor of such a connection, it is clear that the violent interruption of legitimacy (first and foremost, by incest) produces a disaffiliation. Such a detour would not be considered irreparable in the context of other cultures of the world, where legitimacy, and hence filiation as a system and a reference point, does not have such a weight of absoluteness (FM 179).

The Caribbean Sea and Yoknapatawpha County are the paradigms of a new culture no longer in the grip of the fixed idea of its own tradition and the obsession with the legitimacy of its traditions.

So what structure or disorder lie outside the Oedipus complex? What paths to jouissance are not determined by the desire of the mother and the prohibition of the father? Returning to the *Discours antillais*, we find that the slave trade is a tabula rasa; it destroys the past history of the individual and the community, including sexual practices: the collapse of tribal or family structures gives way to a void, where the absent law does not engender transgressions, but aberrations, nonsense.

The master of pre-abolition times, on the other hand, enjoyed the results of the slave's production; he destroyed them for his own pleasure. His material enjoyment (*jouissance*) of the objects of production was the privilege of his position. The slave, in the dialectic of the plantation, is only a tool of production, and this production includes his—or her—sexual activity, which is considered only in relation to the *reproduction* of a servile labor force in the form of his or her offspring. *After* abolition (1848), this particular history, outside the Oedipus complex, will introduce into the space of the plantations a specific mode of jouissance. Let us emphasize from the outset that, for Glissant, the problem is not at all merely sexual, but cultural: everything is a matter of palaver and words, of interlocking languages, as the title of *Discours antillais* highlights. In Martinique, as elsewhere, the dialectic of the master and the slave is also a question of language(s): French (the language of the master), the Creoles (the language of the slave), and the African languages (forgotten and erased by the slave trade), the drama and the struggles between languages are the point where, for Glissant, the negativity of the slavery can reverse the order and rise again in a positivity both creative and poetic.

Glissant invokes the Marxist concept of surplus value to analyze the pre-abolition economy, framing it within the Hegelian master-slave dialectic on a plane that is first (but not primarily) economic: "We know that in this matter anxieties over relationship and surplus-value determine the practice, if not the politics, of the slave-owning colonists. This is a constant throughout the whole black diaspora in all the Americas." Now, Marx's mathematical formulas for calculating surplus value have long been proved to be inconsistent, that is, unreal in mathematical terms.[8] No classical economist can attribute a monetary value to surplus value; what is calculable is income and profits or losses. With the concept of surplus value, however, Marx made a discovery: beyond the calculable profits of invested capital, there is an excess profit related to the position of the master, which must be considered not economically, but symbolically. That is why Lacan replaced surplus value (a noncalculable financial profit) by the symbolic *plus-de-jouir*.[9] There is not only a labor market (which is Marx's innovation and discovery), but also a knowledge market, where merits and values can be assessed, where choices and preferences can be organized. In other words, the *plus-de-jouir* is fundamentally a discourse—it is the jouissance of subjective knowledge. That is exactly what Glissant says: "The slave is the one who does not know, but who desires with all his strength to know and who fights for it at times." On the other hand, "the slave of slavery is the one who does not want to know":[10] the master wants to know nothing, not only of the history of slavery, but in general: and this is, after all, a very relevant description of the position of the Hegelian master in his staticity and immobility. Why would the master want to know when knowledge leads to the abolition of his mastery?

The jouissance of the slave, which did not exist in the eyes of the master, was always a *stolen* jouissance: surreptitiously stolen from his time of work, and hidden from the face of the master. There was no room for this jouissance in the slave economy; it was, strictly speaking, invisible, a diversion of a time and a space that, in principle, belonged entirely to the master. As a result of this initial act of theft, after the slaves' emancipation, the jouissance of the Martinican, now a citizen, was marked by precipitation. It was the short-circuiting of pleasure, on both sides of sexuation: "The Martinican *does not take the time*. In other words, he does not take his pleasure" (DA 296). Because of this impatience, Martinican jouissance is the moment when the subject is alienated and disappears. On the masculine side, the object of desire (a woman) is pulverized in haste: feminine jouissance does not matter in itself, but works only as a recognition of masculine jouissance: "The Martinican man will require the testimony of feminine jouissance, not as belonging to the woman, but as sanctioning the legitimacy of his own theft" (DA 295). As a jouissance without a subject, because it no longer has an object, the destructuration extends to the point where the Martinican becomes the object without subject of sexual tourism: "The Martinicans have convinced themselves that tourists of the female sex are coming here in droves for sexual consumption. [. . .] I invite you to discuss whether this is not an incredible phenomenon of self-reification by which we offer ourselves and boast of ourselves as consumable goods" (DA 301).

On the feminine side, there is the same abolition of the subject; first because female jouissance is not recognized as such; and then because, before abolition, sexual intercourse was barred from leading to reproduction, to children: "Eat the land, do not make children for slavery." After abolition, the response to masculine desire would be the indifference of frigidity and the displacement of feminine desire onto the sons: "After the supposed liberation of the slaves, whereas the Martinican man who thinks himself free erects physiological reproduction as a dramatic and compensatory substitute for economic non-production, the woman crystallizes everything in her sons, especially the eldest, practically avenging the former slave's appetite for jouissance and transferring it to this son" (DA 298). With the reification of the subject, and the substitutionary and matriarchal displacement of jouissance onto the object-offspring, there is no longer any jouissance attached to the subject himself, now alienated to his very depths. The physiological substitute for reproduction has failed to compensate for the lack of economic production.

All this is intimately connected with commodity production, circulation, and consumption; the economy of jouissance corresponds to the "real" economy at every point: "I see 'normal' consumption as an incentive to desire" (DA 458). Normality is here defined by two parameters: consumption in developed countries occurs in a context of production and subjective knowledge of the product to be consumed, in a relative rationality. This structuration is the opposite of consumption in Martinique, where the object is desired immediately, outside the context of production, and it is not its use value that counts, nor its exchange value. Only the social status that the object confers is important: what we see is an expenditure of pure prestige, where the descendants of the slaves regressively mimic the feudal masters or the monarch of the Ancien Régime, and where the object of the expenditure is the direct symbolization of the drive. The Martinican consumer is thus essentially passive, reduced to the reification of an object through which he believes (but it is a pretense) that he can assuage his drive. We may well wonder: does Glissant's analysis not go beyond a "postcolonial" sexuality, that of commodity consumption in the Antillean context? Can this dazzling and specific symptomatology not be extended to the contemporary condition of the developed countries in general? If so, Glissant would have struck a chord, not only in the specific situation of Martinique, but on a much larger scale.[11]

When Glissant expands Martinican jouissance beyond the sexual domain, by applying it to the consumption of commodity objects, he produces a doubly interwoven chiasmatic relationship of commodity and sexuality:

> Indeed, this obsession with immediate jouissance offends almost every field of activity. A customer desires a commodity immediately and absolutely, he will not have the patience to check whether it is suitable for use; a trader who has just set up a business desires absolutely and immediately recover his investments, he will not have the patience to articulate his sales techniques, to spread the profit, even if he guesses that his clientele should increase in proportion to this calculated spread. (DA 295–296)

In other words, in the precipitation of jouissance, the Martinican is a bad capitalist: he spends everything immediately, knowing, prestige, and money, as opposed to the true capitalist who overlooks his jouissance to accumulate and reinvest capital, the golden rule without which he cannot in the long run survive. The Martinican is addicted to the expense of pure prestige found in the Ancien Régime, but in a modern economy that requires the accumulation of capital. After the Revolution and the abolition of slavery, the Martinican is admittedly a citizen (a *Bürger*, a bourgeois) in the Hegelian sense of the term: he can serve in the French army (and kill just like the master); he works or receives unemployment benefits just like the slave (and this is a new figure of enslavement). But in Martinique, this becoming-citizen, which puts an end to the master-slave dialectic, has its periods of dormancy and its failures. Indeed, the Martinican slave did not carry out the Revolution, nor did he become a citizen of the Empire: Napoleon, in the Treaty of Amiens (1802), restored the slavery abolished by the Revolution; slavery would end only in 1848. One crucial fact in this succession of failures and successes is that identity as a citizen was not won; unlike that of the sans-culottes of 1789, it was imposed from outside: "The 'liberation' of the slaves [which] led to the swelling of another trauma arising from a civil status that was allocated, in other words granted, in other words imposed" (DA 277). However, for Glissant, the identity is not the identity that we receive, but the identity that we give ourselves. Moreover, an abolition that is granted, and not conquered, does not lead to a postrevolutionary situation where guarantees concerning private property are extracted from the nobility (or slave-owning planters)—this is one of the essential conditions put forward by Hegel for the Revolution to succeed. The abolition of 1848 did not affect private property; the colonists, now bourgeois and no longer masters, remained the owners of their lands; former slaves did not access the means of production; they were truncated *Bürgers*. The children of slaves only partially gained a citizenship that should have included private property. Hence, according to Glissant, not only a miscognition of the deferred jouissance, something characteristic of a capitalist, but also the appearance of new neuroses, for which the *Discours antillais* boldly puts forward new labels: neuroses of saturation (by the unlimited supply of goods), neuroses of demunition (by the gap between the commodity and its use), and neuroses of stoppage, by which the Martinican overlooks the impossibility of his becoming-citizen. The clinical taxonomy closes with the psychoses of connection, where the de-relation with reality peaks, echoing the "capitalism and schizophrenia" of Deleuze and Guattari: "Thus, to the psychoses of complexion ("de-relating individuals"), more frequent in a technicized environment, we would add the psychoses of connection (of the direct de-relation with the situation-more characteristic of a society like ours)" (DA 291). The psychosis of connection deprives atomized individuals from the chance to participate in Relation: the negativity of De-relation must be answered by the affirmation of Relation.

It is not only individuals who are concerned here, but the community. The neurosis is that of a people, just as the Caribbean unconscious is collective.

On History as Neurosis

> Would it be ridiculous or odious to consider our history as tracing the path of a neurosis? The [word missing] as traumatic shock, settling (in the new country) as a phase of repression, the period of slavery as a latency period, the "liberation" of 1848 as reactivation, the customary delusions as symptoms and even the reluctance "to go back over these things of the past" as a manifestation of the return of the repressed? (DA 133–134)[12]

Whenever he discovers the impasse of a desire that is alienated in the commodity (including sexual commodities), Édouard Glissant always offers the same answer: the *plus-de-jouir* must be fulfilled in a poetics. Thus, the truncated relationship with the land is overcome by a poetics of excess: "The earth is the other's. The poetics of the earth, therefore, cannot be a poetics of saving, of patient clearing, of forecasting. It is a poetics of excess, where everything must be spent at once" (DA 276).[13] In the *Discours antillais*, the clinical picture of neurotic and psychotic symptoms is resolved into words and writings, cataloged in the section "Délire verbal" ("Verbal Delirium"). This delirium is a symptom of the alienation of Martinican jouissance, but it is also its subsumption through a poetic creation; the creation of Évariste Suffrin, who produced Baroque manifestos, is the prime example of what Glissant would later call the "unspeaker" (*déparleur*). To unspeak is, first and foremost, to wax delirious, but in accordance with a regulated rhetoric: "the unspeaker, contrary to what people believe, has his rhetoric and this rhetoric is absolutely impeccable."[14] As symbolic expenditure, de-speaking is also where orality moves into writing.

But Suffrin as an unspeaker does not know he knows. On the contrary, Glissant knows that he knows: there are limits to the way the writer and the psychotic unspeaker, enslaved to psychosis, can be identified with one another.[15] Glissant as an unspeaker opens himself up to poetic freedom only by not submitting to the psychosis of rules and the rules of psychosis. Witness the example of Saint-John Perse: "And I understood that Saint-John Perse was an "unspeaker," that is to say someone who, perfectly mastering the imagery of his words, proposes it by completely hiding the reference to its meaning and by defying anyone to comment on it."[16] Thus, the commentator, like the writer does not need to identify with the cry of the psychotic, the first moment of expression; they must distance themselves from the cry, to give it its full-meaning (*plein-sens*).

In the section of the *Discours antillais* titled "Inconscient, identité, méthodes" ("Unconscious, Identities, Methods"), Glissant rejects any identification: either with the descendants of the slaves, the practitioners of jouissance Martinique-style, or the descendants of the old colonizing masters, known in Martinique as *békés*, who employ the children of former slaves. The new clinical categories prove as much, as they have an explicitly negative connotation. The neuroses of "démunition," "saturation," "stoppage," and the psychosis of "connection" are all labels for Martinican mental imbalance that reject the obligatory empathy of the psychoanalyst clinician or the psychiatrist for his patient, replacing them with an ethical listening that is *situated* (*en situation*).

If Glissant places himself in a position of controlling distance vis-à-vis the Martinican symptom, this is so as to better reveal the control hidden in the psychoanalytic transfer. It will be noted that most psychoanalysts would object to this description of their livelihood; Lacan, in particular, always affirmed that the analyst's discourse was the opposite of the master's discourse, as a discourse of nonmastery. It is, however, in the cunning mastery of sympathy that Glissant reads the case of Georges Payote, a Martinican psychotic, who was analyzed by a Lacanian psychoanalyst, Maud Mannoni: "The problems are 'outgrown.' The gaze of the other 'signals' them, but they are linked to a more encompassing problematic, a psychoanalytic theme for example, where they are diluted. It is reduction by universalism. Sympathy is generalizing (Case of Mme Maud Mannoni)" (DA 304).

Generalization (that of the castration anxiety diagnosed by Maud Mannoni) erased the specific situation of Georges Payote as a Martinican. The identification of sympathy erased the singularities of the case by diluting them in a universal law, of which Payote was merely one of the exemplary variants. In other words, the patient was extracted from his "inextricable place." Payote's psychotic failure lies in the de-relation or the derealization of a signifier and a real: he does not succeed in inscribing into his system the signifier "Martinique" in its alienating reality. The psychoanalyst merely intensifies this failure: "Mme Mannoni says nothing about Georges Payote's attempts to describe his country (the idea he has of it, the conclusions he draws from it)" (DA 310). Taking over from the psychotic and his psychoanalyst, Glissant succeeds where Payote and Maud Mannoni failed: he will describe, better, he will write his country, he will place it in a relation with the world, without erasing its essential characteristics.

In Freud and Lacan, philosophy assumes the very form of the discourse of psychosis: entirely coherent, but entirely intent, in the psychotic, on denying castration, whereas in the master-philosopher the point is the appropriation of the slave's knowledge: "One could almost say that hysteria is a distorted work of art, that an obsessional neurosis is a distorted religion and a paranoid mania a distorted philosophical system," writes Freud.[17] And Lacan notes, with regard to the psychotic President Schreber: "He is just as coherent as many philosophical systems of our time."[18] George Payote, a philosopher suffering in his psychosis, is described in the same terms in *Le Discours antillais*.

Is Glissant the philosopher therefore, in his formidable coherence, psychotic? If for a while Glissant identified with psychosis, he moved away from it, to open psychotic coherence to the questioning of reality, just as his ontics does not close in on itself. The identification with Georges Payote, the producer of a symptom unique to him, must therefore be bypassed, both to grasp its Martinican specificity and to raise it to the level of a poetic model rich in possibilities.

This rule of disidentification can be generalized and must be applied to writings of fiction: Glissant never fully identifies with his characters or, which amounts to the same thing, he identifies with each of them, whoever they may be, masters and slaves, colonists and descendants of slaves. Thus the interpreter cannot adopt any specific fictional position, or identify with any character whatsoever, without betraying Glissant's project; any examination of the "psychology" of Marie Celat or Mathieu Béluse, any repetition of their individual adventures in the commentary are rendered obsolete by the principle of nonidentification that governs Glissant's writing. Making transference impossible means putting an end to the psychological reading of the novel, to the interpretation of Balzac "the generous" or Proust "the sickly" (IL 115) by transference onto such-and-such a character, even the omniscient or subjective narrator. For a long time, *The Red and the Black*, *The Human Comedy*, and *In Search of Lost Time* were read via an identification with a supposed "character psychology" (for Flaubert, it is the opposite, as *Madame Bovary* cannot be read without dis-identifying from the central character, but this ultimately comes down to the same thing, as the countertransference does not in the least abolish identification). This quirk of indulging in psychologizing interpretation is unfortunately very common in francophone studies: it is to be hoped that they will come to maturity by going beyond it and acquiring a theoretical framework of their own; in this respect, it is clear to me that Glissant's theoretical and philosophical work provides us with absolutely indispensable tools.

Ancient philosophy was fundamentally linked to a social structure of slavery, where masters and slaves were completely opposed. The slave's work gave the master the leisure necessary for thought, the *otium philosophicum*. In this respect, the space of plantations, from the sixteenth to the nineteenth century, differed profoundly from ancient societies; it was a regression to social structures that had been swept away in Europe by the disappearance of slavery and serfdom. It is not surprising that this monstrous anomaly (in relation to historical evolution—with or without finalism) produced no philosophers, only popinjays of enjoyment.

For Lacan, the society of the masters of antiquity was not a matter of economics: *otium philosophicum* is also cultural larceny, the grabbing of the slave's knowledge by the master; Lacan takes the example of Plato's *Meno*. In addition, this society extracted the slave's knowledge and hijacked it completely for its own profit: "Philosophy played the role of constituting the master's knowledge, withdrawing it from the slave's knowledge."[19]

Now, in any post-slave-owning society, where the slave has been replaced by the *Knecht* (the servant, in Hegel), and where, democratically, anyone and everyone can pretend to be a philosopher *and* a worker (as in the "philosopher-king" that Glissant reveals in Christianity), philosophy can no longer pretend to be integrated into the discourse of the master and to formulate philosophically the reasons for that discourse.[20] Philosophy becomes the task of every community, in Relation without distinction of class or nation; poetic philosophy is now responsible for laying the basis of an unexpected future: "Thought draws the imagination of the past: a knowledge in becoming. We cannot halt it so as to gauge it, nor isolate it so as to broadcast it. It is a sharing, which no one can divest himself of or, coming to a halt, take advantage of" (PR 13).

In Glissant's fiction, the master-slave dialectic is muted: "The novels I write never *directly* contrast the master with the slave" (DA 286). In this muffled space, thought can arise beyond the philosophical constraints of mastery: "The essence of the connection I attempt to make in these novels is to show precisely that the master-slave opposition in Martinique is always *overdetermined* and it would be misleading to present it as defining" (DA 286). In other words, the Hegelian dialectic is no longer regarded as an absolute of either history or of fiction: it is relativized in a specific context in which it loses its generalizing preeminence. In the same way, there is no longer any "master" of the narrative: identification with the victim, as well as identification with the author, is barred, in the multiplicity of points of view that organize fictions. The question then is whether Glissant, having gone beyond literature, has not also thrown philosophy out of kilter.

Ever since Thales, philosophy has first and foremost tried to understand nature. Much later, modern science destroyed all that the Pre-Socratics had thought of the *physis*. But, as Glissant shows, the first philosophers were not silenced by Galilean science: their writings merely changed status—they were transformed from objective knowledge to subjective knowledge and its imaginary, through which they still speak to us today. Plato and Aristotle imposed silence on the Pre-Socratics, and philosophy committed itself through them to mastery by means of the Beautiful, the True, the Idea, the Concept. Today, a new transformation is taking place, and philosophy, deprived of the symbolic structure that linked it to the master's discourse in antiquity, must be rethought.

Glissant took the full measure of this transformation: leaving behind all mastery, he shares out philosophy; erasing or recomposing Being, the absolute, universality, the concept, his ontics opens new paths to thought; philosophy, now shared and no longer the exclusive occupation of specialists and academics, now dissatisfied with focusing only on the past and present (of systems), emerges from the sterile sphere of the pure concept and commits itself wholeheartedly to the future of our World.[21]

Chapter 14

"I change things, through exchanging with the other, and yet without destroying or distorting myself"

In *Soleil de la conscience*, the loneliness of the individual (the "French," or "Western" individual) is underlined ("Everyone goes back to his room"): "Grandeur and servitude of Paris, which teaches the art of being alone. A hell without seasons," which differs chiasmatically from the solitude of Rimbaud in *A Season in Hell*. As early as 1959, the solution of individual loneliness was an imaginary of Relation: "A hell without seasons. Whence it is necessary for everyone that the *Soleil de la conscience* [sun of consciousness] should arise" (SC 56). This is clarified in *L'Intention poétique* by anticipating the bringing into Relation of opacities: "What is necessary here for all those involved, communities that are heavy with history and communities that are stripped and bare, is not a language of communication (an abstract, emaciated, "universal" language of the well-known kind) but quite the opposite: a possible communication between mutually liberated opacities, differences, languages" (IP 51). The atomization of the modern individual can be remedied only by a renewed sharing.

Now, the singularity of the human subject is a modern and Western notion, born and extended to a range of specific times and spaces: identity and the individual are not eternally self-identical—they have a history or a plurality of histories. Even today, many societies live under social regimes that give the group prominence over the individual. This was for a long time the nature of the social bond in Greco-Roman Antiquity and elsewhere and previously: membership of the community, whether defined as family, ethnicity, language, tribe, nation, people, empire, feudal lineage, or religion were of more importance than individual singularity. In Greek philosophy, as we have seen, the singular is always taken as an illustration of a more general law—witness Aristotle, who "leaves singularity on the margins of logic."[1] Socrates as Plato sees it, is in this respect an exception to the law of groups: he is marked by an *atopia* (*Symposium*, 229c); he is "out of place," an exception to the norm, unclassifiable by the rule that he merely confirms, a quirk or a strangeness that he will pay for with his life (in Plato, *atopia* also designates the singularity of desire, which the lover feels at the sight of the beautiful, a mixture of pain and of jouissance: the soul "is tormented by the strangeness of what it experiences" (*Phaedrus*, 251 d). Apart from a few "out-of-place" individuals, Greek singularity is always merged into the group, even and especially when this group defines itself as an Academy (in other words, a philosophical school).

Everything changes with the New Testament, where a new figure of individuality suddenly arises (as a break). This dramatic change is based on a more general epistemological break, that of incarnation, of the Man-God, the *hapax* that was, according to Saint Paul, "folly for the Greeks and scandal for the Jews," an atopia that neither the Greek polytheistic religion nor the monotheistic Jewish religion could reduce to their categories. The Greek gods had no body, and giving them human flesh would have degraded them; the Jewish god was forever out of the world, incarnating himself solely in the breath of his word. Drawing the consequences of the Incarnation for the social bond, Saint Paul founded, in the Epistle to the Galatians, the modern form of individualism, considered from the point of view of its absolute singularity: "There is no longer any Jew neither Greek; there is no longer a slave or a free man; there is neither male nor female; for all of you are one in Christ Jesus" (Galatians 3:28). The only link that binds the singularities and prevents their definitive atomization is faith. "All one in Jesus Christ": there is simultaneously an inclusion in God and an exclusion of unbelievers.

Glissant reinterprets this inaugural moment of the singularity of the subject: "Individuation is a first mystery, and Christic individuation opens the way to generality. It alone was capable of this. If the whole man, at once flesh, soul and spirit, is in Christ, then the universal can take flight" (MTT 98). This is a paradoxical reading: the moment of singularity coincides with that of generality: when the individual asserts himself, he immediately dissolves into an abstract universal, which could be formulated as follows: "Every man is singular." The origin of individuation, in Glissant, suggests the very dilution of singularity. In the first stage, "What Christ manifests, he and he alone, is incarnation without any falling-off, filiation without any weight of heredity" (PR 62). But things are reversed: "CHRIST—To an undivided ethnic community, legitimized by filiation, is added the act of individuation that inaugurates a History of humanity. The exclusive linearity of this filiation is succeeded by the non-diversifiable linearity of a generalization" (PR 63). Relation objects to this deliquescence in two stages that coincide. First, it takes up St. Paul's universalism that includes all peoples, all natural languages, all individual languages, all cultures; but it objects to the exclusion based on Pauline's "All (one) *in Jesus Christ*," where the universal was limited to the Catholic community.

In the West there is no human sphere unaffected by the redefinition of individuality that Saint Paul promoted. Religion becomes an individual affair (with Protestantism); autobiography, a genre almost unknown in Greco-Roman antiquity, is born with the *Confessions* of Saint Augustine, which will be extended and transmuted into literature by Montaigne and Rousseau. Philosophy, with Fichte and Schelling, establishes subjective individualism, in parallel with the exclusive expression of the self that the romantics turn into their warhorse. In politics, at the end of a long evolution, human rights will be proclaimed; in law, inalienable individual property will make its appearance. I could go on . . .

Recall that for Glissant, "the universal is a lure." As far as Judeo-Christian individualism and singularity are concerned, the postulate is true. These notions are born from a specific soil; they are datable historically, and coextensible, even today, with a precise geography, that of the "West" and its appendages: the singularity of the individual, in the past as in the present, is a principle that is not universal, and one which, for Glissant, Hegel, and Nietzsche, will soon have exhausted all its possibilities—a modernity, by definition, is not an eternity but is destined for twilight and death.

As Eric Voegelin pointed out, the Christic theophany leads to an "egophany" that is the culmination of Judeo-Christian individualism, and gives it its geographical and temporal limits.

However, for Glissant, who returns several times to this theme, egophany has now exhausted its expressive resources: "Everyone finds himself back in his room" (SC 12), the Republic of Letters and its Freemasonry produces truncated, atomized men:

> [. . .] the systematic intellectual attitude of mockery emerges
> in the unconscious refusal to share, to live the world and the
> thought of the world with the other. The unhappy conscious-
> ness then sees any generosity—any seemingly unmotivated
> impulse—as naivety. Stuck in these famous trash cans, the
> last and theatrical refuge of a desperate lucidity, the truncated
> man, who has himself amputated his legs, has obliged himself
> to refuse to *walk*. (IP 28–29)

The shadows of Socrates (derision), Hegel (unhappy consciousness), and Freud (amputation-castration) hover over this paragraph, which describes the apocalypse of egophany, after which there is no longer a "march," that is, a future: "There is no worse calamity than withdrawal (into oneself), reflection (on the other) or abstraction (of everything): it is the unnatural, no longer imposed but intimately assumed" (IP 151). In the twilight of the West, poetry can no longer be satisfied with egophany: "Generality: history is posited by man and imposes itself on him in the modern experience as a ridge of the *I*: a "chamber" poet need not be futile, but will certainly be unfinished [. . .]. [Poetry] cannot summon the solitary man (in a credulously "psychological" lyricism) nor the world as appearance (in a flattened-out realism)" (IP 60).

If the notion of the singular individual is born, it can also die: this is what Glissant notes very early in the course of his œuvre: "The West was constituted in the rule of a spirituality whose most systematic intention was to isolate man, to constantly reduce him to his 'role' as an individual, to confine him to himself: it does not matter here what methodological and technical assets were thus procured" (IP 59). In this death of the Judeo-Christian subject, a philosopher, Hegel (I will return to this later), and two French writers, Mallarmé and Proust, were the main protagonists.[2]

But maybe Arthur Rimbaud precedes them. Just as Glissant institutes, through the Other of thought, a total and profound reassessment of metaphysics, he completely renews the way we interpret the French literary tradition. Of Rimbaud and his "premature effort," he writes: "In other words, his work illuminated latent tendencies, the lesson of his time was not decided, he was materialistic with an idealistic accompaniment, a poet of the world in a context of 'psychological' or descriptive poetry, and he postulated the 'All' by suffering the burden of a long tradition of individualism" (IP 60). Rimbaud is the poet who abandons poetry to devote himself, across the world, to trade; it is he who declares, in a draft of *A Season in Hell*: "Now I can say that art is a piece of stupidity."[3] To which Glissant echoes: "(And it seems that, by today exhausting the total wish by achieving the totality of the world in its density, man is taking art toward its diffuse death—or is it perhaps the unsuspected that is capsizing there?)" (IP 63). The end of European art makes necessary an Other of philosophy and an Other of literature. Arthur Rimbaud is no longer a man of letters (which people find it difficult to forgive)—he drops the Republic of Letters. According to Glissant, this is because he understood that his project was ahead of his time. But the reason is also, perhaps, that in a few years of dazzling activity he found that, after Romanticism, the singular subject had dragged out its possibilities of expression: it was necessary to do something else, and the Whole-World was not there yet to welcome him.

I am here extending what I proposed about the Whole-Book. Mallarmé founds his poetics in a radical and unanswerable negativity (to answer him, we must erase him): "The pure œuvre implies the poet's elocutionary disappearance, as he hands over the initiative to words."[4] The initiative of words creates an "abolished trinket of sonorous inanity" ("Her pure nails very high dedicating their onyx"),[5]—the poet is now nothing but the instrument that makes Language resonate. "Destruction was my Beatrice," writes Mallarmé to Eugene Lefébure. In the Mallarmean paradise, the summit is no longer represented by the Lady or God (Dante's choices), but by nothingness. This disappearance of the subject is concomitant with a fundamental atheism. In a letter to Cazalis, Mallarmé writes: "That old wicked plumage, brought down to the ground, fortunately, God." In the same letter: "This is to let you know that I am now impersonal and no longer the Stéphane you knew—but an aptitude of the spiritual Universe to see itself and develop, through what was once me." The annihilation of the subject (author or reader) quite logically leads to the project of the Book that was to have gathered the Whole of the world and the Whole of the library: "Impersonifed, the volume, as far as one separates from it as author, does not call for a reader's approach. As it is, you must know, between human accessories, it takes place all alone: made, being" (*Quant au Livre*). Glissant comments: "The œuvre-absence is thus (however) the only present, of which books are forever the revelation in a mirror. Mallarmé lived absolutely this tragic and magnificent imbroglio, this unbearable condition" (IP 67). The condition is unbearable because it is a knell—the knell that proclaims both the end of the ("Western") individual and of art. The process of annihilation culminates in the project of the Book, the clear rival of *To Biblion*, the Two Testaments, the end of all books, but also the end of all worlds: "The world is made to end up as a beautiful book." With Mallarmé, Western individuality leads to aesthetic rapture ("a beautiful book"), which confirms its disappearance. This is a proposition that Glissant reverses in all directions, and that could be expressed as: "Books are made to end up as the Whole-World."

The negative poetics of Mallarmé set the stage for the second moment of the exhaustion of the individual Western subject and his reaffirmation in art, Proust's Book, *In Search of Lost Time*. One of the predominant themes of this autobiographical fiction is the vanishing of all the objects of desire, which leads the narrator to an absolute dereliction. Satiety, be it worldly, economic, or sexual, has produced dissatisfaction; commodity pleasure, since it is bought (Proust always paid for his jouissance in hard currency), vanishes in nonsense. Love and desire cannot be fulfilled by objects. But from the depths of the narrator's hell, the author arises, and all love is now transferred to the work, which replaces all the objects of desire, men or women. Through the most minute "psychological" analysis possible (stemming, like jealousy, from obsessional neurosis), Proust's novel saturates and drains the expressive possibilities of the Judeo-Christian subject; there is no longer any shadow zone or "opacity" in which to take refuge. What survives this disaster is once again the Book, which completes Mallarmé's unfinished project in a novelistic form. The novel brings to completion the history of the subject after poetry has abolished itself in the mirror of its own contemplation. This creative destruction itself becomes salvation, outside of the dead ends of desire and jouissance at which the narrator always fails; the displacement of the drive toward the object, which Freud made the mark of modernity, is completed, and the object is always and everywhere found to be faulty, unsatisfactory, failed. Literature and the very volume of *In Search of Lost Time* then become, by sublimation, the sole objects of desire, the only goal to which it is worth dedicating one's life; and this in terms which make it the exact equivalent of Christian redemption, even including the promise of resurrection and eternal life: "I say that the cruel law of art is that people die and that we ourselves die in exhausting all suffering, so that what may grow will be the thick grass not of oblivion, but of eternal life, the thick grass of fruitful works, on which the generations to come will make merry, without caring for those who sleep below, and enjoy their 'picnic on the grass.'"[6] Francois Mauriac, in his famous obituary of Proust, did not fail to point out, as a good Catholic, the idolatry of an author who martyred himself to his work so as to complete it; but Proust's agnosticism precisely prevented him from resorting to the traditional Judeo-Christian forms he had inherited from his family; salvation lay outside the religious "illusion" indexed by Freud, an illusion which for him had no future. If Proust reaches eternity through art, then for him, as for Marcel (who before our very eyes becomes the author himself), time, history, individuality, and singularity are authentically completed and reabsorbed in the creation of *In Search of Lost Time*; and we can participate in this timeless jouissance, enjoying it through reading it and sharing our sublimatory identification.

Any reader of *In Search of Lost Time* may find that the resources for its interpretation are entirely contained in its *volumen*. The Proustian "Book on the book" also thus puts an end to the eternal romanticism that hangs around in Belles-Lettres. The *Search* thus closes down the Republic of the Belles-Lettres: the subject and its book, now merged, have said everything that it was possible to say of themselves; literature can no longer "express the subject"—the adventure of Christian individualism in the chain of the signifier, begun by Saint Augustine in the *Confessions*, and then continued by Montaigne and Rousseau, is accomplished. Everything is brought into the overwhelming light of day—opacity has no refuge. Let me quote Glissant again: "Literary minuteness, however lucid, announces a disintegrated Body. Today, the general character of Western art, what it shares between artists, is the absence of community" (S 62).

It is on the basis of this Proustian End (the exhaustion of all the possibilities of expression of a singularity) that we must read Glissant, to understand the revival, the new throw of the dice by which he wards off the End (of the novel, individuality, Belles-Lettres). Glissant radically rejected Proust:

> The Western novel is not so much a technique—there are many techniques—as a pretense, a belief. It is the belief that we can write history because we are the only ones to control it. This is the fundamental belief. This is a belief shared by the most generous writers, such as Balzac, or the sickliest, like Proust. That is why the novel had become unconsciously and automatically the fundamental element of literature. (IL 115)

I categorically reject the epithet of "sickly" to describe Proust; we need only read *Finding Time Again* to witness the joy of his rebirth, the mystical ecstasy of his salvation and healing in and through the Book. That being said, we must again recognize the sureness of Glissant's symptomatology: reframed by the problematic of the Last Man and the End of History *as figures specific to Europe*, Proust and Mallarmé clearly appear as a *finis terrae*, a Finistère. "They call it Finistère: the end (or edge) of lands. And that was its extremity. [. . .] But it is, there, something else" (IP 18).

In philosophy, it is Nietzsche who perceives most acutely the exhaustion of the Western subject, which he calls the Last Man. The end of European history conceived by Hegel is mocked:

> Behold, I will show you the Last Man: "What is loving? What is creating? What is desiring? What is a star?" Thus will the Last Man speak, blinking. The earth will then become cramped, we will see the Last Man hopping about on it as he shrinks everything. His brood is as indestructible as that of the aphid; the Last Man is the one who will live the longest. "We invented happiness," say the Last Men, blinking. They will have abandoned the lands where life is hard, as they need warmth. They will still love their neighbors and rub up against them, as they need warmth. Illness and mistrust will appear to them as sins; we only have to be careful where we walk! Only fool still stumbles over stones or men! A little poison from time to time; it gives you pleasant dreams; a lot of poison to finish with, in order to have a pleasant death. They will still work, as work is a distraction. But they will take care that this distraction never becomes tiring. They will not become either rich or poor; it's too much of a pain. Who will still want to govern? And who will want to obey? Both are too much of a pain. No shepherd and one flock! All will want the same thing for everyone, all will be equal; anyone who feels differently will gladly enter an asylum. "In the old days everyone was crazy," the smartest will say, blinking. They will be smart, they will know everything that happened before; so they will have something to make fun of endlessly. They will still squabble, but they will soon be reconciled, for fear of spoiling their digestion. They will have their little pleasure for the day and

their little pleasure for the night; but due reverence will be paid to health. "We have invented happiness," the Last Men will say, blinking.[7]

Nietzsche, to free himself from the nihilist impasse of satiety represented by the Last Men, proposes the resolution of the Superman, supposed to overcome the End of History; but the Superman will be, yet again, a singular subject.

In this sense, such a denouement is not suitable for Glissant: his dialectic goes beyond the point of view of the singular subject, the egophany locked in struggle with other individualities, by pooling resources, in a "sociophany" of sharing, through the imaginary of poetics related to specific places, unavoidable and inextricable. (Here, Relation intrinsically constitutes a social bond.)

The imaginary, the place of identities, can also be the space of an irreducible hatred. Glissant is well aware of the problem, and sets it out in terms close to Freud's description, in *Civilization and its Discontents*, of the narcissism of small differences: "Thus too do the calamities of the racist urge exert aim first at the nuances of difference rather than against the radicalities of otherness, of alterity (*altréité*)" (NRM 104).

The narcissism of small differences can be fought on the symbolic level, by absorbing it back into organizations (such as the United Nations) or regions (such as Europe) that are supposed to work for the common good of humanity, but the results leave one doubtful. Glissant takes his stance on a very different ground, that of an imaginary in which Relation reigns, where the subject enters into relationship with the Other without any spirit of conquest, domination, or enslavement. And above all, the mechanism of projections and identifications that supports the self must be dismissed: "It is not necessary for me to become the other (to become other) nor to "make him" in my image" (PR 207). We must escape from narcissistic determinations, by a deliberate decision: Glissant's thought is a voluntarism; Relation can come into being only if it is intentionally imagined and really desired, in common: "Literature, while being deliberate, does not cease to remain a wish. But the wish, by being thus sustained, is finally denied by coming true" (IP 217). The fulfillment of the wish demonstrates that it remains unfulfilled (and unfulfillable): "Any "deliberate" literature (which by definition is soon to be surpassed) is at present in full consciousness preparing its maturity, and arming language with the weapons of knowledge" (IP 43).

Overcoming the aggressive stupidity of a social bond based on narcissism and singularity requires us to give ourselves to the imaginary of Relation, outside of the atavistic rootedness of identity, and in the rhizome of all difference. This is what Glissant calls relation-identity, and he contrasts it with root-identity:

Relation-identity [. . .]

- is given in the chaotic weft of relation and not in the hidden violence of filiation;

- conceives no legitimacy as a guarantor of its own right, but circulates in a new expanse;

- does not imagine a land as a territory, from which we project onto other territories, but as a place where we "give-with" (*donne-avec*) instead of "understanding" (*com-prendre* [Translator's note: literally "to take-with"]) (PR 158).

The constitution of a new notion of identity is a wager and a utopia. It is a generous dream whose function is to break out of the impasse of (Hegelian) egophany and the (Freudian) narcissism of small differences, which has now exhausted its expressive possibilities: "By the thought of wandering we reject those single roots that, by being single, kill all around them: the thought of wandering and that of solidary rootedness and rhizomatic roots. Against the diseases of the single rooted identity, the thought of wandering is and remains the infinite conductor of the relation identity" (PhR 61).

Necessarily requiring at least two terms, relation-identity is inextricably linked to digenesis—it is, from the beginning, a crossbreed of Other and Same: "The thought of the *single root identity*, which kills on the spot, or on the contrary of the *identity which wanders*, which does not go to a single goal, but reinforces all of them, and the here by the elsewhere. The thought of *atavistic cultures*, which have with deadly effect founded legitimacy and territory, and *composite cultures*, the very same which at every moment contrast and mingle their digeneses, crazy primordial births" (PhR 80–81).

Opacity plays its part here; it refuses to make the Other transparent, to index it on the already known, as well as avoiding the imposition of transparency by the Other: "I can therefore conceive the opacity of the other for myself, without my reproaching him for my opacity to him. It is not necessary for me to "understand" him to feel solidarity with him, to build with him, to love what he does. These projected transmutations—without metempsychosis—have resulted from the worst pretensions and the loftiest generosities of the West" (PR 207). Opacity is the sign of the irreducible, not only from individual to individual, but from community to community: "The opaque is the non-reducible" (PR 205). It does not need to be subsumed into a theory or a concept, or to submit to the classifications of psychology or the clarity of a system. Nor is opacity comparable to some Mallarmean "mystery in letters," or to the notion of plot in the novel, which reveals its rebus as a conclusion (there is no plot strictly speaking in Glissant's novels); it is an irreducible moment of the world and of time, pointing to a still unimagined future: "Because the future of literatures is the inextricable, the incomprehensible, the obscure and the too vast, the too bright, the too illuminated" (IL 116). Thus, the refusal of the identitarian is not the dissolution of identity, but the conjoining of at least two opacities: "I claim for all the right to opacity, which is not confinement. This is a way of reacting against so much reduction to the false clarity of universal models" (TTM 29). This does not imply the muddled words of obscurity or the mystery of prophecy, because opacity moves toward a light that is both first (*Soleil de la conscience*) and last: the light of the imaginary.

Ultimately, opacity is a decisive step beyond Hegel. As Eric Voegelin once again saw, in Hegel egophany replaced theophany. The latter always retained some mystery, God remaining hidden and unknowable, even in his incarnation as man. But the self-consciousness of absolute knowledge (egophany) leaves nothing in the shadows: everything is illuminated, everything transparent in *Selbstbewusstsein*. The concept no longer has a shadow zone; the unconscious disappears and, with it, human desire, as singularity merges into the totalizing unity in ideas of the concept. And this dazzling clarity is finalized:

> If the intolerant violence of filiation was once buried in the sacred mystery of the root, if it was tragically given to enter into the opacity of this mystery, if this opacity thus signified mystery and at the same time obscured the latter's violence, —this was always in function of a final transparency, underpinned in the tragic debate. The same transparency, in the history of the West, predicts that there is a general Truth of man and maintains

that what approaches this most closely is the projecting action
by which we realize the world at the same time as we catch
its foundation by surprise. Against this reductive transparency,
a force of opacity is at work. No longer that opacity which
enveloped and reactivated the mystery of filiation, but another
kind, sparing the threatened succulences which join together
(without conjoining, that is, without melting) in the extent
of Relation. (PR 74)

In this respect, in Glissant, opacity represents the revival of desire
and (hi)stories: beyond the Last Man, there is not only a New Man, there
are New Humanities.

Singularity, being individual, is by definition what cannot be said,
as pointed out by medieval scholasticism when it decreed that *individuum
ineffabile est*: what cannot be divided cannot be said. The first elements,
stoicheia, of matter or thought (beginning with the very person who
thinks) are the irreducible residues of thought. Only the generalities of
philosophy or theology are thinkable and can be put into a system. In
Glissant, the *individuum* of scholasticism is replaced by place, detail, difference, "inextricables," "unavoidables," nonreducible singularities.

The function of the thinker and the writer must be rethought: they
are "solitary *and* solidary." Drawing on both Victor Hugo,[8] whose epic
spaciousness he loves, and Albert Camus,[9] whose distrust of any ideology he shares, the writer is for Glissant both "solitary" (the adventure of
thought must be conducted by a singular subject) and "solidary" (with
those who cohabit in his place): "This is what I will summarize by repeating that the writer will be solitary and solidary. Solitary: this means
that he must adventurously live in the thought of wandering, which is
not a collectivist thought or even a collective thought, and solidary: this
means that he must totally grow in the thought of his place. It is only
through this practice of detour and return that the dialectic of Relation
can operate" (EBR 111).

The notions of Same and Other then change: they are at once
irreducible and exchanging, in an incessant dialectic that puts them in
relation while preserving their singularity: "This thought of the Same and
the Other thus sent the poets venturing but it will become frantically
commonplace, once the emergence of peoples has rendered its formulation
obsolete" (PR 43). In the Whole-World, the Same and the Other are in
commutation and in chiasm, both distinct and shared; there is a potential

biography of communities, just as there is an expression of collective history in individual writing: "You can see how the *continuum of the collective*, so difficult to reestablish, ultimately agrees with the discontinuity of the person, who must be supported despite everything" (EBR 62).

The chiasm is concentrated in the quarrel between the thought of the Other and the Other of thought: "The thought of the Other is the moral generosity which would incline me to accept the principle of otherness, to conceive that the world is not made of a single block and that there is not just one truth, mine." On the other hand, the Other of thought is a dynamic becoming, through which it becomes almost synonymous with Relation: "It is an aesthetic of turbulence, whose corresponding ethics is not given in advance. If we admit that an aesthetic is an art of conceiving, imagining, or acting, the Other of thought is the aesthetic implemented by me, by you, to enter into a dynamic process to which we can contribute" (PR 169).

This is indeed a "new dialectic," where identity becomes common, part of the social bond, and otherness is transformed into a quest for this fusion itself:

> In the first place, not to lose oneself as an individual in the rigorous attempt to establish a continuum of the biography of the collective [. . .] in the second place, for a poet, we can see the outlines of both a policy of the maintenance of his individuality and a poetics of the quest for his community. As you will notice, I reverse the function of these terms, "political" and "poetic"—they are no longer as commonly envisaged, but instead I sketch out a new dialectic. (EBR 38)

This implies an ethic of Relation: "The rule of any action, individual or otherwise, would be better if perfected in the experience of Relation" (PR 207). This ethics is the inclusion and totality of transparencies and opacities, whether these be mine or those of the stranger: "I change things, through exchanging with the other, and yet without destroying or distorting myself" (PhR 66).

Glissant thus fights against the fixity of identity and its sociological, economic, and political determinants, as well as those of family and citizenship. Identity in Relation goes beyond an individual definition to extend beyond, in the sharing of different things: "To receive the different things, their encounters, and where beauty infinitely rises, and from which beauty springs infinitely, finally means reaching diversities which are the dimensions and the materials (at the same time) of the Whole-World. We thereby recognize that the identical does not consent to the beauties of this Whole-World, nor does it conceive them" (PhR 30).

We must break away and enter a world that, as always with Glissant, escapes the fateful pressure of predestination: "That is what I call a cultural identity. A questioning identity, where the relation to the other determines Being without freezing it by a tyrannical weight. This is what we see throughout the world: *everyone wants to name himself*" (DA 283, my emphasis).

This self-baptism, which we have already met several times, is an act of freedom in relation to filiations of whatever kind. Moreover, this choice must not be made solely by an individual who self-identifies all by himself; the chosen name must be shared: "The name for us is first collective, not the sign of an I but of a We. It can be undifferentiated (X), its strength derives from its being chosen and not imposed. It is not the parental name, it is the conquered name" (DA 285, note 5.).

What are we to do about imposed names? For they always are imposed, first by family, and then by civil status. The *Traité du Tout-Monde* here provides us with some very useful indications. The "author" first multiplied himself in the names of his characters and in the landscapes he named; his name was "extended," thus breaking with the verticality of filiations: "These names that I inhabit are organized in archipelagos. They hesitate on the edge of some density, one which is perhaps a break, they play tricks with any interpellation, overflowing it infinitely; they drift and meet without my thinking about them" (TTM 77).

The extension of the individual biography to that of the collective challenges the definition of what an author is: "The collective biography, the story that seeks to restore the poem (and which is not a story to be told) can only correspond, not with rigor, but with *poémie*, or *poétrie*, to the individual biography. [. . .] The project of individual existence generally follows the course of the quest for a collective existence" (EBR 36–37). The author is no longer a singularity unfolding the riddles of the world for others: he is these others first and foremost, a member of a community that the poem utters. But, in an antithetical tension, he is also "solitary," "something else," freed as an individual from societal determinants: "What I repeat here allows us to enter into the uncertainty of the individual biography, the biography of a poet, *insofar as, by his absences, he is something else*" (EBR 41, my emphasis). Simultaneously a "we," this "we" who appear everywhere in the work to designate the collectivity of poets not only from the Antilles, but from the world, and also an "I," something else that marks a specific place of utterance, that of the person who, by his utterance, gives form and content to Relation and the Whole-World.

Mahagony gives us a paradigm for dissolution into the collective and escape from the latter. Glissant is, simultaneously and in turn, a character from a book (26), a "brown Negro" (28), an author, a man, a parable (31), a creature, and a creator (31). The uniqueness of point of view is also destroyed by the multiplicity of the narrators in the novels.[10] Glissant himself insisted on this point with regard to *Tout-Monde*:

> The book is made in such a way that one cannot say who is speaking. First, we said that the author speaks. Then we said, "someone is speaking." Then, we even said "it speaks" in the psychoanalytic sense of the word "it" [i.e., id]. [. . .] That or who which speaks is multiple, we cannot know where it/he comes from; it/he may not know it it/himself and it/he does not control or direct the uttering of the discourse. What is projected as spoken words meets another multiple which is the world's multiplicity. When we draw up a poetics of diversity, as I claim to be doing, we cannot speak from the point of view of uniqueness. (IPD 131)

This problematics of identity has a certain deep connection with a series of biographical and historical elements (that is, elements not limited to the individual), against the backdrop of the names that resulted from slavery, then from emancipation. Slaves carried a serial number, and colonists named them at whim. On April 27, 1848, the abolition of slavery was decreed on French territory. The administrators of civil status then set about giving surnames and first names to freed slaves, thus marking identity with a "postcolonial" seal: "To the trauma of being wrenched away was added the trauma of "liberation." The civil statuses provided (or granted) never replace the *Name we have chosen for ourselves*. The uprooted slave is succeeded by the depersonalized citizen. To rediscover oneself as a person is a dramatic act that does not go smoothly" (IP 190).

In 1928, Édouard Glissant was born in a shack in the Morne de Bezaudin near Sainte-Marie. His mother Adrienne Godard gave him the name Mathieu: "Mathieu was the name granted me at baptism (on Saint

Matthew's Day), then abandoned in the customs and the busyness of childhood, reassumed by me (or by a demanding character, that Béluse) in the imaginary; then it grafted itself, to finish or to start again, in Mathieu Glissant" (TTM 77). When he successfully passed his sixth grade exam, his father recognized him, and his official civil status changed from Mathieu Godard to Mathieu Édouard Glissant: "My name has been Glissant since pretty much the age of nine years old, when my father 'recognized' me" (TTM 77). This recognition is in quotation marks: its legitimacy is either suspect or, implicitly and very discreetly, suspected and rejected. He was now nicknamed Ti-Édouard, the "petit Édouard" of filiation and, later, his friends called him Godby, "the young Godby when he parchmented his poems in 1944 on sheets of banana paper" (O 74). These patronymic variations are the sign of the complexity of filiations: the Name-of-the-Father erases the matronym as well as the first name Mathieu (which is still however preserved by the registry office); then come nicknames, which are symbols of belonging to the Antillean community as well as a loophole allowing him to escape patronymic legitimacy: "We incubate within ourselves the instinct of the illegitimate, which here in the Antilles is a derivative of the extended African family, an instinct repressed by all kinds of official regulations, of which the advantages of Social Security are not the least effective" (TTM 78). But the name is always given by others: mother, father, civil status, social security, to be taken literally as that which reassures the well-meaning feelings of an administration and a community when it practices the registration of identities. Moreover, the utopia of the "extended African family" (a fiction in any "modern" state) may reassure the social bond, but in no way guarantees the aspiration to freedom which is one of Glissant's essential demands.

Lacan hammered home the message: foreclosing the Name-of-the-Father means opening the door to a destructuring of the subject that can lead to psychosis, of which President Schreber[11] and, in Glissant, George Payote (DA 305–311) are paradigmatic cases. To reject the symbolic is to fall into mental illness, and this affects not only individuals, but sometimes whole societies; we shall come back to the pages of *Le Discours antillais* in which Glissant analyzes the psychoses of "complexion" and "connec-tion," with "the psychotic violence of the radical choice in madness" (DA 290–292), and we will conclude that the problem has not escaped the author's notice. The solution thus lies not in the outright rejection ("psychotic") of filiation, but in its reinvention. This re-inscription retains *all* the figures of filiation: on the side of civil status and citizenship, a series of surnames and first names: Godard, Glissant, Mathieu, Édouard, a series that comes under the symbolic and the Name-of-the-Father. On the uncivil and non-citizen side, the *same* surnames and first names; but this time poetic utterance confers a *very different* meaning on them. I have already indicated that the whole work could be inscribed, by mulling over the question, as a Moebius strip in which repetition produces something radically new; and the same goes for the problem of identity.

In *Le Quatrième Siècle*, at the time of emancipation, we see civil servants making merry as they transform the slave's registration numbers into invented names: "When the impudence was too visible, they amused themselves by inverting the names, torturing them so as at least to move them away from their origin. Senglis thus became Glissant and Courbaril became Barricou" (QS 178). Senglis was a plantation owner to whom Mathieu Béluse was sold (it was also the atavistic blood [*sang*], starting to slide [*glisser*], to skid from its roots). It must be remembered that these names are surnames invented by a recitative utterance, and thus the first sign of a liberty, even if they designate the slave-owning master, even if they make fun of the civil administration. The second sign of a true emancipation is to turn the master's fictitious name into an anagram: "I once supposed that the name Glissant, probably a granted name, as were most Antillean surnames, was the insolent reverse side of a colonist's name, and thus Senglis. The reverse side of names is significant" (TTM 77).[12] The anagram fictionalizes the very name of Glissant, which becomes thereby the result of a poetics, in the final analysis its only legitimation, outside of any process of filiation, in a Moebius strip. Glissant is thus indeed the "author of himself"; and the same process applies to the first name Mathieu, attributed to Béluse in the *Quatrième Siècle*, but also to the son he had from Sylvie Sémavoine. Through the poetic, Glissant challenges the Name-of-the-Father by repeating it and becoming the Father-of-Names: "I have so many names in me, and so many countries, signified by my name" (TTM 80). Running through the Moebius strip in a mulling over that is only in appearance a banal and simple repetition, Glissant becomes homonymous to himself, while braiding an indestructible link between the poetic and the biographical, the novel and life, history and community, identity and landscape: "*The round* of names is in keeping with the parade of landscapes" (TTM 80; my emphasis). This homonymy would be nothing but a verbal game with no force, if it were not a sign of the coincidence between the man and his work.

Beyond Paul of Tarsus, who invents the singularity of the individual, beyond Hegel, who produces the assumption of the egophany in absolute knowledge, beyond Freud and Lacan, who map the symbolic determinations of the subject, Glissant promotes a redefinition of the individual: a subject shared by the imaginary and divided out by the place, open both to an opacity that resists the clarity of political, psychoanalytic, and bureaucratic taxonomies, and to a future freed from any determinants.

Chapter 15

"And so we bring down (as if literally)
the letter of the world"

In his essays, Glissant never speaks of signifier and signified, rarely of structure, and very often of sign and meaning, and even full-meaning (*plein-sens*) ("The full meaning of an action is given in its place," [PR 217]), expressed by a full-song (*plein-chant*): "The full-song or the howling (in the duration or in the moment) are the preferential places of the poetics of relation, because it views with disdain the casualness in which any presumption of pre-eminence clothes itself" (PR 216). At the same time, the terms "fiction" and "simulacrum" are practically absent, whether in their technical and rhetorical (literary) sense, or, more fundamentally, in a sense that I would call ontological. This ontology of fiction is found, to cite only modern thinkers, in Jeremy Bentham (his "theory of fictions") and Jacques Lacan, who draws inspiration from the latter; for Lacan, linguistic structure is a fiction, a created artefact, outside of nature: "the truth is averred in a structure of fiction."[1] If, as Glissant does, we reject the structure and the signifier, we ipso facto reject the concept of fiction. To reject the signifier is also to deny that the novel, poetry, literature, and language are the unveiling of a truth: it is to reject the ontological conception of language, to refuse the notion that language alone can reveal Being, the True, the Beautiful, the Idea—it is to abandon the One, whether it is conjoined with Being (in metaphysics) or disjoined from it (in structuralism).[2] The rejection of the signifier is synchronous with the displacement that Glissant seeks to effect, from Being to beings, from ontology to the ontic.

241

To reject the signifier is to think against, alongside, or beyond the dominant theoretical movement at the time when Glissant began to publish his first essays: structuralism. It is to avoid making everything begin with language as the truth of Being: for Glissant, there are geneses outside language, in the silence of the chasm or the hardness of the rock. It is, finally, to oppose any conception of reality (not of the Real) that would be homologous to the closed totality of signifiers (which is the Lacanian conception).

The signifier, in Ferdinand de Saussure, is a system of negative differences, an empty form that exists only through the series of these oppositions. But difference, in Glissant, is always a fullness (of matter or thought). It is possible to count and sum the signifiers as beings in the world; this sum would form a closed set. But this taxonomy of negative differences would be no more than an empty form, devoid of any meaning or sense: structure is the possibility of meaning, it does not create it. The meaning (*signification*), though not the sense (*sens*) in the structure comes when, for example, the Same and the Other are imaginatively contrasted in the oscillation of the intersubjective imaginary relation (see Lacan's diagram L). Remember, on the contrary, that the spiral of Glissant's imaginary is in the margin of "any linear projection": apart from the signifier (PR 216). The same and the Other are redistributed there, not by similarity or dissimilarity, but by a relation between one opacity and another opacity.

This is why there is in Glissant's work a clear antistructuralism: reality does not stem from the relative and negative difference that Saussure discovered as being the very nature of language. In *Poétique de la Relation*, structural analysis, what Glissant calls the "poetics of structure," is regularly rejected as "a (subtle) renunciation of the world as it makes itself" (PR 38). The example, not by chance, is here Mallarmé: "A poetics of structure. The text's creator effaces himself, or rather abolishes himself to reveal himself in the texture of what he has created. Just as narrative had been taken out of Mallarmean poetics, History (in the sense that the West has given to this word) is relativised in structuralist opinion" (PR 37; Glissant writes *opinion* and not theory: we must emphasize the difference between them).

Structure as a tool for deciphering the world is a strengthening of determinations, which results in the crushing of the imaginary, that is to say, the exclusion of anything potentially different in its poetic becoming: hence Relation is radically opposed to structure and ideology, and ignores the "protest[s] of models" (PR 187) aimed at covering the world in a grid insofar as it conforms to various archetypes, thus garroting any attempt to listen to the "world as it makes itself": "The use of ideology to build this relationship to the world is doomed to failure; it is the symptom of the loneliness into which individuals are dropped, the symptom of their abandonment. The traditional structures that protected individuals are under threat everywhere, and individuals must fend for themselves, with the sole strength of their intuition of the world, their poetics."[3]

We escape the closed and finite set of the signifier as the constraint of Being, through a poetics that does more than actualize a structure, because it precipitates an unknown future: in other words, it is an open system in contrast to the closed systems of structure. Glissant thus calls for a change in the status of the human sciences, those sciences of analysis and prediction, closed to intuition and the unpredictable, obscuring subjective knowledge and the future with its objective knowledge. This desire for a dynamics already appears, with regard to linguistics, in *L'Intention poétique*, published in 1969; and in 1969, theory is everywhere dependent on Saussurian linguistics and structure, in Barthes, in Lacan, in Lévi-Strauss, to mention only the most important thinkers. Once again, Glissant's independence of mind—he cannot be intimidated by any "school"—should be noted: "Linguistics, inasmuch as it formulates constants and rules, is already behind those wanderings of languages and discourses which in each (collective) being will manifest the presence of Being in the world. Linguistics will need to move from static analysis to dynamic profiles, if it wants to encompass this condition; otherwise it will only confirm an anachronism and show solidarity with the most indiscriminate academic accommodations" (IP 47). Thirty years later, the critique of a model that excludes all evolution and refuses to think of possibilities is extended to all the so-called human sciences, which are reproached for their a priori refusal of the unpredictable:

> The destructurations of today's languages are dramatic, instantaneous, bolts from the blue. The evolutions, too, are dizzying, inventions as stunning as they are ephemeral. There will be no need to consider linguistic fields as analysable and predictable at discretion. Linguistics as a science would perhaps become an art: and soon the human sciences would be redeployed as Arts of the human. Multiplicity and the inextricable would finally enter subjective knowledge, like chaos in the physical

sciences. Objective knowledge and ignorance make us fear this prospect. (EBR 92)[4]

Relation is therefore not the contrast of signifiers; it is the bond of differences; and difference, the "realized quantity" of the logion, is a fullness; moreover, it has a history (philosophical, poetic, political), and *difference differs from itself over time*:

> After which,[5] difference, already considered as a diminution, was viewed as an absolute amputation. Each and any difference. Some contrast with the absolute was required, and difference was established only as eternally a virtuality, on a lower level, constantly repulsed by this dense and radiating brilliance of Being. In accordance with a philosophy of Relation, difference could be very random vis-à-vis the One, as the latter would reflect the Being (of the world), but it is above all the sign and the relay of the unity—diversities, insofar as the different things gather Being-as-beings (of the Whole). Difference contributes to fusion as well as distinction. (PhR 101)

Sartorius, the novel about the Batoutos, was published in 1999. The name "novel" in the subtitle is inadequate to its object. *Sartorius*, indeed, is a transgeneric object, between fiction and reality, essay, narration, and poem. This integration of all discursive types appears minimally, in Glissant, from the publication of the first poems (*Le Sang rivé*) onward, preceded by a commentary; it was continually being extended thereafter. The transgeneric is also a trans-semantic, where contents intermingle as well as forms; this makes books-as-objects irremediably unclassifiable by traditional norms. Glissant's "novels" are not *romans à these* or novels of ideas that would disappear, in an immaterial transparency, to give way to the expression of those "theses." They are rather novels of syntheses or hypotheses, like *Sartorius*, dedicated to a presumptive people, whom Glissant had dreamed up as early as *L'Intention poétique*, before Deleuze put forward the idea:[6] "[Literature] gives an account of the situation of Being, a situation that is part of a nation whose existence is not yet recognized either by the nationals themselves or a fortiori by those who challenge them" (IP 186).

Thirty years after *L'Intention poétique*, the Batoutos realize this imaginary nation, circulating in the past, the present, the future, and in the real geographies of the earth, which they bring into copresence in Relation and the Whole-World. This nation is not a fiction, but an imaginary in which participate all the writers, poets, philosophers appearing in the anthology of the Whole-World, the inhabitants of Easter Island dispersed to the four winds (TM 19), and some choice individuals such as Sylvie Glissant; Glissant made her a citizen Batoutos in my presence—she is now a Batoutoo (the *o* marks the feminine in the language of this people). The Batoutos are undoubtedly the only nation to which Glissant would recognize himself as belonging.

Regarding this additional letter designating the feminine (as in many languages: the *a* in Hebrew and Latin, the *e* in French), Glissant notes: "Aligned in such apparent pairs, *o* and *oo*, they do not here form any irreparable contrast" (S 97). Unlike the Saussurean structure of the signifier, the contrast is neither absolute difference ("irreparable") nor a void of meaning: the differences are in full, and the word "couple" refers to any possible fusion. We are thus in the presence of *letters* that, contrary to the signifier, do not constitute a structure of insubstantial differences, but a fullness, full-singing (*plein-chant*), or full-sense (*plein-sens*) in which the plainchant of the liturgy is stirred up by an *e* replacing the *a*. The letter is not a signifier related to the unconscious "structured like a language" and thus subjected to the rigorous determinism of its parades, but a sign that relates to the *sun* of consciousness, manufactured, without any fatalism, in the imaginary. To imagine a people that is lacking is not a fiction, but an act that forces one to go beyond, onto the margin, outside the signifier, toward the Other of thought. In passing, note that the *o* is the fundamental element of the two favorite exclamations of Glissant and his characters, "Ho!" and "Oho!": the *o*, a mark of the masculine in the Battoutoo language, could be the author's mark, primordial cry, or identity.

Sartorius is built up in and by one of those frequent letter games in the work, for example the "Aa" that baptizes the "first" slave in *La Case du Commandeur* (CM 171). In *Faulkner, Mississippi*, Glissant does not fail to point out that Bill Falkner added a *u* to his last name, having resolved "that this family deserved somehow to be 'transposed' or sublimated by this variant of the name, with this *u* swelling with epic novelty" (FM 52). The additional letter is here the break with the model and ancestral filiation, it is the adoption and deliberate shaping of a new identity, shared, literally, by the work itself. Thus, the *u* added by Glissant to the title of Faulkner's novel as his "novel" *Sartori[u]s* both affiliates with Faulkner's poetics, and suggests an "epic novelty." We must baptize ourselves, both to ward off the heavy curse of families, lineages, traditions, and to give ourselves the possibility of creating a new world: "We have deliberated, we, they, I, accorated (*accorés*) and illuminated, to admit that the Origin is not a Creation but perhaps an undoing, like the fundamental defection of an absolute—so the Batoutos propose [. . .]" (S 95).

In *Sartorius*, the *o* and the *u* structure two swathes of the Whole-World, the African and the Western, in a series of additions from an original act of self-naming: "The *u*'s are as intimidating as the *o*'s. They open onto a sky of which you cannot augur whether it is cursed or brings blessing" (S 269). On the one hand, there is the city of Onkolo, perhaps the imaginary place of origin of this other "Batouto," Ibn-Batouto[u] (Ibn Battuta), who left Tangier to discover the Whole-World at the beginning of the fourteenth century. On the other hand there is Nuremberg, where a friend of Albert Dürer decides to change his surname from Schneider to Sartor (tailor in Latin). The text is arranged in a series, on the Onkolo side, as on the Nuremberg side, by the play of letters that add up and oppose each other. Thus, on the Nuremberg side, they accumulate in a saraband of languages, Latin, German, Italian: Sartor the self-baptized (as the slave Aa) becomes Sartorius (S 210), and thus gives the whole text its title. A slave child, Wilhelm, suddenly appears, strangely similar to a mulatto Hegel; he also changes his name to Guillermo Amo. Might Hegel have been, without knowing it, a mestizo Batouto? The surname's journey ends in America, where the bureaucrat in charge of immigration renames him William Sartoris, the title of the work by Faulkner: "I observe, or at least I suppose, with regard to Wilhelm, that this same *u* which had been removed from his name, from Sartorius to Sartoris, by this too placid government agent, was some sixty years later added by the writer to his family surname" (S 269).

The inextricable letter (irreducible to the signifier) links everything to everything else: it is the very place where Relation appears. Not only from text to text, for example from Faulkner's *Sartoris* to Glissant's *Sartorius*, but from civil identity to an identity of writing, Fa(u)lkner, from place to place, from heaven to earth, of rock in Batouto (see my analysis of kwame, below). It is fusion of irreducibles, outside all paradox. It creates an apparatus of self-interpretation and self-representation, smuggling the world, texts, identities, and places, in a fusion of genres, times, and geographies.

Glissant's entire work must be considered as a letter (and not Belle-Lettre or Beau-Signifiant [Beautiful Signifier], which would reduce it intertextually to the world of signifiers, of literature). This letter unfolds in a Moebius strip on two contrasting and yet united sides: on one side the poetic and the recitative (the "novels"), and on the other side, the essays, "theory," philosophy, and all the interviews, most of them carefully rewritten by Glissant (to take one example, there are enormous differences between the literal transcription of the Baton Rouge interviews and the published version[7]). Beyond forms and genres, a unicity of meanings, contents, and themes circulates consistently from one book to another, whatever its form.

The letter breaks, anchors (*ancre*), and inks in (*encre*) the defiles of the signifier, to produce the marriage of essence and substance, signifier and sense, "where *Being-as-beings* is revealed, the indistinction of essence and substance, dwelling and movement" (PhR 61). This sign that precipitates sense will be what Glissant calls, by a twist through which he appropriates meaning, the "Kwame" of Oko (Kwame is a first name given to a boy born on a Saturday, in the Twi/Akan language in Ghana).

Sartorius is built up from a fundamental act, the engraving of a letter on a pebble, where the orality of the Batoutos goes on to "de-speaking," a writing that is immediately symbol in the etymological sense of the term (*sym-bolon* in Greek: what conjoins, joins a sign to a thing, and therefore not the abstract representation of the thing by an image or a metaphor):[8] "Oko digs up a river rock, in a place where there is no river running. Flat and polished, dark gray, perhaps oval in shape. He engraves his kwame with three lines of flint on the rock and exposes the object at the entrance of the shack he has made for himself, and yet on the inside" (S 66). The stone here speaks to the stone, in a merging materiality. It is impossible not to think of the "sacred poem," primordial, disinterred from the river of the Heraclitean flow, here passing into the light of a first writing. The gesture thus revives the flow of becoming that the absent river had interrupted. Petroglyph, hieroglyph (etymologically "sacred engraving") or cartouche of an absent language, the kwame A, at the same time that it is anchored in the materiality of a rock to which it is married, designates an identity withdrawn from the game of signifiers, although it resembles the A of the alphabets: "The sign that composed this kwame? Let us augur that today, in the diversity of our world that is at last a world, once the multiplicity has been achieved of all things known in their state, which is indeed their relation, this same sign returns to our hands, primordial and natural, as simply dazzling as three flashes of lightning that spell out the ephemeral nature of a sky" (S 73). This flash of lightning is also Heraclitean: "Lightning governs all things" (TFEV 68).

The rock, then, is *lacking* from the river bed, just as the invisible people is lacking in the world: "The expanse speaks to you through the striking absence of these Batoutos." (S 27) But the lack is redeemed, the hieroglyph ensures the transmission of poetic knowledge to our present; engraved in stone, the kwame continues, it is unconquered, *unvanquished*: "The kwame of Oko resisted, its image came down to us" (S 70).

As a letter, it is self-interpreting and self-representing for those who can read: "The kwame of Oko was immediately obvious to the Batoutos. They understood its meaning and did not have to express it" (S 69). It is the starting point of a gathering, since the other members of the tribe come to deposit their kwames in the shack vacated by Oko; it is the core of an original language open to all potentialities: "It was a multiplied alphabet, a collection of all the possibilities of existence" (S 69). The meanings of the primordial kwame are also open to those of all other signs of all other peoples of the earth, past, present, or unforeseeable: Nubians, Egyptians, Sudanese, Italians, Hebrews, Native Americans, Chinese, Japanese, and so on. It brings together the diversity of the Whole-World (see the listing in S 70–71). The kwame rallies multiplicity by means of the letter: "in its turbid simplicity it has inexhaustible echoes. It covers so many visions that you would have recognized or renewed even today" (S 71). Once constituted, written down, it can migrate and spread, to differentiate itself fully: "Do you know that in this country the boys born on a Sunday are called Kwame, a name that they add to their Christian name, Basil or Gervais or Prudence, and to their surname" (S 186). A new, substantial identity is constituted which merges the vertical filiation and the extent of beings. The original *w*, which is also the initial of the first names of Hegel (Wilhelm) and Faulkner (William), finds an echo here: "A boy born on a Sunday and thus named Kwame is perhaps the sign, the kwame of a belonging that can never end" (S 190). We have also, through this game of letters, changed people: we are here among the Baoulé (the practice of naming a Saturday child belongs to the Akan people).

The kwame is then nothing other than the cryptogram of Relation and the Whole-World, thus evoking both all land and all time, and Édouard Glissant's very œuvre in its entirety. Through the kwame, the work is self-representing and self-interpreting, "the quest for poetry through poetry" (IP), a quest for a new thought in the volume of philosophy and art as a whole. The œuvre affirms its dissimilarity positively, as a totality expressing the totality of the world, drawing its authority from itself and depending on itself alone, outside all determinations, including those of Belles-Lettres and philosophy: a radically new ambition!

The games of the letter, in *Sartorius* and elsewhere, those letters *u*, *o*, *i*, *w* that appear and disappear are elementary ontic quantities (not beings, not qualities, not categories), *stoicheia*. Beings, different things, details, and their quantities are self-represented. The *i* would be the kwame of Faulkner's novel *Sartoris*; the *u* would be enough to note both Glissant's *Sartorius* and the new identity of Falkner; the *o* is a spherical absolute similar to that of Heraclitean beings:[9] "the absolute of this letter *o*, which did not make itself heard as such, or of its apogee closed in on itself, as it were" (S 40).[10] The original kwame would bring together in its sign, all together, Oko's identity, the novel *Sartorius*, Glissant's whole way of thinking, as the kwame represents the invisible people of the Whole-World and relation and, in an unlimited extent, the Whole-World as "realized quantity of beings in their difference." The latter must be reevaluated outside Saussurian linguistics, Derrida's deconstruction, and the Lacanian Symbolic: in Glissant, it is inextricable, substance and essence all together, irreducible to any system of negative comparison.

The Republic of Letters is the continuity of signifiers, in submission or revolt. (Just as we should really rename Belles-Lettres as Beaux-Significants or Beautiful Signifiers, the Republic of Letters ought to be known as the Republic of Signifiers.) Glissant's œuvre-letter is a meteor, an inextricable elsewhere, something that arises from itself, unclassifiable, outside of any filiation, outside of the parade of signifiers, outside of genres, outside of the Republic of Letters, outside of the Book, outside of literature, outside of the "Freemasonry" of Belles-Lettres: "little by little we learn to distinguish these invariants a subjective knowledge of which we so much need, and once again we differ by ordering this knowledge, and so we bring down (as if literally) the letter of the world" (TTM 164).

The letter is capable of extension and of becoming: it is not an eternalized and isolated fixity but an integral part of the very movement of Relation: "Literatures express the intuition that this multiplicity is first of all the field of aggregation (not of assembling but of friction), (rubbing returns *literally, to the letter*, which is literature), of all the arts. We propose, to those who are disquieted by so much that is indecipherable, that these are the halting steps, that is, the first pathways, to *Poétique de la Relation*" (PhR 40).

Chapter 16

"Imagine a thousand birds taking flight over an African lake"

How is it that Glissant's work, which constantly incriminates the One, homogeneity and racial and cultural unity, which praises multiplicity and diversity, should present itself with so much homogeneity, coherence, and unity? In fact, from the beginning, this was the writer's "poetic intention"; the whole work is the shadow and the dream of a single text, put in the singular:

> I do not know at what age, in my very young days, I dreamed of having developed a text that wrapped itself innocently but in an abundantly triumphant way over itself, even generating, as and when, its own meanings. Repetition was the thread, with that imperceptible deviance that makes things move forward. In what I write, I have always pursued this text. I am still annoyed that I have not found that turbulent enhalement it created, which seemed to dig around in the bush and hurtle down volcanoes. But I bring back a kind of shadow from it sometimes, which links together the few rocks of words that I gather as I move across such a landscape, yes, a bush, crowned by a volcano. (CL 20)

We can say that this dream came true in the work; but we can just as easily maintain the opposite: the work is only a fragment of a poetic intention that can never reach completion.

How too can a work that challenges universality and the system aspire to them with stubborn constancy, even including all systems and all universals in its deployment?

The apparent contradictions of Glissant's thought are marked by numerous oxymorons ("the non-totalizing totality," the "non-systematic system," relation as simultaneously realized quantity and unnameable), where the terms seem to be defined by their opposites; in the same way, the apparent tautologies ("relation has only the principles of relation") are the signs of a thought that seems to be constructed within an impossibility; and finally, the many chiasms (the thought the Other and the Other of thought, solitary in politics and solidary in poetics, poetic philosophy and philosophical poetry, measure and excess, etc.) are part of this same apparently contradictory logic.

Oxymorons, tautologies, and chiasms directly challenge the norms of rational thought, established from the time of Aristotle's logic with the principles of noncontradiction and the excluded third: A cannot be identical to Non-A; we cannot think of a proposition p and a proposition non-p as being true at the same time. Glissant's oxymorons and tautologies can therefore either appear as easy word games, part of the gossip of the Intellectual, or as in no way being part of a truly philosophical thought. However, their repetition in the work indicates that the contradictions are fully assumed, signaling the certainty that the principle of noncontradiction and the excluded third may be overridden, and that contradictions may constitute (philosophical) thought.

Following Glissant's readings of the past, let us note in the first place how much the geography of Pre-Socratic thought is archipelagic and decentered, albeit within a monolingual framework: "The Ionian archipelago in ancient Greece, well before Alexander, divined both East and West together" (PhR 49). It is only with Socrates and Plato that Athens becomes a major center of thought, so that Aristotle, for example, comes from Macedonia to follow Plato's teaching. Before the preeminence of Athens, we find a scatter of eccentric, inextricable places, Greek colonies, various islands: there is still a great number of places from which the Pre-Socratics and Sophists come. Philosophy is born in a circle of which "the center is everywhere and the periphery nowhere," and the reduction of the periphery to the center coincides with the concentration on a "continental" place, Athens, and with the emergence of the supremacy of rational thought. In fact, the different Greek schools of philosophy bear geographical names: Milesians, Eleatics, and Abderitans, who will then be excluded or brought together in a center, that of fifth-century Athens. Glissant's vision of the opposition between continental thought and archipelagic thought takes on its full meaning here: as often, it allows a new reading of the archeology of thought. Moreover, the great founders, Socrates, Plato, and Aristotle, establish the foundations of rational thought by a refusal of filiation, a parricide, in relation to their Pre-Socratic and Sophist ancestors, in particular, as we have seen, Parmenides of Elea, but also Heraclitus of Ephesus and Gorgias of Leontium, excluded from philosophy by Aristotle the Macedonian who comes to Athens.

The organic thought of Heraclitus is a union of opposites, before or outside of logical supremacy. But these opposites have no fixity—they are in perpetual struggle, in becoming; hence the emergence, in Heraclitus as in Glissant, of many oxymorons: "The opposite is in agreement, from discords arises the most beautiful harmony and everything becomes in the struggle."[1] The only absolutes in the thought of Heraclitus are the Logos and becoming.[2]

From the philosophical generation that follows Heraclitus (544 BCE–480 BCE), the principle of the union of struggling opposites is disputed, in dialogue, in struggle, or in dialectic with Heraclitus, by Parmenides of Elea (520 BCE–440 BCE), who takes the first step in the "rationality" of thought by posing that Being and non-Being are radically contradictory: "One can never prove that non-Being has being" (Fragment B7). After Plato (*Republic* IV, 436b), Aristotle formalized the principle of noncontradiction in logic and philosophy, in clear opposition to Heraclitus: "It is indeed impossible for anyone to believe that the same simultaneously is and is not, as some people imagine that Heraclitus asserted" (*Metaphysics*, Γ 3).

The critique of philosophical poetry and poetic philosophy by Plato (in the *Theaetetus*), in favor of a prosaic rationality, one centered on Being and expressed in one language, is the exact reverse side of the great themes of Glissant's work: digenesis as critic of the One, multiplicity, the rejection of qualities in favor of quantities ("realized"), the wandering of movement, the interbreeding of creolization, the future of becoming, the rejection of Being in favor of beings, the kinship of philosophy and the poetic as thought. Poetry, for Glissant, is not a representation of reality (*mimesis*), but its saying and its very doing—and thought is by no means absent from the poetic, on the contrary. The pitiless critique of the Pre-Socratics and Sophists by Plato is the exile of this primordial poem written by the first philosophers as well as the first poets. This is a tear in the fabric that Glissant stitches back together, at the same time restoring the greatness of the past and bringing back to our present the Pre-Socratics and "sophists" (a very bad label, one that has become pejorative, even though they too are great thinkers).

By drastically simplifying the history of philosophy, we can say that the antagonistic unity of opposites resurfaced when Hegel, in the *Logic*, returned to the Heraclitean source.[3] He was followed on this point by Nietzsche, who affirms in *The Birth of Tragedy* that "contradiction is lodged at the heart of the world" (chapter 9). Everything here pivots, as in Heraclitus, around becoming and time: for Hegel, as for Nietzsche, as for the great Pre-Socratics, becoming is the unity of Being and non-Being. It is in this filiation rejected by Platonism that Glissant builds his dwelling. As early as *Soleil de la conscience*, "subjective knowledge is possible and always future" (SC 70). In *L'Intention poétique*, becoming is affirmed: "We have the opportunity of a literature which will predetermine, by its function as the investigation of a collective consciousness, the works that will illustrate it" (IP 186). Becoming is everywhere and always: "I took things as they never come and I was always ready for the pluperfect of the future" (TTM 50); "It is one of the truths of poetry that an Art of Poetry is always future" (TTM 46); "Neither beings nor wandering have a term, change is their permanence ho! —They continue" (TTM 64); "The writer of today is always a future writer" (EBR 122).

As in Heraclitus, Hegel, and Nietzsche, becoming resolves the oxymorons, tautologies, and chiasms of Glissant: in its movement, what was contradictory becomes thinkable and harmonious ("Socrates was sitting; he has now risen"): the system was closed, it becomes nonsystematic thanks to its future.

Glissant's thought always obeys, in the very depths of its logical form, a universal principle of inclusion, not a logic of exclusion, be this philosophical, aesthetic, political, racial, or poetic. The nonsystematic system, the nontotalizing totality unite the A and the Non-A on the unilateral face of the Moebius strip to synthesize them. Thus, they are paradoxes only on the surface. Becoming sublates (in the Hegelian sense) and resolves contradictions.

In a sense, everything is said in the tenth section of *Philosophie de la Relation*, "La pensée de l'imprévisible" ("The Thought of the Unforeseeable"). We must be careful not to confuse the unforeseeable with disorder (or chaos), because Glissant's becoming appeals to a future that anticipates the realization of notions yet to come, the Whole-World and Relation. On the other hand, we see with what care, philosophical Whole and poetic Whole, Glissant exceeds the binarity of contradictions by projecting it into the future, just as Heraclitus and Hegel had done before him. Ternary thought, where the totality is built up from the union of opposites. Nothing that Glissant has done is conceivable without a fourth dimension, that of the temporality of an open becoming.

The Hegel of the End of History moves away from the deep inspiration he drew from Heraclitus. Its conceptual construction is thought of the present, not of the future; the task of philosophy is not to speculate on becoming:

> To conceive what *is* is the task of philosophy, for what *is* is reason. As far as the individual is concerned, everyone is *the child of his time*; in the same way as philosophy, which summarizes its time in thought. It is just as mad to imagine that any philosophy will surpass the contemporary world as to believe that an individual will leap over his time, will cross Rhodes. If a theory, in fact, goes beyond these limits, if it constructs a world *as it should be,* this world does indeed exist, but only in its opinion, which is an inconsistent element that can take any imprint.[4]

Relative to this Hegelian ukase, Glissant is in the position of a radical heretic. He is not a "child of his time" in that his thought, although historical, rejects the determinations of history. The world that he images and imagines is not an inconsistent and indeterminate opinion, since he takes into account "the realized quantity of all the differences, without any exception." And above all, by a return to the boundless Heraclitean becoming, a figure of the infinite in all its senses, both as *In-finite* (unfinished) and unlimited in its potentialities, Glissant reopens the field of possibilities beyond the Hegelian closure, which was valid, as he saw and as Hegel himself wrote, only for the European West. "The places are repeated from one to the other, there are no limits to Relation, although it is above all a realized (finite) quantity of the different things in the world" (PhR 46). In-finite becoming is named by Glissant as unforeseeable (that which cannot be foreseen) and unforesayable (that which cannot be said, anticipated or determined):

> *The thought of the unforeseeable* (saying this, someone reminded me that Heraclitus guessed the unforeseeable) [. . .]. The

> unforeseeable is not already the unforeseen, the unforeseeable
> offers and comments on itself as perspective, the unforeseen
> imposes itself as consequence and result. [. . .] To frequent the
> thought of the unforeseeable is to be able to escape from these
> upheavals that the unforeseen events of the world raise in us,
> and moreover to make ourselves more and more ingenious
> in arranging within the irruptions of this real a continuous
> possibility for human action. (PhR 68)

That is why there is no name for what is yet to come: "Relation is unnameable."

By giving a final purpose and completion to the history of Europe, Hegel relies on what he calls the "cunning of reason," which works throughout history:

> The particular interest of passion is therefore inseparable from
> the active affirmation of universality . . . It is not the Idea that
> exposes itself to conflict, combat and danger; it stands back
> from all attack and all damage, and sends the passion into battle
> to be consumed there. We may give the name *the cunning of
> reason* to the fact that reason allows the passions to act in its
> place, so that it is only the means by which it comes into
> existence that experiences losses and suffers damage.[5]

Faced with the passive and constraining fate of the cunning of reason, which can only be ascertained, not disputed, Glissant sets up in contrast a poetic rejection of determinations, *the cunning of the poet*:

> But I also believe in the finesse or the instinctive cunning
> of the poet, the finesse and cunning that the practice of the
> poem allots to him. [. . .] A poet does not obey, does not
> conform to general ideas that he has formulated, even to those
> he has formulated for himself. [. . .] It is the innocence or
> the instinctive cunning of the poet that would prevent him
> from finally consenting, or sacrificing, to determinations that
> he himself would have considered very obvious. (EBR 42–43)

Beyond the political and the economic, the poetic thus becomes the first interpretant of the things of the world. The political, in its connection with the poetic, loses its primacy; in particular, the "workers of the world, unite!" does not have to exert its effects of harmonious conformity: "In politics, my highest reference was also the world, not the world conceived as the workers" international, but as a place of encounter, of culture shock, of the clash of humanities. [. . .] For me, poetry and politics were intimately linked by this reference to the world [. . .]."[6] To practice politics in poetry, transversally, is to fall into the prosaicism of Snopes, which amounts to destroying all poetry: "And this meant that poetry was not political, that there was no political poetry, but that great poetry was not conceived without this underlying, subterranean as well as dazzling relation, which was the link to the situation of the world's cultures in relation to each other. In other words, there was no poetry that was not political and there is no political poetry in itself" (Ibid.).

One can doubt the words "innocence" or "instinctive" when they are used by Glissant, as his pen weighs everything systematically and meticulously: the cunning in his work is never innocent—instinct is always well-ordered. The fact remains that the "innocent cunning of the poet" is what compensates for and displaces the constraints of the cunning of Hegelian reason to open History and (hi)stories up to their poetic infinity.

Once becoming is integrated with thought (and how can it not be?), all oxymorons, all chiasms, and all tautologies are resolved, ad infinitum. *Over time*, what was contradictory will become thinkable; *over time*, what seemed to be repetition and mulling over, a tautological self-definition, will produce the radically new, homonyms, something different—and the very form of Glissant's œuvre, in its mulling-over aspect, perfectly marries its content, and thereby projects itself into the future of worlds and books yet to come.

In spite of appearances, Heraclitus and Glissant both constructed philosophies just as systematic, rational, coherent, and homogeneous as Hegel's, whose thinking they anticipate and surpass at once: "the first thought comes back, and it is still the last." That is why, summarizing here all the "philosophical intention" that underlies the present work, I do not hesitate to rank Glissant among the greatest thinkers of all times and all geographies: to tell the truth, it is the only "category" that suits the gigantic ambition, partially achieved, certainly in becoming, of all his work. Becoming is not a talisman of magical thought: it is what integrates all contradiction, which differs all tautology, which resolves all oxymorons in a poetic rationality yet to come: "We see the horizon in imagination, we advance, it constantly retreats and constantly evaporates, because our only way of really conceiving it is through our imaginary" (PhR 148). It should be emphasized that Glissant does not promote an anti- and a-philosophical irrationalism; he is merely integrating rationality into a framework that surpasses it: the imaginary of the many futures that have as yet no names.

The constraints on "old Europe" annoyed Napoleon. The constraints that determine thoughts and cultures, whether of Europe or elsewhere, "annoy" Édouard Glissant just as much, but he challenges them not with thunderous pronunciamientos or political ideologies, and even less by the affirmation of an imperial political and conceptual mastery. He produces a thorough examination of the shortcomings and flaws, munificences and productivities of systems, both in their contents and in their forms; he scrupulously evaluates the possibilities that these constraints contained without knowing it and that each of them in turn suffocated. Glissant knows what he wants to break away from; moreover, he knows that a break preserves the former situation within it, and reinterprets it: "Like literatures, the philosophy of Relation is a mulling over and displacement, all at once" (PhR 94). In no case is it a question of making a clean sweep of the past, a gesture that would empty his whole enterprise of its meaning; we must re-read what has happened, repeat it to transmute it.

Step by step, we have reviewed the constraint of determinations. The discourse of the master—that is, of philosophy and politics frozen in their systematic mastery—is rejected by the imaginary of a living and unnamable becoming; the discourse of the university is transformed by the reinjection of poetic passion and the reassessment of the "great authors"; the classifications, drawers, labels, and ghettos of literary criticism (post-colonialism, francophonie, postmodernism, structuralism, poststructuralism) are rejected; the symbolic-unconscious determinism of the discourse of the analyst is challenged; the discourse of capital is denied in its purely economic constraint; the romantic expression of the individual subject dissolves into a shared poetics. Beyond all discursive categories, the discourses of history, of rhetorical and literary tradition are reorganized by trans-history, trans-rhetoric, and the trans-generic. The discourse of politics is challenged by the refusal of any ideology; the discourse of science awaits its poetics. Also rejected are the folklorism of the soil, utilitarianism in art (which does not mean that Glissant takes refuge in "art for art's sake," since it is "art for the world" and "art of the world"), the literature of notations, and realism. Thus the indeterminacy of the poetics yet to come is positioned as the generalized *reverse side* of the formal causalities of a traditional literature, and political and economic determinations: "This activity can incline us, while continuing the determinations I have mentioned, to take these determinations *backward*. For example, it is poetry and the frequentation of poetry that led me to consider the relation to the earth [as property or non-property—the economic and symbolic relationship]" (EBR 43).

Following the course, point by point, place by place, of all these negativities does not lead to the end of art, which would ultimately be the end of the human. Unlike Hegel, for whom art has nothing more to say to us, the negativities in Glissant are the dawn of all possibilities: "Let us imagine a thousand birds taking flight over an African lake . . ." —the first words of a lecture given at Baton Rouge.[7] The flight takes off, always, from one or more real places, inextricable, inevitable. Taking flight, flying over, are not an escape into an ideal world, a fantasy from the point of view of an out-of-the-world Sirius, the mastery of the unexpected and the event by a conceptual system that has foreseen everything in advance, but the exit from any category whatsoever, the refusal to be accountable to the political, the social, History, the Idea: "But the writer is subject to no duty, in truth. He illuminates his naive and strong lucidities in the fire of an inextricable that he does not govern" (EBR 11).

The cunning of the poet thus surpasses, by incorporating it, the cunning of philosophical reason, the reason(s) of the master. The adultery of philosophy with the discourse of the master, breaking away from the Pre-Socratics, began with Socrates and Plato (*Laws* and the *Republic*). Discussing and contradicting the myth and Homeric poetry, the dialectic that opposes their thoughts, gives birth to Socratic reason.[8] This ostracism gives birth to the discourse of the master who in turn, with Socrates, and through the parricide of Parmenides, makes it possible to affirm Being as reason and principle of identity, without which nothing can be distinguished rationally. Glissant's philosophical return to myth, to the primordial poem, to Parmenides and Heraclitus *before* Socrates, Plato and Aristotle thus amounts to a dismissal of philosophy as the discourse of the master, even a banishment or a parricide in return; this is not the only escape route he offers.

The adultery of philosophy with the discourse of the master ends with Hegel: although this must be qualified by the contradictions of the philosopher himself (Glissant: "Hegel *may* be mistaken"), the Hegelian refusal to think *what will be* is the master's last thought, after which no first thought can return. Glissant's return to Heraclitus must therefore be read as a return to a nondominant control, a noncontrolling domination (since it cannot in any way determine the unpredictability of becoming), both of which Greece created, then forgot or repressed, and that both need to be revived: "The poetics of duration—another leitmotif—that was the principle behind the sacred books or founders of community, reappears and relays the poetics of the moment. The flash of lightning is the trembling of all who desire or dream of the impossible totality, or the totality yet to come; duration exhorts the one who tries to live it, when the joint histories of the peoples draw the contours of its dawn" (PR 45).

In Glissant, there is no question of a regression or a restoration (a form of thought favored by Heidegger). The mulling over of the first thought, of the primordial poem, produces its own transcendence.

Unlike that of Glissant, the thought of Heraclitus is completely intent on the One. The Logos is Unique; it harmonizes opposites and permits multiplicities to be summed up: "It is wise to say [with the Logos] that All is One" (D 50). As Kostas Axelos writes, "the Logos is reason as one, as universal and unifying."[9]

Glissant's becoming rests on this original unity, but this is so as to make it explode (rationally, I would insist) into something unpredictable, which produces ad infinitum Diversity, multiplicity, the Non-Universal, the Whole, and whose only unifying figure is Relation—a "paradoxical" figure, since becoming opens (logically) onto an ultimate form that cannot have a determinate figure. Beyond-Hegel is also Beyond-Heraclitus: Glissant as a philosopher opens new paths to thought, with a boldness and sureness that exceed those of Nietzsche, Derrida, and Deleuze. This assertion may seem insane, but its merit, I hope, is confirmed by my overall interpretation. Glissant never ceases to insist on how the changes of modernity are characterized by its extraordinary speed, facilitated by new technologies, unleashing a chaotic maelstrom: "The destructurations of today's languages are dramatic, instantaneous, bolts from the blue. The evolutions, too, are dizzying, inventions as stunning as they are ephemeral" (EBR 92). Moreover, this speed is not uniform: it is closely linked to the realized quantity of differences: "I think that we are probably all moving toward the Whole-World but that there are different speeds, different times. If we were moving to the Whole-World at the same pace, it would be a form of regimentation and the Whole-World would be weary and boring in its uniformity" (IL 51).

The Internet, which is consubstantial with globalization,[10] is also a valuable opportunity for globality and relationship; it allows us, against the Heraclitean flux, but with the Mississippi, to step twice into the river of change: "Let us say this: the Internet, which we choose as symbol and model for the moment, throws us into the full surge of our totality-world, it would seem, and even if we can click to return to a subject, we would still not know where to step twice into the same water. [. . .] We guess that computer science (there is already one) takes into consideration only the infinitely shifting" (TTM 160).[11]

Glissant espouses the electronic transmission of knowledge, not without a certain reluctance: "Might not this speed itself, which is so precious, actually be a lack? In our increasingly accelerated frequentation with the world's diversity, we need pauses, time for meditation, where we emerge from the flow of information we are provided with, to begin to put our opportunities into order. The book is one of those moments" (TTM 172).

For us to step twice into the same river (that of Heraclitus, or the Mississippi) in order to express change, we need the slow motion of whatever can state this: "The book, project or object, allows me to make the wager of surprising, each time, this same water on my skin. Its current gives me the source and delta, its beginning and end, and in any case as many pages as I want at the same time, it leaves me free to conceive them in the same grasp: what it stretches out between its banks is an evidence of the permanent" (TTM 160). The book is a pause, a repetition, a mulling over of becoming, and makes it possible for us not to be drowned in a passivity that would strip change of all meaning. It is necessary at the same time, another oxymoron, to express the totality in a single stroke, in the immensely rapid immediacy of presence to the world, *and* to mull over change by a constantly renewed writing: "If we are carried away so far as to accumulate the long list of our intuitions in this way, at the risk of exasperating ourselves, as it happened to me at the time of conducting this writing four times, accumulation still does not realize a principle of permanence: this same speed of the world envelops us, we do not have time, and *we have to say everything all at once*" (PhR 82).

Édouard Glissant did not fail to recognize and problematize his thinking as a utopia. But, as always, he is obliged to mark his difference from the utopias of the past, among which he mentions Plato, Saint Augustine, and Thomas More, the inventor of the word in 1516. Calqued on the Greek, *u-topia* means "what is without place," "elsewhere than in the world": from Plato onward, utopia is the very hallmark of idealism.

To Glissant's list, one could add Francis Bacon, Balthasar Gracián, Charles Fourier, Claude-Henry de Saint-Simon, Marx, and many others. It should first be noted that the *Republic*, the *City of God*, *Utopia*, and the *Manifesto of the Communist Party*, like the abbey of Thélème in Rabelais, are all concerned with establishing a city of perfection: it is the social bond that these utopias seek to reorganize. From this long and rich tradition, Édouard Glissant stands out; the utopias of the past are similar to systematic thinking, and so they participate in measure, not excess. As soon as an attempt is made to implement them, or when they are posited as ends, there arises, terrifying, the elimination of present imperfections in the name of the future coronation (Saint Augustine, Islam, and Marx are here exemplary, in the persecution of heretics, infidels, or "bourgeois"): Utopia has at all times required order and measure; it needed them, since it was aimed at a finality of perfection, and thus calculated, without having to impose them, norms, an activity of regency, whose goal was to ensure the eternity of a final result. That is why the thoughts that are considered utopian, and which I see as akin to what I call systemic thoughts, construct in order to maintain themselves such terrifying orders that tolerate no distance, no difference. Everywhere people destroy and massacre, as nobly as anyone could wish, men, women, and children, the cities and paths that lead to them, for the sake of a future humanity (CL 223–224).

Conversely, Glissant proposes a utopia that, with no final goal, accepts imperfection and trembling, denied by an oxymoron that becoming will sublate:

> We understand why our thoughts of Utopia, which are not just simply utopian thoughts, no longer project the reform of a given object, human society or human person: there are all these objects, proposed by all peoples at the same time, and we need to place them in relation rather than to choose one to perfect it while ignoring the others. Our thoughts of Utopia do not conceive of any normative exercise that would incline its object to a perfect form. Where would we take the standard of this perfection from? (CL 224–225)

In *Sartorius*, Glissant gives utopia a narrative form, namely by the invisible and missing people of the Batoutos, to which he returns in *La Cohée du Lamentin*: "Utopia is not the dream. It is what we lack in the world. This is what it is: what we are lacking in the world. Many of us rejoiced that the French philosopher Gilles Deleuze imagined that the function of both literature and art was first of all to invent a missing people. Utopia is the very place of this people" (CL 16). But the Batoutos slip into the real world: early Africa, Renaissance Germany, Faulkner's America. They are like the invisible truth of inextricable and real places. Thus, the Batoutou utopia differs from the whole tradition, whose final goal is the perfection of an ideal "elsewhere" of the world. The Batoutos are grappling with the very negativity of the real world.

It will be objected that they are fictitious, that history has not preserved any traces of their contradictory example; but, in the case of the Glissant's writing, this refutation is invalid: art, the narrative, the poem are for him real objects in the world and actions, not the distance of representation or reproduction by a *mimesis*: the Batoutos are living. The Other of thought, when it is written and enters into representation, is not a conceptual withdrawal, but the place of a making: "The Other of thought is this very movement. There, I must act. This is the moment when I change my thinking, without abdicating its contribution. I change, and I exchange. It is an aesthetic of turbulence, of which the corresponding ethics is not given in advance" (PR 169). Thus Glissant's utopia is both of the world and out of the world, in a virtual elsewhere, the elsewhere of becoming: "With this people [the Batoutos] and this populated country we would be and we are closer to the world, and the world closer to us" (CL 16).

We need to extend to the whole work this oxymoron of a utopia realized by art; all Glissant's texts stem from it: "We are not afraid of Utopia, it is our only Act: it is our only Art" (CL 27).

This explains why, as soon as Glissant's notions begin to materialize historically, they are immediately dismissed as imperfect, incomplete, unsatisfactory: they are not what they should be. Thus the United States—where, in Los Angeles for example, ninety languages are spoken and alive—is a land of multiculturalism and not of creolization (TTM 38–39). Thus, Creority and crossbreeding are not creolization (IL 30–31), globalization is not globality, and the Whole-World, the transcultural and the multicultural, are not Relation, etcetera. In any case, it is a question of systematically rejecting the static nature of present states, frozen into the foreseeable and the trivial, to open them up to the unpredictable and unnamable of the poetic virtual.

Hence the constant appeal to the great inspiration of the dream that sustains Glissant in all his "theoretical" work: "What I am is derived, without any fatalism, from what I will be. The poem too is always yet to come" (TFEV 19). The refusal of any destiny here fits with the unpredictable will of the future. And this future makes it possible to remove the obstacle that currently blocks the notion of totality: "The Whole-World is total to the extent that we all dream it so and its difference from the totality still lies in the fact that its whole is a becoming" (Ibid.). May the Whole-World remain a future! May Relation remain a conjecture! "The poetics of Relation is forever conjectural and does not imply any fixity of ideology" (PR 44). How could becoming be mastered, how could one claim to master it, by naming, prefiguration, prophecy, or the imaginary? Becoming is what opens all discourse and all representation to the unforesayable and the unforeseeable. The different/deferred that Glissant identifies in Faulkner and that he practices in his own writing is the very form of this refusal of any finalizing conclusion: the different/deferred is an opening onto becoming.

Chapter 17

"The continuity of the living is a spiral that does not fear to be interrupted"

"Nothing is true, everything is alive" ("Rien n'est vrai, tout est vivant") is the title of the last presentation of Édouard Glissant's thought, in a lecture he gave on April 8, 2010, at the Institut du Tout-Monde he had founded. This title appears as the conclusion of *La Terre magnétique* (2007) and as an epigraph to *La Terre le Feu l'Eau et les Vents* (2010).[1] In *La Terre magnétique*, the aphorism is a prosopopeia; it is the rocky statues of Easter Island that speak, the signs of a vanished culture that nevertheless re-lives in our present: "Nothing is true in truth, everything is totally alive: yes, it is the translation that these people give of this furied inspiration of the stone, yes yes says Ammy: nothing is true, everything is alive" (TM 118).

"Nothing is true, everything is alive" is also the epitaph chosen by Sylvie Glissant for the writer's tombstone in Martinique: thus the gravestone, through its epigraph, speaks like the Moai of Easter Island. This prosopopeia makes Édouard Glissant's death not a closing, a finality, a completion, but a dawn ready for all flights: words are destined to live, ready for a pluperfect of the future—an immortality. And this dawn, in the work, comes from very far away; the vision was already present in *L'Intention poétique*: "Let us leave behind the dreams of childhood, the dream of the True; let us deny the One" (IP 13).

At first sight, the statement takes the form of a very old paradox, that of the liar, invented, according to the tradition, in the seventh century BC by Epimenides the Cretan, who stated: "All Cretans are liars." How can a liar from Crete tell the truth if all Cretans are deceivers? How, if "nothing is true" and "everything is alive," can any real consistency be found?

Many traditions have reflected on this paradox; in philosophy, Eubulis of Miletus (fourth century BC); in religion, Saint Paul[2] and Saint Jerome, commenting on a passage of the Psalmist;[3] in logic, with Alfred Tarski; in mathematics, with Kurt Gödel. But it is in philosophy that its shadow is the longest, since in our view the principles of noncontradiction and the excluded third are implicitly a refutation of the paradox. However, we know that Édouard Glissant rejects this tradition, born with Aristotle, and instead derives new impetus from Heraclitean becoming. In the *Metaphysics*, Aristotle criticizes Heraclitus: "The Logos of Heraclitus, saying that all is and is not, makes everything true" (Γ 7, 1012 a). This shows that the philosopher, one hundred and fifty years after Heraclitus, having to hand the complete book of the latter (of which only dazzling fragments remain for us), *can no longer understand him.*[4] If we subtract from Heraclitus the all-powerful principle of becoming, and if we force him to obey the principles of noncontradiction and the excluded third, his thought does indeed become absurd. And that is what Aristotle does: for him, becoming, that is to say also the organic growth of the living, is subordinated to the idea, Being and essence: "The domain of becoming is opposed to that of essence, for what comes later in the order of generation comes earlier in nature, and what is first in nature is last in the order of generation" (*Parts of Animals*, II, Chap. I, 646a 24). Henceforth, the Living is subordinate to the idea, to the genus, to the True, and cannot be independent of it. Aristotle, of course, does not ignore the movement of the living; but, subjecting it to the system of the concept, he reduces its unforesayable and unforeseeable autonomy: becoming becomes fundamentally impoverished. "Nothing is true, everything is alive" must be read first as a fundamental questioning of the principles of post-Socratic or post-Platonic philosophy. But also as a questioning of Hegel, who asserts that "the True is the Whole": the living, in such a synthesis, will be only a derivative, one being of the first principles of the Being of truth and totality. Empedocles takes up the antinomy: for him, the One is lost in the world, then gathers itself together again. By choosing the living, Glissant returns to this Pre-Socratic master, while expelling the True and the One from the dialectic. The True is then, by antithesis, on the side of a deadly fixity: *on the side of death,* of what "garrotes and kills"; to reach it, we must go through abstract symbolism or logic. The inspiration here is clearly Nietzschean, as the anthology of the Whole-World shows: "Let me be banished from all truths! Just a madman! Just a poet!" (TEFV 240) or even more clearly: "We have art so as not to perish from the truth" (*The Will to Power* III, § 822.).

Glissant's aphorism rejects the subordination of the living to the Idea, so as to free itself from the limitations of the concept. Moreover, it must be read "in time," in becoming, according to the passage from the first to the second utterance, just like oxymorons and tautologies. Remember the principles of punctuation stated in *Poétique de la Relation* (PR 236): a colon would have indicated a logical consequence ("Nothing is true: therefore everything is alive"). The comma indicates a relation—that is to say, a dynamic process—caught up in a temporality; nothing is true, absolutely, fixedly, from all eternity: the True must be subordinated to the becoming of the living, which grows, changes, and mixes things:

> If we suppose that nothing is True, we go beyond continuity, unless it is the continuous nature of concrete things that do not need capital letters. For the True in capital letters does not pass in any way, the Absolute is nothing. And the Absolute is true only in so far as it goes beyond the absolute. Thus there is no continuity from the True to the True, and all continuity lies in the falsity of the things we have to fight. But the living is the very continuity which, if it ceases, enters into repose, which we call death, to prepare another continuity. Thus, the cessation of continuity in the language of anyone who lays claim to the True is a decisive end, which leaves room only for useful truths.[5]

Thus becoming unties the paradox, just as in all other places it has resolved tautologies and oxymorons: for Relation is in becoming, *is* becoming. The True as absolute, break of continuity, unsurpassable fixity is caught in the growth of the living that challenges and relativizes it. And, at each moment of becoming, another truth emerges. There is no truth that is not related to the movement of thought, to the immobility of a system closed to itself: the True lays a claim to universality that is belied by the growing silence of the living: "That is to say that the language of the True does not exercise and is not exercised in any language, where the living does not know of any natural or other language." Nothing is True, against Aristotle and with Heraclitus, except in the growth of life.

But there is more. One possible way[6] to reduce the paradox of the liar that lies at the heart of "Nothing is true, everything is alive" is to reduce the extension of "nothing is true," a self-destructive reflexive proposition, and to assume that we are in the presence of an uttering followed by an utterance, which could be written as follows: (Glissant says—uttering) Nothing is true: (utterance) "Everything is alive." In fact, this solution is indispensable, so that the "Everything is alive" can be consistent; otherwise we fall into the infinite regression of inconsistent statements. As a consequence of what medieval logicians called *restrictio*, nothing is absolutely, fixedly true from all eternity, not only because the truth depends on the historical or linguistic context in which it is expressed, but because it is transmuted constantly in submission to becoming (the living), which is its only *true* context.

Valerio Adami, in a very fine discussion,[7] noted that Édouard Glissant was an organic thinker. This is perfectly true; he does not produce the thought of the organic, in which the latter is subject to an ideal or scientific control, but the organicity of thought (in a chiasm), which espouses the mixity and growth of the living: "There may be a poetics that draws inspiration from the True, it would be a mystical poetics, or there may be a poetics inspired by the living: it would be a poetics like mine, a poetics of creolization." Glissant's last text, which is also the first, synthesizes all the moments of thought: becoming, negativity, break and continuity, relation, creolization, unachievable, and nondominant totalization, in a profound relation with his rereading of all philosophy. But there is more: a thought that develops by duplication and mulling over and, through the very fact of this repetition, intensifies, grows, and produces the radically new, is a thought that closely espouses the very process of life.

Édouard Glissant's thought is a radical transmutation of all human thought and culture; it takes flight, in a fashion meticulously reflected and weighed, beyond all that has been questioned from the origin of thought to the present day—beyond the One and the Heraclitean Logos (through the multiplicity of the presence of all languages), beyond Parmenidian and Heideggerian Being (through the diversity of beings), beyond the singular and repressed identity of psychoanalysis (through Relation and *Soleil de la conscience*), beyond the universals, be they Catholic, political, or philosophical, beyond the Hegelian system (through the imaginaries of future histories), beyond academic discourse and the discourse of the master (through the unforeseeable nature of becoming), beyond cultural filiations and traditions (through the meticulous and prophetic re-reading of the past, which becomes a future that is exciting in its incompleteness), beyond the partly illusory mastery that philosophy, science, and theory aim to impose on the whole.

Glissant's act, which rejects all causality and all determinism, opens all cultures up to an abysmal and exalting freedom, which is not without its terrors, the "thought of trembling" maybe: "The power of imaginaries is that of the utopia in every day, it is realistic when it prefigures what will long enable us *to sustain actions that do not tremble.* Actions that do not tremble would remain sterile if the thought of the whole world, which is a trembling, did not support them. This is where philosophy exercises, and also the thought of the poem" (PhR 56). The critical rereading of any constraint does not open up to a new domination, but, if I can in turn allow myself an oxymoron, to a nonmastering mastery. This is the lesson of Édouard Glissant: to teach us to live poetically in an unlimited freedom and in the responsibility due to the Other of thought, to open us to the future of an unforeseeable becoming, in which the essential contours of Relation and the Whole-World are being shaped in advance.

The work is systematic, united in its purpose, totalizing, and thus aiming as such at universality. But the system, the Whole, the universal, the one, instead of being excluded, are inclusive and always unfinished, always in the making. Infinite process in which the one and diversity (multiplicity), the Same and the Other, Totality and non-Totality, universality and particularity are constantly exchanging their dialectical positions, and eternally producing chiasms. The places of freedom are exchanged without being confused. This means that the freedom of becoming that Glissant gives himself and gives to the Other is also given to the "West." Beyond ideological, political, or economic divides, Glissant's thinking is also the possibility of "old Europe" becoming or becoming anew. Nothing is more foreign to the notions of the Whole-World and Relation than enclosure in the postcolonial ghetto, the logic of a "naive revenge" (IP 38), a naive and simplistic binarism where everything that originates from the West is poison and all that challenges it is a universal balm for the wounds of the world; even if legitimate or legitimized, the spirit of revenge inevitably renews filiation and the root, and mirrors the hatred that it fights. Interpreted literally, the Whole-World and Relation apply to everyone, everywhere, in the detail and the inextricable of their place.

One can reject Glissant's system in the name of a narrow and impoverished representation of ("philosophical") rationality. But in an extended conception of reason, we must give to the imaginary, to the living, and to change the place due to them; then, the system appears to be perfectly coherent and rational. Because rationality also requires us to question the determinations that limit us, so as to embrace the living with both hands: it is at this price that a life is really worth living. This notionality (and not conceptuality) of the living remains to be explored. Rich with immense potentialities, it is the threshold from which a modern fusion can be expressed, beyond the Socratic fracture of the True and the Idea, but by integrating them. Just as Glissant proposes a beyond of literature and Belles-Lettres, the thought of the living opens onto a beyond-philosophy that renews it from top to bottom and draws us toward a future as yet unfigured.

The "prophetization of the past" that Glissant practiced in his work and the future anterior of the unforeseeable of which he was the great pioneer allow us to rediscover, at the origin of Western thought, a possibility of becoming, proclaimed by Heraclitus and then thrown into a deep oblivion by the triad of the founders of philosophy. As a universal song, Glissant's work is the portico and the conflagration of all potentiality, where the "West," like any other region of the world, can find the resources for multiple revivals and utopias: in Relation.

Chapter 18

"Yes, yes, everything is alive"

In the *Philosophie de la Relation*, Édouard Glissant quotes a sentence from *Mahogany*: "*Truly, my name is Mathieu Béluse. According to the law of narrative, which is in the order of the secret trees, I still have a long life ahead of me.*" He also often said a word to the wise. "Now I am immortal." Not eternal, in the petrification of a divine immobility, but living with a life that will be prolonged ad infinitum beyond the physical death of the body: by the work and the life that it will experience in the many readings to which, from now on, it will endlessly give birth, for centuries.

On the eve of his death, Édouard told Sylvie Glissant: "I dreamed that I had become a living soul of the world."

Notes

Chapter 1

1. We will later be examining in more detail this oxymoron of the "non-systematic system," the concept as enclosure, the system as a necessary opening up, and the pre-eminence of the poetic imaginary. I would like to mention another gift, the most beautiful no doubt: a painting by Sylvie Glissant, where a haiku appears on a white background, a variant of the poem "Lindos" (PC 370)—the variant, changing "bends" to "sighs," turns the poem into a hapax that bestows on the gift a particular tone:

> The undulating earth turns black
> At the feet of the water diviner, sighs
> The prophet of images stumbles
> The blue pucks are finally naked.

2. See Dash, *Édouard Glissant* (Cambridge, 1995), and Britton, *Édouard Glissant and Postcolonial Theory. Strategies of Language and Resistance* (Charlottesville, VA & London, 1999).

3. Milner, back-cover blurb to Glissant, *L'Œuvre Claire* (Paris, 1995).

4. Quoted in Jarczyk and Labarrière, *De Kojève à Hegel: 150 ans de la pensée hégélienne en France* (Paris, 1996), 100.

5. "We are not born alone. To be born (*naître*), in the case of all things, is to know/be-born-with (*connaître*). Every birth (*naissance*) is a knowledge/being-born-with (*connaissance*)": Claudel, "Traité de la co-naissance au monde et de soi-même," *Art poétique,* in *Oeuvre poétique* (Paris, 1957), 150). (Translator's note: Claudel here is making a pun on *connaissance* or subjective knowledge as a *co-naissance* or being-born-with. The distinction between *connaissance*, connoting a more subject-based view of knowledge, and *savoir*, a more objective, scientific knowledge, is crucial to Leupin's discussion of Glissant's work. Sometimes there is an overlap, and *connaissance* can refer quite generally to "knowledge," though

generally with the nuance of "knowledge-by-acquaintance." Where the distinction needs to be highlighted, I have translated *connaissance* as "subjective knowledge" and *savoir* as "objective knowledge," or have added the relevant French word in parentheses.)

6. Glissant hardly ever uses the term "fiction" when he is discussing literature; he reserves the term instead for the big philosophical systems.

7. Montaigne, *Les Essais* (Paris, 1924), book II, chapter XVII, 665.

8. For Lacan, the *plus-de-jouir* is necessarily (logically and historically) linked to surplus value in Marxism. See Lacan, *Séminaire XVI. D'un autre à l'Autre* (Paris, 2006), 16–19. (Translator's note: *Plus-de-jouir*, a complex term in Lacanian psychoanalysis, is often translated as "surplus jouissance.")

9. See Cerquiglini's online article, "Francopolyphonie du Tout-Monde: penser la francophonie avec Édouard Glissant," http://mondesfrancophones.com/espaces/creolizations/francopolyphonie-du-tout-monde-penser-la-francophonie-avec-edouard-glissant/.

10. Exceptions include *Le Discours antillais* as well as pamphlets such as *L'Intraitable Beauté du monde* and *Quand les murs tombent*, which have a particular status in Glissant's œuvre.

11. "We can thus say of subjects who seek to hold a political vision of the world that they are actually seeking a master [. . .]": Milner, *Les Noms indistincts* (Paris, 1983), 92. It is worth reading the whole chapter "La vision politique du monde."

12. In this sense, victimology differs from the Hegelian dialectic, where the master and the slave experience radically opposite desires: the master wants to be recognized as such even at the cost of his own death, but the slave wants to live; there is a future for him—he prefers submission to death.

13. This makes it surprising that Che Guevara occupies a place—too high a place—in the anthology of the Whole-World (TFEV 195).

14. Nesbitt distinguishes between a Glissant who was "politically committed" up until the *Discours antillais* and a Glissant who withdrew from politics in the "quietist anti-politics of Relation" ("Politiques et Poétiques: les errances de l'absolu," in Loichot (ed.), *Entours d'Édouard Glissant, Revue des sciences Humaines* 309 [2013]: 169; see also Nesbitt, "Early Glissant: From the Destitution of the Political to Antillean Ultra-Leftism," *Callaloo* 36, no. 4 [2013]: 932–948). This view is hugely mistaken: Nesbitt criticizes Glissant for not being a new Sartre (or another Nesbitt), putting his pen in the service of the "wretched of the earth." As I said, nothing is more foreign to Glissant than this transitivity and this transparency of writing to politics. His program is thoroughly anti-Sartrean, and resists the Jacobinism of political universality invoked by Nesbitt, and the "transcendence" that would not hesitate to impose its ideal by force, and that has not hesitated to do so. Nesbitt's "political transcendence" would leave no room for art, seen solely as "an aestheticism that deliberately reduces itself to a journey

toward poetry." Nesbitt's properly philosophical criticism is expressed as follows: "The 'philosopher of Relation,' in his implicit ontology, propounds a poetics of the idealist transcendental illusion: the indefinitely repeated statement that our own subjectivity constitutes the unsurpassable horizon of the Whole-World" (Ibid.). Everything about this definition is wrong: Relation is not an ontology, it is not transcendent, and subjectivity is not the horizon of the Whole-World. This will be demonstrated below. A much more accurate view of Glissant's alleged apoliticism is proposed by Prieto, who points out that Glissant's project goes far beyond that of the postcolonial ghetto; according to Prieto, Glissant is therefore "post-postcolonial" ("Édouard Glissant, Littérature-monde, and Tout-Monde," *Small Axe* 63 [November 2010]: 111–119; 114). See also Delpech, "L'insurrection glissantienne: l'imaginaire en action," in Gyssens and Ledent (eds.), *The Caribbean Writer as Warrior of the Imaginary* (Amsterdam, 2008), 215: "The imaginary can become a weapon only if it is turned into an ideology, and the writer becomes a Warrior only if he turns into an ideologue."

15. *Édouard Glissant, Mémoires des esclavages*, with a preface by de Villepin (Paris, 2007).

16. For all publishing details of Glissant's works, see list of abbreviations.

17. *Francophonia* 32 (2012). 209.

18. Interview with *Le Monde*, February 3, 2011. This clichéd anti-Americanism is very widespread among French intellectuals.

19. Interview in *L'Orient-Le Jour* 77, November 2011.

Chapter 2

1. In line with Glissant's lexicon, I will distinguish between two kinds of language: language as langue [translator's note: in the sense of a natural language such as French or English], in its usual sense of what founds a linguistic community, and language as langage [translator's note: as language in the abstract, or as a style or idiom]. Glissant always uses langage to define the idiolect of a poet or a writer: "[The sky (le ciel)] is however enough for you to unleash the words of a childhood that survives. This langage. What does langue matter then, I mean whether you were taught it or if you first knew it? What does that atavism, the flexible science of diction, matter? [. . .] And this langage is the excess of a new and admittedly clumsy langue that seeks to bite" (SC 29). The langue learned is the language of filiation and atavism; langage is the language of disaffiliation and change. Langue, in Glissant's work, is always the framework of a community (national, ethnic, tribal) that draws its authority from that langue. By contrast, langage, although it places itself "in the presence of all langues of the world," is always singular and solitary: it is that of the creator who, for his part, dispenses with any authority or authorization: "Poetics no longer demands

the adequacy of langue, but the precise fire of langage. In other words: I speak to you in your langue, and it is in my langage that I understand you" (IP, 53).

2. See Joubert, "L'archipel Glissant," in *Édouard Glissant* (Paris, 2006), 318, where he applies the Moebius strip to the question of naming in Glissant.

3. Ménil, *Les Voies de la créolisation. Essai sur Édouard Glissant* (Grenoble, 2011), 16ff. This monumental work is indispensable for a reading of Glissant. We can only be saddened by the premature death of its author, one year after Glissant's own.

4. See chapter 11.

Chapter 3

1. For more details, see Kalinowski, "La littérature dans le champ philosophique français de la première moitié du xxe siècle," *Methodos* [online], January 2001, http://methodos.revues.org/53.

2. The strictly "Hegelian" character of this reading of the unhappy consciousness is questioned by Jarczyk and Labarrière in *De Kojève à Hegel: 150 ans de pensée hégélienne en France* (Paris, 1996).

3. Hegel, *Phénoménologie de l'Esprit*, section VII B, "La religion esthétique," vol. 2 (Paris, 1978).

4. Hegel, *Esthétique I* (Paris, 1979), 152.

5. "Solitaire et solidaire," interview of Édouard Glissant by Philippe Artières, *Terrain* 41, September 2003.

6. Fonkoua has shown the influence of Wahl's view of Descartes on the poetics of Glissant in his article "Jean Wahl et Édouard Glissant: philosophie, raison et poésie," in *Poétiques d'Édouard Glissant*, conference proceedings ed. Chevrier (Paris, 1999), 299ff. Wiedorn has explored Glissant's relation to philosophy in *Think Like an Archipelago: Paradox in the Work of Edouard Glissant* (New York, 2018). See also *Theorizing Glissant: Sites and Citations (Creolizing the Canon)*, ed. Drabinski (Rowman and Littlefield, 2015).

7. See Ramnoux, "Héraclite," in *Encyclopaedia Universalis* (Paris, 1985), and Kojève, *Essai d'une histoire raisonnée de la philosophie païenne* (Paris, 1968), vol. 1, 293.

8. "We will give the creative imagination the name of *fantasy* [. . .]. A superficial fantasy never produces a lasting work of art. We do not mean to say that the artist must formulate in *philosophical* thoughts the truth of things which form the basis of religion as well as of philosophy and art. The artist does not need philosophy, and if he thinks as a philosopher, he is actually engaged in a labour that is the complete opposite of the form of knowledge specific to art" (Hegel, *Esthétique I* [Paris, 1979], 354–355). Glissant reabsorbs the Hegelian opposition art/philosophy, and reverses the primacy given to the philosophical over the poetic. However, the philosophical dimension, even if implicit, remains crucial.

9. On the exclusion of poetry by philosophy, see the path-breaking article, essential to an understanding of my own book, by Coursil, "La catégorie de la relation dans les essais d'Édouard Glissant. Philosophie d'une poétique," in *Poétiques d'Édouard Glissant* (Paris, 1999), 87–89. We might add to his thinking the chiasmatic idea of the "poetics of a philosophy."

10. Quoted by Axelos, *Héraclite et la philosophie* (Paris, 1968), 14. Axelos also says: "Hegel was the first to discover the true importance of Pre-Socratic thought in general, and especially the thought of Heraclitus" (227).

11. See Damato, "La répétition dans les essais d'Édouard Glissant," in *Poétiques d'Édouard Glissant* (Paris, 1999), 147–155.

12. As an example, and on a different level: "The interiorization of racism [. . .] is the responsibility of the *metis* himself" (IP 219).

Chapter 4

1. Hegel, *Esthétique I* (Paris, 1979), 97. See also the brilliant work by Lacoue-Labarthe and Nancy, *L'Absolu littéraire. Théorie de la littérature du romantisme allemande* (Paris, 1978). I will here draw a distinction (to be developed in the next chapter) between the *literary* absolute of the Romantics, as the expression of an individual or national genius, and the *poetic* absolute proposed by Glissant—one that is transnational, transindividual, and based on Relation.

2. Hegel, *Esthétique I* (Paris, 1979), 101.

3. There is, ironically enough, no shortage of philosophers who have turned the charge of "chatter" against Hegel himself. One is Schopenhauer, who in *The World as Will and Representation* describes Hegel as "a revolting philosopher over whose empty chatter a sickly tedium hovers."

4. See Kojève, *Introduction à la lecture de Hegel* (Paris, 1971), 86–91, and 151 for the beautiful soul.

5. On the history of this notion, see Fumaroli's preface to *Les Premiers Siècles de la République européenne des Lettres. Actes du Colloque* international, the proceedings of a conference held in Paris in December 2001 (Paris, 2005).

6. Hegel, *Esthétique I* (Paris, 1979), 100–101.

7. Kojève, *Introduction à la lecture de Hegel* (Paris, 1971), 152.

8. As Godin has noted, "The author does not spend his time page after page marveling at his own prowess and his own style, he does not seek to use his novel as a pretext for showing off the huge scope of his knowledge" (*La Totalité* [Seyssel, 1997–2001], vol. 4, 340).

9. Hegel, *Esthétique I* (Paris, 1979), 101.

10. "All poetics is a network": this is clearly akin to the idea of the rhizome.

11. Biondi has emphasized the importance of the commonplace in "Du lieu d'origine au lieu commun," in *Poétiques d'Édouard Glissant* (Paris, 1999),

138–140. On Glissant's distance from nineteenth-century poetry, see Azérad, "Mesure parfaite et réinventée. Édouard Glissant Reinvents Nineteenth-Century French Poetry," in *Thinking Poetry* (London, 2013), 203–220.

12. Hegel, *La Raison dans l'Histoire* (Paris, 1965), 37. The idea that Hegel left Africa out has been questioned; see Okonda, *Hegel et l'Afrique: thèses, critiques et dépassements* (Puteaux, 2010).

13. Buck-Morss, *Hegel, Haiti and Universal History* (Pittsburgh, 2009).

14. See the detailed study by von Arnim, *Hegel contre le racisme, invitation à lire Hegel dans ses textes*, online: http://www.hegel.net/fr/f311112contre_le_racisme.htm. For Hegel's run-ins with the Prussian government, see Pinkard, *Hegel: A Biography* (Cambridge, 2000), 486 and passim. See also the remarks of Châtelet in *Hegel* (Paris, 1981), 160–161, indicating that the philosopher never saw the Prussian monarchy as the perfect incarnation of the rational state.

15. For Castro, see EBR, 40; for Che Guevara, see TTM, 155.

Chapter 5

1. Lacan, "Radiophonie," in *Autres écrits* (Paris, 2001), 440.

2. "[The Sophists] were the teachers of Greece. It is through them that philosophy came into being" (Hegel, *Leçons sur l'histoire de la philosophie* (Paris, 2000), vol. II, 244).

3. On this question see Axelos, *Héraclite et la Philosophie* (Paris, 1968), 72–75.

4. This ban was highly praised by Saint Augustine, in his utopian city: "Here we must award the palm to a Greek, to Plato who, when designing the ideal model of a perfect Republic, expelled from it the poets, as enemies of the truth" (*City of God*, II, XIV; see Plato, *Republic*, X, 595b–c, 598d, 605c, 607a).

5. For further details, see Cassin, *Le Plaisir de parler* (Paris: Éditions de Minuit, 1986). She comments on a passage in the *Gorgias*: "An interweaving of literature, pedagogy and politics: that is where the plasma leads us. The world-effect is produced on two levels: that of the establishing of the human world, of the consensus formed by the city, culture as opposed to nature; and that of literary fiction, of the patrimony that constitutes the idea of a people, culture as opposed to lack of culture . . ." (19–20).

6. See chapter 12.

7. "Heraclitus lays bare the deep meaning of the mysteries, while vehemently attacking the pseudo-religious sentiments of ordinary folk" (Axelos, *Héraclite et la Philosophie* [Paris, 1968], 142).

8. Hegel, *Esthétique II* (Paris, 1979), 35.

9. "Hegel's perspicacity grasped the hidden harmony. Hegel envisages the Heraclitean fire as a process, a becoming: 'fire is physical time,' he writes" (Axelos, *Héraclite et la Philosophie* [Paris, 1968], 100).

10. See Bachelard, *La Psychanalyse du feu* (1938), *L'Eau et les Rêves* (1941), *L'Air et les Songes* (1943), *La Terre et les Rêveries du repos* (1946), *La Terre et les Rêveries de la volonté* (1948), all published in Paris.

11. When Glissant talks about the chaos-world, he transforms Hesiod's original Chaos into another "element" of this world and connects it to the scientific theory of chaos.

12. Pinkard, *Hegel* (Cambridge, 2000), 582.

13. Axelos, *Héraclite et la Philosophie* (Paris, 1968), 80ff.

14. Axelos, *Le Jeu du monde* (Paris, 1969). See the commentary on the *Discours antillais* by Oakley in her *Common Places: The Poetics of African Atlantic Postromantics* (Amsterdam, 2011), 42. Note, however, in the light of the preceding chapter, that it is wrong to categorize Glissant as a postromantic.

15. "It is Socrates's dialectic that destroys everything, with its relativism, its critical irony, and its use of empty ('abstract') notions of the Beautiful and the Good" (Kojève, *Introduction à la lecture de Hegel* [Paris, 1971], 255).

16. Godin, "Prologue," in *La Totalité* (Seyssel, 1997–2001), vol. 1, 25.

17. Hegel, *Phénoménologie de l'Esprit* (Paris, 1978), 18. As opposed to the Truth as Totality, we need to emphasize the idea that "Nothing is true, everything is alive," the final stage in Glissant's thought (see my analysis below).

18. Hegel, *Phénoménologie de l'Esprit* (Paris, 1978), 38.

19. Ibid.

20. See Koyré, *From the Closed World to the Infinite Universe* (Radford, 2008), in which he discusses the epistemological break between modern science and the ancient world.

21. Brøndal, "*Omnis* et *totus*: analyse et étymologie," in *Essais de linguistique générale* (Copenhagen, 1943). On the relevant etymology, here is what Brøndal writes: "1. *Tōtus*, the culminating term of the integral series, the expression of the coherence or indivisibility of a body, appears to come from a noun that emphasizes the political or ethnic solidarity of a social group (political in Italy: Oscan *touto*, 'civitas,' ethnic north of the Alps: Gothic *Þiuda*, a 'people'). —Just as *saeculum*, which properly means '(human) generation,' shifts to the sense of 'world' (human or not) and is translated into Gothic by *manaseÞs* 'human seed,' hence 'κόσμος,' and in West Germanic by **wer-ald* 'human generation,' hence 'world' (German *Welt*, English *world*). 2. *Omnis*, the culminating term of an arithmetical construction, the expression of an ordered whole, appears however to come from the very name of man—the being that is both social and rational. The model of any organized group is the human group—This is substantially analogous to the way in which κόσμος, which first meant 'adornment,' 'toilette' (an order of a purely human nature) came generally to designate the order that unites all things, the harmonious universe dear to the Hellenic spirit. *Mundus* (whence, by scholarly borrowing, the French 'monde' for 'world') is a docile calque of this: it first meant 'adornment,' then 'the set of celestial bodies,' the 'world.' "

22. Christ also puns on *mundus* in Saint John: "*Dicit ei Iesus qui lotus est non indiget ut lavet sed est mundus totus et vos mundi estis sed non omnes.*" (Contextual and literal translation: "And Jesus said to him, "Whoever has bathed does not have to wash, he is wholly pure. And you are pure too, but not all of you." "Creolizing" translation: "Who has bathed is all world/whole world. You are worlds, but not all of you.")

23. Céline, *Rigodon, in Romans IV* (Paris, 1974), 887.

24. Blanchot, *Le Livre à venir* (Paris, 1959), 14–15.

25. See Oster, "D'un statut d'évangéliste: Maurice Blanchot," *Littérature* 33 (1979): 111–128.

26. Mallarmé and his Book, figured as an œuvre resembling an ammonite or a Moebius strip, already occupies a significant place in *L'Intention poétique*, 64–67.

27. Hegel, *Phénoménologie de l'Esprit* (Paris, 1978), 18.

28. Hegel, *Esthétique I* (Paris, 1979), 17.

29. Kojève, *Introduction à la lecture de Hegel* (Paris, 1971), 393.

30. Quoted in Jarczyk and Labarrière, *De Kojève à Hegel* (Paris, 1996), 109.

31. See Lauro, "Le frémissement de la lecture, parcours littéraire d'Édouard Glissant," *Francophonia*, XXXII, Autumn 2012, 200.

32. Hegel, *Phénoménologie de l'Esprit* (Paris, 1978), 130.

33. Id., *Esthétique IV*, 63.

34. Id., *Esthétique IV*, 23 (my emphasis).

35. Id., *Phénoménologie de l'Esprit* (Paris, 1978), 12.

Chapter 6

1. The very title of the work, *Introduction à la poétique du divers*, shows the *diversum* as the complete opposite of the *universum*.

2. See the French version of Aristotle's *Poetics*: *Poétique*, trans. Dupont-Roc and Lallot (Paris, 1980), especially 222, note 1.

3. For further details, see "Catholique," in *Les Pères apostoliques* (Paris, 2001), 507–509.

4. "I do not speak of the catholic universal in the solely religious sense" (EBR 23).

5. The question has been partly discussed by Carminella Biondi and Elena Pessini, "La quête du sacré dans Tout-Monde," in *Rêver le monde, écrire le monde: Théorie et narrations d'Édouard Glissant* (Bologna, 2004), 77–90.

6. On the theme of the unspeaker, see Dash, "No Mad Art: The Deterritorialized Déparleur in the work of Édouard Glissant," *Paragraph* 24, no. 3 (November 2001): 113–116.

7. See Cailler, "Interfaces: Walt Whitman et Édouard Glissant," *Francofonia* 32 (2012): 81–82; Delpech, "Édouard Glissant à la cheminaison du Tout-Monde,"

Francofonia 32 (2012): 183. See also Delpech, "L'insurrection Glissantienne: l'imaginaire en action," in Gyssens and Ledent (eds.), o cit., 214.

8. "The Son of God died: it is believable because it is absurd; and, having been buried, he rose from the dead; it is certain because it is impossible" (De carne Christi, 5).

9. This is a convincing example of creolization within a "single" language, since the Hebrew of the Torah and the Hebrew of the Mishnah are different and yet related.

10. For further details, see my *Passion des Idoles* (Paris, 2000), 120–130.

11. See Paul, "Le christianisme," in *Grand Atlas des religions* (Paris, 1990), 228ff.

12. For further details on this "white" or blank language, or on language as non-language, see my *Fiction et Incarnation. Littérature et théologie au Moyen Âge* (Paris, 2000), chapter 3.

13. Gauvin ponders this formula in "L'imaginaire des langues," in *Poétiques d'Édouard Glissant* (Paris, 1999), 275–284.

14. See below my remarks on the word "*poétrie*," derived from the English word "poetry."

15. See chapter 12.

16. "The poetic imaginary that [Glissant] develops has a decisive speculative role in thinking about relation [. . .] The poetics of relation proposed by Glissant draws on a non-analogical imaginary and does not depend on a logic of imitation" (François Noudelmann, "Pour une pensée archipélique," in Harvey, Kaplan, and Noudelmann [eds.], *Politique et Filiation* [Paris, 2004], 199–200).

17. This also applies, in the political and juridical domains, to the words, "every man born on this territory is a citizen of the Republic"; Glissant clearly marks the limits of this false universality: "And even if you say "republican citizenship," it comes down to the same thing, as it is still a matter of French citizenship, of the French Republic." The same is true of the Universal Declaration of Human Rights: "For me [. . .], this is the declaration of the rights of just one part of the French people." Likewise with the "universality" of the law: "Law is not universality, but the jurisprudential calculation of all particular situations. It is not universality—we must be fully aware of that" ("La Relation imprédictible et sans morale," interview with Noudelmann, *Rue Descartes* [online] 37 (2002): 190. http://www.cairn.info/revue-rue-descartes-2002–3–page-76.htm#pa4). Interestingly, Glissant here subscribes to a definition of customary law that is of Anglo-Saxon origin, as opposed to the normative law found for example in France.

18. See chapter 12.

19. This ontics probably draws on Wahl's *Vers la fin de l'ontologie* (Paris: Vrin, 1956).

Chapter 7

1. As Milner puts it, "There is never synonymy between a notion from Antiquity and a modern notion"; "Lacan and the Ideal of Science," in Leupin (ed.), *Lacan and the Human Sciences* (Lincoln, NE, 1991).

2. See Milner, "Lacan and the Ideal of Science," where he notes that Foucault's position involves an absolute nominalism. So Foucault is very different from Édouard Glissant, who wrote: "[. . .] we should here beware of nominalism. In other words, we must not believe that revelation lies in words or in the letter of the text or the spoken word" (EBR 101).

3. Hegel, *Esthétique IV* (Paris, 1979), 63.

4. Ibid., 23–24.

5. For further details, see Kojève's commentary in *Introduction à la lecture de Hegel* (Paris, 1971), 133–141.

6. However, it is a more complex problem, as Hegel is equivocal (not-one, non-total). For Kojève, Hegel is an atheist, while for Labarrière he is still a Christian ("Le Dieu de Hegel," in *De Kojève à Hegel* [Paris, 1996], 138ff.). Bruaire claims that Hegel is a Christian while still suggesting that Hegel's philosophy is incompatible with any Christian philosophy ("Conclusion," in *Logique et Religion chrétienne dans la philosophie de Hegel* [Paris, 1964]). We will discuss Hegel's equivocal relation to the question of the End of History.

7. See my discussion of Hegel's view of poetry earlier in this chapter.

8. Nietzsche, *Untimely Considerations*, 2, section 8.

9. Nietzsche, *The Joyful Wisdom*, V, § 357.

10. Rousset, *G. W.F. Hegel. Le Savoir absolu* (Paris, 1998), 47.

11. François Noudelmann points out that the rejection of filiation by the flesh is also a rejection of conceptual filiation: "As against genealogical legitimacy, Glissant would emphasize random encounters, nicknames, and names acquired after marriage or adoption. This counter-model is true not only for human groups, but also for the representation of ideas, *because it is also an epistemological paradigm of the syntax of relations*" ("Édouard Glissant's Legacy: Transmitting without Universals?," *Callaloo* 36, no. 4 (2013): 873, my emphasis. Similarly, John Drabinski writes, "Glissant generates a new conceptual language. In that sense, he is the author of a paradigm shift" ("Shorelines, in Memory of Édouard Glissant," *Journal of French and Francophone Philosophy* 19, no. 1 [2011]: 7).

12. Barnabé, Chamoiseau and Confiant, *Éloge de la créolité* (Paris, 1989).

13. Bachelard had a tiny frying pan for one egg, which fascinated Édouard.

14. Fragment 40, quoted in Kessler, *L'Esthétique de Nietzsche* (Paris, 1998), 163.

15. Thanks to Raphaël Lauro for drawing my attention to this point.

16. *Chronicques abregées des roys de France.*

17. In classical Latin, *poetria* refers to the woman poet, the poetess; so medieval Latin weaves, interweaves, and interbreeds the word. See my study "Absolute Reflexivity," in *Barbarolexis* (Cambridge, MA, 1989).

18. For further details, see de Lubac, *Exégèse médiévale* (Paris, 1959), I, 1, 305ff.

19. Char, *L'Âge cassant* (Paris: José Corti, 1995). For Glissant's affinities with Char, see Glissant's chapter on Char in *L'Intention poétique*, 84–91, as well as the obituary he wrote on him in *Le Courrier de l'Unesco* XLI, no. 6 (1988): 33.

Chapter 8

1. At this point I also recall another of Édouard's chiasms; speaking of scholars, he said: "Those people write to live, I live to write."

2. While English has the common word "inclusivity," it is notable that French needs to resort to a neologism (*inclusivité*) to express the opposite of "exclusivity."

3. See the "psychoses of complexion" and the "psychoses of connection" mentioned in *Le Discours antillais* (DA 291).

4. Hegel, *Esthétique IV* (Paris, 1979), 138–139 (I emphasize the related notions).

5. On all these epic moments, see *Faulkner, Mississippi* (Paris, 1996).

6. The abolition of the slave trade (not of slavery itself) dates from 1807. Great Britain had got there first, and was also the first to abolish slavery, in 1833.

7. Chevrier (ed.), *Poétiques d'Édouard Glissant*, 55.

8. But not always completely: the Danes and the Portuguese recorded their machinations. But these were based on departures from Africa, not arrival in America or the Antilles, where the origins and filiation of the slave as object was of little importance and was soon forgotten.

9. The novel (*roman*) covered everything that was not written in Latin, but in the "romance" language.

10. Blanchot, *Le Livre à venir* (Paris: Gallimard, 1959), 265ff.

11. See FM 51–52. See also Azérad, "Édouard Glissant and the Test of Faulkner's Modernism," in *American Creoles* (Liverpool, 2013), 197–215.

12. See Madou, "L'un et le Divers, comment repenser le lyrique, l'épique, le tragique, le politique?," in *Poétiques d'Édouard Glissant* (Paris, 1999), 192–202. See also his *Édouard Glissant: De mémoire d'arbres* (Amsterdam, 2004) and *Errance et épopée: Glissant, Segalen, Walcott* (Paris, 2016).

Chapter 9

1. See the collection of pieces *Autour d'Édouard Glissant* (Paris, 1988). For the particular case of his relation with Lam, see Samia Kassab-Charfi, "Les "épaisseurs têtues" du sens. L'intime dialogue entre Wilfredo Lam et Édouard Glissant," *Francofonia* 32 (2012): 135–146.

2. Glissant contradicts Leroi-Gourhan, who saw common characteristics in the art of caves scattered across prehistoric Europe (see Leroi-Gourhan, *Préhistoire de l'art occidental* (Paris, 1977). Glissant's reconstruction does not obey the rules of archeology, but those of a foundational myth.

3. We can draw a contrast between the respective approaches of Glissant and Bataille in *Les Larmes d'Éros* (Paris, 1971). For Glissant, Lascaux was the foundation of an open, tightly bound community; for Bataille, it was the initial affirmation of an individualized Eros.

4. The Greek word used by Heraclitus has a threefold connotation: fitting separate pieces together, as in carpentry; a military or social accord drawn up between potential opponents; and the tuning of a musical instrument. In Plato, it becomes a synonym for "symphonia" (the harmony of musical sounds) and loses its material connotations. See Kahn, *The Art and Thought of Heraclitus* (Cambridge, 1979), 196 and note 260; see also Axelos: "What we provisionally call an 'aesthetic vision' is the vision that grasps a totality without ever losing sight of everything that manifests itself in a fragmentary way" (Axelos, *Le Jeu du monde* (Paris, 1969), 204).

5. Hegel, *Esthétique I* (Paris, 1979), 34 (my emphasis).

6. Ibid., 27 (my emphasis).

7. The nickname "Apocal" is simultaneously the title of the last poem written by Édouard Glissant and that of a narrative that remained an unfinished project; only the title page exists, as Glissant's death prevented him from pursuing it.

8. Hegel, *Esthétique I* (Paris, 1979), 10. This declaration yet again displays Hegel's anti-romanticism: Rousseau, of course, had educated Europe to appreciate the beauty of Nature.

9. Contrary to a common view, see Nesbitt, "Politiques et poétiques: les errances de l'absolu," in *Entours d'Édouard Glissant, Revue des sciences humaines* 309 (January 2013): 155–169.

10. Anti-Kantian or anti-sublime: in Kant, reason and the idea always eventually triumph over the uncanny effect of the sublime by affirming the beauty of what is horrible (Kant, "Observations on the Sentiment of the Beautiful and the Sublime," in *Critique of Judgement*, §§ 25–26).

11. A brief gallery, with commentaries, of some of Glissant's favorite painters can be found in *Autour d'Édouard Glissant* (Paris, 1988).

12. Hegel, *Esthétique I* (Paris, 1979), 16. Hegel inverts Plato's elevation, but in this inversion it is still transcendent Spirit (or Being) that rules the work of art.

13. Nietzsche, *Le Livre du philosophe* (Paris, 1969), 185.

Chapter 10

1. "It is this positive interpretation of the principle of negativity that has made the thought of Heraclitus so congenial to Hegel and his followers" (Kahn, *The Art and Thought of Heraclitus*, 188). See also Kojève, *Introduction à la lecture de Hegel* (Paris, 1971), especially 455ff.

2. Hegel, *Phénoménologie de l'Esprit* (Paris, 1978), 256; see also Kojève, *Introduction à la lecture de Hegel* (Paris, 1971), 255.

3. Nietzsche, "Le problème de Socrates," § 2, in *Twilight of the Idols*. There is a second moment of agreement with Hegel, in the section on "The Last Man" at the end of *Thus Spoke Zarathustra*; but where Hegel sees a consummation, Nietzsche interprets it as a catastrophe. I will be returning to this.

4. See Hegel, *Leçons sur l'histoire de la philosophie* (Paris, 2004), vol. 1.

5. Axelos, "La pensée d'Héraclite dans l'histoire de la pensée," in *Le Jeu du monde* (Paris, 1969), 227.

6. See Kojève, *Introduction à la lecture de Hegel* (Paris, 1971), 455.

7. Hegel, *Phénoménologie de l'Esprit* (Paris, 1978), 19, note 34. Kojève, in *Introduction à la lecture de Hegel* (Paris, 1971), 457, suggests that the word has a threefold meaning: suppression, conservation, and sublimation. See also Nancy, *Hegel, l'inquiétude du négatif* (Paris, 1997), 76, who discusses Derrida's translation of this term into French as *relève*; for further details, see also the chapter in Kojève's Introduction called "La dialectique du réel et la méthode phénoménologique chez Hegel" (447ff) and Nancy (*Hegel*, 79–81). See also "Comment traduire les philosophes allemands? Entretien avec Jean-Pierre Lefebvre," *Genèses* 7 (1992): 150–162.

8. As we have seen, we need to set the real universality of mathematics (as in Galilean science) to one side: to begin with, a theorem or an algorithm is always strictly localized to a single field of application. Second, most of the time, human life cannot be grasped by it. In each case, neither Galilean science nor its method can lay claim to universality.

9. See my discussion of *Soleil de la conscience* in chapter 2.

10. See chapter 12.

11. Diawara, "Conversation with Édouard Glissant aboard the Queen Mary II (August 2009)," in Barson and Gorschluter (eds.), *Afro Modern: Journeys through the Black Atlantic* (Liverpool, 2010), 63.

12. See Rousset's discussion in *G.W.F. Hegel. Le Savoir absolu* (Paris, 1998).

13. Hegel, *Esthétique I* (Paris, 1979), 43.

14. "La Relation imprédictible et sans morale," 192.

15. Leupin, "L'œuvre mangrove," *artpress* 229 (November 2000), reprinted as Coda in EBR.

16. See del Fiol, "Édouard Glissant/Salah Siété: immanence ou transcendance de la relation?," in Kassab-Charfi, Zlitni-Fitouri, and Céry (eds.), *Autour d'Édouard Glissant. Lectures, épreuves, extensions d'une poétique de la Relation* (Bordeaux, 2008).

Chapter 11

1. As far as I know, the capital letter for Relation first appears in 1969 in *L'Intention poétique* (IP 217). *Le Tout-Monde* ("Whole-World") is initially written as "Tout-monde" ("Whole-world"), then the two nouns are both capitalized.

2. See chapter 6.

3. See the table of contents, 157: "V. Archipelagic thought, the thought of the essay; VI. The thought of trembling; VII. The new thought of borders; VIII. The thought of wandering; IX. The thought of creolizations; X. The thought of the unforeseeable; XI. The thought of the world's opacity; XII. The thought of Relation; XIII. The thought of the trace."

4. "'Relation' has no outside: it is a thought-out space, closed by the finiteness of the earth's geometry and the overall character of the 'Project.' Different for everyone, it is the same for everyone. [. . .] In Relation, there is no pure detachment" ("La catégorie de la relation dans les essais d'Édouard Glissant. Philosophie d'une poétique," in *Poétiques d'Édouard Glissant*, 99).

5. Substance (or essence), quantity, quality, relation, place, time, position, possession, action, passion.

6. In the history of philosophy, Glissant probably has only one predecessor, the Dominican anti-Thomist Durand de Saint-Pourçain (c. 1270–1334), for whom relationship is a mode of being itself (*esse ad aliud*, "being toward the other"), not an addition that qualifies it: "Knowledge, for him, does not consist of a reality added to the soul from the outside to perfect it, but is a relation to the object, 'apprehension' or judgment, emitted by pure whenever the soul moves out to any object that presents itself to it. Thus the Thomistic notion of truth as *adaequatio rei et intellectus* appears absurd: truth cannot be an adequation between the known object and the *verbum mentis* produced in the act of knowing, but an agreement between the object insofar as it is known and the same object as existing" (*Encyclopaedia universalis*, Thesaurus I, article on Durand de Saint-Pourçain). In all likelihood, Glissant was not aware of this predecessor, whose quasi-heretical positions caused him considerable difficulties with the ecclesiastical hierarchy. See Gilson, *La Philosophie au Moyen Âge* (Paris: Payot, 1962), 624.

7. See Milner's definition of the logion: "[The *logia*] are at once recurrent, true, essential, and capable of being fully interpreted by themselves. They are neither anodyne, nor inconsistent, nor incomplete. They are not enigmatic" (*L'Œuvre Claire* [Paris, 1995], 27).

8. "La Relation imprédictible et sans morale."

9. See Deleuze, *Le Pli. Leibniz et le Baroque* (Paris, 1988), from which this quotation is taken.

10. Hegel, *Science de la logique*, trans. Jankélévitch (Paris, 1949), vol. I, 332.

11. This is close to the Deleuze of *Différence et répétition*.

12. Diawara, "Conversation with Édouard Glissant aboard the Queen Mary II (August 2009)," in Barson and Gorschluter (eds.), *Afro Modern: Journeys through the Black Atlantic* (Liverpool, 2010).

13. Kassab-Charfi, Zlitni-Fitouri, and Céry (eds.), *Autour d'Édouard Glissant. Lectures, épreuves, extensions d'une poétique de la Relation* (Bordeaux, 2008), 348.

14. The status of the being of the unconscious in Lacan is more complex than Glissant says: the antinomy between these two gigantic thoughts of the

twentieth century does not, I think, lie at the level of being, but at that of the unveiling of the truth. Remember Lacan's rewriting of the cogito: "I think where I am not, therefore I am where I do not think" (*Séminaire XVII. L'Envers de la psychanalyse* [Paris, 1991], 118). Or again, "either I think, or I am": to be is to be without words (without thoughts)—in analytical terms, being is therefore on the side of the unconscious. It does not follow that the unconscious itself is a being: "We do not even know if the unconscious has a proper being, and it is because we can't say "it's that" that it was given the name "it" (*ça*) (*Es* in German, or: "it," in the sense we say "it's kicking off" or "it's a right farce" [Translator's note: i.e., "people are kidding around"])" (*Autres écrits* [Paris, 2001], 333.)

15. Jacques Lacan, *Séminaire XV. L'Acte analytique*, January 10, 1968.

16. "In the proper sense of the words, it is language which speaks. Man speaks only insofar as he replies to language by listening to what it says" (Martin Heidegger, "[. . .] L'homme habite en poète . . . ," in *Essais et conférences* (Paris, 1958), 227–228 [lecture of October 6, 1951]).

17. "The unconscious is not when we lose our memory; it's when we can't remember that *of which* we know" (Lacan, *Autres écrits* (Paris, 2001), 333).

18. "La Relation imprédictible et sans morale," 177.

19. This notion is proposed by Deleuze and Guattari, *Mille plateaux. Capitalisme et Schizophrénie* (Paris, 1980), 31–33; this passage is quoted at length in the *Anthology of the Whole-World* (TEFV 155–159).

20. Ibid., 31.

21. But not in the civic ethics of Hegel as set out in *The Philosophy of Right*; here again, Glissant preserves the process, not the contents.

22. "La Relation imprédictible et sans morale," 179 (my emphasis).

23. Ibid.

Chapter 12

1. Parmenides, *Sur la nature ou sur l'étant. La Langue de l'être?*, ed. Cassin (Paris, 1998).

2. Heidegger, "Que veut dire penser?" and "Moîra (Parménide, VIII, 34–41)," in *Essais et conferences* (Paris, 1958).

3. Ibid., 90. This notion of Heidegger's earned him a rap on the knuckles—deservedly so, in my opinion—from Ernst Bloch: "Heidegger, the most static thinker imaginable . . ." (*L'Athéisme dans le christianisme* [Paris, 1978], 86.)

4. See Cassin's comments in *Sur la nature ou sur l'étant. La Langue de l'être?* (Paris, 1998), 67.

5. "The concept of being! As if the most miserable empirical origin did not already appear in the word's etymology! *Esse* basically means *to breathe*: if man uses this word when speaking of all things, it is because, by metaphor, that is to say by an illogical process, he transports the conviction that he is breathing

and that he is living to all other things, whose existence he conceives of as a kind of breathing analogous to his" (Nietzsche, *La Naissance de la philosophie à l'époque tragique des Grecs*, chapter 11).

6. Wahl, *Vers la fin de l'ontologie* (Paris, 1956), 255.

7. See Cassin, *L'Effet Sophistique* (Paris, 1995), 26ff.

8. See Cassin's remarks in *Sur la nature ou sur l'étant. La Langue de l'être?* (Paris, 1998), 33, note 1.

9. See chapter 16.

10. For further details, see *Les Présocratiques*, ed. Dumont (Paris, 1988), 1002–1026 and the presentation on 1520.

11. Dupréel, *Les Sophistes* (Neuchâtel, 1948), 69.

12. Cassin, *L'Effet Sophistique* (Paris, 1995), 43.

13. Fragments VI, VII, and VIII, in *Les Présocratiques*, 259–261. However, there is little agreement between the specialists: see the presentation on Parmenides, 1261–1267.

14. Unlike several others, Wahl never forgave Heidegger's support for National Socialism.

15. Wahl, *Vers la fin de l'ontologie* (Paris, 1956), 257.

16. Ibid., 102 (my emphasis).

17. Nietzsche, *The Joyful Wisdom,* "Foreword." And also: "All philosophical systems are outdated: the Greeks shine brighter than ever, especially the Pre-Socratic Greeks. It is not surprising that it takes a few millennia to resume things from where they had got to—a few millennia is very little!" (Posthumous fragments, X 26 [43] and 26 [105]).

18. "The essence of being (*être*) involves disappearing (*disparaître*), and this disappearing, far from dissolving in dispersion, is Being" (Axelos, *Héraclite et la philosophie* [Paris, 1968], 52).

19. On the very precise system of punctuation marks, see PR 236 (already quoted): a colon means a logical consequence, a dash means a contrast.

20. "Kant, in the *Critique of Pure Reason*, presents what he says about Relation in these terms:

> Unconditioned unity
> of RELATION
> that is to say
> itself, not as inherent
> But as
> SUBSISTENT.

Whether this relation contributes to the systematic unity of ends (the moral principle) or to the unity of knowledge (the architectonic principle), two qualities can be affirmed here: first, that Relation is the binding agent that ensures the permanence of thought in the individual: second, that Relation has no part in substance. This difference that Kant seems to establish between substance and subsistence is highly significant. Be that as it may, the idea of relation in his work does not act as an opening up to plurality, insofar as it is a totality. For Kant, plurality takes place in time, not in space. In space, there is existence, which does not seem to be differentiated within itself" (PR 229).

This expresses Glissant's distance, in the wake of Hegel, from German idealism in its deepest expression.

21. Axelos, *Héraclite et la Philosophie* (Paris, 1968), 52.

Chapter 13

1. See Demoulin, "L'Œdipe rêve de Freud," *Psychoanalytische Perspectieven* 20, no. 3 (2002): 397–414.

2. Lacan, *Séminaire XVII. L'Envers de la psychanalyse* (Paris, 1991), 135.

3. What is universal, for Lacan, is castration, and this depends on language—on the "no" affixed to the desire—and not on an act, whether it be the death of Laius in *Oedipus the King* or the murder of the father of the primitive horde in the myth proposed by Freud in *Totem and Taboo*, whose last sentence "In the beginning was the act" is contradictory to Lacanian theory. Oedipus, for Lacan, is above all the man who solves the enigma of the sphinx, a more fundamental moment than the murder of the father and incest.

4. Perse, "Amers," in *Œuvres complètes* (Paris, 1972), 380.

5. As Glissant interprets it: "[Saint-John Perse] thought that the condition of freedom was for everyone not to be governed by a (hi)story, other than of the generalizing kind, or limited by a place, unless it was spiritual" (PR 53).

6. This is true only if we ignore the phallic cults that were widespread outside the West (India, pre-Columbian America, etc.) and in the West (the cult of Priapus, Dionysos, etc.).

7. "(It is appalling to note, however, the number of incestuous rapes carried out on daughters or stepdaughters, often of pre-pubertal age, by their fathers or stepfathers in the Antillean countryside; we cannot just say that this is a phenomenon linked to modes of cultural misery or lack of structure, or to conditions of country life and just plain poverty)" (FM 179).

8. See von Bortkiewicz, "Wertrechnung und Presirechnung im Marxschen System," *Archiv fur Sozialwissenschaft und Sozialpolitik*, 1907.

9. Lacan, *Séminaire XVI. D'un autre à l'Autre* (Paris, 2006), 17 and passim.

10. Chevrier (ed.), *Poétiques d'Édouard Glissant* (Paris, 1999), 56.

11. Note the similarity between the analysis in the *Discours antillais* and Lacan's discourse: "Buying from a rich man, from a developed nation, you believe—this is the sense of the wealth of nations—that you will simply enjoy

the level of a wealthy nation. Only, in this case, what you lose is your knowledge, which gave *you* your status" (Lacan, *Séminaire XVII. L'Envers de la psychanalyse* [Paris, 1991], 94).

12. "Path of a neurosis": remember Freud, for whom the "primitive" man can tolerate his neurosis very easily (he is therefore not neurotic) because he puts it into action or representation, while it makes a modern man ill; he cannot translate it into action: "In the neurotic, action is completely inhibited and completely replaced by the idea. The primitive, on the contrary, knows no obstacle to action: his ideas are immediately transformed into actions; you could even say that with him the action replaces the idea" (Freud, *Totem et Tabou* (Paris, 1970) 185).

13. There is a kinship here with Bataille's notion of expenditure.

14. Glissant's intervention at the round table "Parler et déparler," in *Autour d'Édouard Glissant. Lectures, épreuves, extensions d'une poétique de la Relation* (Bordeaux, 2008), 347.

15. This is the objection that can be laid against the study, with its many examples, by Chancé, *Édouard Glissant, un traité du "déparler." Essai sur l'œuvre romanesque d'Édouard Glissant* (Paris, 2002).

16. Ibid., 349.

17. Freud, *Totem et Tabou* (Paris, 1970), 88.

18. Lacan, *Séminaire III. Les Psychoses* (Paris, 1981), 66.

19. Lacan, *Séminaire XVII. L'Envers de la psychanalyse* (Paris, 1991), 173; see also 21–22. For Hegel, the *otium philosophicum* ends with the figure of Christ, who is both a thinker and a carpenter: work is no longer servile, and thought is no longer the privilege of the masters.

20. It was Heidegger's mistake to have believed that National Socialism provided the opportunity for a return to the social structure of the philosophy of Antiquity. And it was in complete consistency with this belief that he joined the Party (and kept his card until the German defeat) and placed the university at the service of the Nazis. The illusion persists, in happily more benign forms: examples include Barthes dining at the Élysée with François Mitterrand, and Bernard-Henri Lévy advising Nicolas Sarkozy during the invasion of Libya.

21. It is in this respect that Glissant's project differs from that of Deleuze: for Glissant, the task of philosophy is not only to create new concepts. (In thinking that this *is* philosophy's task, in the final analysis Deleuze and Guattari, despite their intentions, fall back within the traditional history of philosophy.)

Chapter 14

1. Milner, *Clartés de tout* (Lagrasse, 2011), 44.

2. I am here leaving aside Céline, who is part of the same problematic, which he solves through paranoia, in contrast to the obsessive neurosis of Proust;

a full demonstration would require too much space. Note merely that Glissant never mentions Céline, although the latter is one of the greatest prose writers in the French tradition. We spoke together just once about Céline's panic at the rise of racial and cultural mixing.

3. Arthur Rimbaud, *Œuvres complètes* (Paris, 1972), 171.

4. Mallarmé, "Crise de Vers," in *Œuvres complètes* (Paris, 1945), 366.

5. This is—not by chance—the only one of Mallarmé's poems that appears in the anthology of the Whole-World (TEFV 249).

6. Proust, *À La Recherche du temps perdu* (Paris, 1989), vol. IV, 615.

7. Nietzsche, *Thus Spoke Zarathustra*, Prologue, 5.

8. "My life can be summed up in two words: Solitary-Solidary" (Hugo, *Post-scriptum de ma vie*, from the 1870 notebook).

9. Camus, "Jonas ou l'artiste au travail," in *L'Exil et le Royaume:* "Rateau looked at the entirely white canvas, in the center of which Jonas had only written, in very tiny writing, a word that one could decipher but that might have read either 'solitary' or 'solidary'" (*Théâtre, Récits, Nouvelles* [Paris, 1963], 1652).

10. Britton, "La poétique du relais dans *Mahagony* et *Tout-Monde*," in *Poétiques d'Édouard Glissant* (Paris, 1999), 169–178.

11. Lacan, "D'une question préliminaire à tout traitement possible de la psychose," in *Écrits* (Paris, 1966), 531–583.

12. On the process of naming, see Dash, *Édouard Glissant* (Cambridge, 1995), 88ff., and Loichot, "Plural, Illegitimate and Uncertain Fathers," in Bueno, Caesar, and Hummel (eds.), *Naming the Father. Legacies, Genealogies, and Explorations in Fatherhood in Modern and Contemporary Literature* (New York, 2000), 102–117.

Chapter 15

1. "The significance of the message can accommodate—we need not hesitate to go that far—all of the falsifications imposed on the furnishings of experience, occasionally including the very flesh of the writer. The only thing that matters is a truth which insists that in its unveiling the message condenses. There is so little contrast between this *Dichtung* and the *Wahrheit* in its nudity that the fact of the poetic operation must rather arrest us at this feature that we forget in all truth, namely that it turns out true in a structure of fiction" (Lacan, *Écrits* [Paris, 1966], 742–743).

2. Structuralism is, according to Jean-Claude Milner, a new ontology (but still, yet again, an ontology): "structuralism defines a new mode of being. [. . .] The One and the being were now separated; whence it followed that the theory of what comprises a being changed: to be is not to be identical to oneself and, by this identity, to count for One; to be is to be opposable and, because of this opposition, to count for One only at a second stage, through the mediation of several" (Milner, *Le Périple structural* [Paris, 2002], 234–235).

3. Interview with *L'Orient-Le Jour*, no. 77, November 2011.

4. The contrast with Lacan is obvious: for him, either the human sciences come under modern science, in which case they are not human, since science abolishes the singularity of the subject; or they deal with the human, in which case they cannot be sciences, but *arts*, as Glissant notes, thereby calling for the total recomposition of the so-called "human sciences" to make them nonreductive, nonpartitioning instruments, open to the unpredictable.

5. After what? After Heidegger: "(Then, much later, and according to perhaps one of many possible Heideggers)": "Difference is the avatar that Beings try to impose on Being" (PhR 100). On the next page, therefore, the Heideggerian "ontological difference" between Being and beings is called into question, along with the hierarchy in which Being comes first and dominates beings.

6. The epigraph to *Sartorius* is a homage to Gilles Deleuze: "Health as literature, as writing, consists in inventing a people that is missing. It is the task of the function of storytelling to invent a people. You do not write with your memories, unless you turn them into the origin or the collective destination of a people still to come, still buried under its betrayals and denials" (Deleuze, "La littérature et la vie," in *Critique et Clinique* [Paris, 1993], 11).

7. Dedications to friends are also part of the apparatus of writing and subjective knowledge; see the both visual and poetic capsules by "Édouard Glissant & Hans Ulrich Obrist," *Documenta* 13, no. 38 (2012).

8. Metaphor": another word that is just as absent from Glissant's lexicon as "signifier."

9. "For the beginning and the end coincide in the circumference of the circle" (D 103). Cassin shows that the poem of Parmenides was a path, based closely on the epic of Odysseus, leading from Being to the sphere of beings (Cassin, *Sur la nature ou sur l'étant. La Langue de l'être?* [Paris, 1998], 59 and 65, note 2).

10. See Chancé, *Édouard Glissant, un traité du "déparler." Essai sur l'œuvre romanesque d'Édouard Glissant* (Paris, 2002), 193ff., and Cailler, "Sartorius, le roman des Batoutos, ou la brisure de l'O/eau," in Gafaïti, Lorcin, and Troyansky (eds.), *Migrances, Diasporas et Transculturalités francophones. Littératures et Cultures d'Afrique, des Caraïbes, d'Europe et du Québec* (Paris, 2005), 257–275.

Chapter 16

1. See the commentary by Axelos, *Héraclite et la philosophie* (Paris, 1968), 48–50.

2. "To re-say it in a semi-modern and pseudo-Schellingian language, we can say that, for Heraclitus, the Absolute is Relativity itself, or as such. Or, more simply, that *only change is permanent* in the world we live in and talk about, as

well as in what we *say* when we talk about it (which is as it should be)" (Kojève, *Essai d'une histoire raisonnée de la philosophie païenne*, vol. 1 [Paris, 1968], 266).

3. The problem is admittedly complex, as Hegel employs the notion of contradiction in contradictory ways, as has been demonstrated by Grégoire, "Hegel et l'universelle contradiction," *Revue philosophique de Louvain* 44 (1946): 373, and, more recently, Nodé-Langlois, "Métaphysique et logique spéculative: la critique hégélienne du principe de contradiction": http:// www.philopsis.fr/.

4. Hegel, *Principes de la philosophie du droit* (Paris, 1940), 39.

5. Hegel, *La Raison dans l'Histoire* (Paris, 1965), 129.

6. "Solitaire et solidaire," interview between Glissant and Artières, *Terrain* 41 (September 2003).

7. Unpublished English version, dated April 2002. The theme recurs several times in *La Cohée du Lamentin*: "Like a flight of thousands of birds drifting unpredictably, in vivid splendour, over this lake of China or Africa" (CL 17).

8. See Kojève, *Introduction à la lecture de Hegel* (Paris, 1971), 456.

9. See Kojève, *Introduction à la lecture de Hegel* (Paris, 1971), 59.

10. See my "Heurs et malheurs de l'asujet. Note sur les histoires à la fin de l'Histoire," *Conférence* (Autumn 2013): 39ff.

11. Heraclitus: "You cannot step twice into the same river" (D 91); Glissant: "The river governs no linearity, you cannot put your feet twice into the same water" (FM 209).

Chapter 17

1. See the commentary by Loichot, "Édouard Glissant's Graves," *Callaloo* 36, no. 4 (2013): 1025ff.

2. Titus 1:12.

3. "All men are liars," Psalms 116:11, *Homélie sur le Psaume 115* [116b]).

4. In his *Rhetoric* (Γ 5, 1407 b, 11), he criticizes the Ephesian for his obscurity, due to the difficulty of punctuating his works, as there are not enough grammatical (logical) conjunctions.

5. From "Francofonia: Studi e ricerche sulle letterature di lingua francese," 63. In Le frémissement de la lecture. Parcours littéraires d'Édouard Glissant (2012), 215.

6. For an overview of the solutions, see Recanati, "Une solution médiévale du paradoxe du menteur," in Vance and Brind'Amour (eds.), *Archéologie du signe* (Toronto, 1983).

7. Institut du Tout-Monde, September 2012.

Bibliography

Aristotle, *Poétique*, trans. Roselyne Dupont-Roc and Jean Lallot (Paris, 1980).

Autour d'Édouard Glissant (Paris, 1988).

Axelos Kostas, *Héraclite et la Philosophie* (Paris, 1968).

————. *Le Jeu du monde* (Paris, 1969).

Azérad, Hugues, "Mesure parfaite et réinventée. Édouard Glissant Reinvents Nineteenth-Century French Poetry," in *Thinking Poetry* (London, 2013), 203–220.

————. "Édouard Glissant and the Test of Faulkner's Modernism," in *American Creoles* (Liverpool, 2013), 197–215.

Barnabé, Jean, Patrick Chamoiseau, and Raphaël Confiant, *Éloge de la Créolité* (Paris, 1989).

Bataille, Georges, *Les Larmes d'Éros* (Paris, 1971).

Bertrand, Dominique, *Les Pères apostoliques* (Paris, 2001).

Biondi, Carminella, "Édouard Glissant: du lieu d'origine au lieu commun," in Jacques Chevrier (ed.), *Poétiques d'Édouard Glissant* (Paris, 1999). http://www. ÉdouardGlissant.fr/biondi.pdf

Biondi, Carminella, and Elena Pessini, *Rêver le monde écrire le monde. Théorie et narrations d'Édouard Glissant* (Bologna, 2004).

Blanchot, Maurice, *Le Livre à venir* (Paris, 1959).

Bloch, Ernst, *L'Athéisme dans le christianisme* (Paris, 1978).

Bollack, Jean, *Héraclite et la Séparation* (Paris, 1972).

————. *Parménide. De l'étant au monde* (Paris, 2006).

Bortkiewicz, Ladislaus (von), "Wertrechnung und Preisrechnung im Marxschen System," *Archiv fur Sozialwissenschaft und Sozialpolitik*, 1907.

Bourgeois, Bernard, *Le Vocabulaire de Hegel* (Paris, 2011).

Britton, Celia, *Édouard Glissant and Postcolonial Theory. Strategies of Language and Resistance* (Charlottesville/London, 1999).

Brøndal, Viggo, *Essais de linguistique générale* (Copenhagen, 1943).

Bruaire, Jean-Claude, *Logique et Religion chrétienne dans la philosophie de Hegel* (Paris, 1964).

Buck-Morss, Susan, *Hegel, Haiti and Universal History* (Pittsburgh, 2009).

Cailler Bernadette, "Sartorius, le roman des Batoutos, ou la brisure de l'O/eau," in Hafid.

Gafaïti, Patricia M. E. Lorcin, and David G. Troyansky (eds.), *Migrances, Diasporas et Transculturalités francophones. Littératures et Cultures d'Afrique, des Caraïbes, d'Europe et du Québec* (Paris, 2005).

———. "Interfaces: Walt Whitman et Édouard Glissant," *Francofonia* 32 (2012).

Camus, Albert, *Théâtre, Récits, Nouvelles* (Paris, 1963).

Cassin, Barbara, *L'Effet Sophistique* (Paris, 1995).

———. (ed.), *Le Plaisir de parler* (Paris, 1986).

Céline, Louis-Ferdinand, *Rigodon*, in *Roman IV* (Paris, 1974).

Chancé, Dominique, *Édouard Glissant, un traité du "déparler." Essai sur l'œuvre romanesque d'Édouard Glissant* (Paris, 2002).

Char, René, *L'Âge cassant* (Paris, 1995).

Châtelet, François, *Hegel* (Paris, 1981).

Chevrier, Jacques (ed.), *Poétiques d'Édouard Glissant* (Paris, 1999).

Claudel, Paul, *Oeuvre poétique* (Paris, 1957).

Coursil, Jacques, "La Catégorie de la relation dans les essais d'Édouard Glissant, philosophie d'une poétique," in Jacques Chevrier (ed.), *Poétiques d'Édouard Glissant* (Paris, 1999). http://www.ÉdouardGlissant.fr/coursil.pdf

Damato, Barbara, "La répétition dans les essais d'Édouard Glissant," in Jacques Chevrier (ed.), *Poétiques d'Édouard Glissant* (Paris, 1999). http://www.ÉdouardGlissant.fr/damato.pdf

Dash, J. Michael, *Édouard Glissant* (Cambridge, 1995).

———. "No Mad Art: The Deterritorialized Déparler in the work of Édouard Glissant," *Paragraph* 24, no. 3 (November 2001).

Deleuze, Gilles, *Critique et Clinique* (Paris, 1993).

———. *Le Pli. Leibniz et le Baroque* (Paris, 1988).

Deleuze, Gilles, and Félix Guattari, *Mille plateaux. Capitalisme et Schizophrénie* (Paris, 1980).

———. *Qu'est-ce que la philosophie?* (Paris, 1991).

Delpech, Catherine, "L'insurrection Glissantienne: l'imaginaire en action," in Kathleen Gyssens and Bénédicte Ledent (eds.), *The Caribbean Writer as Warrior of the Imaginary* (Amsterdam, 2008).

———. "Édouard Glissant à la cheminaison du Tout-Monde," *Francofonia* 32 (2012).

Demoulin, Christian, "L'Œdipe rêve de Freud," *Psychoanalytische Perspectieven*, 20, no. 3 (2002): 397–414.

Diawara, Manthia, "Conversation with Édouard Glissant aboard the Queen Mary II August 2009," in Tanya Barson and Peter Gorschluter (eds.), *Afro Modern: Journeys through the Black Atlantic* (Liverpool, 2010).

Drabinski, John, "Shorelines, in Memory of Édouard Glissant," *Journal of French and Francophone Philosophy* 19, no. 1 (2011).

Dupréel, Eugène, *Les Sophistes* (Neuchâtel, 1948).

Fonkoua, Romuald, "Jean Wahl et Édouard Glissant: philosophie, raison et poésie," in Jacques Chevrier (ed.), *Poétiques d'Édouard Glissant* (Paris, 1999). http://www.ÉdouardGlissant.fr/fonkoua.pdf

Freud, Sigmund, *Totem et Tabou* (Paris, 1970).

———. *Malaise dans la civilization* (Paris, 1971).

Fumaroli, Marc, *Les Premiers Siècles de la République européenne des Lettres. Actes du Colloque international* (Paris, December 2001) (Paris, 2005).

Gauvin, Lise, "L'imaginaire des langues," in Jacques Chevrier (ed.), *Poétiques d'Édouard Glissant* (Paris, 1999). http://www.ÉdouardGlissant.fr/gauvin.pdf

Gilson, Étienne, *La Philosophie au Moyen Âge* (Paris, 1962).

Glissant, Édouard, "Mondialité, diversalité, imprévisibilité, concepts pour agir dans le chaos-monde," interview in *Les périphériques vous parlent* 14 (Summer 2000).

———. "La Relation imprédictible et sans morale," interview with François Noudelmann, *Rue Descartes* 37 (2002). http://www.cairn.info/revue-rue-descartes-2002-3–page-76.htm#pa4

———. *Sur l'imaginaire*, Baton Rouge, Mondes Francophones, April 20, 2002.

———. "Solitaire et solidaire," interview with Philippe Artières, *Terrain* 41 (September 2003).

———. "Édouard Glissant avait fait le vœu d'une unité caribéenne," interview with Jacques Denis, *Le Monde*, February 3, 2011.

———. "Entretien avec *L'Orient-Le Jour*" 77 (November 2011).

———. "Entretien avec Christian Tortel," *Francophonia* 32 (2012).

———. "Francofonia: Studi e ricerche sulle letterature di lingua francese." In Le frémissement de la lecture. Parcours littéraires d'Édouard Glissant (2012).

Godin, Christian, *La Totalité* (Seyssel, 1997–2001).

Grégoire, Franz, "Hegel et l'universelle contradiction," *Revue philosophique de Louvain*, vol. 44, 1946.

Hegel, Georg Wilhelm Friedrich, *Esthétique* (Paris, 1979), 4 vols.

———. *Principes de la philosophie du droit* (Paris, 1940).

———. *Science de la logique*, trans. Samuel Jankélévitch (Paris, 1949).

———. *La Raison dans l'Histoire* (Paris, 1965).

———. *Le Savoir absolu* (Paris, 1977).

———. *Phénoménologie de l'Esprit*, trans. Jean Hyppolite (Paris, 1978).

———. *Leçons sur l'histoire de la philosophie*, trans. Pierre Garniron (Paris, 2004).

Heidegger, Martin, *Essais et Conférences* (Paris, 1958) [lecture of October 6, 1951].

Hondt, Jacques d', *Hegel* (Paris, 1998).

Jarcyzk, Gwendoline, and Pierre-Jean Labarrière, *De Kojève à Hegel. 150 ans de pensée hégélienne en France* (Paris, 1996).

Joubert Jean-Louis, "L'archipel Glissant," in Jacques Chevrier (ed.), *Poétiques d'Édouard Glissant* (Paris, 1999). http://www.ÉdouardGlissant.fr/joubert.pdf

Kahn, Charles A., *The Art and Thought of Heraclitus* (Cambridge, 1979).

Kalinowski, Isabelle, "La littérature dans le champ philosophique français de la première moitié du xxe siècle," *Methodos* (January 2001). https://journals.openedition.org/methodos/53

Kant, Immanuel, *Idée d'une histoire universelle d'un point de vue cosmopolitique* (Paris, 1993).

Kassab-Charfi, Samia, "Les 'épaisseurs têtues du sens,' l'intime dialogue entre Wilfredo Lam et Édouard Glissant," *Francofonia* 32 (2012).

———, Zlittni-Fitouri, Sonia, and Loïc Céry (eds.), *Autour d'Édouard Glissant. Lectures, épreuves, extensions d'une Poétique de la relation* (Bordeaux, 2008).

Kessler, Mathieu, *L'Esthétique de Nietzsche* (Paris, 1998).

Kojève, Alexandre, *Essai d'une histoire raisonnée de la philosophie païenne*, vol. 1 (Paris, 1968).

———. *Introduction à la lecture de Hegel* (Paris, 1971).

Koyré, Alexandre, *L'Idée de Dieu dans la philosophie de saint Anselme* (Paris, 1984 [reprint of 1923 ed.]).

———. *From the closed world to the infinite universe* (Radford, 2008).

Lacan Jacques, *Écrits* (Paris, 1966).

———. *Séminaire XV. L'Acte analytique*, January 10, 1968.

———. *Séminaire III. Les Psychoses* (Paris, 1981).

———. *Séminaire XVII. L'Envers de la psychanalyse* (Paris, 1991).

———. *Autres écrits* (Paris, 2001).

———. *Séminaire XVI. D'un autre à l'Autre* (Paris, 2006).

Lacoue-Labarthe, Philippe, and Jean-Luc Nancy, *L'Absolu littéraire. Théorie de la littérature du romantisme allemande* (Paris, 1978).

Lauro, Raphaël, "Le frémissement de la lecture, parcours littéraire d'Édouard Glissant," *Francophonia* 32 (2012).

Lefebvre, Jean-Pierre, "Comment traduire les philosophes allemands?" *Genèses* 7 (1992): 150–162.

Les Présocratiques, ed. Jean-Paul Dumont (Paris, 1988).

Leupin, Alexandre, *Barbarolexis. Medieval Writing and Sexuality* (Cambridge, MA, 1989).

———. *Fiction et Incarnation. Littérature et Théologie au Moyen Âge* (Paris, 2000).

———. "L'œuvre mangrove," *Artpress* 229 (November 2000).

———. *La Passion des Idoles* (Paris, 2000).

———. "Heurs et malheurs de l'asujet. Note sur les histoires à la fin de l'Histoire," *Conférence* 37 (Autumn 2013).

Loichot, Valérie, "Plural, Illegitimate and Uncertain Fathers," in Eva Paulino Bueno, Terry Caesar, and William Hummel (eds.), *Naming the Father. Legacies, Geneologies and Explorations in Fatherhood in Modern and Contemporary Literature* (New York, 2000).

———. "Édouard Glissant's Graves," "Special Issue: Édouard Glissant," *Callalo* 36, no. 4 (2013).

Madou, Jean-Pol, "Édouard Glissant: voix créoles, écritures médiévales," *Francofonia* 32 (2012).

Mallarmé, Stéphane, "Crise de Vers," in *Œuvres complètes* (Paris, 1945).

Ménil, Alain, *Les Voies de la créolisation. Essai sur Édouard Glissant* (Grenoble, 2011).

Milner, Jean-Claude, *Les Noms indistincts* (Paris, 1983).

———. "Lacan and the Ideal of Science," in Alexandre Leupin (ed.), *Lacan and the Human Sciences* (Lincoln, 1991).

———. *L'Œuvre Claire* (Paris, 1995).

———. *Le Périple structural* (Paris, 2002).

———. *Clartés de tout* (Paris, 2011).

Montaigne, Michel de, *Les Essais* (Paris, 1924).

Nancy, Jean-Luc, *Hegel, l'inquiétude du négatif* (Paris, 1997).

Nesbitt Nick, "Early Glissant: From the Destitution of the Political to Antillean Ultra-Leftism," *Callaloo* 36, no. 4 (2013).

———. "Politiques et Poétiques: les errances de l'absolu," in Valérie Loichot (ed.), *Entours d'Édouard Glissant, Revue des sciences humaines*, no. 309 (2013).

Nietzsche Frederich, *Zarathoustra*, 1883.

———. *Le Gai Savoir* (Paris, 1989).

Nodé-Langlois, Michel, "Métaphysique et logique spéculative: la critique hégélienne du principe de contradiction." http://www.philopsis.fr

Noudelmann, François, "Édouard Glissant's Legacy: Transmitting without Universals?" *Callaloo* 46.4 (2013).

———. Harvey, Robert, and Elizabeth Ann Kaplan, "Pour une pensée archipélique," in *Politique et Filiation* (Paris, 2000).

Oakley, Seanna Sumalee, *Common Places: The Poetics of African Atlantic Postromantics* (Amsterdam, 2011).

Okolo, Onkonda Benoît, *Hegel et l'Afrique: thèses, critiques et dépassements* (Puteaux, 2010).

Oster, Daniel, "D'un statut d'évangéliste: Maurice Blanchot," *Littérature* 33 (1979).

Parmenides, *Sur la nature ou sur l'étant. La langue de l'être?*, ed. Barbara Cassin (Paris, 1998).

Paul, André, "Le christianisme," in *Grand Atlas des religions* (Paris, 1990).

Perse, Saint-John, *Œuvres complètes* (Paris, 1972).

Pinkard Terry, *Hegel, a Biography* (Cambridge, 2000).

Popaïoannou, Kostas, *Les Présocratiques* (Paris, 1988).

———. *Hegel* (Paris, 2012).

Prieto, Éric, "Édouard Glissant, Littérature-monde, and Tout-Monde," *Small Axe* 63 (2010).

Proust, Marcel, *La Recherche du temps perdu* (Paris, 1989).

Ramnoux, Clémence, "Héraclite," in *Encyclopaedia Universalis* (Paris, 1985).

Recanati, François, "Une solution médiévale du paradoxe du menteur," in Eugène Vance and Lucie Brind'Amour (eds.), *Archéologie du signe* (Toronto, 1983).

Voegelin, Éric, *Order and History*, vol. 4: *The Ecumenic Age* (Baton Rouge, 1974).

Wahl, Jean, *Vers la fin de l'ontologie* (Paris, 1956).

Index

Abolition, of the subject 75, 215; of
slavery, 116, 139, 213, 214, 215,
217, 237, 283n6
Absolute, the, 32, 63, 70, 78, 145,
162, 192, 222, 244; the Absolute
contrasted with the absolute, 267;
the Absolute in Heraclitus, 292n2
Abstract, the, 163; Abstract Being,
163; Glissant's suspicion of, 29; and
the universal, 33, 34, 74, 92, 105,
141, 189, 224
Abstract art, 156
Abstraction, Glissant's critique of, 34,
47, 76, 105; and beauty and truth,
153; Glissant criticized for, 179; and
knowledge, 75; and the universal,
179
Adami, Valerio, 156, 268
Africa, and Hegel, 16, 62–63, 76,
278n12; slavery in, 139, 283n8
African family structures, 211, 238
African languages, 214
African societies, 210
Albert the Great (Saint), 98, 101
American Civil War, 139, 144
Anaximenes of Miletus, 70
Andronicos of Rhodes, 196
angelism, 78, 192
animal kingdom of the spirit (Hegel),
9, 55

Anselm (Saint), 97, 98, 101
anthropology, 41, 43, 132, 136;
Glissant's philosophical, 5
anti-Americanism, 275n18
anticolonialism, 12, 15, 20, 63
Antilles, the, colonization in, 21;
contemporary situation of, 9; and
Francophonie, 11; and Paris in
Glissant's life, 23, 26, 27, 31, 36, 44,
120, 160; poets from, 237
Antillean culture, 12, 25; and
psychoanalytical categories, 182,
185, 210, 213; and slavery, 139, 144
Antillean-Guyanese Front, 17, 160
Antillean naming system, 238–39
antiquity (Greco-Roman), 69, 223,
225; Heidegger and, 290n20;
philosophical language of, 77, 111,
197, 282n1
apoliticism, Glissant's alleged, 275n14
archipelago, Glissant's metaphorical
use of the term, 80, 124, 203, 236,
276n6
Aristotle, 45, 48, 76, 97, 197;
criticizes Gorgias, 202; criticizes
Heraclitus, 48, 67, 204, 266–67;
criticizes Parmenides, 68; and
ethics, 189; and logic, 252–53; and
ontology, 173–74, 176, 178, 195,
196; and poetry, 8, 91; *Rhetoric*, 67,